TO MY FATHER

Politics in England

POLITICS IN ENGLAND
An Interpretation for the 1980s

RICHARD ROSE
Centre for the Study of Public Policy
University of Strathclyde

We live under a system of tacit understandings.
But the understandings are not always understood.

Sidney Low, *The Governance of England*

faber and faber

First published in 1965
by Faber and Faber Limited
3 Queen Square London WC1N 3AU
Second edition published in 1974
Third edition published in 1980
Reprinted 1982
Printed in Great Britain by
Redwood Burn Ltd, Trowbridge, Wiltshire
and bound by Pegasus Bookbinding, Melksham, Wiltshire
All rights reserved

© Richard Rose 1965, 1974, 1980

British Library Cataloguing in Publication Data

Rose, Richard, b.1933
    Politics in England. – [New ed.].
    1. Great Britain – Politics and government – 1964 –
    I. Title
    320.9′41′0857   JN234

    ISBN 0–571–18021–3
    ISBN 0–571–18023–X Pbk

Contents

Tables and Figures

Acknowledgments

This book sums up the author's experience of a quarter-century of studying politics while moving back and forth between Britain and America. As an American with an English wife and bi-national children, I have found this work personally congenial as well as professionally stimulating.

In this third edition of *Politics in England*, every chapter has been thought through afresh in the light of events of the 1970s, from the controversial 1971 Industrial Relations Act to the 1979 general election. In turn, these events pose major questions for the 1980s. By drawing upon the experience of England under confident Conservative and Labour governments as well as under governments that have lost both self-confidence and national confidence, this study tests to what extent generalizations about British government are particular to a given time, or true regardless of circumstances. Reviewers can debate whether English politics, the study of political science or the author has changed most since the first edition of this book appeared. Readers are invited to approach the text as the author has done: as a new product.

As the copious footnotes emphasize, evidence has been drawn from many different sources. Unpublished machine-readable survey data have been kindly made available by the Gallup Poll; by Dr. Ted Tapper of the University of Sussex; by the Inter-University Consortium for Political Research, custodian of the voting studies undertaken by David Butler and Donald Stokes, 1963–70; and by the SSRC Data Archive at the University of Essex, custodian of the 1974 British Election Studies. The facilities of the University of Strathclyde Social Statistics Laboratory have been invaluable in processing machine-readable data, and Dr. Ian McAllister and Miss Ann Mair have provided helpful and prompt assistance there. Where the train of thought leads beyond available evidence, the discussion explores the implications of more general ideas not yet confirmed by formal research. Understanding can be advanced by raising questions as well as by answering them.

Many debts have been accumulated in writing a book as wide-ranging as this. The suggestion that started it all came from Gabriel Almond. In preparing the original study, and in much else, I have benefited specially from sharing thoughts with J. A. T. Douglas and W. J. M. Mackenzie. The following have kindly commented upon portions of the manuscript of this edition: Nicholas Deakin, Dennis Kavanagh, Richard Parry, Laurence Pollack and Kenneth Wald.

Mrs. R. West and Mrs. M. McGlone have promptly and accurately turned an amalgam of typed and handwritten papers into a neatly typed book manuscript.

None of the individuals or organizations mentioned by name necessarily endorses any particular point in this study. They share responsibility for merits, not demerits.

Richard Rose
Bennochy, Helensburgh

6 June 1979

Only connect . . .

E. M. Forster, *Howards End*

Introduction

There is a great difficulty in the way of a writer who attempts to sketch a living Constitution, a Constitution that is in actual work and power. The difficulty is that the object is in constant change.

England today suffers from the after-effects of early success. Once the leading nation in the world, it now has nowhere to go but down—if success is judged in relative terms. The difficulties are most evident in the economy. Two centuries after originating the first Industrial Revolution, England labours with an industrial system less modern than that of later industrializing Germany and Japan. Whereas Americans write about the problems of living in a technologically advanced post-industrial society, in England there is a greater worry about de-industrialization.

More than a century ago, the Victorian governors of England successfully adapted traditional, even medieval institutions of government to the imperatives of urban, industrial society. The results are embodied in stable institutions of representative government. Today England runs the risk of becoming over-institutionalized. Initiatives of government can be inhibited by the resistance of established institutions reflecting England's past interests rather than its present or future needs. To speak of the continuity and stability of England's political institutions may be another way of describing political stagnation.

Understanding politics becomes more important as a nation's problems accumulate. Even if ordinary citizens turn their backs on government when things go wrong, problems persist, or are even exacerbated by civic indifference. In the contemporary mixed-economy welfare state, the problems of government are not confined to government; they affect almost everybody. Public policies influence the cost of living and unemployment, and changes in education, health and pensions affect, for better or worse, the lives of tens of millions of people.

[1] The epigraphs in this book are taken from Walter Bagehot's classic *The English Constitution*, first published in 1867.

As England enters the 1980s, there is a danger that past political achievements may be taken for granted, and contemporary difficulties dismissed out of hand. The problems facing England in the 1980s are neither transitory nor imported. They reflect the cumulation of problems that have been sidestepped or grappled with unsuccessfully by British governments for a generation. In Victorian times, the governors of England successfully faced the challenge of modernization. Today, their heirs face the challenge of 're-modernizing' many of the country's institutions.

England in comparative perspective

A distinctive feature of this book is that England is viewed in an international perspective. We can better appreciate the continuity of political institutions and political liberties in England if we compare its record with, say, Germany's or Italy's political history. Such a comparison also calls attention to England's relative low rate of economic growth. Viewing England in comparative perspective is justified by history, for England has long been influential internationally.

Understanding England is important, because for generations it has been the prototype of a country enjoying both stable representative government and relative economic wealth. British political institutions have served as a model on every continent. As the author of *The Origins of American Politics* has emphasized, 'The pattern of political activity in the colonies was part of a more comprehensive British pattern, and cannot be understood in isolation from that larger system.'[2] Parliaments can be found in India, Kenya and Canada, as well as in London. Even the Republic of Ireland, which owes its independence to armed revolt against the Crown, has modelled many of its governing institutions upon British examples.

In the mid-1970s the alleged weaknesses of England gained such international notoriety that it became an important negative reference group, that is, an example of a good country *not* to imitate. In a farewell interview as President, Gerald Ford cautioned his fellow Americans, 'It would be tragic for this country if we went down the same path and ended up with the same problems that

[2] Bernard Bailyn, *The Origins of American Politics* (New York: Vintage, 1970), p. ix.

Great Britain has.'[3] British and American writers contributed to a state-of-England symposium entitled *The Future That Doesn't Work*. Its editor proclaimed, 'The United Kingdom has become the latest version of the Sick Man of Europe and, as the United States has been on a similar diet, one might well ask if this nation is fated to go the way of the United Kingdom, and what, if anything, can be done to duck such a fate.' Such remarks prompted a former Labour Cabinet minister, Barbara Castle, to comment, 'It is a curious form of special relationship that casts the United States as mourner-in-chief over Britain's corpse.'[4]

Memories are short. Ten years previously Americans were seen and saw themselves as a land with worse problems than any other modern nation. An American journalist in London, Anthony Lewis, then wrote:

> Of course there are things wrong in Britain today. What seems unjustified is any national sense that in these sins Britain is worse than other countries, and must therefore suffer. A moment's consideration of the United States, with its terrifying problems of war and poverty and social division, should make clear the absurdity of any such guilty notion. . . . In Britain, after all, the problem is only money.[5]

Comparison need not imply global judgments about the superiority of one society to another. The author has lived too long on each side of the Atlantic to believe that this is practicable. As any traveller can verify, the grass *is* greener on the moister, cooler, and English side of the Atlantic. But the machinery for gardening is more advanced in America. Moreover, the heat of a Continental climate means that an *Englischer Garten* in Munich or a *giardino all'Inglese* in Florence is not the same as the equivalent in its more temperate home island. Comparison must always involve careful specification of the topic: different (or better) in what respect?

Evaluating the state of England is difficult, for there is no agreement about how the performance of government should be evalu-

[3] Quoted in 'Ford Fear of Carter Promises', *Daily Telegraph* (London), 4 January 1977.

[4] Cf. R. Emmett Tyrrell Jr., in his editor's introduction to *The Future that Doesn't Work: Social Democracy's Failures in Britain* (Garden City, N.Y.: Doubleday, 1977), p. 2, and 'Americans told Britain Still Lives', *The Times* (London), 17 April 1978.

[5] 'QE2 and other Sore Points', *Sunday Times* (London), 12 January 1969.

ated. The most favourable judgments are likely to be those that emphasize what England has done; achievements of the past are a great source of pride and reassurance to the nation's governors. The least favourable are Jeremiah statements that extrapolate future disaster from present difficulties.[6] For example, British government is often condemned for failing to generate a high and persisting rate of economic growth. Yet few would recommend growth at any price, a fashion popular in Eastern Europe and in modernizing dictatorships in the Third World. English people do not want government by coercion, whatever its purported economic advantage.

If reconciling conflict is the chief criterion of success, then England's government can claim a record of success that none of its major Continental neighbours—France, Germany or Italy—can match. Twentieth-century England has been better at governing with consensus than in mobilizing economic resources. England differs fundamentally from more prosperous Continental neighbours, such as Germany and France, in having a long tradition of stable representative government. If the price of this is a relatively stagnant economy, it is a price that many who have lived through war and revolution are prepared to pay.

In the 1980s the chief political concern of England is not the achievement of economic growth, for this will-o'-the-wisp has eluded both Conservative and Labour governments for more than a generation. It is how to adapt political institutions long a byword for liberty and representative democracy to changing circumstances.

The book's objectives

The primary object of this book is deceptively simple: to describe how politics in England works today. It starts by examining the historical and geographical setting of contemporary England. Chapter I considers the mixed inheritance of modern England, and the following chapter the constraints of place. The structure of the political system is considered in chapter III, which analyses the institutions by which the Crown-in-Parliament rules, and chapter IV, which examines the political culture central to the exercise of authority. Three crucial functions of any political system—the

[6] Bernard D. Nossiter's *Britain: A Future that Works* (Boston: Houghton Mifflin, 1978) attacks fallacies found in the argument of Tyrrell's *The Future that Doesn't Work*, but itself paints a gloomy picture of many aspects of United Kingdom politics. For a more balanced view, see William B. Gwyn and Richard Rose, eds., *Britain —Progress and Decline* (London: Macmillan, 1980).

socialization of individuals into the political culture, recruiting political participants and communicating and withholding political information—are the subjects of the following chapters. The articulation and aggregation of interests by the interrelated actions of pressure groups and parties are the subject of chapters VIII and IX. The final three chapters of the book consider how parts of the political system combine to make and implement policies, and the adaptation of government in a world of change, and constraints upon change.

To analyse politics in its social context is to follow a tradition that goes back to Bagehot's late-Victorian study of *The English Constitution*, and is as up to date as contemporary social science.[7] The boundaries between different parts of society are not so clear as the boundaries between academic disciplines. Whereas professors can easily be divided into political scientists, economists and sociologists, ordinary English people cannot be separated into citizens, consumers and friends: they combine all of these roles in their everyday lives.

The second object of this book is to understand the chief influences upon politics in England today. To study relations of cause and effect is to move from a static to a dynamic view of politics; the policy process is a world of movement, like a ballet, rather than the object of a still-life photograph. The exchange of influence is a two-way street; those who exercise influence are also subject to it. For example, a Cabinet minister influences citizens by making policies, and is also the object of influence from pressure groups and the electorate.

Thirdly, this book asks: What impact does government have upon life in England today? When government levies taxes equivalent to upwards of 50 per cent of the national product, its actions are bound to have an impact upon the economy. But the actions of government may not have the impact that governors intend. For example, in 1966 the Labour government of Harold Wilson abandoned plans to promote faster economic growth in order to give priority to maintaining the international value of the pound; a year later, devaluation followed. In 1972, the Conservative government of Edward Heath launched an incomes policy to combat inflation;

[7] Cf. G. A. Almond and G. Bingham Powell Jr., *Comparative Politics: System, Process and Policy* (Boston: Little Brown & Co., 2nd ed., 1978) and works cited therein.

eighteen months later inflation was rampant and the government was turned out of office by the electorate.

Finally, this book seeks to identify how politics in England is changing. To do this we must free ourselves from the blinkers imposed by the conventional wisdom of the past. As J. M. Keynes wrote nearly half a century ago:

> Madmen in authority, who hear voices in the air, are distilling their frenzy from some academic scribbler of a few years back. I am sure that the power of vested interests is vastly exaggerated compared with the gradual encroachment of ideas.[8]

Keynes himself now threatens to become one of the 'defunct economists' whose writings he railed against. There is no particular reason to expect that the ideas, evidence and conclusions of major studies of British government written twenty-five or thirty years ago will necessarily be relevant to England in the 1980s. The events of the 1970s have challenged many received ideas. While some challenges may be evanescent, others are almost certain to loom still larger in the years ahead.[9] A concern with emerging problems as well as with current and past events informs the whole of the book; each chapter concludes by posing a specific question about the 1980s.

A half century ago, the distinguished French writer André Siegfried diagnosed England's position thus: 'To turn the corner from the nineteenth into the twentieth century, there, in a word, is the whole British problem.'[10] Since then, England has successfully accomplished great changes. In the turbulent world of today, it faces a new challenge: the need to prepare for entry into the twenty-first century.

[8] J. M. Keynes, *The General Theory of Employment, Interest and Money* (London: Macmillan, 1936), p. 403.

[9] See Dennis Kavanagh and Richard Rose, eds., *New Trends in British Politics* (London & Beverly Hills: Sage Publications, 1977), and Dennis Kavanagh, 'New Bottles for New Wines: Changing Assumptions about British Politics', *Parliamentary Affairs* XXXI:1 (1978).

[10] *England's Crisis* (London: Jonathan Cape, 1931), p. 11.

I
The Constraints of History

Each generation describes what it sees, but it uses words transmitted from the past. When a great entity like the British Constitution has continued in connected outward sameness, but hidden inner change for many ages, every generation inherits a series of inapt words—of maxims once true, but of which the truth is ceasing or has ceased.

Every country is constrained by its history, for past actions limit the choices open to present-day governors. Present choices, in turn, have consequences that constrain the future. For example, the 1921 Anglo-Irish Treaty gave *de facto* independence to two-thirds of the population of Ireland, but it left a virulent challenge to political authority in Ulster. Past events can also be important when they leave no heritage. In the eighteenth century, English slave traders exported slaves to the New World but not to England, thus avoiding the legacy of racial problems that has tormented America.

To understand politics in England, it is necessary to understand the origins of institutions, as well as their current rationale. A deductive approach, inferring an explanation of institutions and processes from their contemporary consequences, cannot provide an accurate explanation of politics in England. English people have never had to sit down under pressure of military defeat or domestic revolution to deduce a constitution from first principles. This has been the twentieth-century fate of all the major powers in Europe: France, Germany, Italy, Russia and the successor states of the Habsburg and Ottoman Empires. The government of England has developed inductively and organically. Old institutions have been adapted to new tasks, and new institutions have been grafted to old.

England has been fortunate in resolving many of the fundamental problems of governance before the onset of industrialization. The Crown was established as the central political authority in late medieval times, and the supremacy of secular power over spiritual power was settled in the sixteenth century, when Henry VIII broke with the Roman Catholic Church to establish a national Church of England. The power struggle between Crown and Parliament in the civil war of the 1640s was followed by a Restoration. The monarchy continued—but not as before. The Constitution prevailing in England at the time of the industrialization in the late eighteenth century was a mixed Constitution, with authority divided between Crown and Parliament. The result was limited but not ineffectual government.

The continuity of England's political institutions is outstanding in the world. Unlike America, England has never been able to contemplate the future free from the constraints of a feudal past. Nor have Englishmen turned to revolution to destroy traditional institutions of government in favour of a new order. The major features of the British Constitution reflect forms from the distant past, as well as contemporary innovations. That central institution of democracy—elections—involves procedures dating back to the seventeenth century. In apportioning electors into constituencies, the Boundary Commissioners are not expected to apply mechanically the formula: One person, one vote, one value. They are also expected to make allowance for the representation of 'communities that are integral, human entities which have both a history and a very lively sense of corporate feeling'.[1]

History is more than a record of past events; the residues of history constitute what we familiarly term the present. Nowhere is this more true than in the politics of England, where the heir to an ancient Crown pilots jet aircraft and a medievally styled Chancellor of the Exchequer tries to steer the pound through the deep waters of the international economy. Clement Attlee aptly summarized the interpenetration of different periods of the past in a tribute to Winston Churchill:

> There was a layer of seventeenth century, a layer of eighteenth century, a layer of nineteenth century and possibly even a layer of twentieth century. You were never sure which layer would be uppermost.[2]

Symbols of continuity often mask great changes in English life. Nowhere is this more true than in what Bagehot described as the 'undergrowth of irrelevant ideas' gathered around the Constitution. For example, Parliament was once a supporter of royal authority;

[1] Chuter Ede, quoted in Vincent Starzinger, 'The British Pattern of Apportionment', *Virginia Quarterly Review*, XLI:3 (1965), p. 328.
[2] *The Guardian*, (London), 21 April 1963.

then it was a restraint upon it, deposing monarchs, and making laws in its own right. Today it is primarily important as an electoral college making or unmaking Cabinets. The persistence of an institution for centuries usually indicates that it has altered greatly—sometimes out of all recognition—to meet changes in the country's circumstances.

The history of England is normally taught in schools as a success story. The first part of this chapter emphasizes that the making of modern England resolved many fundamental political problems successfully, but also has contributed to contemporary problems. The second section evaluates the contemporary significance of the mixed political inheritance of modern England. A long and continuous political history is neither good nor bad of itself; failures as well as successes can endure.

The making of modern England

There is no agreement among social scientists about when England developed a modern system of government. A political historian might date the change at 1485, an economic historian from about 1760, and a frustrated egalitarian reformer might proclaim that it hasn't happened yet.[3]

Industrialization, not political revolution, was the great discontinuity in English history. England was the first industrial nation. By the early eighteenth century it had already developed the commercial skills and resources needed to transform an agricultural and handicraft economy; by the middle of the nineteenth century, England had become the world's first modern industrial society. The repeal of the Corn Laws in 1846, signifying the shift from an agrarian society producing its own food to an industrial economy exchanging manufactured goods for food imported from other countries, symbolizes this change.

The Constitution of England at the time of the Industrial Revolution was designed for a rural society, and justified by tradition. Until 1834 the Treasury kept the nation's accounts in Roman numerals and Latin prose. Reformers declared that this 'Gothic' constitution

[3] For a much fuller development of points discussed herein, see Richard Rose, 'England: A Traditionally Modern Political Culture', in Lucian W. Pye and Sidney Verba, eds., *Political Culture and Political Development* (Princeton: University Press, 1965). See also Keith Thomas, 'The United Kingdom', in Raymond Grew, *Crises of Political Development in Europe and the United States* (Princeton: University Press, 1978), pp. 41–97.

could not meet the problems of modern (i.e. early nineteenth-century) English society. The governors of Old England adapted slowly but realistically to political change. The Prime Minister, Earl Grey, endorsed the landmark 1832 Reform Act with the argument that 'Unless the privileged sections of the community were prepared to adapt and to improve, waves of dangerous and uncontrollable innovation would completely drown the existing social order.'[4]

The simplest way to date the advent of modern government is to say that it came about in Victorian times. During this era, from 1837 to 1901, the principal features of the old Constitution were altered and supplemented by new devices enabling government to cope with the problems of a society that was increasingly urban, literate and critical of unchanged traditions. England was also a much larger society, for the population nearly doubled from 1790 to 1850, and had trebled by 1900.

The 1832 Reform Act started a process of enfranchising the masses that led to the grant of the vote to a majority of English males by 1885. As the electorate expanded, party organization began to develop along recognizable modern lines too. Innovations promoted by followers of the rationalistic philosophy of Jeremy Bentham led to the development of a large, bureaucratic and effective civil service. England's constitutional bureaucracy was capable of organizing everything from the economical saving of candle ends to prototype laws of the modern welfare state.[5]

By the middle of the nineteenth century British government had demonstrated that not only could it cope with the military threat of Napoleon's armies, but also with the novel challenges of industrialization. Government provided the political stability and security within which industry and commerce could flourish, and began to make public provision for welfare too. The first minister responsible for health was appointed in 1854, for education in 1857, and for local government, a major institution delivering welfare services, in 1871. The institutional foundation for the twentieth-century mixed-economy welfare state was established.[6]

[4] Cf. G. Kitson Clark, *The Making of Victorian England* (London: Methuen, 1962).

[5] See Henry Parris, *Constitutional Bureaucracy* (London: George Allen & Unwin, 1969).

[6] On the establishment of the major functional institutions of British government in comparative perspective, see Richard Rose, 'On the Priorities of Government: A Developmental Analysis of Public Policies', *European Journal of Political Research*, IV:3 (1976).

The nineteenth-century growth of government and the growth of the economy resulted in public expenditure rising greatly in absolute terms, while falling as a proportion of the Gross National Product (see Table I.1). In 1820, after the end of the Napoleonic wars, public spending accounted for more than one-sixth of the national product. By 1880, it accounted for only one-tenth of the national product. Yet this smaller proportion of a greatly expanded national product gave a far larger amount of money to government. In 1820 the British government spent £70 million; by 1880 it was spending six times as much in constant prices. The whole of the cost of increased public spending in the nineteenth century and well into the twentieth century could be financed by the fiscal dividend of economic growth.[7]

TABLE I.1 **The growth of the economy and of public expenditure, 1790–1961**

Year	Population (Million)	Gross national product		Total public expenditure	
		At constant price	Per capita	Per capita	As % of GNP
1790	14.8	100	100	100	12
1820	16.1	169	120	169	17
1850	27.3	356	193	179	11
1880	34.6	679	290	232	10
1910	45.0	1,383	455	444	12
1938	47.5	1,900	592	1,444	30
1961	52.8	2,871	805	2,468	38

Source Jindrich Veverka, 'The Growth of Government Expenditure in the United Kingdom since 1790', *Scottish Journal of Political Economy*, X:2 (1963), p. 114.

The creation of a modern system of government did not make the problems of governing disappear. What it did do was give politicians institutions useful in responding to the challenges that have confronted twentieth-century England.

The first of these challenges has been national defence in a war-torn world. In the First World War, Britain and France held Germany at bay in a trench war of bloody attrition, finally winning in 1918 with latterday American support. In the Second World War

[7] See Alan T. Peacock and Jack Wiseman, *The Growth of Public Expenditure in the United Kingdom* (London: Oxford University Press, 1961).

Britain stood alone against Nazi Germany in 1940–41, until the outbreak of a global war including Russia, America and Japan. Britain once again emerged on the winning side.

The second great challenge of the century, the granting to the working class of full rights of citizenship, was accomplished gradually. The bulk of the popular political demands made by the Chartists in 1837 were met by 1918. The supremacy of the elected House of Commons, as against the aristocratic and hereditary House of Lords, was established by legislation in 1911. The right to vote was granted all adult men in 1918, as well as to women aged 28 or above.[8] The Labour Party, founded in 1900 to secure the representation of manual workers in Parliament, first formed a minority government briefly in 1924. Ironically, the non-violent General Strike of 1926 demonstrated the commitment of trade union leaders to constitutional action. When union leaders saw the potentially revolutionary implications of a general strike, these implications were disowned, and the strike collapsed.[9]

Thirdly, government has increasingly been concerned with distributing and redistributing the fruits of economic growth through welfare policies benefiting the mass of citizens. In Victorian England, government was primarily concerned with the regulation of social affairs by public health policies from which all citizens, rich and poor, collectively benefited, and compulsory education, introduced in 1870. The Liberal government of 1906–14 laid twentieth-century foundations for the welfare state by guaranteeing pensions in old age. Inter-war governments expanded the provisions of welfare services. From 1890 to 1932, public spending per head on social services rose nine times, a larger increase in real terms than that achieved from 1932 to 1951. In this era the British government was relatively well placed to increase public spending, notwithstanding inter-war unemployment rates fluctuating between 11 and 23 per cent. The country's national product more than doubled between 1913 and 1938, a rate of economic growth faster than that of France, Germany or Sweden.[10]

[8] The voting age for women was lowered to 21, the same as that for men, in 1928, and to 18 for both sexes in 1969.

[9] Cf. Krishan Kumar, 'Can the Workers Be Revolutionary?', *European Journal of Political Research*, VI:4 (1978).

[10] See Jindrich Veverka, 'The Growth of Government Expenditure in the United Kingdom since 1790', *Scottish Journal of Political Economy*, X:2 (1963). Cf. B. R. Mitchell, *European Historical Statistics 1750–1970* (London: Macmillan, 1975), Table K1.

The Second World War and its aftermath brought about great changes within England. The wartime all-party coalition government of Winston Churchill sought to provide fair shares for all when mobilizing the population for all-out war. From the wartime coalition emerged the Beveridge Report on Social Welfare, Keynes's Full Employment White Paper of 1944 and the Butler Education Act of 1944. These three measures—the first two named after Liberals and the third after a Conservative—remain major landmarks of the mixed-economy welfare state today.

The fair shares policy was continued by the Labour government of Clement Attlee elected in 1945. It maintained rationing and controls to ensure that everyone observed postwar austerity while rebuilding the economy. The National Health Service was established, providing medical care for all. The mines, gas, electricity, the railways, road transport and the steel industry were nationalized as part of Labour's programme of increasing government power in the economy. By 1951 the Labour government had accomplished the measures on which there was agreement within the party, and its economic policies had yet to produce prosperity. A much reformed Conservative Party under Winston Churchill was returned to power by the electorate.

For three decades since, Conservative and Labour governments have sought economic prosperity, a generous provision of welfare services, and increasing take-home pay for ordinary citizens. The 1950s saw a marked rise in living standards, after years of wartime scarcity and postwar austerity. Consumer goods once thought the privilege of a relative few, such as cars and refrigerators, became widespread. Some observers interpreted the boom in mass consumption as the start of a 'classless' society, as the Conservatives won general elections with unprecedented increases in their parliamentary majorities in 1955 and 1959. The Prime Minister, Harold Macmillan, summarized the economic record of the 1950s by saying, 'Most of our people have never had it so good.' But Macmillan was cautious about the future. When praising current prosperity in 1957, he warned:

What is beginning to worry some of us is, 'Is it too good to be true?' or perhaps I should say, 'Is it too good to last?' Amidst all this prosperity, there is one problem that has troubled us—in one way or another—ever since the war. It's the problem of rising prices.[11]

The 1960s cast a shadow of doubt upon the government's ability to guarantee continued affluence, for the British economy grew more slowly than the government wished and more slowly than its European or overseas competitors. The Macmillan government turned to economic planning measures in hopes of stimulating steady growth, and in 1961 applied unsuccessfully to join the European Common Market. Labour in opposition argued that, in an era of technological change Socialism provided a better means to develop the economy. But the promises of the 1964–70 Labour government under Harold Wilson were shattered by a classic economic dilemma: how to stimulate a domestic economic boom without simultaneously risking the devaluation of the pound because of foreign creditors' reactions. The Wilson government tried to prevent the devaluation of the pound, but failed. By the time Labour left office in 1970 the nation's economy was growing more slowly than at any time in its post-1945 history.

The 1960s were also important as the beginning of an era of disillusionment with British government. Continuities with the past were attacked as evidence of the dead hand of tradition. The choice of the 14th Earl of Home, then a member of the House of Lords, as Prime Minister in 1963 by a small clique of Conservative notables seemed to epitomize the hold of history. Sir Alec Douglas-Home replied to the attack by remarking, 'I suppose Harold Wilson must be the fourteenth Mr. Wilson.' Satire was deployed—on television, the stage and in periodicals such as *Private Eye*—to mock what was formerly held in esteem. A stream of books, pamphlets and articles were published on the theme: What's wrong with Britain?

A series of Royal Commissions and enquiries proposed reforms of the civil service, local government, Parliament, education, the mass media, industrial relations and the Constitution. Governments have enacted a number of the institutional changes recommended. New titles were given Whitehall offices in response to a desire for change for its own sake. Behind the entrance way, the same people went through the same administrative routines as before.

[11] Quoted in Dennis Kavanagh and Richard Rose, 'British Politics Since 1945: The Changing Field of Study', in Kavanagh and Rose, eds., *New Trends in British Politics* (London and Beverly Hills: Sage, 1977), p. 13.

The 1970s intensified anxieties about the government (or even, some argued, the governability) of England. Taken together, the experience of Conservative government under Edward Heath from 1970 to 1974 and of a Labour government under Harold Wilson and James Callaghan from 1974 to 1979 has demonstrated that the difficulties of governing England are not the fault of particular individuals or parties. The Heath government was noteworthy for introducing major changes in policies as well as in institutions of government. But the biggest changes of the decade were neither intended nor desired by the Prime Ministers who presided over them.

In pursuit of a policy of limiting wages in the midst of a then unprecedented rate of inflation, Edward Heath risked the authority of his office in 1974 by a confrontation with the National Union of Mineworkers, which was defying the government's pay policy in pursuit of wage increases. The impasse was broken by the general election of 28 February 1974, called by the Prime Minister to ascertain: Who governs? The electorate returned a vote of no confidence in both major parties. The Conservative share of the vote dropped by 8.1 per cent, and the Labour vote by 5.8 per cent, reducing both parties to their lowest level of popular support in generations. Neither party won a parliamentary majority. A minority Labour government was formed under Harold Wilson.

In October 1974 Labour won a bare parliamentary majority with 39.2 per cent of the vote, the lowest percentage poll of any majority government in British history, and little more than the vote attracted by Senators Barry Goldwater and George McGovern in their landslide defeats in the 1964 and 1972 American Presidential elections. By 1977 the Labour government had lost its majority, because of by-election defeats and defections by sitting MPs. It required a pact with the Liberals to guarantee it a House of Commons majority on a vote of confidence.

The major achievement of the 1974–9 Labour government was to maintain a political consensus in the face of the country's most severe economic difficulties since the inter-war depression. Instead of confrontation with the unions, the Labour government sought a so-called social contract. Initially, this was intended to provide higher levels of government welfare benefits, and avoid any government restrictions upon wage increases. In July 1975 the first of a series of pay policies was adopted, limiting wage increases to £6 a week. In 1976, the exigencies of sterling were such that the government was forced to seek a loan from the International Monetary Fund, and impose severe cash limits upon public sector spending. By the beginning of 1979, the economy continued to fare ill. Unemployment stood at 1.5 million, the highest since the 1930s; prices had doubled since 1974; real wages had fallen, notwithstanding a nominal increase in money wages of more than 100 per cent; and the economy had actually contracted, instead of grown, in two of the preceding four years.

The British general election of 3 May 1979 saw the two major parties in a reversal of roles. The Labour government under James Callaghan argued against the risk of change. The nominally Conservative party led by Margaret Thatcher called for a radical change in the country's economic policy. The Conservatives won an absolute majority in Parliament, but the party gained only 43.9 per cent of the vote. Labour's share of the popular vote fell to 36.9 per cent, its lowest since 1931. The electorate's greater confidence in Mr. Callaghan's personality could not overcome the unpopularity of the Labour government's record. The Liberals and Nationalists continued to poll relatively well, together taking 18 per cent of the popular vote. Mrs. Thatcher became the first woman Prime Minister of a major European country.

Judged against the experience of European governments across the time span of centuries, the government of England has a record of great achievement. England, unlike Germany or Italy, has no modern experience of Fascist dictatorship; unlike Czechoslovakia, no experience of a Communist *coup d'état*; unlike Spain, no experience of military dictatorship arising from civil war; and unlike France, no modern experience of military occupation, the collapse of a regime and the creation of a constitution around a charismatic leader.

A mixed inheritance

One great premise of English politics is the assimilation of the past in the present. Change for its own sake has had little appeal to English politicians; they have preferred to adapt rather than abolish ageing political institutions. The monarchy is the outstanding example of adaptation. Given great past advantages, the implicit premise of political change becomes the assimilation of past and present, rather than the radical rejection of the past on behalf of an unknown and untested future. The spirit is summed up in the motto of Lord Hugh Cecil's study of Conservatism: 'Even when I changed, it should be to preserve.'[12]

History constrains any British government. Past events must today be taken as given, limiting what any British government can do. For example, the housing policy of any government is constrained by the housing decisions of its predecessors. In the lifetime of a Parliament, only 10 per cent of the population at most can be placed in new houses. Nine-tenths of all English families must live in houses that were not built under the government of the day. No government of the day can write off the inertia commitments of past policies.

In the course of time, assets can turn into liabilities. For example, England's industrial eminence has owed much to the fact that it was the first country in the world to have an industrial revolution. It was for long the world's leading industrial nation because it was the world's *only* industrial nation. Today, changes in technology have made obsolete England's pioneering advantages in such industries as textiles and shipbuilding. The rapid industrialization of Continental Europe and Japan has also limited the exports of newer industrial products, such as cars and mass consumer goods. Today, England simultaneously faces the problem of 're-modernizing' its economy, and caring for the workers and regions hit hardest by the decline of traditional industries.

When the inheritance of the past appears benign, it provides great reassurance to governors and governed. Today, an increasing number of people question whether it should. In the caustic words of one left-wing writer, E. P. Thompson, 'We lie upon our heritage like a Dunlopillo mattress, and hope, in our slumbers, those good, dead men of history will move us forward.'[13]

There is a limit to which past success can be extended into the future. The House of Commons in 1980 has only one member who sat in a Cabinet of Clement Attlee or Winston Churchill more than a quarter century before. It is full of MPs who hope to be Cabinet ministers in the twenty-first century. Today, we are far closer to the

[12] *Conservatism* (London: Williams & Norgate [*c.* 1912], p. 243.
[13] E. P. Thompson, 'An Open Letter to Leszek Kolakowski', in Ralph Miliband and John Saville, eds., *The Socialist Register 1973* (London: Merlin, 1974), p. 24. See more generally, J. E. S. Hayward, 'Institutional Inertia and Political Impetus in France and Britain', *European Journal of Political Research*, IV:4 (1976).

year 2000 than to 1900 or, for that matter, to 1945. There is no longer good reason to refer to contemporary England as in the postwar era. Future generations will not characterize our time by what it followed, but by what it is a prelude to.

II
The Constraints of Place

Are they [the English] not above all nations divided from
the rest of the world, insular both in situation and in mind,
both for good and for evil?

The island position of England is its most significant geographical
feature; insularity is one of its most striking cultural characteristics.
London is physically closer to France than it is to the geographical
centre of England, but the English Channel has for centuries fixed a
deep gulf between England and the continent of Europe. Although
there is no other continent to which the island could conceivably be
assigned, the English do not think of themselves as Europeans. In
the words of a French writer, 'We might liken England to a ship which,
though anchored in European waters, is always ready to sail away.'[1]

When Europe was the centre of world affairs, England held aloof
from commitments there, intervening only when necessary to maintain a balance of power. Today the country's military dependence
upon America is as meaningful politically as its geographical prop-
inquity to France, Belgium and the Netherlands. Entry to the European Community has occurred in spite of perceived differences
between Englishmen and Europeans. Historic links with Commonwealth countries in other continents further reduce the significance of physical geography. Politically, the English may claim to be
equally close to or distant from Europe, America and the nations of
a global Commonwealth.

When English people are asked to say what they think of other
major nations, the largest proportion (74 per cent) gives a favourable rating to the United States; West Germany comes second,
France third, and Japan fourth. All of these countries receive the
esteem of English people, although they are culturally and geographically heterogeneous, and two were enemies in the Second
World War. The one thing that they have in common is a much more
dynamic economy than England.[2]

[1] André Siegfried, *England's Crisis* (London: Jonathan Cape, 1931), p. 303.
[2] *Gallup Political Index* (London: Social Surveys Ltd.), No. 215 (June
1978), p. 16.

Yet, when English people think of emigration, they do not think first of moving to prosperous and nearby countries of the European Community or to ex-colonial cousins in America. Instead, surveys consistently show that 77 per cent of English, if emigrating, would wish to settle in Canada, Australia, New Zealand or Southern Africa. Only 9 per cent mention America and 7 per cent a Continental European country.[3] In spite of geographical remoteness, these old Dominions appeal because they are perceived as closest in outlook to what the English know and like at home.

Whereas England claimed to lead the world in many things in the nineteenth century, today its politics are dominated by the constraints of political, economic and social geography. In a world of global interdependence, England is more dependent than many other nations. Moreover, within the United Kingdom, Englishmen can no longer take for granted the willingness of Scots, Welsh and Ulstermen to act as if they too were English. The multi-racial Commonwealth poses a problem too, for it has sent to England more than a million people, facing England with the problems of adapting an all-white society to a multi-racial life. This chapter reviews in turn England's place in the world, its place in the United Kingdom, and the place of black Britons in a society that is overwhelmingly English.

Insularity and involvement

England's insular position has been a great asset, saving it from military invasions that have cost European countries so much in the twentieth century. The last successful foreign invasion of England was the Norman conquest of 1066; in France, it was the German invasion of 1940. In both world wars of this century, England was free from occupation, while the continent of Europe was a battlefield. Unlike France, Germany, Italy and Japan, contemporary England has not had to build new political institutions after the havoc of war.

Insularity is not to be confused with isolation. As an island with a long seafaring tradition, the country has been, in the words of Sir Eyre Crowe, 'a neighbour of every country accessible by sea'. By acts of policy and by the adventurous initiatives of public officials and private traders, England came to administer an empire that at one time included nearly one-fifth of the population and land area

[3] *Gallup Political Index*, No. 200 (March 1977), p. 10.

of the world. The British Empire drew together territories as scattered and various as India, Nigeria and Palestine, as well as the old Dominions of Canada, Australia, New Zealand and South Africa. The success of empire builders left Britain at the end of the Second World War with political commitments on every continent. The end of the empire began with the grant of independence to India and Pakistan in 1947. In the decades since, British governments have accepted that they could no longer enforce their authority at a distance of thousands of miles against colonial peoples demanding independence. Nearly three dozen independent states today, with a population of 800 million, were part of the British Empire in 1945.

The British Empire has been replaced by a free association of more than two dozen sovereign states, the Commonwealth. The independent status of its chief members is shown by the removal of the word 'British' from the title of the Commonwealth. A number of Afro-Asian nations have exchanged loyalty to the Crown for the status of a republic, and the old Dominions of Canada and Australia have symbolically abandoned 'God Save the Queen' as their national anthems. Only a miscellany of island colonies and small trading enclaves such as Gibraltar and Hong Kong remain from days of the Empire. Meetings of Commonwealth countries today often emphasize the political and social conflicts among its very heterogeneous membership.[4]

The story of postwar British foreign policy is a story of gradually contracting commitments. Initially, the United Kingdom played an important role as a partner of America in organizing major alliances. In 1946, Winston Churchill took the lead in stimulating a Western military alliance against the advance of the Soviet Union; this culminated in the creation of the North Atlantic Treaty Organization (NATO) three years later. In 1947, the Labour government took the lead in organizing a European response to the United States offer of economic aid in the Marshall Plan. After the outbreak of the Korean War in 1950, Britain took the lead in European rearmament. The inability to pursue an independent foreign policy was revealed in 1956. In collaboration with France, it organized an abortive military invasion of Egypt to seize the Suez Canal,

[4] On the significance of this change, see A. P. Thornton, *The Imperial Idea and its Enemies* (London: Macmillan, 1959) and Sir Nicholas Mansergh, *The Commonwealth Experience* (London: Weidenfeld & Nicolson, 1969).

regarded by the Prime Minister, Sir Anthony Eden, as vital to England's trade lifeline. The military force was withdrawn in the face of joint American and Russian opposition, its objective unachieved.

The contraction of diplomatic commitments has been matched by a decline in military strength.[5] Initially, the United Kingdom sought to develop an independent nuclear weapon system. By 1962 it was reduced to dependence upon the United States for the sophisticated research and development technology required for modern armaments. In 1965 the Labour government showed itself unable (or unwilling) to use force against 200,000 white settlers in Southern Rhodesia, who unilaterally declared independence in defiance of London's preference for a multi-racial government. By the start of the 1970s, the country's military force of 332,000 was so limited that it needed to withdraw troops from its principal overseas bases in NATO in an attempt to contain violence in Northern Ireland.

As part of a heritage from an imperial past, the United Kingdom remains one of the five permanent members of the Security Council of the United Nations. Like France, its influence is of a different and lesser order than that of the three Council super-powers: America, Russia and China. It is a member of 126 different international organizations; this ranks it third among nations in membership in international organizations. But British government officials now question whether the country needs—or can afford—diplomatic commitments taken for granted a half century ago. Official reports suggest that embassies should be closed down in lands where the benefits are not perceived as equal to the cost, and one report has even recommended the abolition of a separate diplomatic service.[6]

While no longer a diplomatic or military great power, England continues to belong to that very small group of nations that is both big and rich. It ranks eleventh among nations in the world in population, and in terms of gross national product, the conventional measure of economic wealth, it ranks seventh in the world. Most of

---

[5] See e.g. Kenneth Waltz, *Foreign Policy and Democratic Politics* (London: Longman, 1969); Richard E. Neustadt, *Alliance Politics* (New York: Columbia University Press, 1970) and Gavin Kennedy, *The Economics of British Defence* (London: Faber & Faber, 1975).

[6] Cf. the *Report of the Review Committee on Overseas Representation* (Chairman: Sir Val Duncan) (London: HMSO, Cmnd. 4107, 1969); the Central Policy Review Staff, *Review of Overseas Representation* (London: HMSO, 1977) and Max Beloff, 'The Think Tank and Foreign Affairs', *Public Administration*, LV (Winter 1977).

the countries that outrank it, such as America, Japan and Russia, are far bigger in population. When national wealth is related to population, England remains a prosperous nation, but on a *per capita* basis its international ranking falls to twentieth place. It is not only behind such oil-rich sheikhdoms as Saudi Arabia, but also behind such small, prosperous Continental countries as the Netherlands, Belgium, Austria and Norway. The economy remains far wealthier than that of the typical member state of the United Nations, which is both small and poor. Overall, English people are among the wealthiest ten per cent of the world's population.

The economy is unusually integrated with the world economy. In a literal sense, England must export to live. Since the repeal of the Corn Laws in 1846, England has depended upon importing much of the food that it eats; today, major industries are also dependent upon the import of many raw materials as well. To pay for these imports, England exports a wide range of manufactured goods, as well as such 'invisible' services as banking and insurance. The City of London is one of the world's great financial centres. England disperses its trade more widely among the countries of the world than any other trading nation.[7]

Like all Western nations, in the past generation England has experienced real and substantial economic growth. From 1951 to 1978, the economy grew in 24 of 27 years. In the 1950s and 1960s, the annual rate of growth was relatively steady, tending to fluctuate between 2 and 3 per cent per year. The economy has, however, grown less than that of any other Western nation. As a result, while England has been getting richer in absolute terms, its economic position has been declining relative to that of other major Western nations (see Table II.1). England has grown an average of 2.5 per cent annually since 1951, but America has grown 3.2 per cent annually and Germany by 5.8 per cent.

In the 1970s, the entire world economy has suffered a recession, with growth rates falling, and prices rising everywhere. Britain has felt these difficulties more than most countries. The 1.8 per cent average annual growth in the British economy from 1971 to 1978 was lower than that of any other major Western nation except Sweden. Moreover, the more than 100 per cent increase in prices

[7] For detailed rankings, see Charles L. Taylor and Michael C. Hudson, *World Handbook of Political and Social Indicators* (New Haven: Yale University Press, 2nd ed., 1972).

was greater than that of any other major Western nation, and more than double the rate of inflation in America or Germany (see Table II.1).

TABLE II.1 **Economic growth and inflation in comparative perspective, 1951–1978**

	Annual growth, GNP		Annual change, prices	
	1951–70	1971–78	1951–70	1971–78
	%	%	%	%
Britain	2.7	1.8	4.0	13.5
France	5.1	3.4	5.4	8.9
Germany	6.3	2.6	3.0	5.5
Italy	5.4	2.4	3.4	13.0
Sweden	3.8	1.5	4.5	9.0
United States	3.6	2.8	2.7	6.7

Sources OECD, *National Accounts of OECD Countries, 1950–1968* (Paris: OECD, 1969), annual change tables; OECD, *National Accounts of OECD Countries, 1975*, Vol. 1 (Paris: OECD, 1977), annual change tables; OECD, *Main Economic Indicators*, 79/5 (May 1979).

The high rate of inflation reflects the desire of English people to increase their consumption, both private and public, faster than the nation's economic growth. Increased demand is met in part by increasing such imports as cars, which British manufacturers cannot produce in sufficient quantity and at the right price to meet demand. When imports run well ahead of exports the government seeks foreign loans in an effort to avoid a balance of payments crisis. In the words of James Callaghan shortly after becoming Prime Minister:

> No one owes Britain a living, and may I say to you quite bluntly that despite the measures of the last 12 months we are still not earning the standard of living we are enjoying. We are keeping up our standards by borrowing, and this cannot go on indefinitely.[8]

While the British government's influence upon the national economy has been growing, the influence of international market forces upon the British economy has grown even more. To meet balance of payments problems, the United Kingdom has had to go

[8] Prime Ministerial broadcast, 5 April 1976.

to the International Monetary Fund time and again in order to secure international loans permitting it to meet major trading obligations. In the course of negotiating these loans with this international agency, British governments have had to give undertakings to take economic measures that they knew would be unpopular with the national electorate, e.g. squeezing consumption and increasing unemployment, in order to forestall other difficulties, e.g. inflation or a large-scale international devaluation of the pound.[9]

Because Britain's inflation rate has been higher than that of other major Western nations, the value of the pound has declined relative to other major international currencies. Until 1949, the £ was worth (U.S.) $4.20, and from then until 1967, $2.80. It was then devalued to $2.40, and since 1972 it has been allowed to 'float' in international exchange markets. Its price is basically determined by pressures of supply and demand. At one point in 1976, the pound floated to a value of less than $1.60, before rising above $2.00 in 1979, with an improvement in the British economy and continued troubles with the American economy. Since 1949, the pound has fallen even more in value in comparison with European currencies. From 1953 to 1967 the £ was worth about eleven German Deutsche Marks. At the end of 1979, it was worth less than four Deutsche Marks. At the request of a German plaintiff, an English High Court judge rendered judgment against a British company in Deutsche Marks, because 'Sterling floats in the wind, it changes like a weathercock with every gust that blows.'[10] From 1972 to mid-1979 the pound fell by 32 per cent in relation to a basket of currencies of its major trading partners. (Cf. Table XI.7.)

As the United Kingdom's relative position has declined in the world, government has looked to Europe, hoping to secure continued economic growth and a share of diplomatic influence by joining with the six increasingly prosperous countries of the European Community (or Common Market as it is often called in Eng-

[9] On Britain's dealings with the IMF in 1976, see the series of articles by Stephen Fay and Hugo Young, 'The Day the £ Nearly Died', *Sunday Times*, 14, 21, 28 May 1978. On the political economy generally, see the writings of Samuel Brittan, e.g. *Steering the Economy: The Role of the Treasury* (London: Secker & Warburg, 1969), J. Dow, *Management of the British Economy 1945–1960* (London: National Institute of Economic & Social Research 1970), and F. T. Blackaby, ed., *British Economic Policy, 1960–74* (Cambridge: University Press, 1978).

[10] See the statement by Lord Denning in *Shorsch Meier* v. *Hennin* (1974), cited in Richard Vaughan, ed., *Post-war Integration in Europe* (London: Edward Arnold, 1976), p. 191.

land, to stress its economic rather than political significance). Britain did not join the Community when it was established in 1957, considering its position superior to that of Continental neighbours ravaged by the effects of wartime. In 1961, the Conservative government of Harold Macmillan first sought British entry. Concurrently, many changes in European societies were drawing the island nation into closer links with its Continental neighbours. These ranged from joint participation in televised Eurovision song contests and European Football Cup matches to the impact of American multi-national corporations. Jet aircraft have made the English Channel less a barrier to travel than city traffic. A businessman travelling from London to Paris, Brussels or Frankfurt spends twice as long getting to and from the airport as in flight.

The United Kingdom joined the European Community on 1 January 1973, but there has been a question mark behind its membership since, for ordinary voters and politicians have continued to disagree about whether the decision was the right one. Parliament approved entry by 112 votes; divisions about membership cut across party lines. A majority of Conservative and a minority of Labour MPs voted for entry, and were opposed by a majority of Labour and a minority of Conservative MPs.[11]

Economic arguments were the chief reasons given for entry to the Common Market. The British economy was pictured as likely to benefit from the stimulus of wider markets and competition. Exclusion from Continental markets, if the United Kingdom remained outside the Community, was depicted as a risk that the country could not afford to run. Benefits did not follow as expected. Instead, in October 1973 the oil crisis triggered a world recession. The Common Market has been blamed by its critics for many of the economic difficulties that have befallen Britain since.

In 1975 the Labour government took the unprecedented step of calling a national referendum to determine whether or not the United Kingdom should remain a member of the European Community. The referendum showed a majority of 67 to 33 per cent in favour.[12] But the one-third that voted against have not abandoned their opposition, and support for the Community has waned. By

[11] For details, see Uwe Kitzinger, *Diplomacy and Persuasion* (London: Thames & Hudson, 1973).
[12] See David Butler and Uwe Kitzinger, *The 1975 Referendum* (London: Macmillan, 1976) and Anthony King, *Britain Says Yes* (Washington, D.C.: American Enterprise Institute, 1977).

July 1978, only 29 per cent of the respondents in a British Gallup Poll thought the country's membership in the Community a good thing, as against 38 per cent thinking it bad, and 33 per cent with no opinion. Moreover, many English people still regard Continentals as alien or remote. No Community nation has been visited by more than 38 per cent of the British people, and only 13 per cent claim to know enough French to read a French newspaper.[13]

By signing the Treaty of Rome and becoming a member of the European Community, the British government has increased its involvement in Continental European affairs.[14] Direct election of the European Parliament in June 1979 has increased the legitimacy of relatively weak Community decision-makers against national governments, including the British government. Virtually every government department must at some point now take European Community policies into account, and British politicians and civil servants are increasingly involved in the bargaining process that produces vast numbers of small-scale Community regulations that become binding laws in Britain. Yet even after experience of membership, neither proponents nor opponents of the Community can agree about how much influence the Community has upon Britain, or Britain upon the Community.

Public opinion actively favours England withdrawing from its historic great-power position in the world, and adopting a more isolationist 'Little England' role. In 1978, 51 per cent of respondents told the Gallup Poll that they would like to see the country become more like Sweden or Switzerland, as against 31 per cent wishing England to be a leading world power.[15]

But England's future place in the world is not determined by popular wish alone. The constraints of history and of place limit the extent to which the government can insulate the country from world economic trends. Today, the effective choice of government is not whether England should be big and rich or a small rich country like Switzerland, but whether it can remain a big, rich country, or whether it gradually becomes a big, and relatively poor, Western

[13] See *Euro-Barometre* (Brussels: Commission of the European Communities, No. 9, July 1978), Annex Table 1 and *Gallup Political Index*, No. 209 (December 1977), p. 12.
[14] See e.g. Helen Wallace, William Wallace and Carole Webb, eds., *Policy-Making in the European Communities* (London: John Wiley & Sons, 1977) and sources cited therein.
[15] *Gallup Political Index*, No. 216 (July 1978), p. 14.

nation. By refusing to face this choice, England's governors demonstrate the aptness of the judgment of the American diplomat, Dean Acheson: 'Great Britain has lost an empire and has not yet found a role.'[16]

One Crown and many nations

The English Crown is the oldest and best known in the world, yet there is no such thing as an English state. In international law as in the title of the Queen, the state is the United Kingdom of Great Britain and Northern Ireland. The island of Great Britain, the principal part of the United Kingdom, is divided into three parts: England, Scotland and Wales. England constitutes 55 per cent of the land area of Great Britain. The other part of the United Kingdom, Northern Ireland, consists of six counties of Ulster that remained under the Crown rather than join an independent Irish Republic ruled from Dublin. In so far as territorial contiguity is politically significant, one might expect a state to occupy an island to itself or a pair of neighbouring islands. (See Figure II.1.) Irish nationalists have always argued that geography implies the existence of two island states, Ireland and Britain. Unionists have argued for a United Kingdom of the two islands. The international boundary of the United Kingdom today cuts across the northeast of Ireland, the one arrangement that is not implicit in insular geography.

The constraints of geography make England only a part of the United Kingdom. As elsewhere in Europe, the boundaries of the United Kingdom are the result of centuries of diplomatic negotiations, battles won and lost, and the accidents of dynastic succession. Wales was joined to England by dynastic inheritance, formalized by legislation in 1536. Scotland was similarly joined in two stages in 1603 and 1707. England has intermittently been sending troops to Ireland from 1169 to the present, in an effort to maintain some sovereignty in at least part of the island. While the ancestry of the Crown may be traced back to Alfred the Great in the ninth century, the current boundaries of the United Kingdom date only from 1921.

In social and political terms, the United Kingdom is a multinational state.[17] The great majority of Welsh people think of them-

[16] 'Britain's Independent Role about Played Out', *The Times*, 6 December 1962.
[17] See Richard Rose, 'The United Kingdom as a Multi-National State', in R. Rose, ed., *Studies in British Politics* (London: Macmillan, 3rd ed., 1976). For documenta-

selves as Welsh, and Scottish people think of themselves as Scots. In Northern Ireland there is no agreement about national identity; nearly two-thirds see themselves as Irish or Ulstermen. Except in Northern Ireland, these distinctive identities can be harmonized with a British identification.

In Scotland the established church is presbyterian in form, whereas the Church of England is episcopal; the Queen, by a political compromise that long antedated the ecumenical movement, worships as a Presbyterian in Scotland and as an Anglican in England. Scotland also maintains a separate and distinctive legal system, influenced by the Roman law tradition. Its educational system also differs from that of England in important ways, such as state subsidies for Roman Catholic schools and university entrance requirements. The industrialized Scottish Lowlands concentrates most of Scotland's population around Glasgow and Edinburgh. The area is distinct from England in everything from architecture to drinking habits. The vastness of the Scottish Highlands to the North is outside industrial civilization, except for the occasional incursions of North Sea oil activities. The Highlands has less than five per cent of Scotland's population.

The existence of a separate legal system and separate social institutions has meant that Scotland has always had some political institutions separate and distinct from England. Since 1885 there has been a separate minister at the head of a Scottish Office, and since 1939 the administrative headquarters of the Scottish Office has been in Edinburgh. The Scottish Office gradually acquired responsibilities for health, education, agriculture, housing and economic development.

With responsibilities parallel to those of more than half a dozen other departments in the Cabinet, the Scottish Office is sometimes referred to as a 'mini-government' for Scotland. But this statement is incorrect for two reasons. First of all, the Scottish Office is not accountable to a separately elected Scottish Assembly, and the Secretary of State for Scotland remains a member of the British Cabinet. The decisions of the Scottish Office reflect the judgments of the British government, whether or not the party governing

tion of institutional variations from a semi-official viewpoint, see the Crowther–Kilbrandon Royal Commission on the Constitution *Report*, Vols. I–II, and the associated *Minutes of Evidence* and *Research Papers* (London: HMSO, Cmnd. 5460, 1973). Note also, Richard Rose and Ian McAllister, *United Kingdom Facts* (London: Macmillan, 1980).

FIGURE II.1 **England and the British Isles**

Great Britain represents a majority of Scottish constituencies as well as English constituencies.[18] In May 1979 the Conservative government won only 22 of Scotland's 71 seats in the House of Commons.

The most distinctive feature of Welsh society is language. The proportion of people in Wales speaking Welsh has declined from 53 per cent in 1891 to 27 per cent, according to the 1971 census. Many with Welsh ties, like the Prince of Wales, show a little knowledge of Welsh in tribute to the very different cultural values implied by the gulf between the English and Welsh languages. In religion Welsh people tend to belong to a variety of Protestant non-conformist denominations. Welshmen campaigned for generations against the established episcopal church in Wales; it was finally disestablished in 1920. Within Wales there are sharp contrasts between the English-speaking, industrial and more populous South and Welsh-speaking, rural North West.

Since the sixteenth century, when Wales was amalgamated with England, it has almost invariably been governed by the same laws as England. In 1746, Parliament declared that the word 'England' in an Act of Parliament was deemed to include Wales, a provision not repealed until 1967. The introduction of compulsory education in the nineteenth century was incidentally a cause of Anglicization in Wales, for Welsh-speaking children were by law required to attend English-language schools. In 1907, the first step was taken to treat Wales distinctively for administrative purposes, with the establishment of a separate Welsh Secretary of Education. In 1964, a separate Welsh Office was established, with its head a Cabinet minister. The Welsh Office has progressively been given administrative responsibility for education, local government, housing, roads, health, social work and industrial development, matters previously administered by a variety of London-based departments treating Wales like a region of England.[19]

By the common agreement of both English and Ulster people,

[18] For basic information, see James G. Kellas, *The Scottish Political System* (Cambridge: University Press, 2nd ed., 1975).

[19] On the social background, see K. O. Morgan, *Wales in British Politics, 1868–1922* (Cardiff: University of Wales Press, 1963); and Kevin R. Cox, 'Geography, Social Contexts and Voting Behaviour in Wales, 1861–1951', in Erik Allardt and Stein Rokkan, eds., *Mass Politics* (New York: Free Press, 1970). On political institutions, see J. A. Cross, 'The Regional Decentralization of British Government Departments', *Public Administration*, XLVIII (Winter 1970); E. Rowlands, 'The Politics of Regional Administration: The Establishment of the Welsh Office' and

Northern Ireland is the most un-English part of the United Kingdom.[20] Formally, Northern Ireland is a secular state, but in practice differences between Protestants and Catholics dominate its politics. Protestant loyalty to the Crown rests upon the English monarch's historic status, proclaimed in the Bill of Rights of 1689, as 'the glorious instrument of delivering this kingdome from Popery and arbitrary power'. Protestants constitute two-thirds of the population. They held power locally from the establishment of a 'home rule' Northern Ireland Parliament in 1921, following the secession of Southern Ireland from the United Kingdom, until 1972. Most Catholics have refused to support this regime, holding that national identity justifies Ulster's merger in a 32-county Republic of Ireland, with its capital in Dublin. Such a merger would result in a society in which Catholics outnumbered Protestants approximately three to one. Protestants reject the idea of belonging to a United Ireland.

Since 1968, Northern Ireland has been in turmoil. In that year, Ulster Catholics began demanding what they regarded as the normal civil rights of Englishmen. In the absence of any means for pursuing these claims through the courts and any electoral influence because of their minority status, Catholics turned to internationally publicized street demonstrations to advance their aims.[21] Successive British Labour and Conservative governments forced the Stormont government to make token concessions, which created a backlash among Protestants fearful of being forced into a United Ireland. Demonstrations turned to street violence in 1969, and the British Army intervened. The Irish Republican Army was revived, and in 1971 it began a military campaign to remove Northern Ireland from the United Kingdom. In retaliation, Protestants have also organized illegal forces.

In the first ten years since the killing started in August 1969, more than 1,900 people have died in political violence in Northern Ireland, the equivalent in population terms of more than 65,000 killed in Britain. The dead include hundreds of civilian bystanders, as well

<hr>

Public Administration, L (Autumn 1972) and *Studies in Public Policy* (University of Strathclyde Centre for the Study of Public Policy).

[20] See Richard Rose, *Governing without Consensus: An Irish Perspective* (London: Faber & Faber, 1971) and Richard Rose, Ian McAllister and Peter Mair, *Is There a Concurring Majority about Northern Ireland?* (Glasgow: University of Strathclyde Studies in Public Policy, 1978). On conventional welfare issues see R. J. Lawrence, *The Government of Northern Ireland* (Oxford: Clarendon Press, 1965).

[21] For the logic of such actions, see Richard Rose, 'On the Priorities of Citizenship in the Deep South and Northern Ireland', *Journal of Politics*, XXXVIII:2 (1976).

as hundreds of British soldiers, Ulster policemen, and Irish Republicans and Protestant Loyalists killed 'on active service' with illegal military units.

British policy has been erratic and unsuccessful since it became actively involved once again in Northern Ireland affairs. Initially, British troops provided full support for the Unionist (and Protestant) Northern Ireland government at Stormont. In 1971 the Army helped to intern hundreds of Catholics without trial in an unsuccessful attempt to break the IRA. The IRA flourished. In 1972 the British government abolished the Stormont Parliament, and took direct responsibility for affairs there, creating a Northern Ireland Office under a British Cabinet minister. In reaction, Protestant violence flourished. In 1974 the British government temporarily succeeded in creating a Northern Ireland Executive sharing power between one faction of the Unionists and the pro-Irish unity Social Democratic and Labour Party. The Executive collapsed in the face of a political general strike organized by Protestants. The British government refused to grant the strikers' demand for a general election to test whether there was majority support for the biconfessional power-sharing government. In 1975 Britain authorized the election of a constitutional Convention. When the Unionist majority in the Convention recommended the adoption of an Ulster constitution modelled on British parliamentary practice, the British government rejected it as unsuitable for the least united part of the United Kingdom.[22]

For generations, political differences between England and non-English parts of the United Kingdom were confined to differing levels of support for the Conservative and Labour parties, which have had 'national' as well as class images. In Northern Ireland, the Conservatives' ally, the Unionists, normally swept the majority of working-class as well as middle-class votes, because Unionism was the primary issue of concern to the Protestant majority. In Scotland and Wales, Liberal and subsequently Labour candidates have done disproportionately well, because of the Conservative Party's identification with English institutions and values.[23]

In the 1970s, nationalist parties challenged the monopoly of

[22] See Richard Rose, *Northern Ireland: Time of Choice* (London: Macmillan, 1976) and Robert Fisk, *The Point of No Return* (London: Andre Deutsch, 1975).

[23] See William L. Miller, *Electoral Dynamics in Britain since 1918* (London: Macmillan, 1977), especially Ch. 6, and, for detailed nation-by-nation breakdowns of voting figures, see Rose and McAllister, *United Kingdom Facts*, chs. 3–4.

votes of British parties. (See Table II.2.) The challenge has been most successful in Northern Ireland, where neither the Conservative nor Labour parties were prepared to contest seats at the 1974 or 1979 parliamentary elections. The chief parties are all unique to Northern Ireland: on the Protestant side, the Official Unionists, and the Democratic Unionists led by Dr. Ian Paisley, and on the Catholic side, the pro-Irish unity Social Democratic and Labour Party. In Scotland, in October 1974, the Scottish National Party came second in popular votes with 30 per cent of the Scottish total, only 6 per cent less than that won by the front-running Labour Party. The idiosyncrasies of the electoral system gave Labour 41 of the 71 Scottish seats in the House of Commons, against 11 for the Scottish Nationalists. In Wales, Plaid Cymru has consistently polled about one-tenth of the vote since 1970. In October 1974 it reached a high point in parliamentary terms, winning three of the Principality's 36 seats. The most distinctive feature of Welsh politics continues to be the disproportionately high Labour vote.[24]

In response to the rise in Nationalist votes in Scotland and Wales, the Labour government in August 1974 pledged to devolve some government responsibilities to popularly elected Assemblies in Scotland and Wales. The implementation of these pledges by legislation provoked strong reactions in Parliament. MPs jealously sought reassurance that the devolution of powers to Assemblies in Edinburgh and Cardiff would not detract from Parliament's authority. Moreover, many MPs considered the Labour government was over-reacting to nationalists, pointing out that in October 1974 89.2 per cent of Welsh voters rejected the Nationalist party, and 69.6 per cent of Scottish voters did likewise.

Parliamentary opposition forced a referendum asking Welsh and Scottish voters whether they wished the Devolution Acts approved by Parliament to go into effect. A novel feature of the referendums was the requirement that if 40 per cent of persons deemed eligible to vote did not approve devolution, the government would be compelled to present a motion to repeal the Acts. In the referendum of 1 March 1979 Welsh voters unequivocally rejected devolution; 79.7 per cent voted against and 20.3 per cent in favour. In

[24] On the Nationalist parties, see Jack Brand, *The National Movement in Scotland* (London: Routledge & Kegan Paul, 1978); Keith Webb, *The Growth of Nationalism in Scotland* (Harmondsworth: Penguin, 1978); Alan Butt Philip, *The Welsh Question* (Cardiff: University of Wales Press, 1975) and Ian McAllister, *The Northern Ireland Social Democratic and Labour Party* (London: Macmillan, 1977).

TABLE II.2 The division of the vote in the United Kingdom, 1974–1979

	Conservative %	Labour %	Total, two main parties %	Liberal %	Nationalist %	Population millions
England						
October 1974	38.9	40.1	79.0	20.2	n.a.	46.4
May 1979	47.2	36.7	83.9	14.9	n.a.	
Scotland						
October 1974	24.7	36.3	61.0	8.3	30.4	5.2
May 1979	31.4	41.5	72.9	9.0	17.3	
Wales						
October 1974	23.9	49.5	73.4	15.5	10.8	2.8
May 1979	32.2	48.6	80.8	10.6	8.1	
Northern Ireland						
October 1974	0	0	0	0	100.0[a]	1.5
May 1979	0	0	0	0	100.0	
Totals						
October 1974	35.8	39.2	75.0	18.3	5.5	55.9
May 1979	43.9	36.9	80.8	13.8	4.3	

Note[a] All Northern Ireland parties are classified as Nationalist here, because, while they disagree about many things, none runs as part of a British party ticket.

Scotland, a narrow majority of Scots who voted gave approval to devolution; 51.6 per cent voted yes, and 48.4 per cent voted no. But the proportion of eligible voters endorsing devolution was only 32.8 per cent of the Scottish electorate. In consequence, Parliament repealed the devolution acts for both Scotland and Wales, reversing the decision of the Commons a year previously.

The May 1979 general election confirmed the strength of Unionist (that is, pro-United Kingdom) sentiment in all the non-English parts of the United Kingdom. The Scottish National Party share of the vote dropped to 17.3 per cent, and it lost nine of its eleven Members of Parliament. The vote of the Welsh Nationalists dropped by 2.7 per cent, and it lost one of its three MPs. In Northern Ireland, Unionists of different party labels once again swept ten of the Province's twelve seats, and could look forward to a bigger voice thereafter, since the next Parliament is meant to add up to half a dozen more Ulster MPs to match its representation to population.

The United Kingdom today is constrained by both history and geography. Its institutions do not define political relationships in a logically structured written Constitution. The government of the United Kingdom is the product of conquests, dynastic accidents and bargains occurring at different times and in different places. As the United Kingdom enters the 1980s, the government of England continues in a pattern long familiar. In 1978 Parliament voted novel ways of devolving powers to Scotland and Wales, only to find them rejected the following year. In Northern Ireland, the British government's position is noncommittal. It has pledged that Northern Ireland should remain a part of the United Kingdom as long as a majority of its inhabitants so wish. But the institution of direct rule in the Province, the Northern Ireland Office, enjoys authority only on an annually renewable basis. Northern Ireland is governed by 'temporary' direct rule.

The triumph of particular customs over general principles is demonstrated by the absence of any standard terminology to describe the United Kingdom. For example, British politicians promoting devolution to Scotland and Wales proclaimed themselves anxious to defend the integrity of the United Kingdom, while simultaneously accepting that the people of Northern Ireland have the unilateral right to withdraw from it and join the Republic of Ireland, if a majority would so vote. A typical 'British' government department based in London will exercise some of its powers on a

United Kingdom basis, others in Great Britain only, many only in England and Wales, and some for England alone. Inconsistencies in the very structure of government must be reflected here.[25]

Politics in England is the subject of this book, because England dominates the United Kingdom in so many ways. Its people constitute five-sixths of the population of the United Kingdom. The remainder is divided unequally among three non-contiguous nations. The largest, Scotland, has but one-ninth the population of England—though it is more populous than three member states of the European Community, Denmark, Ireland and Luxembourg. On occasions of conflict, non-English people are expected to adapt to English ways. The term 'British' reflects this asymmetry. When an Englishman calls something British, the chances are he thinks of things English, whereas Scots, Welsh and Ulster people have a pluralistic frame of reference. What is central to England will never be overlooked by any United Kingdom government. Politicians who wish to prosper in Parliament must accept English norms if they wish to advance. It is thus appropriate to talk about British government and English society.

The significance of national differences within the United Kingdom is further underscored by examining the regions of England, most of which have more people than Wales or Northern Ireland. The absence of a politically meaningful sense of regional identity is shown by the government's lack of any single, standard definition of region used for all purposes. There are no regional assemblies or regional elections, nor are regional offices of central government perceived as centres of political power. Regions tend to be so large and dispersed that there is limited opportunity for people to meet.

Some of the differences between regions reflect differences in class composition. Southern regions, including London, tend to be more middle-class. This has resulted in the Conservatives winning a majority of parliamentary seats in Southern England at every general election but two since 1900, and Labour winning a majority of seats in Northern England at every election since 1945. But differences among English regions are of less consequence politically than differences between Scotland or Wales and England.[26]

[25] See also below, pp. 301–4.
[26] See Ian McAllister, Richard Parry and Richard Rose, *United Kingdom Rankings* (Glasgow: Strathclyde Studies in Public Policy, No. 44, 1979).

Within England, London occupies a pre-eminent place. With 7 million people, Greater London is seven times larger than Birmingham, the second largest city in England. Only four other English cities have more than half a million people: Liverpool, Manchester, Sheffield and Leeds. New York City is as large as London, but it does not similarly dominate American cities. New York contains less than one twenty-fifth of the population of America, but London contains one-sixth the population of England. Unlike Washington, Bonn, Ottawa and many other capitals, London is simultaneously the centre of government, finance, the mass media and the arts. Nearly three-quarters of people meriting a biography in *Who's Who* live within a 65-mile radius of the capital.[27] Most of society's leaders are thus geographically segregated from the bulk of the English people, who do not live within commuting distance of the capital. They live in what are symbolically called the provinces.

The pre-eminence of London has increased in the past century with the political decline of an aristocracy based upon landed interests and of business leaders in industrial cities that burgeoned in Victorian times. Social distance between governors and governed is reinforced by the fact that more than half the Members of Parliament have not lived in their constituency before election. Among civil servants, a similar distance is apparent. Successful administrators expect to rise within London offices, and not be posted to an office in the provinces. Moreover, civil servants are disproportionately likely to have gone to a secondary school and university in the area around London. Their only experience of England north of Oxford and Cambridge may be short business trips or holidays in the most rural and most atypical parts of the United Kingdom.[28]

Black Britons

As citizens of a world power, British people have long been able to move throughout the world without constraint. For centuries England also received a small but noteworthy number of immigrants from other lands, principally Europe. The present Royal Family is the most notable of English immigrants. The Queen is immediately

[27] Mark Abrams, quoted in Lord Windlesham, *Communications and Political Power* (London: Jonathan Cape, 1966), p. 234.
[28] See Edwin Hammond, *An Analysis of Regional Economic and Social Statistics* (Durham: Rowntree Research Unit, 1968), Table 2.7.3.

descended from the heirs of the Princess Sophia of Hanover. George I came from this German princely state to assume the English throne in 1714, succeeding the Scottish-bred Stuarts. German connections were maintained by Queen Victoria's marriage to Albert, Prince of Saxe-Coburg and Gotha, and by marriages of their offspring. Until the outbreak of anti-German sentiment in the First World War, the surname of the Royal Family was Saxe-Coburg-Gotha. By Royal Proclamation, George V changed his name to Windsor in 1917.

Through the centuries less eminent immigrants have also come; as a great port and trading centre, London has been accessible to all of Europe. The chief influx of immigration in the first half of the twentieth century consisted of Jews from Eastern Europe before the First World War, refugees from Nazi Germany in the 1930s, and Poles and Hungarians afterwards. By the standards of America, Canada or Australia, immigration has always been numerically small.[29]

As a result of its imperial status, the United Kingdom has never had a clear-cut definition of who is and who is not a British citizen. Almost all the nearly one billion residents of the Commonwealth from India to the Falkland Islands are British subjects, even though they have never come within five thousand miles of the White Cliffs of Dover. These nominal subjects are also citizens of their country of residence. Moreover, citizens of the Irish Republic, which left the Commonwealth in 1949, are allowed to enter Britain freely, to vote at British elections and to sit in the House of Commons while retaining their Irish citizenship.

In the late 1950s, small numbers of British subjects from populous (and non-white) parts of the Commonwealth, especially the West Indies, Pakistan and India, began migrating to England, to benefit personally from their country's historic connection with England. Since 1955, the net inflow of non-white immigrants has fluctuated between 16,000 and 110,000 annually. The great majority of immigrants have been attracted to England by the prospect of a job, whether as a doctor, a factory worker or a hospital orderly. Those who disliked England and returned home have been fewer than those who liked it and have sent for their relatives and friends

[29] See C. Holmes, ed., *Immigrants and Minorities in British Society* (London: Allen & Unwin, 1978) and E. Krausz, *Ethnic Minorities in Britain* (London: Paladin, 1972).

to join them. By the 1971 census, the estimated non-white population of the United Kingdom rose from 74,000 (0.2 per cent) twenty years previously to 1,500,000 (2.3 per cent).[30]

The immigrants had little in common upon arrival. British West Indians came as native English speakers, albeit some spoke with a calypso accent. The bulk of the early immigrants from the Indian sub-continent—whether from India or Pakistan—came with alien cultures. While some were bilingual graduates of schools and universities, the majority were uneducated, unskilled and often ill at ease in speaking English. Muslims and Sikhs follow religious practices that have made them especially distinctive. In several cities Sikhs have had to fight political campaigns to become bus conductors, because municipally owned bus companies said they would not be employed unless they wore caps rather than ritual turbans.[31] African immigrants have been distinctive from other immigrants, as well as divided among themselves by tribe and citizenship. These cultural differences and differences in skin colour have made it difficult to establish an American-style black political movement. Instead, there is a heterogeneous assortment of non-white groups.

The variety of immigrants is indicated by a proposal for the 1981 census to ask immigrants to identify their racial or ethnic origins as: White (European), African, Arab, Chinese, Indian, Pakistani, Bangladeshi, Sri Lankan or other. Persons in the latter four groups are also to be asked to indicate their religion as well: Hindu, Sikh, Muslim or other. The director of the Central Statistical Office commented, 'The question does look funny and must seem extraordinary to any logician or philosopher. The only defence is, it works.' The English use of the term 'race' to refer to skin colour, nationality or religion exemplifies the uncertainty and inconsistency with which cultural differences are defined.[32]

The entry to England of a relatively small number of coloured immigrants has had a significance far out of proportion to their number. The constraints of history have allowed Englishmen to regard themselves as a 'race' apart from the inhabitants of alien

[30] On the first wave of immigration, see E. J. B. Rose and associates, *Colour and Citizenship* (London: Oxford University Press, 1969).

[31] See David Beetham, *Transport and Turbans* (London: Oxford University Press, 1970).

[32] 'Planning for the 1981 Census of Population', *Population Trends*, 10 (December 1977), pp. 8–9, and *New Society* (London), 21/28 December 1978, p. 697.

European countries and from Scots, Welsh and Irish, as well as from the non-white world.[33] Yet the same history has created political ties within a Commonwealth in which whites are a small minority, and has led non-white British subjects to immigrate to England. From the first, public opinion has opposed coloured immigration. In 1958 two-thirds endorsed stricter controls upon immigration and by 1968 95 per cent wished stricter controls on immigration, a position that has not altered substantially since. In 1964 Members of Parliament were shocked out of a complacent belief that their fellow countrymen were free of racial animosity, when a racialist candidate, running on the Conservative label, won an upset victory at Smethwick. By 1970, Enoch Powell could become prominent as a proponent of a 'white England' policy, and leaders of both parties feared the alleged electoral impact of his pronouncements.[34]

Successive Conservative and Labour governments have responded in 1962, 1968 and 1971 by passing laws intended to limit the number of Commonwealth immigrants entering the United Kingdom. In 1968 the Labour government placed strict controls upon the entry of tens of thousands of Asian residents of East Africa holding British passports, on the grounds that they were not connected with Britain by birth or descent. The law now allows entry on a quota basis to dependants of immigrants already settled in Britain, persons with approved jobs to come to, and United Kingdom citizens unconnected by birth or descent with Britain. Patrials—that is, white persons with close family connections with the United Kingdom—have a free right of entry. As a consequence of these restrictions, immigration by coloured Commonwealth subjects is now running at a lower rate than in the 1960s. The exact number remains a subject of continuing, and sometimes emotional political dispute, averaging annually about one-tenth of one per cent of the population of the United Kingdom.[35]

[33] See e.g. L. P. Curtis Jr., *Anglo-Saxons and Celts* (Bridgeport, Conn.: Published for the Conference on British Studies by the Universities, 1968) and Ivor Crewe, ed., *The Politics of Race* (London: British Political Sociology Yearbook, Vol. II, Croom Helm, 1975).

[34] Cf. Douglas E. Schoen, *Enoch Powell and the Powellites* (London: Macmillan, 1977), William L. Miller, 'What is the Profit in Following the Crowd?', *British Journal of Political Science* (forthcoming) and Z. Layton-Henry, 'Race, Electoral Strategy and the Major Parties', *Parliamentary Affairs*, XXXI:3 (1978).

[35] On numbers, see *Ethnic Minorities in Britain: Statistical Data* (London: Community Relations Commission, 6th ed., 1976) and frequent contributions to the journal, *New Community*.

In domestic politics, the most important questions concern coloured immigrants who have settled in England and their English-born children. While numbers are relatively small, they challenge residents of major English cities to abandon their traditional assumption that England is an all-white society, and to accept the emergence of a multi-racial England. By comparison, Americans have never doubted that their country is a multi-racial society; the only question has been the terms of black and white relationships. Surveys of public opinion consistently emphasize that while there is an overwhelming majority against sustained immigration, a significant fraction accept the idea of a multi-racial society in principle. But there is no consensus about race relations at present. When English people are asked what effect immigrants have had upon England, 20 per cent emphasize benefits, 23 per cent say they have made no difference, and 45 per cent think immigrants are harming England.[36] The strong sense of English identity leads politicians to treat coloured Britons as alien, even when born in England. Immigrants who retain a strong attachment to Hindu, Muslim or Sikh religious values wish to emphasize their cultural differences too.

Characteristic English political values tend to support a non-interventionist government policy on race relations at a time when the government increasingly seeks to regulate most economic and social relationships. English politicians have long prided themselves on their tolerance, and do not wish to admit that discrimination can occur in England. In so far as it is known to occur, this may be interpreted as an argument against passing laws to benefit a small percentage of blacks, at the risk of alienating a potentially larger number of white voters. Laws intended to improve race relations have been passed in 1965, 1968 and 1976, largely modelled upon American legislation, except that their scope is less, and provisions for the judicial enforcement of rights are much weaker than in America.[37] A government-sponsored Commission on Racial Equality combats discrimination, relying primarily upon investigation and conciliation, rather than judicial prosecution.

The leaders of the major parties differ in degree, not principle, about race relations questions. The two crucial issues are defined as:

[36] See National Opinion Polls *Review* (London: NOP No. 6, 1976), pp. 36–8; *Gallup Political Index*, No. 211 (February 1978), p. 10.
[37] See Donley T. Studlar, 'Political Culture and Racial Policy in Britain', in R. Rose, ed., *Studies in British Politics* (3rd ed.).

how few coloured immigrants should be admitted to Britain in the coming years, and how much (or how little) should government do to promote good race relations within England? While nearly every other conceivable minority is found in the House of Commons, no political party has a black Briton as a member there. The only blacks in Parliament are appointed to the House of Lords. In a limited number of constituencies efforts are made to court the immigrant vote; to date, the vote appears to have favoured Labour. When blacks have stood independent of party, their vote has been derisory.

From time to time, anti-coloured groups attract public attention by protest marches and the counter-demonstrations they invite. But their electoral impact has been very slight. In 1970, ten National Front parliamentary candidates averaged only 3.6 per cent of the vote in their constituencies. In October 1974, 90 National Front candidates polled 0.4 per cent of the total vote, and in 1979, 0.6 per cent, losing its deposit in each of 303 seats it contested. The small amount of electoral support for the National Front appears to come from both Labour and Conservative ranks.[38]

The constraints of an imperial heritage have made England a multi-racial society in fact, but not yet in political values and affirmative action legislation. Politicians have concluded that the transition from an all-white to a multi-racial society is so difficult that the slower the pace and the fewer people involved, the less the friction. The question for the 1980s is whether this characteristically gradualist approach will lead to the pluralist acceptance of the children of Commonwealth immigrants as Black Britons or even their assimilation as Black English, or whether a reaction will create a small but politically alienated group who first and foremost identify as blacks rather than Britons.

[38] See Michael Steed, 'The National Front Vote', Parliamentary Affairs, XXXI: 3 (1978) and Martin Walker, The National Front (London: Fontana, 1977).

III

The Constitution of the Crown

'On all great subjects', says Mr. Mill, 'much remains to be said', and of none is this more true than of the English Constitution. The literature which has accumulated upon it is huge. But an observer who looks at the living reality will wonder at the contrast to the paper description. He will see in the life much which is not in the book; and he will not find in the rough practice many refinements of the literary theory.

Before studying what governments do we must first understand what government is. The conventional way to describe a government is to discuss its constitution. This cannot be done here, for England has no written Constitution. At no time in the past was there a break with tradition, as in the American Revolution, forcing politicians to think about the basis of their authority, and to write down how the country should be governed henceforth. The English Constitution exists today because it has persisted since medieval times without every having been rejected completely by the people of England. In the modern world its authority derives from the antiquity of its origins.

The theory of sovereignty emphasizes that government should be unitary and powerful. The symbol of the Crown in Parliament, the lawyer's name for government, is a mace. In practice, the several and different powers and functions of government are divided among a multiplicity of institutions. The Prime Minister, the Cabinet, Parliament and individual departments such as the Treasury and the Foreign Office are separately impressive, but they do not constitute anything as coherent and powerful as that which Europeans have in mind when they refer to the *state*. As Bagehot emphasized, central features of the English Constitution cannot be distinguished from society, as the ideas of state and society are juxtaposed in Continental Europe. In extreme cases, writers can refer to the Constitution as embodied in something as broad and vague as the English way of life.

When the Constitution is invoked, the writer usually has in mind a mixture of Acts of Parliament, judicial pronouncements, customs and conventions about the rules of governance. Some of these elements are three centuries or more old, for example, methods by which Parliament can limit the Crown's right to tax and spend public monies. Others are less than a decade old, and their full meaning has yet to be tested, like the power granted the European Community in 1973 to make laws binding in England. Because of the jumble of unwritten and written elements in the Constitution, an introduction to a collection of constitutional (i.e. fundamental) documents remarks, 'It would be foolish to suppose that this mode of systematising the material gives a complete picture of the British Constitution.'[1]

The absence of a written Constitution is often said to be a great advantage, because it allows the government of the day to adapt institutions and actions to changing circumstances without the procedural difficulties of amending a written constitution. Laws of constitutional significance are not entrenched; they are no more difficult to alter than any ordinary statute. The flexibility of the constitution is undoubted; it has been a condition of its survival through the centuries. The flexibility arises in part from vagueness about what exactly are the customs and conventions that politicians are bound to accept. As a result of this vagueness, when there is a major dispute about the actions of the government of the day, both sides can appeal rhetorically to constitutional principles. Neither can refer to any document that binds the government of the day. Disputes about the introduction or repeal of laws of constitutional status are resolved by political power. The party with a united majority in Parliament carries the day. As the immediate cause of controversy recedes into the past, all sides usually come to accept yesterday's disputed actions as part of today's constitutional practice.

Increasingly, critics are heard questioning whether an unwritten and sometimes vague set of ideas rooted in assumptions of very different historical periods is suitable for England in the 1980s. Critics allege there is a 'constitutional wasteland' because there is no single and supreme charter of government and citizens' rights; there are merely fragmentary acts, customs and conventions.[2]

[1] Leslie Wolf-Phillips, *Constitutions of Modern States* (London: Pall Mall, 1968), p. 182. For a Continental view, see Gianfranco Poggi, *The Development of the Modern State* (London: Hutchinson, 1978).
[2] Nevil Johnson, *In Search of the Constitution*, p. 35.

Proponents of a written Constitution are unlikely to secure their objective. But persons hoping for changes by accident if not design may take heart from Sir Leslie Scarman's view, 'Momentous legal events have a way of happening in our society without anyone troubling much about them at the time. Later, when the event is beyond recall and its consequences seen, the debate begins.'[3]

In everyday political discourse, people do not talk about the Constitution but about government. The term government may be used in many different senses, as is shown by the variety of familiar adjectives that can modify it. One may speak of the Queen's government, to emphasize its enduring and non-partisan features. Alternatively, using the name of the Prime Minister of the day, e.g. the Thatcher government, stresses personal and transitory features. Reference to a Conservative or Labour government emphasizes partisanship. The phrase government officials usually refers to civil servants rather than elected politicians. Collectively, the executive agencies of government are often referred to as Whitehall, after the London street in which many major government offices are located. Downing Street, the home of the Prime Minister, is a small lane off Whitehall, and the Houses of Parliament—the home of both the House of Commons and the House of Lords—is at the bottom end of Whitehall. The historic clustering of government offices in Westminster symbolizes the centralization of government, just as the increasing dispersal of government offices throughout London symbolizes the growing complexity of so-called central government.

This chapter explores the chief ways in which the stone-and-mortar of institutions and the flesh-and-bones of individuals give substance to the complex idea of government. The world of Whitehall—the home of the Prime Minister, the Cabinet and civil servants—is explored in the first section. Parliament and Members of Parliament are the subject of the second section, and the role of law the third. The concluding section considers the informal but real community of interest pervading the whole government in Westminster.

[3] Quoted in the review article by K. C. Wheare, 'Does it Really Exist? Some Reflections upon the Contemporary British Constitution', *Parliamentary Affairs*, XXXI:2 (1978), p. 214.

Whitehall[4]

In the words of a leading constitutional authority, 'The Crown represents the sum total of governmental powers.'[5] This does not mean that the monarch of the day personally determines the major activities of what is referred to as Her Majesty's Government. Instead, the Crown symbolizes the institutions of government. For example, government property is held in the name of the Crown, rather than in the name of someone as transitory as a Prime Minister, something as abstract as the state, or as diffuse as the people of England. In the law courts, criminal actions are similarly entered as the case of *Regina* (i.e. Queen Elizabeth II) against the person accused of offending against the Queen's peace.

The question thus arises: What constitutes the Crown? No simple answer can be given. The Crown is an idea to which people are asked to give loyalty. Like postage stamps bearing the face and emblem of the reigning monarch, the Crown has no name. It is also a concept of indefinite territorial domain, and it refers to no particular primordial community of people. Today as in Bagehot's time, the idea of the Crown confuses the dignified parts of the constitution, which sanctify authority by tradition and myth, with the efficient parts that actually carry out the work of government.[6]

The reigning monarch, as distinct from the Crown, is almost exclusively concerned with dignified aspects of government.[7] The duties of Queen Elizabeth II are few in relation to what is formally called Her Majesty's Government. The Queen must give formal assent to laws passed by Parliament, but she may not state publicly her opinion about legislation. The Queen is also responsible for naming the Prime Minister and dissolving Parliament before a

---

[4] In this book, the term Whitehall will be used to refer to government departments, their ministers and civil servants; because the ministerial heads are also MPs, Whitehall is not normally referred to by the American phrase, the executive branch of government. The term Parliament usually refers to the House of Commons, and the term MP always refers to a Member of the Commons. Westminster refers to these two sets of institutions and all who cluster around them in and around Whitehall and the Houses of Parliament.

[5] See E. C. S. Wade and A. W. Bradley, *Constitutional Law* (London: Longman, 8th ed., 1970), p. 171.

[6] Cf. Geoffrey Marshall, *Constitutional Theory* (Oxford: Clarendon Press, 1971) and Richard Rose, *From Steady State to Fluid State: The Unity of the Kingdom Today* (Glasgow: Strathclyde Studies in Public Policy No. 26, 1978).

[7] For the best informed description, see the study by Dermot Morrah, Arundel Herald Extraordinary, *The Work of the Queen* (London: William Kimber, 1958).

general election. In these actions, the Queen is expected to act consistently with the will of Parliament, as communicated to her by the leader of the governing party of the day.

The Queen receives major government papers, including reports of Cabinet meetings. She usually receives the Prime Minister once a week to discuss current affairs. The monarch has the opportunity to encourage the Prime Minister or to warn privately about points that Cabinet deliberations have overlooked. No Prime Minister in modern times has suggested that a policy was followed because of the monarch's wishes. The effective responsibility for government remains with elected politicians.

When no party has a majority in the House of Commons, the Queen could conceivably be faced with conflicting advice about calling an election from a minority Prime Minister and a majority of MPs. In 1931 the monarch did collaborate in the dismissal of a minority Labour government and its replacement by a coalition government without a general election. In the uncertain circumstances of minority government in the 1970s, the Queen was not confronted with such conflicting advice. It was fortunate for the Queen to be left ratifying decisions taken elsewhere, for a monarchy faced with a real choice would lose its status as an institution above the battle of party politics.[8]

The ceremonial role of the Queen as head of state consumes a substantial portion of royal time. The Queen or other members of the Royal Family appear at a great range of public functions, from horse races and air shows to the laying of cornerstones for new local government buildings. The Royal Family is also in demand for goodwill tours abroad. Because these time-consuming tasks are performed by the Royal Family, leading elective politicians have more time for the efficient work of government. The differentiation of roles also establishes a clear distinction between national and partisan aspects of government. In America, by contrast, the President is not only the ceremonial symbol of national unity, but also the head of a political party that divides the electorate by competing for votes.

The formal responsibilities of the Queen are necessary though unimportant. In the absence of a hereditary monarch, England might have a president, like Germany or Italy, to commission each new government and to undertake ceremonial tasks. In the absence

[8] See 'Mr. Short and Left Wing in Dispute over Queen's Right to Spurn Wilson advice', *The Times*, 11 May 1974.

of a monarch or a figurehead president, the ceremonial duties and the symbolic aura of the head of state would be invested in the Prime Minister of the day. A Gallup Poll survey reports that 81 per cent of English people prefer a Queen, as against 10 per cent favouring a president.[9]

If British government is to be characterized in a simple phrase (a practice that may be questioned, see chapter X), it is best described as Cabinet government, for the powers and prerogatives nominally vested in the Crown in Parliament are effectively vested in the Cabinet.[10] The Cabinet was described by Walter Bagehot as the efficient secret of the English constitution, securing 'the close union, the nearly complete fusion of the executive and legislative powers'.[11] Fusion results from the fact that Cabinet ministers come from the majority party in the House of Commons, thus assuring control of legislation; concurrently they are the executive heads of the major departments of central government. By contrast, American politicians are constitutionally debarred from simultaneously being Congressmen and members of the presidential executive. Because the Conservative and Labour parliamentary parties normally vote as cohesive blocs, no Cabinet is likely to be turned out of office by losing a vote of confidence. The Labour government's fall on a vote of confidence in 1979 was without twentieth-century precedent.

The endorsement of Cabinet is the strongest sanction that a policy can have. Many major contemporary decisions, especially in economic and foreign affairs, do not require an Act of Parliament. Cabinet can approve policies for inflation or economic growth within existing broad statutory grants of authority. Once Cabinet has approved a policy, endorsement of action by the House of Commons can normally be taken for granted, and civil servants are expected to work faithfully to carry out the decision, however much they may disagree with it on personal or political grounds. Cabinet ministers often disagree among themselves, and if enough disagree with a proposal, even the Prime Minister may be unable to carry a policy, because of the threat of a mass of Cabinet resignations

[9] *Gallup Political Index*, No. 190 (May 1976), p. 12.
[10] For overviews of the Cabinet, see Valentine Herman and James E. Alt, eds., *Cabinet Studies: A Reader* (London: Macmillan, 1975) and, historically, Hans Daalder, *Cabinet Reform in Britain, 1914–1963* (London: Oxford University Press, 1963).
[11] Bagehot, *The English Constitution*, p. 9.

leading to the collapse of the governing party's majority in the House of Commons, and to electoral defeat.[12]

The convention of Cabinet responsibility requires that all ministers, including many too junior to sit in Cabinet, give public support to a Cabinet decision, or at least refrain from making public criticism. Cabinet ministers usually go along silently with their colleagues, even when they disagree with a decision, in return for colleagues endorsing their departmental actions. If a minister does not wish to go along with colleagues, the constitutional convention is that the minister should resign. But such is the political pain and risk of giving up office that only eight members of Cabinet have resigned on political grounds since 1945.[13] Normally, disagreements in Cabinet are masked by a public and dignified show of unity, even if private controversies within Cabinet continue. Ministers in strong disagreement with a Cabinet decision may try to form an alliance with colleagues to overturn a decision, and leak to the press differences of opinion with their colleagues in an attempt to influence Cabinet deliberations or to curry favour in the party by showing they do not really accept responsibility. Exceptionally, in the 1974–9 Labour Cabinet, divisions about British membership in the European Community were so deep that Cabinet ministers were allowed to disagree publicly on this issue, for neither Harold Wilson nor James Callaghan felt that he could safely continue as Prime Minister if anti-Market ministers resigned.[14]

As long as the electoral system normally gives a majority to one party in the House of Commons, the Cabinet is secure. If the party in office lacks an absolute majority in the House of Commons, then the Cabinet cannot be certain of securing a parliamentary majority for every decision that it endorses. From March 1974 to 1979, the Labour governments of Harold Wilson and James Callaghan intermittently lacked a majority in the House of Commons, and in March 1977 took the unusual step of concluding a pact with the Liberals to

[12] For a study of Harold Wilson being frustrated as a Prime Minister see Peter Jenkins, *The Battle of Downing Street* (London: Charles Knight, 1970).

[13] See David Butler and Anne Sloman, *British Political Facts, 1900–1975* (London: Macmillan, 4th ed., 1975), pp. 75f.

[14] Violations of the doctrine of collective responsibility attract attention precisely because they are departures from the norm. See Dennis Kavanagh, 'New Bottles for New Wines', pp. 14f and, for a personal account of intra-Cabinet machinations from the viewpoint of a mercurial minister with a liking for intrigue, see R. H. S. Crossman, *The Diaries of a Cabinet Minister* (London: Hamish Hamilton and Jonathan Cape), Vol. I (1975), Vol. II (1976) and Vol. III (1977).

ensure support for government legislation. Labour Cabinet ministers had the enormous advantage of backing by civil servants, and because their Liberal partners were distant from and lacked knowledge of how Whitehall works they could not promote legislation on their own.[15]

Notwithstanding its formal importance, meetings of the Cabinet normally ratify rather than make decisions. One reason for this is the pressure of time. The Cabinet usually meets only one morning a week, and its agenda is extremely crowded with routine business. A second reason is bureaucratic: the great majority of matters going up to Cabinet have normally been discussed in great detail beforehand in Whitehall committees. Any major measure is likely to be considered first by senior civil servants from the departments affected by it. Civil servants are meant to confine their discussions and recommendations to technical matters, so that ministers can concentrate upon controversial political acts. The distinction is easier to state than to apply. Ministers meet in Cabinet committees to review the preliminary reports of civil servants, and to dispute and resolve outstanding political issues. On crisis issues of the economy and foreign affairs, committees may be constituted informally, meeting late at night at 10 Downing Street, with the Prime Minister conferring with chosen advisers from within and outside the Cabinet.

Ministers prefer to resolve their differences by bargaining in committee or by informal negotiations in order to present Cabinet an agreed recommendation difficult to challenge. In Cabinet, a minister finds it difficult to upset a recommendation agreed by informed and affected colleagues. A minister is more likely to let settlements hammered out in committee go through without great debate, in anticipation of having decisions affecting his department similarly endorsed another time.[16]

[15] On the parliamentary response of the Labour Cabinet to its weakness in the Commons, see the annual surveys of Ivor Burton and Gavin Drewry, e.g. 'Public Legislation: Survey of 1975/76 and 1976/77', *Parliamentary Affairs*, XXXI:2 (1978). Cf. Alistair Michie and Simon Hoggart, *The Pact* (London: Quartet Books, 1978).

[16] For views of the same Cabinet by different members, see accounts of the 1964–70 Labour Cabinet by e.g. Patrick Gordon Walker, *The Cabinet* (London: Jonathan Cape, 1970); Richard Crossman, *Inside View* (London: Jonathan Cape, 1972) and *Diaries*; Sir Richard Marsh, *Off the Rails* (London: Weidenfeld & Nicolson, 1978); George Brown, *In My Way* (London: Victor Gollancz, 1971); and Harold Wilson, *The Labour Government 1964–70, A Personal Record* (London: Weidenfeld & Nicolson, 1971).

Within the Cabinet, the Prime Minister occupies a unique position, sometimes referred to as *primus inter pares* (first among equals). But as Winston Churchill once wrote, 'There can be no comparison between the position of number one and numbers two, three or four.'[17] As leader of the majority in the House of Commons as well as chairman of the Cabinet, and the party's chief campaigner in elections the Prime Minister personally represents the fusion of parliamentary and executive authority. Status in one place reinforces status in another.

The Prime Minister's authority arises first of all from the fact of being the elected leader of the largest party in the House of Commons and the legitimate spokesman for all the party's MPs. In both the Labour and Conservative parliamentary parties, the leader is elected by a process of elimination.[18] In the first ballot, the candidate with the fewest votes must retire, and others may withdraw in favour of other candidates if their support is low. The balloting continues until one of the field of contenders secures an overall majority. In 1975, Mrs. Thatcher successfully challenged the incumbent Conservative party leader in opposition, Edward Heath, on the first ballot securing a plurality of votes in a field of three candidates, and winning an absolute majority on the second. In 1976, six Cabinet ministers sought election as Labour leader, following the retirement of Harold Wilson. On the third ballot James Callaghan was elected Labour Party leader, thus automatically becoming Prime Minister. Of Prime Ministers since 1945, five—Winston Churchill, Sir Anthony Eden, Harold Macmillan, Sir Alec Douglas-Home and James Callaghan—initially entered Downing Street by selection when their party was already the government. Four—Clement Attlee, Harold Wilson, Edward

[17] Winston S. Churchill, *Their Finest Hour* (London: Cassell, 1949), p. 14. For judicious summaries of the role of the Prime Minister, see A. H. Brown, 'Prime Ministerial Power', in Mattei Dogan and Richard Rose, *European Politics* (London: Macmillan, 1971) and George W. Jones, 'The Prime Minister's Power', *Parliamentary Affairs*, XVIII:2 (1965). For analysis of the debate about Prime Ministerial power, see ch. X, below.

[18] Previous to 1965 the Conservative leader was selected by extremely informal and private consultations among senior party leaders, a process that led to great controversy in the party when Sir Alec Douglas-Home emerged as Prime Minister in 1963, and to surprise when Harold Macmillan, rather than R. A. Butler, became Conservative Prime Minister in 1957. On the history of the 'emergence' of Conservative leaders, see R. T. McKenzie, *British Political Parties* (London: Heinemann, 2nd ed., 1963), ch. 2.

Heath and Margaret Thatcher—took office after leading their party in a victorious election campaign.

Patronage is the second source of a Prime Minister's influence over colleagues. The Prime Minister of the day determines which of several hundred MPs serve as Cabinet ministers. In addition to appointing about twenty Cabinet Ministers, the Prime Minister also appoints sixty or more MPs to junior posts, in charge of minor departments outside the Cabinet or in two types of subordinate posts within departments, minister of state, or parliamentary secretary or undersecretary of state. Collectively, these ministers constitute the front-bench of the governing party. In addition, another thirty or so back-bench MPs act as unpaid parliamentary private secretaries to individual ministers, keeping the minister in touch with rank-and-file back-bench opinion in the House of Commons. As the work of government has grown, the number of ministerial appointments has also increased. In 1900 ministerial jobs were given to 42 of the 402 MPs in the governing Conservative Party. In 1975 Harold Wilson had 118 MPs in jobs as ministers, junior ministers, or as parliamentary private secretaries. This totalled more than one-third of the membership of the Parliamentary Labour Party. It also constituted more than two-thirds of the votes required to give the Prime Minister a majority if a vote of no confidence were moved against him in the Parliamentary Labour Party.[19]

Because the Prime Minister has the sole discretion to sack ministers, losing the leader's favour can cause a minister to lose office. The hope of preferment encourages back-bench MPs wishing office to support the Prime Minister. In making ministerial appointments, the Prime Minister is formally free to name or exclude anyone. In practice, a Prime Minister must include most of the major parliamentary politicians of his party. Potential critics and successors are thus bound to give public support (or at least, avoid public criticism), because they are jointly responsible for all that the Cabinet does. The more widely a Prime Minister distributes jobs among various groupings within the parliamentary party, the broader the base of support. Many MPs regard office as a fair exchange for support.

The policies and ambitions that lead persons into the Cabinet can

[19] See Richard Rose, *The Problem of Party Government* (London: Macmillan, 1974), Table XIV.1.

lead them to resign. A minister who resigns on an issue of policy always runs the risk that colleagues find that they can govern without him. But a resignation does not inevitably blight a rising minister's career. The ups and downs of political events may retrospectively make a resignation look justified, or a Prime Minister may decide that it is not prudent to allow a major party figure to remain untrammelled by responsibility indefinitely. While most ministers who resign have gone into oblivion, a few, such as Winston Churchill, Anthony Eden and Harold Wilson, have become Prime Minister subsequent to resigning or refusing office.[20]

In Whitehall terms, the Prime Minister's authority derives from chairmanship of the Cabinet when it is meeting, and being its authorized spokesman at times when it is not meeting, or in circumstances—such as question-time and debates in the House of Commons, television interviews or discussions with foreign governments—when the Cabinet cannot collectively enunciate policy.

As chairman of the Cabinet, the Prime Minister can, in Clement Attlee's words, 'extract the opinion of those he wants when he needs them'. Votes are virtually never taken in Cabinet. A discussion is concluded by the Prime Minister summing up thus:

> The job of the Prime Minister is to get the general feeling—collect the voices. And then, when everything reasonable has been said, to get on with the job and say, 'Well, I think the decision of the Cabinet is, this, that or the other. Any objections?' Usually there aren't.[21]

Cabinet discussion does not focus upon precisely phrased resolutions leading to a vote, and a discussion can be stopped by a Prime Minister because differences of opinion are intense.

As the recognized spokesman of British government, the Prime Minister's political leeway is far greater when the Cabinet is not in session. In such circumstances, the Prime Minister can make statements that collectively commit Cabinet colleagues, requiring any who disagree to resign or overthrow him. In a crisis, when there is no time to call Cabinet meetings, the Prime Minister can deal personally with affairs, consulting or advising ministers in affected Cabinet departments as is deemed best. While the Prime Minister can make

[20] See Peter Madgwick, 'Resignations', *Parliamentary Affairs*, XX:1 (1966).
[21] Clement Attlee, quoted in Francis Williams, *A Prime Minister Remembers* (London: Heinemann, 1961), p. 81.

statements on behalf of the government in domestic policy, she or he must consult the affected minister first because it is the minister who is immediately responsible for a particular act of policy.

The Prime Minister's role as the party's leading election campaigner is of increasing importance. By entering Downing Street as the victor of a general election, a Prime Minister can claim to have the personal backing of the electorate, for general election campaigns concentrate great attention upon the personality and statements of the party leaders.[22] Once in office, a Prime Minister with demonstrated popularity in opinion polls can intimidate colleagues by pointing out that this personal stature is the party's chief electoral asset, and that colleagues must accept the Prime Minister's leadership as the price of ensuring victory at the next election.

A Prime Minister who relies upon electoral authority is vulnerable to ejection from office. For example, Edward Heath, elected leader by Conservative MPs in 1965 and made Prime Minister in 1970 by the national electorate, lost his post in 1975, after twice leading the Conservatives to defeat in the general elections of 1974. Harold Wilson served as Labour leader in opposition and government for thirteen consecutive years from 1963, but his influence within the party fluctuated greatly, depending upon whether parliamentary colleagues viewed Wilson's leadership as an electoral asset or liability. The resignation on grounds of ill health by Harold Macmillan in 1963 was widely welcomed by Conservative colleagues as saving them the difficulties of trying to eject a leader who had become an electoral liability.

The formal powers of the Prime Minister change slowly if at all, but the effective significance of the office varies according to the political circumstances of the day and the way in which the incumbent of the moment defines the role. Woodrow Wilson's words about the American presidency are equally apt in England; a chief executive can strive 'to be as big a man as he can'.

Individual Prime Ministers set very different sights. Clement Attlee, for five years deputy Prime Minister in wartime and Labour Prime Minister from 1945 to 1951, was an unassertive spokesman for the lowest common denominator of views within the Labour Cabinet. This self-denying role kept him apart from the clash of

---

[22] See David Butler and Donald Stokes, *Political Change in Britain* (London: Macmillan, 2nd ed., 1974), ch. 17 and Dennis Kavanagh, *Constituency Electioneering in Britain* (London: Longman, Green & Co., 1970), pp. 52–5.

personalities among his senior ministers. When Winston Churchill succeeded in 1951, he was almost 77 years old and in ill health. Churchill wished to remain in office to conduct foreign affairs as he had done in the wartime Coalition government. But Churchill

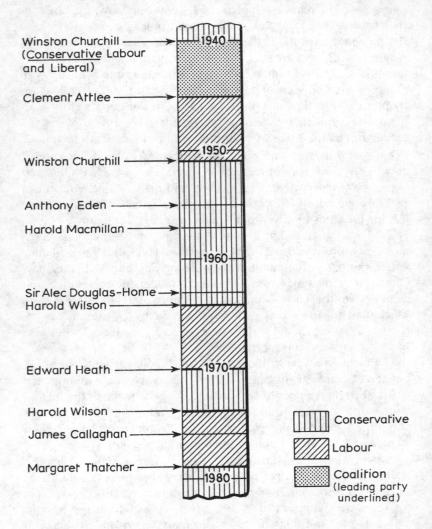

FIGURE III.1   **British Prime Ministers and governments, 1940–1979**

exerted little influence upon domestic policy, and was increasingly remote from his Cabinet. Anthony Eden, notwithstanding long experience of office, failed to define a role for himself in domestic politics after succeeding Churchill in 1955. In foreign affairs Eden took initiatives without consulting colleagues, leading to the Suez War of 1956. Eden's health broke when the attack was halted, and resignation followed in 1957. Harold Macmillan was ready to intervene strategically in both domestic and foreign policy, but his directives were not so frequent as to cause friction with his Cabinet. Exceptionally, Macmillan had held major posts previously concerned with both the economy and foreign affairs. After five years in office, however, political setbacks and ill health weakened Macmillan's ability to set policy guidelines; the party welcomed his resignation on health grounds in October 1963. Sir Alec Douglas-Home had the good health to take an active part in government, but lacked any knowledge of economic affairs, the chief political problem of government. Sir Alec was also distrusted by many Cabinet colleagues because of the way in which an inner-party caucus had secured him the post.

Both Harold Wilson and Edward Heath assumed office committed to an activist definition of the Prime Minister's job. In 1964, Wilson encouraged British journalists to compare him with John F. Kennedy, perceived in London as a powerful doer of things. Wilson's fondness for publicity led critics to describe him as more interested in managing the public relations of government than its policies. In reaction, Edward Heath entered office in 1970 with the declaration intention of stressing 'action not words'. Heath stated major objectives, both domestic and in Common Market policy, and sought to reorganize the Whitehall machine to enhance the powers of the Prime Minister.

The events of 1974 marked a retreat from the ideal of an activist Prime Minister. Heath's aggressive direction of the economy was rejected by the electorate, and Harold Wilson abandoned the rhetoric of mobilizing the nation under Prime Ministerial leadership. Instead, Wilson appeared as a political conciliator, promoting consensus in place of confrontation. The Labour government's unique links with trade unions made it easier to do this. Although Wilson's successor James Callaghan had held all three major departmental offices—Foreign Secretary, Chancellor of the Exchequer and Home Secretary—he avoided any claim to expertise.

Instead, Callaghan emphasized reconciling diverse interests in the face of severe economic difficulties. Emollient words replaced the promise of action as the dominant element in the image of a Prime Minister. The election of Margaret Thatcher in 1979 once again returned to Downing Street a Prime Minister who wished to play an activist role in promoting policies.

As an individual politician, a British Prime Minister has less formal authority than an American President. The President is directly elected by the nation's voters for a fixed term of office. A Prime Minister, by contrast, is chosen by colleagues in the Commons for an indefinite term, and is as likely to enter office through the resignation of a predecessor midway between elections as to enter office by leading a party to electoral victory. The President is thus more secure than a Prime Minister. A President can dismiss Cabinet appointees with little fear of the consequences, whereas a Prime Minister sees potential rivals for the leadership among senior colleagues. The President is the undoubted head of the federal executive. The most commanding phrase in Washington is: the President wants this. The equivalent phrase in Whitehall is: the Cabinet has decided that.[23]

The Prime Minister is more powerful than an American President in so far as British government is more subject to central Cabinet direction. Armed with the authority of Cabinet and support from the majority party in the House of Commons, the Prime Minister of the day can be certain that virtually all legislation introduced in the course of a year will be enacted into law. By contrast, a President must suffer the slings and arrows of Congressional delays, amendments and opposition, nullifying much of his annual legislative program. Moreover, the Prime Minister is on top of a unitary government, embracing local as well as central government, and without judicial limitations on its powers. By contrast, the President is only the leading person in the executive branch of federal government, without formal authority over Congress, and with even less authority over state and local governments and the judiciary.

Every Prime Minister, however much influence is sought and

[23] For a post-Watergate account of the offices that places both in their constitutional setting, see William S. Livingston, 'Britain and America: The Institutionalization of Accountability', *Journal of Politics*, XXXVIII:4 (1976). For an analysis emphasizing political attitudes, see Richard E. Neustadt, 'White House and Whitehall' in Richard Rose, ed., *Policy-Making in Britain* (London: Macmillan, 1969).

gained, must live with the fact that, while on top of the Whitehall machine, the number of things he or she can do is limited by the number of hours in the week (see pp. 28ff.). The things that can be done by 'her' government are determined within the departments headed by individual members of the Cabinet.

While the Cabinet is the keystone of the arch of central government, the departments are the building blocks.[24] Departments, singly or in collaboration, administer the collective responsibilities of Cabinet. Because of the limits of Cabinet time, the great bulk of decisions are taken within departments, especially if the subject matter is not expected to be a matter of political controversy. An individual minister's standing in Cabinet depends upon the ability to show other ministers that he knows the answers to questions and criticisms and, when necessary, can co-ordinate actions with colleagues in other departments.

From time to time, politicians or professors suggest that the involvement of Cabinet ministers in departmental affairs prevents the Cabinet from being a proper planning body. These critics usually advocate a small Cabinet of half a dozen persons to act as overseers of Whitehall. No Prime Minister has accepted this view, except in wartime. The majority have agreed with Herbert Morrison that 'a Cabinet without departmental ministers would be deficient in that day-to-day administrative experience which makes a real contribution to collective decisions'.[25]

There is no agreement among Prime Ministers or political scientists about the best way in which to organize or classify the work of government into departments. The last major review of the departmental structure of government, Lord Haldane's Report of 1918, noted two alternative principles: division in terms of client groups such as pensioners, employees and Welshmen, or organization according to the services to be performed, e.g. dividing responsibility for children among Education, Health and custodial sections of the Home Office.[26]

[24] Ministerially headed departments are not the whole of central government agencies; see Christopher Hood, Andrew Dunsire and K. Suky Thompson, 'So You Think You Know What Government Departments Are. . .?', *Public Administration Bulletin*, (Exeter) No. 27 (August 1978). See also ch. X, below.

[25] Lord Morrison of Lambeth (Herbert Morrison), *Government and Parliament* (London: Oxford University Press, 3rd ed., 1964), p. 48.

[26] For classification schemes, see W. J. M. Mackenzie, 'The Structure of Central Administration', in Sir Gilbert Campion *et al.*, *British Government since 1918* (London: Allen & Unwin, 1950).

Every Cabinet has had some departments organized primarily in terms of clients, and other departments organized by services. When Mrs. Thatcher formed her Cabinet in May 1979, the departments were :

Economic Affairs: The Treasury; Trade; Industry; Employment; Energy; Transport; Agriculture, Fisheries & Food

External Affairs: Foreign & Commonwealth Office; Defence

Social Services: Health & Social Security; Education & Science

Territorial and Environmental: Environment (including English Local Government and Housing); the Scottish Office; the Welsh Office; the Northern Ireland Office

Law: Lord Chancellor's Department; Home Office; the Attorney-General and the Solicitor-General for England & Wales; the Lord Advocate; the Solicitor-General for Scotland

Managerial and Non-departmental: Leader of the House of Commons (job doubled with the non-departmental portfolio of Chancellor of the Duchy of Lancaster); Lord President of the Council; Paymaster-General; Lord Privy Seal (and Leader of the House of Lords); Parliamentary Secretary of the Treasury (i.e. Chief Whip in the House of Commons); Civil Service Department.

The compound labels emphasize the complexities of departmental structure. This is accentuated by the readiness of Prime Ministers to put new labels on old or rearranged government functions, or to abolish old titles by merging responsibilities in super-departments such as that of the Environment.

One reason why departmental titles and duties can easily be altered is that government departments are not usually single-purpose institutions with a clear hierarchy of tasks, but rather an agglomeration of more or less related administrative units brought together by government expansion, fusion and fission. Because of this, since 1952 successive Prime Ministers have merged nineteen old departments in five mammoth super-departments.[27] For example, the creation of a new Ministry of Technology launched by the Labour Government in 1964 simply placed a new Cabinet minister on top of a collection of government bureaux previously responsible to a variety of ministers. Reciprocally, the abolition of

[27] Cf. Sir Richard Clarke, *New Trends in Government* (London: HMSO, 1971) and L. J. Sharpe, 'Whitehall—Structures and People', pp. 54ff in Dennis Kavanagh and Richard Rose, eds., *New Trends in British Politics* (London and Beverly Hills: Sage, 1977).

the Ministry of Technology by the Conservatives in 1970 did not mean the wholesale dismissal of civil servants, but rather the reassignment of the parts of the Ministry of Technology to other ministries, especially the new Department of Trade and Industry. In 1974 Labour divided this super-department into separate departments of Trade, Industry, and Prices and Consumer Protection: and in 1979 the Conservatives abolished the last named.

The limiting consideration in the creation of a government department is the political controversy that its work is expected to generate. A department cannot be any larger than a single minister can answer for in the Cabinet and in the House of Commons. For example, a department dealing routinely with a heavy volume of work, like the Post Office, required so little ministerial attention that its work was hived off to a separate Post Office Corporation outside the department framework of Whitehall. By contrast, as troubles in Northern Ireland became progressively greater following civil rights demonstrations of 1968, the duty of monitoring events there shifted from a junior minister to the Home Secretary, and then led to the creation of a separate Northern Ireland Office in 1972.

The ability of a minister to answer for a department also depends upon the coherence of its subject matter. For example, Education and Science concerns a number of integrated services, whereas the Home Office is responsible for a heterogeneous set of policies. The smaller and more homogeneous the groups being served by a department, the more coherent its work becomes. For example, the centralization of agricultural pressure groups makes the Ministry of Agriculture, Fisheries and Food much more easily administered than the departments of Trade and of Industry, which lack comparably centralized business pressure groups. The danger of having a well-organized client group is that the minister may become its captive if it is politically powerful. If many different groups make demands upon a minister, it is easier to play one off against another.

Established departments such as the Treasury and the Home Office illustrate another important proposition: the difference between Whitehall departments. The Home Office has a staff of approximately 25,000 and the Treasury, 1,000. The Home Office has many tasks that can be kept administratively separate: police, fire, prison, drugs, cruelty to animals, control of obscene publications, and race relations. The Treasury, by contrast, has a few major interrelated tasks: management of the economy, protecting the balance of payments and control of public expenditure. Because of the importance of its tasks, the Treasury has more senior civil servants than the Home Office. The Home Office has more staff at lower levels, because of the much greater volume of its routine work.

The job of Home Secretary is much more burdensome. More paper work is required, and the Home Secretary is always vulnerable to adverse publicity, e.g. if a convicted murderer escapes from prison or a newspaper stirs up concern with drug taking. Responsibility for the economy is much more diffuse, and the Chancellor of the Exchequer has a ministerial colleague, the Chief Secretary, to carry the burden of managing public expenditure.

The two departments also vary greatly in procedure and style.[28] In the Home Office, there is a tradition of advice moving slowly up through the civil service hierarchy; recommendations reflect concern with consistency in the details of administration. For example, when the abolition of capital punishment was being debated, one senior Home Office official opposed it on the ground that it would be manifestly unfair to those who had already been executed. In the Treasury, by contrast, the Chancellor is more likely to receive a variety of opinions from his civil servants, and they, in turn, are likely to be almost as varied and changeable in their outlook as academic economists. Not least in significance is the difference in power. A Home Secretary, by virtue of his domestic responsibilities, can expect that his decisions will usually be enforced. By contrast, any Chancellor of the Exchequer has to accept that whatever he decides can easily be upset by international economic trends over which British government has no control.

Every minister has a multiplicity of roles, but ministers differ in the relative emphasis given to each.[29] In policy terms, a minister may initiate policies, select among alternative policies brought forward from within the department, or be a minimalist, not making any policy decisions at all. Making policy initiatives sounds appealing, but in practice much time, energy and political capital are risked in trying to move from a ringing declaration of good intentions to an

[28] For an insider's view, see Roy Jenkins, 'The Reality of Political Power', *Sunday Times*, 17 January 1972.

[29] The typology of ministerial roles is taken from the major study by Bruce Headey, *British Cabinet Ministers: The Roles of Politicians in Executive Office* (London: George Allen & Unwin, 1974).

Act of Parliament. Many ministers prefer to allow their civil servants to identify policies regarded as administratively practicable, selecting among them ones to sponsor. To influence policy, a minister must have a point of view broad enough to be relevant to many problems, yet sufficiently defined so that civil servants can draw the correct inference about what the minister would wish done with the dozens of issues that cannot be referred to him for lack of time. In default of a clearly defined ministerial viewpoint, civil servants tend to fall back upon the departmental point of view about issues.

A Cabinet minister is also the executive head of a large bureaucracy, formally responsible for all that is done in his name by thousands of civil servants.[30] A minister is expected to spend time in oversight of departmental activities, scrutinizing files and memoranda to ensure that nothing is said or done in his name that will prove politically embarrassing to justify in Parliament. In addition a minister may seek to encourage departmental morale by meeting with officials in the field as well as in Whitehall, to understand their problems better and to see that they understand his point of view too.

A third role of a minister is departmental ambassador to the world at large. Success in this role determines the relative influence of a minister's department in a world where many compete for influence. A minister is first of all the department's ambassador to the Cabinet, needing Cabinet endorsement for the department's handling of controversial issues, for legislation the department wishes to promote and, not least, for the department's claims for money. Secondly, a minister is the department's spokesman in the House of Commons, defending its actions from criticism, as well as promoting legislation there. Thirdly, a minister is the department's chief spokesman in consultations with pressure groups, including groups within the government party, determining which demands are rejected or accepted, and seeking group support for departmental initiatives. Last and not least, a minister also represents the department in the press and on television, promoting its policies, praising its work and defending it from critics when things appear to go wrong.

A minister also acts as a politically ambitious individual and a

[30] On the concept of ministerial responsibility, see S. E. Finer, 'The Individual Responsibility of Ministers', *Public Administration*, XXXIV (Winter 1956) and Maurice Wright, 'Ministers and Civil Servants', *Parliamentary Affairs*, XXX:3 (1977).

ministerial job is often viewed in terms of its career impact. A minister considered good in heading a lesser department may hope for promotion to a major post, such as the Treasury, the Home Office or the Foreign Office, and senior ministers will often nurture an aspiration to become Prime Minister. In career terms, a minister can prosper within Whitehall by gaining a reputation for being good at understanding the work of the department, and in winning battles in Cabinet on its behalf. In Parliament, a minister can rise in esteem by skill in debating, dominating critics by the adroitness and quickness of his replies. The development of a good reputation within the party requires careful attention to endless committee meetings, and the ability to demonstrate that whatever a department is doing, it is consistent with party policy and principles. Skill in garnering newspaper headlines and frequent invitations to appear on television enhance a politician's visibility outside the world of Westminster.

Every Cabinet minister is assisted by several junior ministers assigned to the department by the Prime Minister. Junior ministers are sometimes delegated the oversight of substantial chunks of departmental work, such as prisons in the Home Office or university affairs in Education. But a junior minister cannot take a major decision of political significance. The doctrine of individual ministerial responsibility formally fixes the whole responsibility for the department upon its chief minister. While the doctrine has been increasingly infringed by the growth of large departments, no Cabinet minister can remain indifferent to receiving blame for errors made by his subordinates.

Government could continue for months without new legislation, but it would collapse overnight if hundreds of thousands of civil servants stopped administering prosaic laws concerning taxes, pensions, housing, health and other responsibilities of the welfare state. Because English government is centuries old, the accumulation of laws is especially great. Because it is 'big' government, even a middle-rank civil servant may be responsible for a staff of several thousand people or for spending tens of millions of pounds. Only if these duties are executed routinely—that is, quietly and effectively—will leading ministers have the time and opportunity to make new policies.

Civil servants perform the great bulk of work done in the name of a Cabinet minister. There are substantial legal and theoretical problems in defining precisely the boundaries of the civil service. A legal textbook concludes that in order to determine whether a given official is a civil servant or not, 'The facts of each appointment must be considered.'[31] Whatever their work, the jobs normally have a few things in common: recruitment by examination; long-service employment guaranteed by public funds; and an inflation-proof pension upon retirement. Many of the bureaucratic characteristics attributed to civil servants, such as concern with paper work, obedience to rules and promotion by seniority, are increasingly found outside as well as inside government, as large organizations—both public and private—become increasingly bureaucratic. Similarities of public and private employment are further increased when civil service advantages are gained by private sector employees (e.g. long holidays and protection against dismissal) or government accepts an obligation to match private sector wage increases funded by higher productivity, with public sector wage increases funded by higher taxes.

Nearly three in every ten British workers is paid by public money. The overwhelming proportion of Englishmen paid by government funds do *not* work for what is conventionally defined as the civil service, yet about 750,000 workers are officially classified as part of the civil service. (Cf. Table X.1.)

Civil servants are divided into a variety of classes unequal in size and political significance. The most important group within the civil service is also the smallest: the administrative class that advises ministers and oversees the work of operating bureaux. It consists of about 7,500 persons. In turn, it is served by a staff of about 70,000 executive class officials, who undertake substantial burdens but exercise little political discretion. The administrative class is itself subdivided into hundred of senior civil servants who see ministers frequently, and the several thousand who hope to win such posts by a combination of merit and seniority. The administrative class consists of individuals whose primary skills are political rather than legal, economic, scientific or technological. The motto of the administrative class has long been: 'The expert should be on tap but not on top.' While there are many professional civil servants drawing salaries equal to those of senior administrative class officials, their expertise has traditionally confined them to specialized tasks.

[31] See Wade and Bradley, *Constitutional Law*, p. 218. Note also the discussion in W. J. M. Mackenzie, 'The Civil Service, the State and the Establishment', in Bernard Crick, ed., *Essays on Reform* (London: Oxford University Press, 1967).

In total, the civil service has about 80,000 professional, scientific and technical staff, engaged in fields as different as engineering, accountancy, psychology, soil conservation and looking after museums. The largest single category in the civil service (about 200,000) consists of clerical staff, typing and filing the paper work that is the stuff of bureaucracy, undertaking tasks with little discretion. The civil service also includes about 170,000 industrial workers, primarily in such defence industries as munitions making.[32]

One major role of administrative class civil servants is to look after the needs of ministers. These high-level civil servants are intimately involved in the formulation and marketing of policies. Within Whitehall offices, these civil servants scrutinize the continuous flow of information coming into the centre to decide what papers should go up to the minister for consideration, and which can be disposed of without showing to the minister for comment. Senior civil servants spend little time in administering particular programmes; most of their time is spent screening information for possible ministerial attention, and making recommendations for action on the bulky departmental files that come up to their desks from subordinates. In addition, they comment (often negatively) upon the administrative practicality of any policy proposal emanating from the minister, or the governing party. A minister is not bound to accept advice about the drawbacks of a proposed policy, but it would be foolish of a minister to ignore warning signals from those who have served far longer than he in his department. Administrative-class civil servants are also involved in helping the minister prepare parliamentary and extra-parliamentary speeches to promote new policies, and prepare briefs to answer criticisms of departmental actions when political storms break out.

The second major concern of senior civil servants is to maintain what are considered principles of good government, whatever the party in power. While civil servants report to a minister, they are also servants of the Crown, that is, committed to seeing that the Queen's government is carried on without rapid disruption or disturbance because of the wish of a passing politician. As permanent members of the permanent institutions of government, civil servants are concerned with protecting long-term interests of govern-

[32] For up-to-date details of the civil service, see the annual report of the Civil Service Commission. The terminology used here follows older terminology, which continues to influence the status hierarchy of the civil service today.

ment. Moreover, as their long-term career prospects are determined by the decisions of the most senior civil servants rather than by politicians, each individual wishes to cultivate a reputation for adhering to civil service standards of good behaviour, rather than adopting unorthodox means in order to score a departmental triumph for a minister on a given issue. Civil servants are also conscious that, in the course of a forty-year career in Whitehall, individuals whom they face in opposite positions in one interdepartmental committee may be close colleagues another year.[33]

There are many roles undertaken by civil servants elsewhere in Europe or America that senior British civil servants do not perform.[34] For example, they are rarely responsible for the 'hands-on' management of major government activities, such as the provision of health services, education or industrial production. Nor do British civil servants engage in overt political activity; the good (or ill) they do is done anonymously, and not by engaging in public controversies; this task is left to ministers. Traditionally, administrative-class civil servants have regarded their job as a lifetime career, and not as a stepping stone to a well-paid job in industry, as can be the case in Washington, or to election to Parliament on a party ticket, as can happen in Continental Europe.

The work of the administrative class is more political than administrative, for the theoretical distinction between politics and administration cannot be sustained at the point at which ministers and civil servants meet face to face to discuss issues. At the apex of Whitehall, civil servants are remote from the routine activities of government that can be prescribed by rules and regulations. Civil servants are expected to give advice about policies, the very stuff of what government does. Any issue worth calling to the attention of a minister is by definition political, that is, likely to be the subject of differences of opinion. In reviewing alternative policies, a civil servant is making political and not purely administrative judgments. Whitehall administrators accept this fact; a survey found that 76 per cent consider political considerations more important than technical considerations, 79 per cent regard clashes between interest

[33] For a discussion of relations between civil servants (and much else), see Hugh Heclo and Aaron Wildavsky, *The Private Government of Public Money* (London: Macmillan, 1974).

[34] For elaboration, see James B. Christoph, 'Higher Civil Servants and the Politics of Consensualism in Great Britain', pp. 48ff and other selections in Mattei Dogan, ed., *The Mandarins of Western Europe* (New York: Halsted Press, 1975).

groups as inevitable, and 89 per cent do not resent politicians being concerned with administrative issues. On all three of these points, senior British civil servants more readily accept political roles than do their counterparts in Germany, Italy, the Netherlands or Sweden.[35]

Ministers and civil servants need each other. A minister looks to civil servants first of all for information about what is happening within the department, especially things that are (or could quickly become) politically controversial. Secondly, when controversies arise, a minister wants civil servants to identify practicable alternatives and to point out the difficulties as well as the attractions of each. Thirdly, a minister needs civil servants to translate the broad policy objectives of the governing party into concrete policy alternatives, and eventually into a bill that can be enacted by Parliament. Once a policy is determined by the minister or by Cabinet, civil servants are expected to carry it out loyally, even if they disagree with it. In the words of one anonymous official, 'The soul of the service is the loyalty with which we execute ordained error.'[36] The chief criticism that ministers make of civil servants is that they lack expert knowledge. Another criticism is that the civil servant's viewpoint is too cautious and unimaginative, and tends to reduce unnecessarily the range of policy alternatives put to a minister.[37]

Civil servants want their minister to give clear and prompt decisions about problems that they present, and to stick to a decision when, as is usually the case, it attracts criticism as well as praise. Given a clear lead by their minister, civil servants are safe in exercising authority in his name. Civil servants also like a minister to be successful as the department's ambassador, winning battles in Cabinet, defending the department from criticism in Parliament and the press, and securing public recognition and praise for its achievements. A minister who is indecisive when action is imperative, or who is inconsistent and unpredictable, makes life difficult for civil servants. A minister who is unsuccessful as an ambassador makes the department a loser in the Cabinet competition for scarce

[35] See S. J. Eldersveld, Sonja Hubee-Boonzaaijer and Jan Kooiman, 'Elite Perceptions of the Political Process in the Netherlands Looked at in Comparative Perspective', in Dogan, ed., *The Mandarins of Western Europe*, p. 159. For another analysis of the same British data, see Robert Putnam, 'The Political Attitudes of Senior Civil Servants in Western Europe: A Preliminary Report', *British Journal of Political Science*, III:3 (1973).

[36] See Ian Gilmour, *The Body Politic* (London: Hutchinson, 1969).

[37] See Headey, *British Cabinet Ministers*, p. 112.

public funds and legislative time, and will depress departmental morale by failing to answer public criticism effectively.

Ministers and senior civil servants are both deeply involved in political administration. Within a department, their shared responsibility gives them common interests, and their high position gives them—jointly or singly—the power to influence major policies. As civil servants rise in the administrative hierarchy, they become increasingly skilful in anticipating the political concerns of their minister, and in undertaking political responsibilities, such as preparing Cabinet papers, writing speeches and policy documents, and drafting answers to politically embarrassing questions. As ministers gain experience in Whitehall, they learn to accept or anticipate the administrative objections that civil servants raise about politically attractive initiatives. In so far as each can understand the other's job, they constitute a single team advancing departmental interests. One persisting difference remains: ministers owe their transitory Whitehall position to party favour and electoral good fortune, whereas civil servants owe their permanent posts to good fortune in recruitment and to favour in Whitehall.

The difficulties of British government have made reform of the civil service a perennial topic on the political agenda. It is assumed that changing the institutions or personnel of government would be sufficient to change the impact of policies on society. In 1968, the Fulton Committee on the civil service delivered sweeping criticisms of it, and recommended a host of reforms, mostly concerning the recruitment, grading and training of civil servants. Nine years later, the House of Commons Expenditure Committee published another review of the civil service, recommending many of the same reforms again, as well as calling for changes in the relationship of Whitehall departments and Parliament.[38]

The dissatisfaction of the reformers can easily be explained: the responsibility for changing the civil service is in the hands of the civil servants themselves. They are readiest to promote changes congenial to themselves and to oppose changes supported by outsiders. The government rejected the Commons proposals in a report that was described as 'more notable for the changes it rules out than the

[38] See the Fulton Committee, *Report: The Civil Service*, Vol. I (London: HMSO, Cmnd. 3638, 1968) and related publications; and the report of the House of Commons Committee chaired by Michael English, MP (London: HC 535–I, 1976–7, HMSO).

reforms it proposes'.[39] Permanence, not rapid change, is the essence of a civil service.

One purposeful change[40] that has taken place in the 1970s is the introduction of special advisers to Cabinet ministers, performing political functions that civil servants are barred from, or not specially suited for. Special advisers, usually one to an individual Cabinet minister, were first introduced in the 1970 Conservative government, and generalized by the 1974 Labour government.[41] Special advisers provide political companionship to ministers who may feel lonely surrounded by civil servants in a vast Whitehall office; they read Cabinet papers from other departments, commenting upon them in the light of broad party concerns; they act as a liaison between the minister and party groups specially concerned with the work of the department; and they can read files, attend meetings and hold political discussions for which the minister lacks time. In extreme cases, special advisers may question the fundamental assumptions of policy advice sent to the minister through departmental channels, or promote alternative policies in competition with those officially recommended.

Special advisers have fitted into Whitehall because most of their roles complement rather than compete with the principal concerns of civil servants. A single policy adviser in a department with ten or twenty thousand staff does not present a threat to established civil service practices. The adviser can also be asked to do political tasks from which civil servants are debarred, e.g. making contacts with party officials. Because most special advisers are not experts in the subject matter of their minister, they do not provide technical expertise, which the Fulton Committee said was lacking in Whitehall. Instead, they provide partisan political expertise.

Notwithstanding much talk and some action, the criticisms of the 1960s reformers can still be heard in 1980. It is particularly signifi-

[39] Peter Hennessy, 'Prime Minister Rules out Reorganization of Central Government', *The Times* (16 March 1978), reporting the issuance of a Government White Paper HMSO, Cmnd. 7116, 1978, as a response to the English Committee report cited in footnote 38 above.

[40] Many limited and unintended changes occur gradually in formal and informal political practices in Whitehall. For analytic reviews, see particularly Maurice Wright, 'Ministers and Civil Servants', and Sharpe, 'Whitehall—Structures and People'. The Sharpe article is also valuable as a citation to additional sources.

[41] See Rudolf Klein and Janet Lewis, 'Advice and Dissent in British Government: The Case of the Special Advisers', *Policy and Politics*, V:1 (1977) for a full discussion of many points summarized here.

cant (though little noted) that most of the criticisms of civil servants are equally applicable to ministers. For example, both are generalists; neither is expected to have professional skills or expertise relevant to the substantive problems of the department, whether it is the Treasury, education, agriculture or social services. Neither MPs nor civil servants have training or experience of managing large organizations, except what they learn on the job in Whitehall. Ministers are shuffled from department to department in response to the political exigencies of the moment, and civil servants are often sent to another post soon after mastering technical details of a job. Civil servants appear expert in their subject by comparison with Cabinet ministers, and they are truly expert if their subject is defined as political administration. Civil servants often lack expertise in the substance of the problems confronting them, by comparison with many specialists outside government.

Because Whitehall is run by a combination of ministers and civil servants working hard sixty hours a week or more, anything that affects either group affects the whole system. If the calibre or skills of the civil service deteriorate, this affects what the Cabinet can achieve. If a Prime Minister or his Cabinet is uncertain or unrealistic in setting policy objectives, this affects what civil servants can achieve. When one falters, the whole falters. In so far as the skill of civil servants and/or ministers are not adequate to today's problems, then the aggregate capability of government is diminished.

The role of Parliament

In its dignified aspect Parliament is very impressive. The Palace of Westminster, the meeting place of the House of Commons and the House of Lords, is a familiar symbol throughout the world. Parts of the building date back to the eleventh century; the bulk is of Victorian Gothic design, as massive as it is non-utilitarian. Officers of the House emphasize its dignity by wearing elaborate formal dress, including wigs. The late Aneurin Bevan, a left-wing Labour MP, described his first impression of Parliament as a church dedicated to 'the most conservative of all religions—ancestor worship'.[42]

In terms of efficient power, Parliament is not so impressive, because its role in policy-making is strictly limited. The Cabinet controls most of its proceedings; by convention, the Leader of the Opposition is also allowed to fix topics for debate on a limited

[42] Aneurin Bevan, *In Place of Fear* (London: Heinemann, 1952), p. 6.

number of days. The Prime Minister can be sure that any proposal the government puts forward will be promptly voted on in Parliament and voted on in the form desired by the executive, for the government drafts legislation and controls amendments. Furthermore, Cabinet enjoys the powers of the purse. While the budget prepared by the Treasury is debated at length in Parliament, it is rarely altered.

The limited influence of Parliament is made clear by a comparison with the United States Congress. In America each of the houses of Congress controls its own proceedings, independently of the other and of the White House. When one party controls the presidency and the other Congress, party loyalties reinforce Congressional independence. An American President can ask Congress to enact a bill, but he cannot compel it to vote on a measure, let alone endorse it. Moreover, a bill that is finally approved may receive many amendments that reduce or destroy its value to the White House. Last and not least, Congress can increase or decrease presidential requests for appropriations. The budget that the President presents is not a final document, but an attempt to get Congress to provide funds. Congressmen invoke their budgeting powers to monitor closely executive activities throughout the year. Parliament lacks each of these powerful Congressional checks upon the executive.

In a year's parliamentary business, the government of the day can secure the passage of up to 100 per cent of the bills it introduces; this has happened eight times since 1945. Since 1945 a government has secured an average of 97 per cent of the legislation that it introduces during a full Parliament. (See Table III.1.) The ability of the government of the day to get its way is not influenced by party colours: the 1945–50 Labour government secured passage of 99.1 per cent of the 310 bills it introduced, and from 1970 through 1973, the Conservative government enacted 98.4 per cent of its proposals. Even in the 1974–6 sessions of Parliament, when Labour had no sure overall majority, it none the less enacted 91.2 per cent of the 159 bills that it introduced.

The bills that government promotes are often amended in the House of Commons, but the government of the day almost invariably determines whether or not proposed amendments will be enacted into law. In three full sessions from 1967 to 1971, the government moved a total of 1,772 amendments at committee and

TABLE III.1   **The proportion of government bills approved by Parliament**

Parliament (Government)	Bills introduced	Approved	Percentage approved
1945–50 (Labour)	310	307	99.0
1950–51 (Labour)	99	97	98.0
1951–54* (Conservative)	167	158	94.6
1955–59 (Conservative)	229	223	97.4
1959–64 (Conservative)	251	244	97.2
1964–65* (Labour)	66	65	98.5
1966–69* (Labour)	215	210	97.7
1970–73 (Conservative)	192	189	98.4
1974–78* (Labour)	260	236	90.8
Total	1,789	1,729	96.6

*Omits final session of Parliament, interrupted by government calling a general election, voiding all pending bills.
Sources 1945–69: Calculated from Valentine Herman, 'What Governments Say and What Governments Do: An Analysis of Post-War Queen's Speeches', Parliamentary Affairs, XXVIII:1 (1974/75) Table 1.
1970–78: Calculated from Gavin Drewry, 'Legislation', in S. A. Walkland and Michael Ryle, The Commons in the Seventies (London: Fontana, 1977), Table 1, and Ivor Burton and Gavin Drewry, 'Public Legislation: a Survey of the Sessions 1977/8 and 1978/9', Parliamentary Affairs (forthcoming).

report stages of legislation; 1,770 were approved by Parliament. By contrast, Opposition MPs and back-bench MPs in the government party moved 4,198 amendments; of these, only 210 were approved by the government. Of the government amendments, 365 were moved as a result of undertakings given at the committee stage of legislation to look again at a specific and often non-controversial detail of a bill. Overall, the government of the day introduces and enacts 89 per cent of amendments to laws, as well as securing the passage of nearly all substantive legislation. This reflects a state of mind summed up by a Labour Cabinet minister: 'It's carrying democracy too far if you don't know the result of the vote before the meeting.'[43]

[43] Eric Varley, quoted in Michie and Hoggart, The Pact, p. 13; research by J. A. G. Griffith, cited in The State of the Nation (London: Granada Television, 1973), pp. 124–5.

The government of the day consistently wins votes in the House of Commons because of party loyalties. The government represents the majority party in the Commons, and MPs in the majority party are expected to support Cabinet measures (and vote against motions of the opposition) in order to maintain their party in control of government. The principal division in central government does not run between Parliament and Whitehall, but rather within the House of Commons, separating the majority party—which controls both the Commons and Cabinet—and the opposition.

When there is a major vote in the House of Commons, it is normally treated as a vote of confidence in the government. The party line on voting in the Commons is stated officially in a weekly memorandum issued by the party's Chief Whip. MPs of the governing party accept the whip, because they recognize that only by voting as a block can their party continue to control government. To defy the whip on a given issue by abstaining, or even more voting for the other side, is acceptable only if it does not lead to the downfall of the government. Cabinet ministers benefit most from party discipline, for their proposals are supported by the feet of back-bench colleagues tramping through the division lobbies, even when some MPs do not accept a measure with their hearts and minds.

Back-benchers of the governing party go along with the Cabinet because of trust in leaders, a belief that frequent rebellion may cost them chances of promotion to a ministerial role and, above all, because of an acceptance of the overriding claims of party loyalty. While party discipline is often criticized by independent commentators, the great majority of MPs consider it necessary and desirable. In the blunt words of a Labour MP, George Darling:

> There is a lot of nonsense talked about party discipline, usually by so-called Liberals who haven't got a party and have the quaint notion that if they had it would work effectively as a sort of anarchists' federation.[44]

Within the governing party in the Commons, there are opportunities for back-bench MPs to influence government, individually and collectively. The Whips office is expected to listen to the views of back-bench MPs dissatisfied with a particular government pro-

[44] Quoted in Rudolf Klein, 'What MPs Think of their Jobs', in Bernard Crick, *The Reform of Parliament* (London: Weidenfeld & Nicolson, 1st ed., 1964), p. 212.

posal, and convey their concerns to ministers.[45] In the corridors and club-rooms as well as the committee rooms of the Commons, backbenchers can tell ministers what they think is wrong with the party's measures. Disagreement can be carried to the debating chamber of the Commons as well, and may lead individual MPs in the governing party to abstain, or even vote against the government whip on a particular amendment, and occasionally on the principle of a bill. The threat of withholding support is intended to make ministers think again about government policy, for ministers do not wish to put too much strain on the loyalty and confidence of their backbench supporters.[46]

From 1945 to 1974, voting was strictly along party lines (that is, not one of the 600-plus Conservative or Labour MPs voted with the other party) in seven-eighths of all parliamentary divisions. When an MP did vote with opponents, this almost invariably occurred when a rebel would not affect the overall outcome. In other words, an individual MP could express distinctive personal or constituency views, when he knew that stepping out of line would not hurt the party's cause.[47] The extent of cross-party voting fluctuates, and when it rises, as in the 1970s, there is a tendency to proclaim this as evidence of the independence of MPs. But even when individual rebel votes are at their height, the great majority of divisions are strictly along party lines—and rebels have an inconsequential effect upon the result.

An individual MP who makes a habit of rebellion or threatens to rebel to the party's collective damage faces the risk of expulsion from the party and almost certain electoral defeat, since MPs are elected primarily on the basis of their party label, and not on a personal basis. Knowing this, Harold Wilson, as Prime Minister, could threaten Labour MPs thus:

[45] See Anthony King and Anne Sloman, *Westminster and Beyond* (London: Macmillan, 1973), ch. 8 and Donald Searing and Chris Game, 'Horses for Courses', *British Journal of Political Science*, VII:3 (1977).

[46] For a sophisticated contemporary study of the variety of ways in which MPs can divide, especially when dissent is present, see Anthony King, 'Modes of Executive–Legislative Relations: Great Britain, France and West Germany', *Legislative Studies Quarterly*, I:1 (1976).

[47] For an exhaustive analysis of individual MPs' behaviour, see Philip Norton, *Dissent in the House of Commons* (London: Macmillan, 1975). Note also Robert Jackson, *Rebels and Whips* (London: Macmillan, 1968). On the logic of 'position taking' without influencing the result, see David R. Mayhew, *Congress: The Electoral Connection* (New Haven: Yale University Press, 1974).

All I say is 'watch it'. Every dog is allowed one bite, but a different view is taken of a dog that goes on biting all the time. If there are doubts that the dog is biting not because of the dictates of conscience but because he is considered vicious, then things happen to that dog. He may not get his licence renewed when it falls due.[48]

By definition, the Opposition party cannot expect to alter major government decisions, because by itself it does not have enough votes in the House of Commons. The Opposition accepts the defeat of nearly every one of its motions for a period of up to five years, the maximum life of a contemporary Parliament, because it hopes for victory at the next election. As long as the two major parties alternate in winning control of a parliamentary majority at elections, each can expect to enjoy all the powers of British government at least part of the time.[49]

The experience of the minority Labour government in the 1974–9 Parliament emphasizes the importance of party discipline. While Labour was the largest single party in the Commons, it did not have an absolute majority of votes for the bulk of the period. Because it could not rely upon its own votes to carry any measure introduced, the government was less willing to make divisions into votes of confidence, for fear of being forced to resign. For that reason, Labour back-benchers were readier to rebel, especially as there were differences within the party about government policies. At times, Labour rebels augmented Conservative, Liberal and Nationalist opposition votes to defeat the government.

In March 1977, the Prime Minister emphasized the importance of having a secure parliamentary majority, concluding a pact with the Liberals in the House of Commons. The pact promised the Liberals consultation about legislation in return for a Liberal promise to refrain from defeating the government on a vote of confidence. Inter-party agreement thus temporarily replaced intra-party solidarity as the basis of government domination of Parliament. After the pact expired, the government, with a majority of about 30 over the Conservatives, relied upon divisions among the seven other parties opposing it to maintain itself in Parliament until March 1979.

The daily routine of the House of Commons is that of a 'talking

[48] Quoted in *The Times*, 3 March 1967.
[49] On the role of the Opposition party, see R. M. Punnett, *Front-Bench Opposition* (London: Heinemann, 1973).

shop'. Its procedural forms allow discussion in a variety of different ways. A typical day may begin with a number of MPs at morning committee meetings, others attending to correspondence or gossip in the Palace of Westminster and a few, especially lawyers, pursuing normal jobs. At 2.30 p.m. the House assembles for prayers, followed by an hour of parliamentary questioning of departmental ministers and the Prime Minister about topics notified in advance. At 3.30 p.m. ministers, opposition leaders or back-benchers may briefly raise exceptional or urgent items, e.g. an international or economic crisis. By 3.45 p.m. the House is usually dealing with pending legislation or debating policy issues, with ministers and front-bench opposition spokesmen speaking first. By the time the ordinary back-bencher rises to speak, many MPs will have left the chamber to have their evening meal, or for meetings in the Palace of Westminster with other MPs or visitors. The chamber is likely to fill up again for major speeches (and perhaps a vote) at the end of the major debate of the day at 10 p.m. If the governing party has difficulty in limiting debate about controversial measures, the Commons may continue sitting until after midnight. In 1975–6, it continued sitting until midnight or after on 84 of 190 days.[50] The final half-hour of each day is reserved for an adjournment debate, in which an individual back-bencher can air a grievance about a particular issue and receive a reply from a junior minister.

The House of Commons spends far more time each year talking than does the Parliament of any other major Western nation. In 1975–6 it sat for a total of 190 days. It also spends more time each day in talking than do other major Parliaments. For example, in the period 1968–73, it spent one-third more time in full session than did the United States Senate, three times more than the French Assembly, and nearly five times more than the West German Bundestag.[51] Because of long sessions, MPs have limited time to spend in their constituencies, or to see things and people outside London.

In the course of a year, the House of Commons spends more time talking about non-legislative than legislative matters. In a typical year, only 32 per cent of the time is devoted to discussing govern-

---

[50] 'The Late Parliamentary Show', *The Economist*, 22 October 1977, pp. 15–17.
[51] For comparative data about Parliaments, see Valentine Herman with Françoise Mendel, *Parliaments of the World* (London: Macmillan, 1976), especially Table 24. For time-series data on Britain, see Butler and Sloman, *British Political Facts, 1900–1975*, pp. 156–8.

ment bills, and another 7.5 per cent is devoted to statutory instruments promulgated by government departments but theoretically subject to veto by Parliament. In addition, the government must find time for debates about which it has yet to crystallize its own views into legislative form. About one-fifth of the time of the Commons is given to the Opposition to initiate debates criticizing government action or inaction. Another sixth of the Commons' time is spent discussing motions brought forward by individual back-bench MPs, many on issues unrelated to party.[52]

The variety of procedures for discussing public questions reflects the fact that many important responsibilities of contemporary government cannot be determined by Acts of Parliament. Government actions concerning the economy, industrial disputes and foreign affairs are usually determined by a ministerial or Cabinet decision rather than by Acts of Parliament. Such decisions are typically framed as statements of intent, since government cannot unilaterally determine the outcome of international negotiations, domestic bargaining about wages or prices, or trends in the national and international economy. In advance of government action, parliamentary debates register the mood of the House, indicating to ministers what decisions or statements of intent would be popular with the government party, and what would be vulnerable to criticism. After the event, MPs debate the wisdom of these discretionary decisions.

Among all the functions of parliamentary activity, the first and foremost is weighing men, not measures. MPs continually assess their colleagues as ministers and potential ministers. A minister may win a formal vote of confidence but lose standing among colleagues if his arguments are demolished in debate, or if he shows little understanding of the case that his civil servants have briefed him to argue. The club-like atmosphere of the Commons also permits MPs to judge through the years the personal character of their colleagues, separating those who merit personal confidence from those who do not. By this continuing assessment of persons, MPs make uncoerced judgments of the Cabinet and Opposition leadership. While this is not recorded in division lists, party leaders note carefully which of their colleagues have the confidence of

---

[52] See R. L. Borthwick, 'The Floor of the House', in S. A. Walkland and Michael Ryle, eds., *The Commons in the 70's* (London: Fontana, 1977), p. 53.

THE CONSTITUTION OF THE CROWN 93

back-benchers, and journalists write reputations up and down according to fluctuations in this intangible mood.

Scrutinizing the administration of laws is a second major function of Parliament.[53] An MP may write directly to a minister, questioning a seemingly anomalous or unfair departmental decision or policy called to his attention by a constituent or a pressure group. If the MP is not satisfied with the results of this review, he can raise the issue with the responsible minister at question time in the Commons. MPs can also raise administrative issues in the daily adjournment debate. The knowledge that dissatisfaction with a private reply can lead to public debate ensures that correspondence from back-bench MPs is given special attention within the minister's private office. The minister may reaffirm departmental policy so convincingly that his questioner will not wish to pursue the matter further. He may decide to alter policy to avoid a repetition of embarrassing questions on a point. In more than one-fifth of adjournment debates, a minister makes a positive response to his critic. If a minister is persistently in trouble with back-benchers on administrative issues and fails to convince his colleagues by his replies, the Prime Minister may resolve the difficulty by changing the minister.

MPs can request the Parliamentary Commissioner for Administration (also known as the Ombudsman, after the Swedish prototype) to investigate complaints about maladministration by central government departments. But many fields of inquiry are excluded by the Commissioner's terms of reference; in the first two years of work (the office was created in 1967), nearly three-fifths of all complaints received were rejected as outside the Commissioner's jurisdiction. The Commissioner's findings are reported to Parliament for debate, but he has no power to order the reversal of a government decision.[54]

British entry to the European Community has challenged Parliament to find a means of scrutinizing legislation that is binding upon British subjects, but is not enacted by an Act of Parliament. The laws and regulations of the Community are normally proposed by the European Commission in Brussels, and agreed following bar-

[53] For detailed discussion of many methods of parliamentary scrutiny, see chapters in Walkland and Ryle, eds., *The Commons in the 70's*.

[54] See e.g. Roy Gregory and Peter Hutchesson, *The Parliamentary Ombudsman: A Study in the Control of Administrative Action* (London: George Allen & Unwin, 1975).

gaining among representatives of the nine national governments, including the British government of the day.[55]

MPs, particularly those opposed to the principle of British membership in the Community, have criticized this procedure as a violation of the sovereignty of Parliament. In this they are technically correct, since the Community Treaty establishes a supra-national body. The practical diminution of parliamentary influence is easily overstated. Since government ministers rather than Parliament make national legislation, its influence is little lessened if these ministers do so in international negotiations rather than national negotiations. Ministers remain accountable to Cabinet and ultimately to votes of confidence in the House for the Community actions. MPs have established committees to scrutinize Community legislation; their ineffectualness differs little from those of many Commons groups concerned with domestic legislation. The direct election of a European Parliament in 1979 will increase the accountability of the Community to the electorate but, by the same token, could diminish the potential influence of national Parliaments.

The House of Commons also uses committees to scrutinize administration. A small group of MPs can give more time to an issue than can the whole House. Moreover, committees can interview civil servants and other experts, as well as receive written reports. One type of committee is primarily concerned with reports from expert staff about matters of administration. For example, the Public Accounts Committee, always chaired by a leading Opposition MP, reviews government expenditure after the event, publicizing instances of waste and financial mismanagement. Its existence as a watchdog is a caution to administrators of public money. The Statutory Instruments Committee scrutinizes regulations laid down by the executive under powers delegated by Act of Parliament. It can call the attention of the House to statutory instruments that it believes inconsistent with parliamentary practice and legislation. A Select Committee on Expenditure, introduced in the 1970–1 session of Parliament, reviews the long-term expenditure implications of the annual government budgets, as well as examining the priorities established in the budget. It has yet to establish itself as an

[55] See David Coombes, 'British Government and the European Community', in Kavanagh and Rose, eds., *New Trends in British Politics*; and Martin Kolinsky, 'Parliamentary Scrutiny of European Legislation', *Government and Oppostion*, X:1 (1975).

effective influence upon the spending policies of the executive. The Select Committee on Nationalized Industries scrutinizes a major field of public administration not amenable to normal forms of parliamentary investigation, because nationalized industries are managed by boards appointed by ministers. Select committees are also established on an *ad hoc* basis to deliberate upon such matters as electoral law reform, or to enquire into unusual events, such as a parliamentary scandal.

In response to demands by back-bench MPs and academics, since 1966 specialist committees also scrutinize government activities. The specialist committees are concerned with such topics as Science and Technology, Education and Science, Race Relations and Defence. In a typical session of the House in the 1970s, some 40 committees or subcommittees met each session, and slightly more than half of all back-bench MPs served on one or more of these committees.[56]

While the select committees have the attributes of important bodies—questioning ministers, civil servants and outside experts; making field trips; and publishing reports—they lack significant political influence. As a committee moves from discussions of detail to more general questions, it raises the issue of confidence in the government. Party discipline then makes the government secure against dictation from specialist bodies.

The scrutiny of administration by Parliament does affect ministerial behaviour, because the need to answer criticisms publicly concentrates attention upon the 'presentational' aspects of policy. A department or a minister may, however, become more concerned about what is said about its activities than what actually gets done. The Head of the Civil Service relates the following experience.

I happened to be visiting the Welsh Office in Cardiff on the day when there had been an oil slick in the Bristol Channel. So naturally there was a great deal of activity going on, and when I arrived at the office the man in charge there was beginning to get people in to start assessing the situation.

The first question dealt with was—what was to be said in the House? It was not—how much mess was there on the beaches and

[56] Many reformers have had second thoughts about the value of committees. See Nevil Johnson, 'Select Committees as Tools of Parliamentary Reform: Some Further Reflections', in Walkland and Ryle, eds., *The Commons in the 70's*.

what damage had been done, and how progress could be made in clearing it up? That came next.[57]

Talking about legislation is a third function of the House of Commons. It is not concerned with actually writing legislation. The general principles of bills are decided by ministers. Bills are prepared by specialist parliamentary draftsmen acting on instructions in memoranda prepared by civil servants seeking to give detailed expression to broad ministerial wishes. Particular details are discussed at length with affected and interested parties *before* being introduced in the Commons. Laws are described as Acts of Parliament, but it would be more accurate if they were stamped: made in Whitehall.

Such influence as the Commons exerts upon legislation is felt at the drafting stage, when Whitehall seeks to anticipate what MPs will and will not attack when a bill comes forward for debate. Inevitably, Whitehall officials are less able than MPs in assessing the collective opinion of Parliament. That is why both government and opposition amendments are brought forward during various stages of parliamentary deliberation.

The actual process of enacting legislation is complex. A bill is introduced to the House of Commons by a minister at first reading, and published without debate. In the second reading debate that follows subsequently, the general principles of the bill are meant to be discussed. Major bills are then usually referred to the Committee of the Whole House (all MPs meeting under distinctive rules of procedure). Lesser legislation is considered by standing committees containing a fraction of the House. Party discipline is effective in both places. There must then be a report stage, giving all MPs a chance to discuss it once again. A third reading debate follows.

A bill can then proceed to the House of Lords. If it is passed in the same form as in the Commons, it receives the formality of royal assent, and becomes the law of the land. If the Lords make amendments or vote against a bill, it returns to the Commons for further consideration, unless it is a money bill, which automatically becomes law within a month after leaving the Commons. The Commons may accept the amendments of the Lords. If the Commons rejects them, the Lords may bow to the wishes of the Commons, or insist again upon its amendments. If this happens, the

[57] Quoted in *The State of the Nation*, p. 99.

deadlock can be resolved and the Commons version of the bill
becomes law, if it is approved by the Commons twice in a period of
more than one year at successive annual sessions. The Lords has the
power to delay a bill, but not the power to filibuster it to death.[58]

The fourth function of MPs is expressive—articulating political
ideas and values, privately as well as in public, and outside the
House of Commons as well as inside it. An MP has much readier
access to the mass media than does an ordinary citizen, and is also
better able to raise issues in the party outside Parliament. Within
Parliament, an MP can communicate ideas to a minister informally
or through the minister's parliamentary private secretary, an MP
responsible for collecting views about departmental policy from
back-benchers. Both parliamentary parties have specialist committees that meet privately; these committees shadow government
departments. If rebuffed in private conversations and meetings,
back-benchers can carry their disagreements to the floor of the
Commons, putting down early-day motions critical of their leaders.
While these motions are not debated, they will get publicity if a
substantial number of MPs sign. MPs can also speak against their
own front-bench in a debate, even though whips will expect them to
vote with the minister in the division that ends it.

It is sometimes suggested that Parliament also has a fifth function: mobilizing consent for particular government measures, as
well as mobilizing votes for the party most successful in educating
voters to prefer its approach to government. But Parliament cannot
sway mass opinion, because the mass of the electorate is not nearly
as interested in the work of Parliament as are MPs or professors of
politics. The average daily sale of *Hansard*, the journal containing a
verbatim report of parliamentary debates, is about 2,500 copies. Only
the quality newspapers read by one-tenth of the electorate report in
any detail speeches made in the Commons. In 1978, the House of
Commons allowed broadcasting of its proceedings, but excerpts
played on radio attract a limited number of listeners.

The public's lack of interest or exposure to debate is matched by
that of MPs. Only one-sixth of back-benchers regularly listen to
their colleagues making speeches in the House of Commons, and
another two-fifths regularly listen to speeches on topics of particular

---

[58] See S. A. Walkland, *The Legislative Process in Great Britain* (London: George
Allen & Unwin, 1968) and, for the definitive statement of procedure, Erskine May,
Parliamentary Practice (London: Butterworth & Co., 19th ed., 1976).

personal interest. Less than one-third of MPs read or skim *Hansard* regularly. The majority of MPs rely on press reports or conversations with other MPs to find out what is said on the floor of the House.[59]

A newly elected MP, contemplating his or her role as one among 635 individuals in the House of Commons, immediately notices the advantages that election brings. Remarks of an MP unnoticed when a private citizen now appear in print. An MP is able to direct enquiries to any branch of British government and expect prompt, courteous and full answers. As an MP, a person will have the opportunity to meet people in many different walks of life, and travel at government expense or at the expense of an interest group. Entering Parliament opens opportunities to do free-lance journalism, or take a variety of part-time consulting posts. The Palace of Westminster also provides most of the facilities of a first-class London club.

By the time an MP has drawn a first year's salary, he or she begins to note the shortcomings of parliamentary life. The pay is calculated to permit MPs without outside earnings 'to live and maintain themselves at a modest but honourable level'.[60] The expense allowance of MPs often fails to cover costs arising from maintaining a home in London and in a constituency distant from London. Back-bench MPs and Opposition front-benchers lack the personal staff that U.S. Congressmen enjoy. Office and secretarial facilities are made available grudgingly and may involve extra expense.

The lack of services for MPs reflects the historic definition of the role as a part-time job for a wealthy person. A 1967 survey found that two-thirds of Conservative MPs had part-time jobs, whereas three-quarters of Labour MPs made politics their sole occupation. Conservatives usually argue that work outside the Commons keeps them in touch with the 'real-world' problems of an ordinary citizen. Labour MPs argue that it is a full-time job to keep in touch with the world of politics. Differences in occupational background help explain differences in party attitudes. Many Conservative MPs

[59] See Anthony Barker and Michael Rush, *The Member of Parliament and his Information* (London: George Allen & Unwin, 1970, for PEP & the Study of Parliament Group), pp. 135ff.

[60] See *Report of the Committee on the Remuneration of Ministers and Members of Parliament* (London: HMSO, Cmnd. 2516, 1964), paragraph 35; and, latterly, *Remuneration of Ministers and Members of Parliament* (London: HMSO, Cmnd. 4836, 1971). On back-bench life generally, see Peter G. Richards, *The Backbenchers* (London: Faber & Faber, 1972).

combine being an MP with their previous occupation as a professional person, or as a company director. By contrast, only a third of Labour MPs can pursue professional work simultaneously with serving in the Commons, for Labour MPs are more likely to be ex-school teachers than lawyers or accountants. Nearly half of Labour MPs can, however, supplement their allowances by drawing upon trade union sponsorship.[61]

Once in the House, every back-bencher is faced with a wide choice of alternative roles. He may decide to do no more than meet the whip's expectation of a party loyalist, voting as the leadership decides, without taking part in deliberations about policy. If he does wish to be more than a name in a division list, an MP must decide whether to make a mark by brilliance in debate, willingness to attend routine committee meetings, as an acknowledged spokesman for a pressure group, or in a non-partisan way, e.g. as a House wit or chairman of its kitchen committee.[62]

The chief political role open to every MP is that of advocate. MPs can use the facilities of the House of Commons to publicize causes that they feel are neglected or misunderstood. Individual MPs have become known as advocates for causes as disparate as world government (not yet realized) a revolving toothbrush (realized without legislation), or abortion law reform (realized without implicating the parties in a controversial matter). MPs may get together with like-minded colleagues to form ginger groups to push the Labour leadership to the left or the Conservative leadership to the right, according to their ideological views. Many MPs are recognized spokesmen for an interest group, and some represent interests with which they were identified long before entering Parliament. An accountant may speak for an association of accountants, and a former miner may receive financial aid from the National Union of Mineworkers. An MP can accept a retainer to advocate a point of view in Parliament as long as he declares this interest before speaking.

An MP is expected to speak for constituency interests, but constituents accept that party discipline will prevent their MP from voting with a constituency interest against the party policy when these are in conflict. An MP can speak on behalf of individually

---

[61] See the *Annual Register of Members Interests* (London: HMSO).
[62] See the discussion in Richard Rose, *People in Politics* (London: Faber & Faber, 1970), pp. 98ff.

aggrieved constituents. Most MPs also hold 'surgeries' in their constituency at least once a month. Constituents can see them there to pour out personal problems, even if it is a problem that central government cannot put right.[63] When in the constituency, an MP visits party officials to make sure that whatever their views, they do not voice grievances about the work of their MP.

Ironically, the one role that an MP will rarely undertake is that of legislator. Each year the government sets aside a small amount of time for MPs to introduce private members' bills. MPs ballot for this privilege. Because government support is not assured, less than a dozen of such bills pass in a session.[64] A number are non-controversial, concerning such things as unsightly litter. A few concern issues so controversial that neither front-bench will take responsibility. For example, private member bills secured the legalization of abortion and homosexuality. A controversial private member's bill will take many years to pass or may never be adopted, because, in the absence of whips to enforce disciplined voting, a small group of MPs opposed to a measure can obstruct its passage.

The House of Lords is unique among the upper chambers of modern Western parliaments because it is primarily an hereditary institution. In addition to hereditary peers, whose recent or remote ancestors have been ennobled for their activities, the Lords include up to eleven judges sitting as Lords of Appeal in Ordinary, twenty-six bishops of the Church of England, peers who have had hereditary titles conferred for their public services, and, since 1958, distinguished men and women appointed to life peerages. (Members of the Royal Family do not sit in the Lords, although holding titles.) Hereditary peers are three-quarters of the membership of the Lords, but they do not dominate its proceedings. About one-third of the hereditary peers attend the Lords less than once a year. Only one-seventh of the Lords attend at least half its sessions. Many of the active peers are retired members of the House of Commons who find the three-afternoons-a-week pace of the Lords suited to their advancing years. Life peers, numbering about 300, can speak from extra-parliamentary experience in varied walks of

---

[63] See Robert E. Dowse, 'The MP and his Surgery', *Political Studies*, XI:3 (1963); Barker and Rush, *The Member of Parliament and his Information*, pp. 173ff.

[64] See Dick Leonard, 'Private Members' Bills since 1959' in Leonard and Valentine Herman, *The Backbencher and Parliament* and P. G. Richards, 'Private Members' Legislation', in Walkland and Ryle, eds., *The Commons in the 70's*.

life: industry finance, trade unions, education, and the mass media.[65]

Like the House of Commons, the Lords is an electoral chamber, weighing men as fit or unfit for ministerial office. Because of the high average age of peers, few expect office; only in the Conservative ranks are there usually younger peers seeking to establish themselves politically. Since 1963 the most politically ambitious can disclaim a hereditary peerage and stand for the House of Commons. Because convention requires that every minister be in Parliament, a seat in the Lords can be given a minister brought in from outside Westminster to contribute expertise to government. Once in office, the minister will have to prove his worth in debate in the Lords, a less difficult audience than the Commons. The absence of constituency responsibility gives a peer an advantage in a post requiring much travelling, such as the Foreign Office, or in a post in which freedom from constituency pressures might be useful, such as race relations.

The Lords' power to reject bills passed by the House of Commons was formidable until the Parliament Act of 1911 abolished its unlimited right of veto, substituting the power to delay the enactment of legislation. Since the Parliament Act of 1949, this delay can be little more than one year, a power only significant in the year before a general election. The Lords wish to avoid rejecting measures from the Commons, for this would raise questions about their status. The Lords cannot claim to represent the nation, because they are neither elected popularly, nor are they drawn from anything like a cross-section of the population. Moreover, the Lords have always had a Conservative majority. Before the passage of the Life Peerages Act, Conservatives outnumbered Labour peers by about eight to one; since then, the Conservative advantage over Labour has been three to one.[66] Occasionally, the predominantly Conservative Lords have used their powers to delay the passage of a major Labour government bill, or to oppose a non-party measure, e.g. the abolition of capital punishment. The use of delaying powers is exceptional; the threat of their use occasionally worries a government, especially a Labour government.

The Lords can initiate or amend legislation. The government of

[65] See Bernard Crick, *The Reform of Parliament* (London: Weidenfeld & Nicolson, rev. 2nd ed.), p. 137.

[66] *Ibid.*, p. 108. See also, Butler and Sloman, *British Political Facts, 1900–1975*, pp. 174–9.

the day often introduces legislation in the Lords if it deals with technical matters, such as the consolidation of previous Acts of Parliament. Other Lords' bills deal with non-party matters, such as legislation affecting animals. The government of the day can use the Lords as a revising chamber to incorporate amendments suggested in debate in either chamber. Members of the upper house can also introduce private peers' bills. In the 1974–79 Parliament, 140 of the 315 government bills were initially introduced in the Lords.

Like the Commons, the Lords can discuss public issues without reference to legislation. The government or opposition may initiate a debate on foreign affairs, or individual back-benchers may raise on their own initiative such topics as pornography or the future of hill farming. Peers may scrutinize administration by questioning ministers. Because peers have no electoral constituency, it would be considered constitutionally improper for peers to interfere with elections to the Commons. Press coverage is slight. A peer who wishes to influence public opinion is more likely to get publicity if he makes his remarks on a public platform outside the Palace of Westminster than if he records his thoughts in the little-read House of Lords *Hansard*. MPs are distant and unenthusiastic about the Lords. Five-sixths of Labour MPs and half of Conservative MPs say they pay little or no attention to its debates.[67]

The limiting influence of both Houses of Parliament perennially stimulates demands for reform by back-bench MPs, active peers and political commentators. The strongest demand is for the reform of the House of Lords. But there is fundamental disagreement about the direction of change. Labour critics talk about abolishing the House of Lords, regarding its functions as an undesirable hindrance rather than a necessary help or check upon the elected House of Commons. Conservatives have promoted the idea of removing or reducing the hereditary element of the Lords membership, in order to increase its political status. As long as its composition is an anachronism, the House of Lords cannot compete successfully for influence against the House of Commons.[68]

[67] See Barker and Rush, *The Member of Parliament and his Information*, pp. 144–7 and Peter Bromhead and David Shell, 'The Lords and their House', *Parliamentary Affairs*, XX:4 (1967), pp. 342ff.
[68] On the difficulties that Labour faces within its own ranks in trying to reform the Lords, see Janet Morgan, *The House of Lords and the Labour Government, 1964–70* (Oxford: Clarendon Press, 1975).

The criticisms of the House of Commons are multiple. It is said to do a bad job of reviewing legislation, scrutinizing administration, representing and educating public opinion, and preparing younger MPs for the tasks of ministers. The possible remedies prescribed are equally varied. Since 1964, many minor reforms have been introduced into the work of Parliament, affecting the procedures of the House and the facilities of individual MPs. But a decade later an academic survey of these reforms concluded with 'pronounced pessimism' that the changes were 'puny . . . in the extent to which they have failed to grip the essential problem': the need to diminish the power of the government of the day, if Parliament is to become more effective in the government of England.[69]

Another reason why reform has languished is that public opinion is not only critical of Parliament but also favours reforms unpopular with MPs. Gallup Poll surveys taken in 1976 found that 41 per cent felt that the House of Commons as a whole was not representative of the views of the public, as against 36 per cent believing it was. The largely hereditary House of Lords was thought unrepresentative by 42 per cent, and representative by 27 per cent. A majority of people do not want to reform Parliament by providing MPs with better office space and secretarial help or higher salaries. Instead, a majority of the public favoured reducing the number of MPs, bringing in persons from outside Parliament to look after government, and including members of the opposition in committees directing government.[70]

One reason why reform proposals have languished is that proponents of reform disagree about the part that Parliament should play in government. Some reformers believe that Parliament should have powers to prevent executive actions, whereas others simply wish greater powers to scrutinize and criticize. The former group wishes to transfer power from Whitehall to the House of Commons; the latter, to improve the work of Whitehall by the Commons correcting its oversights and errors. Reformers also disagree about the role of an individual MP. Some assume that being an MP is a full-time job and that facilities should be appropriate. Others argue that day-and-night immurement in the Palace of Westminster

[69] S. A. Walkland, 'Whither the Commons?', in Walkland and Ryle, eds., *The Commons in the 70's*, pp. 239, 243. Cf. John P. Mackintosh, ed., *People and Parliament* (Farnborough: Saxon House, 1978).

[70] *Gallup Political Index*, No. 193 (August 1976), p. 8, No. 197 (December 1976), p. 9.

threatens to make MPs very remote from those they claim to represent.

The most important obstacle to reform reflects the principal grievance of back-bench proponents of change: powers of decision effectively rest with the leaders of the governing party in Cabinet, and not with the House of Commons as a whole. Whatever MPs say from the back benches or in opposition, once in Cabinet they argue that the present powers of Parliament are all that can be granted to it. For example, in 1978 the Labour Prime Minister rejected a Commons committee recommendation to expand the work of select committees with the argument that this would 'involve a fundamental change in our parliamentary system and in the relationship between the Executive and Parliament'.[71] Back-bench MPs of both parties are rightly sceptical of the readiness of Cabinet ministers to give them greater influence. Only one-sixth think that ministers wish to see MPs well informed about the work of government in Whitehall.[72]

The result is that Whitehall rather than Parliament is the prime law-making institution in England. As long as it enjoys a majority in the Commons, a government can be virtually certain of securing parliamentary approval of a major piece of legislation within a single annual session. In the course of a year, a government can enact 60 to 70 bills. In an emergency, it can pass a major piece of legislation in weeks, or even days. While Whitehall is more powerful than the Palace of Westminster, it is not all-powerful. It can only govern through Parliament, for the government of the day must win parliamentary votes of confidence to stay in office, and put legislation to Parliament for a vote before it becomes law.

Collectively and individually, Members of Parliament, especially in the governing party, influence government by voicing demands that it 'do something' about an issue that they believe to be important. If the clamour is persistent enough, the government may amend a policy, or even withdraw it for further consideration. But it is up to the government to decide whether or not to let the Commons talk it out of action; a majority of MPs will rarely veto action by votes. In a complementary fashion, MPs can talk a government into acting upon a current issue, but it remains up to the government

[71] Quoted in 'Prime Minister Rules out Reorganization of Central Government', *The Times*, 16 March 1978.
[72] Barker and Rush, *The Member of Parliament and his Information*, p. 363.

to decide how to respond to a general clamour to do something about a problem with a specific policy.

Institutionally, the procedures of the House of Commons limit the amount of legislation that a government can enact in a year. These procedures make the introduction of a major bill a lengthy and tiring process, which can take up to three years from the time a Cabinet decides in principle to promote legislation to a bill receiving the Royal Assent. MPs waiting unsuccessfully for time to speak in a debate have as their counterparts Cabinet ministers waiting to get authorization from Cabinet to put a major bill forward in Parliament. Some 300 proposals are put to Cabinet annually by ministers; only a fifth or a sixth succeed in gaining a place in the year's crowded parliamentary timetable.[73] Once a bill gets in the House, critical MPs can harass a minister through hours of technical and difficult debate on its clauses. A minister can, however, reckon that once a bill is in the Commons, it will pass. If necessary, the government can invoke the guillotine, that is, a timetable motion that cuts off debate on a measure, and force a whipped vote that the government can confidently win.

The experience of the minority Labour government in 1974–9 underscores the limitations of Parliament. Votes in the House of Commons were important only because one of the crucial assumptions of British politics was not met: namely, that a single party would have a majority of seats there. The dispersion of opposition strength by a multiplicity of small 'third' parties gave the Labour government room to manoeuvre, and Harold Wilson and James Callaghan did just that, securing the bulk of the legislation they wished, and an above-average tenure of office. The Commons gained influence because of an accident of the electoral system denying any party a majority, not because of actions of MPs. The 1979 general election returned things to normal: a party with less than half the popular vote won 100 percent control of government by gaining a comfortable majority in the House of Commons.

Because Parliament is a necessary part of British government, it must concur in what government does. But its power to scrutinize and criticize the men and measures of government should not be confused with the ability to exercise the powers of the Crown.

[73] See D. N. Chester, 'The British Parliament, 1939–1966', *Parliamentary Affairs*, XIX:4 (1966), p. 429; Lord Morrison of Lambeth, *Government and Parliament*, ch. 11, Valentine Herman, 'What Governments Say and What Governments Do', p. 30.

The role of law

Courts have relatively little influence upon Westminster government, because the role of law is narrowly defined. Whereas, in centuries past, judges proclaimed the doctrine of the rule of law to restrain royal absolutism, twentieth-century English judges do not see themselves as arbiters of what government may or may not do. Instead, they assert that it is up to Parliament (acting under the direction of the Cabinet) to decide what government can do. Unlike American counterparts, English courts claim no power to declare an Act of Parliament unconstitutional, nor will they accept a claim that an act should be set aside because it conflicts with a previous Act of Parliament or with what claimants describe as natural rights.[74] English judges believe that an unwritten Constitution must be constantly made and unmade, but they want no part of the job. That is for Parliament and the electorate. The final court of appeal is political rather than judicial.

Judicial avoidance of political matters is specially noteworthy inasmuch as the highest court is a committee of the House of Lords, consisting of the Lords of Appeal in Ordinary. These law lords are entitled to participate in debates and divisions of the upper chamber, but when they do speak it is usually about legal matters. Even when judicial opinions have drawn attention to defects in existing statutes, law lords have hesitated to campaign to modify defective statutes. The task of suggesting amendments and improvements in the large mass of statute law that has accrued through the centuries belongs to the English Law Commission, established in 1965. However, most statutes, like the great majority of court actions, concern criminal cases or civil actions far removed from major questions of constitutional law.

While the courts avoid party political disputes, judges themselves are often used by the government of the day to conduct quasi-judicial inquiries into matters of current political concern. Their status as arbiters is a positive attraction to a government seeking to dispose of a political hot potato. So too is the fact that judges, in so far as they have political biases, tend to favour established author-

[74] See Louis L. Jaffe, *English and American Judges as Lawmakers* (Oxford: Clarendon Press, 1969), p. 4. For other American views of English law, see Fred L. Morrison, *Courts and the Political Process in England* (Beverly Hills: Sage Publications, 1973) and Lawrence Baum, 'Research on the English Judicial Process', *British Journal of Political Science*, VII:4 (1977).

ity. The covert political use of judges assists the government of the day, but may reduce the judges' claim to political impartiality. In the words of the *Solicitor's Journal*, 'Each time a judge is misused by being put up as a face-saver behind whose report a government can hide . . . a little of the long-standing esteem in which judges are held and some of their authority is undermined.'[75]

The principal public function of judges in the courts is to determine whether a government has acted within its statutory powers. If an action of central government or a local authority is *ultra vires* (outside its powers), the courts may order it to desist. The courts may also quash an action because it is undertaken in a procedurally improper manner. If a statute delegates discretion to a public authority, the courts do not question the motives of the executive exercising discretion.

In the great majority of cases in which Englishmen believe the government is acting wrongly, the point at issue is not a charge of treason or the denial of *habeas corpus* but the administration of welfare benefits, planning permission for a house, or similar questions. Administrative tribunals hear complaints by citizens against a government department. These specialized tribunals deal with problems such as land and property, pensions and national assistance, the health service, the military, transport, and income tax.

An Englishman who believes that the government has denied basic rights will find it difficult to get the courts to redress this grievance. There are no primary rules in the unwritten constitution that the citizen can invoke in pleading against an Act of Parliament. The United States Constitution entrenches individual rights superior to statute law in a Bill of Rights. By contrast, the English Bill of Rights of 1689 is primarily concerned with limiting royal power *vis à vis* Parliament, and ensuring a Protestant Crown. As long as the government has statutory authority for its actions, the courts will uphold them.

The government's statutory powers can be so broad as to sanction almost anything. In 1940 Parliament passed in one day an Emergency Powers (Defence) Act that authorized the government to compel persons 'to place themselves, their services and their property at the disposal of His Majesty'. In 1968 the Labour Government enacted a bill to restrict the entry to Britain of persons of

---

[75] Quoted in Gavin Drewry, 'Judge and Political Inquiries: Harnessing a Myth', *Political Studies*, XXIII:1 (1975), p. 60.

Asian origin domiciled in Kenya, notwithstanding the fact that they held British citizenship. A member of the Labour Cabinet, R. H. S. Crossman, later commented that the measure 'would have been declared unconstitutional in any country with a written constitution and a Supreme Court'.[76]

Even if the courts rule against the executive, the effect of a judgment can be cancelled by a subsequent Act of Parliament giving retroactive statutory justification for what the courts ruled should not be done. For example, in 1965 the Burmah Oil Company won a law suit claiming government compensation for property damaged in the Second World War. The government promptly passed a retrospective act abolishing the grounds for claiming compensation. On 23 February 1972, a Northern Ireland High Court, in deciding a case brought by a Catholic MP, John Hume, declared that the British Army had no authority to carry out a variety of actions against civilians in Ulster. That afternoon the Home Secretary introduced a bill in the House of Commons to legalize British Army actions retrospectively. The bill, overriding the Court's judgment, was approved by both Houses of Parliament the same day.[77]

The ability of the governing party of the day to use the doctrine of the supremacy of Parliament to ride roughshod over judicial opinions and the absence of judicial protection for minority rights has led in the 1970s to calls for such reforms as a written bill of rights or a Constitutional Court. While admitting that 'these ideas are strange to the present generation', Sir Leslie Scarman, head of the English Law Commission, has called for action to remedy 'the helplessness of the law in face of the legislative sovereignty of Parliament . . . to accommodate the concept of fundamental and inviolable human rights'.[78]

Today, as in the past, the chief constraints upon British government are cultural norms concerning what government should and should not do. Written formulae cannot themselves restrain gov-

---

[76] R. H. S. Crossman, 'Understanding the Profusion of Shrinking Violets', *The Times*, 6 September 1972.

[77] See House of Commons, *Debates*, Vol. 831, cols. 1285–1454 (23 February 1972) and Harold Wilson's approving comments in his *The Governance of Britain* (London: Sphere Books, 1977), p. 217. Subsequently, Ulster civil rights groups have sought relief from the European Commission on Human Rights at Strasbourg rather than appeal to a British High Court.

[78] Sir Leslie Scarman, *English Law—The New Dimension* (London: Stevens & Sons, 1974), p. 15.

ernment. In England, little attempt is made to employ formal constitutional constraints. In the words of a High Court judge:

> The safeguard of British liberty is in the good sense of the people and in the system of representative and responsible government which has been evolved.[79]

The role of the police illustrates the importance of behavioural norms. In England, police operate on the assumption that their authority will be popularly accepted, and those they seek to apprehend will be shunned by society at large. Police patrol unarmed; criminals are expected to be unarmed too. To a remarkable extent police in England are respected. This does not mean that the police are never criticized, but the mass of the population consider a policeman guilty of wrongdoing to be an atypical rather than a normal figure, in an urban landscape.[80]

England has no paramilitary security force to compel obedience to the law, or anything like the American national guard for use in the event of domestic political disorder. The internal security forces of England are, in proportion to population, one-third smaller than in America, France or Italy. The navy is England's premier armed service; by its nature, the navy cannot be deployed within Britain. The army is almost never used to enforce public order within England; it is a source of ready manpower in a flood or a railway wreck, or it is very occasionally used when a strike threatens essential services.

The importance of English attitudes in maintaining law and order is best demonstrated by a comparison with Northern Ireland, the most disorderly part of the United Kingdom. Parliament has never been successful in efforts to export English institutions of police, courts, or military organization to any part of Ireland, because these institutions can operate only with the full consent of the population. Irish Republicans have always refused such consent. Ulster Protestants, determined to maintain their own political hegemony, have given consent only with reservations.

Westminster's first reaction to civil rights disorders in Ulster was to encourage the Northern Ireland government to imitate English

[79] Lord Wright, in *Liversidge* v. *Sir John Anderson*, quoted in G. Le May, *British Government, 1914–1953* (London: Methuen, 1955), p. 332.
[80] See *Gallup Political Index* No. 196 (November 1976), p. 8; the Royal Commission on the Police (London: HMSO, Cmnd. 1728, 1962) and Jenifer Hart, 'Some Reflections on the Report', reprinted in Rose, ed., *Policy-Making in Britain*.

procedures. For example, following the 1969 Belfast riots, the Hunt
Committee on the Royal Ulster Constabulary recommended that
the police divest themselves of arms and change their uniforms from
Irish green to English blue. Its recommendations failed to bring
order. The British Army increasingly adapted its attitudes to Irish
circumstances. In August 1971 the British government justified the
internment of hundreds of Catholics without the right of *habeas
corpus* on the ground that internment was authorized by an Act of
Parliament. By February 1973 it was interning Protestants too.
England's rule of law, it is painfully clear, is not for export to all
parts of the United Kingdom.[81]

A community of interests

Government is a community of people. Group values and expectations tend to determine what individuals in office can do, and what
they wish to do. Whereas the federal government in Washington
may be described as 'a government of strangers', because so many
people in it are unfamiliar with each other, Whitehall is like a
village, where most people feel that they belong to a single community. Like any group of villagers, they are much more interested in
maintaining the standards of their community than in worrying
about what happens in cities as distant as Birmingham or Bonn.[82]
  The public is the intended beneficiary of government policies.
But the public is distant from the world of Westminster. MPs, civil
servants and ministers immediately respond to the demands of their
offices and to the demands that each makes upon the others so that
the Queen's government can be carried on.
  Whitehall is in many respects a small community.[83] While few
ministers or civil servants live in the vicinity of Whitehall, the people
who work there spend most of their waking hours together, developing an intimacy like that found within an Oxford college. At the
top, Whitehall is not a vast sprawling impersonal institution like the
University of London. Within this village, everyone knows or
knows about everyone else's strengths, weaknesses, opportunities

[81] See Richard Rose, 'On the Priorities of Citizenship in the Deep South and
Northern Ireland', *Journal of Politics*, XXXVIII:2 (1976) and sources cited therein.
  [82] Cf. Hugh Heclo, *A Government of Strangers* (Washington, D.C.: The Brookings
Institution, 1977), and Heclo and Wildavsky, *The Private Government of Public
Money*.
  [83] See F. M. G. Willson, 'Policy-Making and the Policy-Makers' in Rose, ed.,
Policy-Making in Britain.

and ambitions. Ministers may find the life trying, as they compete against each other for scarce resources: money, parliamentary time, press headlines and Prime Ministerial favour.

Civil servants can take a different view; while ministers (and governments) come and go, they remain forever. The ethos of Whitehall is set by civil servants rather than ministers, because they are more numerous as well as more durable. At any one time, there are likely to be twenty times as many senior civil servants as there are ministers working in Whitehall. Of these, it can be reckoned that only a dozen or two dozen ministers carry much political influence; they must work in tandem with several hundred very influential civil servants. The hundreds of thousands of civil servants meant to carry out the decisions of the several hundred top people are kept at arm's length by considerations of protocol and hierarchy within government.

In the village of Whitehall, civil servants are not anonymous. Each has a reputation to maintain with peers and with the civil service superiors who determine promotion. What is it that gives a civil servant a good repute? First and foremost, be trustworthy. One must be scrupulously honest in money matters and in keeping private knowledge of public affairs. One must not try to 'pull a fast one' on colleagues in other departments by withholding information that makes a department look bad or that colleagues in other departments should know. A senior civil servant should also be reliable; predictability of actions is important when time is pressing and a short conversation cannot discuss every point. Co-ordination can best occur if officials in each department know what their colleagues elsewhere expect them to do.

Soundness is another cardinal virtue. A civil servant who repeatedly voices clever but controversial ideas will become a bore if more experienced hands must explain, for the ninety-ninth time, why a particular bright idea is simply 'not practical politics'. Intelligence is demonstrated by showing an awareness of the complexities of a problem, by finding one more snag than anyone else has found, or by finding one more objection to an awkward proposal for change. Whitehall (like much English university education) prizes the critical intelligence.

Within the community of Whitehall, ministers' reputations are determined by different criteria than in Parliament. Of course, a minister who is known to be good at presenting or defending a department in parliamentary debate is always welcome, as is a minister who can secure favourable press publicity, or counter unfavourable publicity. But civil servants are also concerned with what a minister is like in private. A minister who values the good repute of civil servants will be willing to listen to and understand complex briefings about administrative and technical matters, intervening selectively upon points important in party political or policy terms, but not trying to overturn the work of months of committee meetings and endless drafting and redrafting of documents. Ministers value colleagues who are easy to do business with about inter-departmental matters affecting the day-to-day workings of government. Once a decision is made, a minister who wishes a good reputation should not job backwards, or heap blame on others if things go wrong.

The knowing impassive figure of the mandarin is the symbol of the English civil service, just as the Washington counterpart is symbolized by the aggressive athlete, the man with clout. 'Why are your officials so passionate?' a British Treasury official once asked presidential adviser Richard Neustadt.[84] Neustadt turned the question around, asking why British civil servants are so dispassionate about the outcome of their activities. He concluded that American civil servants care about policies because their careers are wrapped up with the success of their departments and, even more, their reputation for getting things done. To win a political battle is to advance personally, as well as to advance the commonweal. In England, by contrast, civil servants know that their minister will get the credit (or the blame) for the result of their work. They are personally detached because they have no career stake in the outcome of what they are doing. A good reputation for upholding the Whitehall code is more important than winning any specific struggle for policy. The style of governing is that of the relaxed amateur, rather than the determined, ruthless professional. British civil servants do not play to win; the important thing is how you play the game.

Whitehall civil servants are perennially sceptical of politicians' claims to reform the world within the lifetime of a single Parliament. Their day-dream of paradise is not of megalomaniac power, but of a world in which there are few decisions to make, because ministers,

---

[84] Richard E. Neustadt, 'White House and Whitehall' in Rose, ed., *Policy-Making in Britain*, p. 292.

MPs and subjects have left them undisturbed in the orderly administration of routine affairs of state. In the words of Sir William Armstrong, former permanent head of the civil service, the chief danger in government is not 'that obstructive bureaucrats will drag their feet' but that ministers' 'optimism will carry them into schemes and policies which will subsequently be seen to fail—failure which attention to the experience and information available from the service might have avoided'. An experienced minister, Roy Jenkins, concluded that a minister looking back on decisions in which personal preferences conflicted with civil service advice would regret some decisions 'made with advice and some made against it'.[85]

The constitution of the Crown is not a mechanism for resolving problems, but for coping with them, or adapting to them, if the problems are inevitable or perennially recurring. Whitehall officials talk about the machinery of government, but the last thing that they actually believe is that government is a machine, capable of manufacturing engineering-type solutions to pressing problems, or being improved by advances in machine technology. The language of Whitehall mandarins is meant to obscure thought rather than hone it.

Gardening metaphors are much more suitable to describe Whitehall attitudes toward their institutions of government. Within a given year, there is a familiar cycle of planting, cultivating and reaping the results of a year's work in Acts of Parliament, white papers or the prevention of measures that could have spread like weeds. A gardener does not expect to control the environment, but to respond to it, watering plants when rain is short, pulling weeds when and where they sprout, pruning back plants that grow too fast, and treating those that show blight.

The work of a well-planted garden is continuous: things are always sprouting or blooming or growing. But the yield is also uncertain. Civil servants cannot be sure of the product of their work until after it is accomplished, just as gardeners may see their efforts rewarded by a good summer, or ruined by too much or too little rain. As in gardening, the great bulk of Whitehall work consists of daily and recurring routines: preparing briefs for committee meetings or answers to parliamentary questions, repairing the damage

[85] Cf. Sir William Armstrong, 'The Role and Character of the Civil Service', text of a talk to the British Academy, London, 24 June 1970, p. 21 and Roy Jenkins, 'The Reality of Political Power'.

done by past mistakes, planting ideas or proposals that may blossom a year or two hence. Just as there are thousands of gardeners for every plant geneticist trying to improve the breed, so there are hundreds of civil servants trying to preserve the garden of Whitehall, for every person consciously trying to improve it.

Both ministers and civil servants see themselves as persons with great responsibilities. Ministers are ultimately responsible to the electorate; immediately, they are responsible to their colleagues in Cabinet and to their patron in Downing Street. The longer they remain in office, the more they are likely to develop a sense of responsibility to their department and its servants; it is their position as head of a department that gives them status in government. Civil servants are ultimately responsible to the Crown; immediately, they are responsible to their minister and to the head of the civil service. Civil servants have little personal contact with party politics and even less with the electoral hurly-burly of representative government. A comparative European-American study found that senior British civil servants ranked sixth and last in terms of frequency of contact with MPs, political party leaders or ordinary citizens.[86]

The closeness of the community of Whitehall has its dangers. Heclo and Wildavsky, generalizing from a study of financial control by the Treasury, argue:

> Political administration in Great Britain is profoundly narcissistic, because each participant must and does care greatly about what his fellows are doing and thinking. To be more precise, it is not so much the individuals who are self-absorbed as the governmental apparatus of which they are a part and to which they must necessarily respond. To say that British political administrators care more about themselves than about the country would be wrong; to say that more of their time and attention is devoted to themselves than to outsiders would be closer to the truth.[87]

The strength of the Whitehall community is the ease with which it can dispatch business. The method of governing emphasizes the morale of government more than the substance of policies. The

---

[86] See Bert A. Rockman, 'Linkages at the Top: Cross-National Perspectives on Elite Interaction' (Chicago: Annual meeting of the Midwest Political Science Association, 20–22 April 1978), p. 27.

[87] Heclo and Wildavsky, *The Private Government of Public Money*, p. 9.

community is thus vulnerable to events outside Whitehall, particularly when they threaten changes that are unpleasant or cannot readily be accommodated within standard Whitehall operating procedures. A good policy is considered as one that both ministers and civil servants of different departments find acceptable: it is not necessarily a policy that produces the desired result. For example, from 1964 to 1967, maintaining the pound against devaluation was regarded as the only possible or desirable policy; to speak of anything else was considered 'anti-British' if not actually treasonable. Yet the policy proved merely impossible to sustain against the pressure of outside events that could not be controlled by the village of Whitehall.

The denizens of Westminster enter the 1980s with ample evidence of their inability to control central events, both domestic and international. Like villagers everywhere, they are vulnerable to decisions made in cities elsewhere, such as Zurich, Washington or Tokyo. At times of economic crisis, such as 1974–5, there are signs of a community of despair. The crucial question for the 1980s is whether this community can adapt to the pressures of the world outside Whitehall, or whether, in that characteristic locution of reactive mandarins, Whitehall will only respond when a problem threatens to become too 'disastrous'.

IV

Political Culture and Political Authority

It is the dull traditional habit of mankind that guides most men's actions and it is the steady frame in which each new artist must set the picture that he paints.

The political culture of England consists of those values, beliefs and emotions that give meaning to politics. Political *values* are important because these ideas about society justify actions and guide political choices. Political values cannot be isolated from political beliefs and emotions. For instance, freedom of speech may be regarded as a value in itself; it may be believed to lead to the best choice of public policy; or it may be cherished as a symbol of good government. A political culture is a more or less harmonious mixture of the values, beliefs and emotions of a society.

Beliefs in the political culture concern what ought to happen. The idea of oughtness combines empirical and normative expectations. For example, people think that there ought to be a general election, even if the governing party is likely to lose. They think this ought to happen because it is morally right that a government, especially an unpopular government, should periodically submit itself to electoral judgment. Moreover, no government in past experience has illegally prolonged its stay in office. Even when expectations are unambiguously clear, they do not necessarily determine events. Twice in this century, in the exceptional circumstances of wartime, governments have postponed general elections with the consent of all parties in Parliament.

Emotions significant in the political culture concern the fundamentals of government, such as the identity of the society to be governed and the strength of political commitment. Tradition has given the English an extraordinarily strong sense of national identity. Its strength is shown by the absence of nationalistic symbols, which can betoken a late or frustrated sense of nationhood. In two world wars of this century, the British people have shown a commitment to country strong enough to make great sacrifices for national survival, and hundreds of thousands laid down their lives, often in battles against great odds.

The cultural outlooks of Englishmen are not inherited biologically, but they are transmitted from generation to generation. Through a process of political socialization, Englishmen learn about events of the remote past and political outlooks formulated before they were born. In the course of a lifetime, every citizen learns new ideas, in keeping with individual and national experience. Elderly Englishmen may combine many strata of beliefs, ranging from those prevalent in Victorian times to the present. The outlook of young voters will be greatly influenced by events of the 1970s; the eras of Sir Winston Churchill and Clement Attlee will be part of their history.

The values, beliefs and emotions that constitute the political cultural of England are collectively 'a system of tacit understandings'.[1] They are tacit because they are taken for granted. Ordinary citizens do not speak the language of political theorists or political sociologists, nor do they readily articulate their thoughts about government. The discussion that follows thus draws upon a mixture of materials in an effort to depict the political culture of England today. It gives particular attention to the views of the politically active minority. This group is not only articulate, but also has a disproportionate influence upon government.

The most important elements of a political culture concern the very nature of political authority. The first section of this chapter examines the extent of popular allegiance to authority. The reasons for the acceptance of authority are the theme of the second section. A third important issue is: who should exercise authority? Cultural norms not only support authority but limit it. The final section of this chapter discusses cultural norms about what government should *not* do.

The legitimacy of authority

Of all the cultural attitudes affecting government, the most important concern allegiance to political authority. Authority is fully legitimate if citizens support the regime and also comply with its basic political laws, that is, laws that the governors say must be obeyed as a condition of the regime's survival. If people refuse to support the regime but comply with its laws, then it is coercive. A regime that loses both the support and compliance of many citizens,

---

[1] Sidney Low, *The Governance of England* (London: Ernest Benn, revised edition, 1914), p. 12.

for example, the Stormont Parliament in Northern Ireland, is headed toward repudiation.[2]

Support for a regime is not a judgment about the effectiveness or efficiency of government. People may simultaneously support the forms of representative government, while making many specific criticisms of how it works. There is the risk of confusing desire for reforming particular institutions, such as Parliament, with unconditional rejection of authority. Reform may assist in maintaining a regime by adapting old institutions to new conditions. This is pre-eminently true in England, for contemporary British government includes many institutions whose names have remained the same but whose functions have changed through the centuries.

The continuity of authority in England makes the idea of overthrowing the existing regime inconceivable to many people. When a sample of public opinion is asked what it thinks of government by elected representatives, 94 per cent support it as a very good or fairly good way of governing; only 3 per cent consider it a bad way to run the country. Politicans too almost unanimously support the established system of governing by elected representatives; only 2 per cent of MPs say there should be big changes in the way England is governed.[3]

The political difficulties arising from the world-wide oil crisis of 1973, two indecisive elections in 1974 and the country's continuing economic problems have reduced the confidence of citizens in the effectiveness of England's government. But it has not thereby made people doubt the legitimacy of parliamentary institutions. Even when Nationalist parties in Scotland and Wales reject the idea of government by Westminster, they do not reject the idea of parliamentary government. It is the locus of authority—London —rather than its forms that draw Nationalist criticisms.

Popular support for constituted authority is also evidenced by the rejection of left- and right-wing extremist movements. The Communist Party of Great Britain has always polled a derisory vote. Its best (sic) election was in 1945, when Communists won 0.4 per cent of the vote; in October 1974, at a time of considerable industrial tension and militancy, Communist candidates polled only 0.06 per

---

[2] For a fuller discussion of the concept of legitimacy, see Richard Rose, *Governing without Consensus* (London: Faber & Faber, 1971), ch. 1.

[3] See Committee on the Management of Local Government Vol. 3, *The Local Government Elector* (London: HMSO, 1967), pp. 66ff; Robert D. Putnam, *The Beliefs of Politicians* (New Haven: Yale University Press, 1973).

cent of the vote, and none of the 29 Communist candidates secured as much as one-eighth of the vote in a constituency. In 1979, the Communist Party again polled less than one-tenth of one per cent of the popular vote. The Communist Party today does not advocate the armed overthrow of the established regime, and surveys have found that individual Communists differ little from Labour activists in their acceptance of political authority. The British Communist Party has even been described as 'overwhelmed by the British political culture and forced to accommodate to the country's political tradition'.[4]

From time to time, self-styled Fascist movements appear and nominate candidates for parliamentary elections; their popular support is also miniscule. In the 1930s the British Union of Fascists, led by a former Labour MP, Sir Oswald Mosley, failed to gain any support at a time of high unemployment and impending world war. In the 1970s, the National Front sought to stimulate support for a radical reaction against established parties and institutions. When anti-immigrant marches have been organized in areas with many black immigrants, violence has resulted. But electorally, the National Front has been a failure. In 1979, 303 National Front candidates could poll only 0.6 per cent of the vote.[5]

It is sometimes argued by political opponents of the former Conservative MP, Enoch Powell, that his political activities constitute a threat to political authority. It is undoubtedly the case that Powell's pronouncements in favour of patriotism and against immigration, British membership in the EEC, and many programmes of the mixed-economy welfare state stir up considerable political controversy. But surveys show that each of his pronouncements has support from a substantial fraction of the public, including some Cabinet ministers. When, for example, the British government of the day has imposed racial restrictions upon immigration there is an identification of the law of the land with Powellite views. Powell's political influence has been limited, moreover, since

[4] Roberty Kilroy-Silk, in a book review in *Political Studies*, XVIII:4 (1970). See also D. T. Denver and J. M. Bochel, 'The Political Socialization of Activists in the British Communist Party', *British Journal of Political Science*, III:1 (1973) and Kenneth Newton, *The Sociology of British Communism* (London: Allen Lane, 1969).

[5] See Martin Walker, *The National Front* (London: Fontana, 1977); Michael Steed, 'The National Front Vote', *Parliamentary Affairs*, XXXI:3 (1978) and Robert Benewick, *The Fascist Movement in Britain* (London: Allen Lane, 1972).

his 1974 self-imposed isolation in an Ulster Unionist constituency in Northern Ireland has left him without a political party base in England.[6]

The scope of authority

The readiness of English people to comply voluntarily with basic political laws confirms the legitimacy of government. The very idea of a political crime—in East European countries, called 'a crime against the state'—is unknown in England. Crimes such as bank robbery or murder are considered anti-social acts, not crimes against the state. By contrast, in Northern Ireland, many illegal actions, including robbery and violence, are undertaken with political intent. They are not viewed as anti-social actions, but as political deeds done for 'the cause', and the British government at one point granted political status to hundreds of imprisoned IRA men and Protestant para-militants.

Even when political stakes are high, people believe that losers as well as winners should comply with basic political laws. During the Suez War of 1956, the then leader of the Opposition, Hugh Gaitskell, told the House of Commons that the Labour Party would be

... bound by every constitutional means at our disposal to oppose it. I emphasise the word 'constitutional'. We shall, of course, make no attempt to dissuade anybody from carrying out the orders of the government, but we shall seek, through the influence of public opinion, to bring every pressure to bear upon the government to withdraw from the impossible situation into which they have put us.[7]

When a few supporters of unilateral nuclear disarmament advocated civil disobedience as a method for advancing their views in the 1960s, they found that even within this radical group politically motivated violation of the law failed of support.[8]

The rise of unorthodox methods of political activity in the late 1960s—protest marches, rent strikes, sit-ins at public buildings and

[6] On Powell, in addition to his own published writings, see Douglas E. Schoen, *Enoch Powell and the Powellites* (London: Macmillan, 1977).

[7] House of Commons, *Debates*, Vol. 558, col. 1462 (31 October 1956). More generally, see Leon D. Epstein, *British Politics in the Suez Crisis* (London: Pall Mall, 1964).

[8] See Frank E. Myers, 'Civil Disobedience and Organization Change', *Political Science Quarterly*, LXXXVI:1 (1971).

violence to property and persons—has reaffirmed the commitment of the great majority of English people to compliance with basic political laws. A nation-wide survey concentrating upon unorthodox political protest found little support for political action outside the law (see Table IV.1). A majority approved of signing petitions and lawful demonstrations but disapproved of eight other forms of political protest, ranging from boycotts and rent strikes to violence. The level of approval is low (16 per cent) for unconventional but legal protest measures such as unofficial strikes, as well as for measures that are illegal but not uncommon in the 1970s, e.g. occupying buildings or blocking traffic.

TABLE IV.1   **The limits of support for unorthodox political behaviour**

	Approve %	Believe effective %	Have done %
Sign petitions	86	73	23
Lawful demonstrations	69	60	6
Boycotts	37	48	6
Rent strikes	24	27	2
Unofficial strikes	16	42	5
Occupying buildings	15	29	1
Blocking traffic	15	31	1
Painting slogans on walls	1	6	–
Damaging property	2	10	1
Personal violence	2	11	–

Source Alan Marsh, *Protest and Political Consciousness* (London: Sage Publications, 1977), Table 2.1.

The commitment of the English to lawful political actions reflects values about how people ought to act, and not simply calculations about what will work. The proportion approving lawful protest is higher than that believing such measures will be effective. Equally, the minority believing unorthodox measures are effective is consistently larger than that approving such measures. For example, 11 per cent believe violence is effective, but only 2 per cent approve of using violence. (Table IV.1.) Given that most people disapprove of unorthodox political behaviour and do not believe it effective, it follows that very few have engaged in such protests: the highest (*sic*) number is 6 per cent reporting involvement in boycotts, and 5 per cent in unofficial strikes.

The commitment of English people to established political authority is also shown by popular readiness to support the government in taking strong measures to defend itself, if its authority is challenged by the violation of basic political laws. Surveys show that 80 per cent approve courts giving severe sentences to protestors who disregard the police, and 73 per cent approve police using force against demonstrators. A similarly large majority believe that this tough line on law and order would also be effective. (See Table IV.2.)

TABLE IV.2   **Support for actions in defence of established political authority**

	Approve %	Believe effective %
Courts giving severe sentences to protestors who disregard the police	80	71
Police using force against demonstrators	73	78
Government using troops to break strikes	46	60
Government passing laws to forbid all public protest demonstrations	25	35

Note   Approve includes all voicing strong approval or approval; effectiveness column combines persons considering action very or somewhat effective.
Source Alan Marsh, *Protest and Political Consciousness*, Table 3.2.

Most English people reject unorthodox or illegal political activities, but they also reject the government of the day amending or 'bending' the law to repress lawful disagreement with public policies. Only a minority would endorse the government using troops to break strikes, and only one-quarter would favour a law infringing rights of free speech by making political protest demonstrations illegal. (See Table IV.2.) The median English person takes a middle of the road position, wanting public officials as well as anti-government protestors to support the institutions of government and comply with basic laws.

Why obey authority?

The legitimacy accorded authority is not the result of carefully calculated policies pursued by English politicians. Politicians try to avoid raising constitutional issues, because they are so difficult to resolve, especially in the absence of a written Constitution. As one political commentator, Hugo Young, notes:

> Preserving constitutional order could be called the highest task of politics. Yet the effort applied to it has been derisory. Half of Whitehall devotes itself to the economy, which it can but slightly tinker with. Virtually none of Whitehall has been concerned with the constitution . . . to almost all concerned, constitutional issues exist in order to be denied, circumvented or reduced to an administrative inconvenience.[9]

For centuries, English political philosophers have speculated about the causes of political authority, and many different reasons have been offered in explanation. But collectively these ideas cannot provide a satisfactory explanation, for the best-known philosophers have disagreed fundamentally. Thomas Hobbes, writing at the time of the seventeenth-century English civil war, saw society tending toward the 'war of every man against every man'. Government must, if need be, compel compliance, so that public order (and much else) could be secure, he declared. Any regime that assured order itself deserved support. John Locke, writing almost contemporaneously with Hobbes, had a very different view of authority, claiming that it should rest upon the agreement of intelligent persons, independently seeking to secure their natural rights by collective political action. Edmund Burke, an eighteenth-century observer of the American and French revolutions, sought to reconcile contrasting views. Burke emphasized the importance of tradition as a sanction for consent: 'People will not look forward to posterity who never look backward to their ancestors.' Yet he also accepted the need for change: 'A state without the means of some change is without the means of its conservation.'

Writing in the early years of the Industrial Revolution, Jeremy Bentham emphasized the improvement of social conditions by the conscious reform of government. Bentham's touchstone was 'the greatest happiness of the greatest number' of the citizenry. John

---

[9] 'Into the Golden Future', *Sunday Times*, 7 August 1977. Note the maladept manner in which Westminster has handled the two chief constitutional problems of the 1970s—civil war in Northern Ireland and non-violent Nationalist pressures in Scotland and Wales.

Stuart Mill also argued for individual rights. Mill held that the state could demand compliance with laws only when this was necessary to restrict individual behaviour to avoid greater harm to others. Although German by birth, upbringing and intellectual outlook, Karl Marx wrote most of his major works while living in London, and expected England to be in the vanguard of a working-class revolution overthrowing an allegedly oppressive state. Latterday English Marxists have awaited this revolution against authority for more than a century. They disagree in their explanations about why it has yet to come about.[10]

English political philosophy is notable for the absence of certain schools of thought prominent in many Continental European countries. For example, modern England has produced few thinkers who glorify authoritarian government on nationalist or religious grounds. Anarchists advancing philosophical arguments against the very idea of the state have not had the significance of a Rousseau in France. The empiricism of English philosophy inhibits the creation of totalitarian political philosophies that turn questions of art, morality and private beliefs into political issues, as occurred in Nazi Germany or Communist Russia. The worldly-wise journalist Walter Bagehot did not emulate Machiavelli by glorifying the pursuit of power. Instead, his treatise on the English Constitution celebrates the conditions necessary to maintain government by consent.

The great books of English political philosophy have had little effect on mass opinion, because for centuries most English people could not read these books: they were illiterate. Even after a century of compulsory education, these texts are studied by only a small minority in society. Popular political outlooks tend to be derived from experience, and not from books.

Past traditions are sometimes cited as an explanation of the unreflective, even unconscious, English acceptance of political authority. Given the variety of events in a thousand years of English history, traditions can be cited to justify political revolt as well as political allegiance. Regicide is a far older habit than parliamentary government. Well-placed Englishmen have been committing treason against the Crown at least since the time of Thomas à

[10] See e.g. Ralph Miliband, *The State in Capitalist Society* (London: Quartet Books, 1973); James Harvey and Katherine Hood, *The British State* (London: Lawrence & Wishart, 1958) for an orthodox Communist view; and Tom Nairn, *The Break-Up of Britain* (London: New Left Books, 1977), for a critique that is Scottish Nationalist as well as Marxist.

Becket in the twelfth century. Lowly Englishmen have been revolting against the Crown at least since Wat Tyler's peasant rising of 1381.

Three models of English politics summarize the contrasting 'lessons' of history. The model most used in public discussion is liberal: English people govern themselves through responsible parliamentary government. Another traditional model is elitist: Political power reflects social and economic power. A third model is that of dissent: Englishmen recognize and, after the event, often endorse the views put forward initially by a few radicals speaking according to their conscience against the majority.[11]

The symbols of a common past, transcending divisive elements, are also cited as causes of popular allegiance to authority today. The monarchy is the most prominent and personal symbol of political authority. Public opinion overwhelmingly favours having a King or Queen as head of state. Moreover, this positive regard is common throughout society: a majority of the young and old, Labour and Conservative, working class and middle class respond positively to the Queen.[12]

But survey evidence rejects the theory that positive regard for the Queen creates or strengthens allegiance to political authority.[13] One reason for this is that the Queen is viewed as a non-political figure, above the everyday activities of government. Another reason is that the positive emotions inspired by a monarch are not strong. The shallowness of emotional responses to a monarch is evidenced by the fact that the institution remains popular, whatever the behaviour of the incumbent. The hurried abdication of King Edward VIII in order to marry an American divorcee occurred without difficulty in 1936 because popular regard was immediately transferred to the next incumbent of the office, King George VI.

The greatest difficulty in explaining political allegiance by invoking symbols is that there is no way to separate cause and effect. One can as easily say that the Queen is a popular symbol because she heads a legitimate regime as argue that the Queen causes support for

[11] See W. J. M. Mackenzie, 'Models of English Politics' in Richard Rose, ed., *Studies in British Politics* (London: Macmillan, 3rd ed., 1976).

[12] See Richard Rose and Dennis Kavanagh, 'The Monarchy in Contemporary Political Culture', *Comparative Politics*, VIII:4 (1976). Note also, *Gallup Political Index*, No. 190 (May 1976), p. 12.

[13] Rose and Kavanagh, 'The Monarchy in Contemporary Political Culture', pp. 560ff.

the regime. Similarly, the regard in which Englishmen hold their Crown, their traditions, and their institutions can be a consequence of centuries of legitimate government. There is nothing compelling in the existence of symbols *per se*. In Northern Ireland the symbols of royalty and British government stimulate conflict between Irish Republicans and Protestants proclaiming loyalty to the Crown.[14]

When surveys ask people to evaluate reasons for giving allegiance to authority, the reason most often endorsed is pragmatic: 77 per cent believe 'It's the best form of government we know.' Such a judgment does not regard authority as perfect or even trouble free. British government is regarded as good enough, or simply as the least of many possible evils. 'It's the kind of government the people want' is also viewed as a good reason for supporting government by 66 per cent. A majority (65 per cent) also recognizes the inevitability of government: 'we've got to accept it whatever we think'.

The effectiveness of government in providing the right things for people is relatively unimportant; 49 per cent think it is a good reason for accepting authority. Contrary to what is sometimes argued by economic determinists of differing political views, popular allegiance is not bought by the provision of public benefits. A government that is ineffective in managing a mixed-economy welfare state can still enjoy authority if people consider it the best form of government that they know.[15]

Whose authority?

Identifying those subject to authority is no problem, for English people have shared a common national identity for centuries. This identity is so taken for granted that the government does not think it necessary to put the name of the country on its postage stamps; the head of the Queen is regarded as sufficient. In Scotland and Wales, the great majority of people identify themselves as British as well as Scottish or Welsh, and the Protestant majority in Northern Ireland also identifies itself as British. Thus notwithstanding Nationalist challenges, the overwhelming mass of the electorate—95 per cent in 1979—voted for British political parties upholding the authority of the United Kingdom. (See Table II.2.)

Governors constitute a small and select fraction of the popula-

---

[14] See Rose, *Governing without Consensus*, p. 244.
[15] See Richard Rose and Harve Mossawir, 'Voting and Elections: a Functional Analysis', Part II.

tion. Their power is justified because governors are believed to represent the country as a whole. The authority that governors exercise is not theirs alone. There is, however, no agreement about whose authority it is. Three different theories of representation are important today.[16]

1. The *trusteeship* theory of political authority emphasizes the traditional duty of leaders taking the initiative in determining what government does. Writing before the First World War, A. L. Lowell described England's governors as holding office 'by the sufferance of the great mass of the people, and as trustees for its benefit'. According to this doctrine, MPs and Cabinets are not expected to ask what the people want, but to use their independent judgment to determine what is in the best interests of society. In the words of L. S. Amery, a Conservative Cabinet minister writing after the Second World War, England is governed 'for the people, with but not by the people'.[17]

In pre-democratic times, trustees were thought necessary because the majority of the population was considered unfit—by birth, upbringing and interests—to participate in government. Writing in 1867, Bagehot argued that anyone who doubted this had only to go into his kitchen to talk with the cook. Bagehot thought that a democratic franchise would work well only if the mass of the electorate showed deference to their 'betters'. Today, only an ageing and very small (less than one-tenth) fraction of English people are prepared to defer to others on grounds of social status.[18]

The electors' choice of MPs shows that university education rather than high birth is now the most important requisite for securing selection to a place among the nation's trustees in Parliament. Concurrently, there has emerged a group of educated left-wing political activists who seek power to do what they want to do, not what the mass of voters wish. A survey of youthful ideological technocrats concludes that their radical outlook 'has less to do with altruism and much more to do with their urge to hasten

[16] For a wide-ranging review of these theories, see A. H. Birch, *Representative and Responsible Government* (London: George Allen & Unwin, 1964).

[17] L. S. Amery, *Thoughts on the Constitution* (London: Oxford University Press, 2nd ed., 1953), p. 21; A. L. Lowell, *The Government of England*, Vol. II (London: Macmillan, 1908), p. 508.

[18] Cf. Bagehot, *The English Constitution*, and evidence cited in Dennis Kavanagh, 'The Deferential English: A Comparative Critique', *Government and Opposition*, VI:3 (1971).

the day when the existing elites have been ousted by themselves'.[19]

The trusteeship view of government is summed up in the epigram: The government's job is to govern. The outlook is popular with any party in office, because it justifies government doing whatever it wishes. Reciprocally, the opposition is critical, because it does not enjoy the prerogatives of Her Majesty's government. Civil servants find the doctrine congenial too, because they permanently serve the governing party, and can therefore see themselves as the permanent (and non-elected) trustees of the public interest.

2. *Collectivist* doctrines of representation assume that social groups are the constituent units of politics; individuals are considered politically important in so far as they are members of groups. Collectivists argue that the aggregation of individual preferences by groups is inevitable in decision-making in a country with more than 55 million citizens. In addition, they usually assume that the chief political interests in society are organized into groups, particularly economic interests.

The Conservative version of group politics emphasizes the inclusiveness of group interests. Conservatives believe that all the different interests of groups can be accommodated by government. Socialists, by contrast, tend to emphasize an exclusive doctrine of groups. In the words of Frank Cousins, formerly leader of the Transport and General Workers, the country's largest trade union, 'We represent Britain, we represent the working class of Britain and they are Britain.'[20]

In the collectivist conception of politics, public policy is seen as the result of group conflicts. Whitehall, Parliament and sometimes party meetings, are the chief arenas of group conflict. Trade unions and business organizations are viewed as the most important groups exerting pressure within the policy process. If carried to its logical extreme, this view of the policy process reduces government to an institution simply 'squaring' powerful group interests. In the words of W. J. M. Mackenzie, 'The state is submerged by the interests; it continues, but only as a form of contest. The so-called

[19] Alan C. Marsh, *Protest and Political Consciousness* (London: Sage Publications, 1977), p. 197.
[20] *Labour Party Conference Report* (1962) p. 182. For a detailed historical examination of the collectivist outlook, see Samuel H. Beer, *Modern British Politics* (London: Faber and Faber, 1965).

government is like a medieval king amid the barons' wars; his body is a symbol and a prize that the factions strive to possess.'[21]

The collectivist approach raises but does not answer important questions about whom group leaders represent. Trade unions claim little more than one-third of the labour force among their membership, and an even smaller proportion of the labour force are businessmen or own shares in companies. Political parties seek the votes of the whole electorate, but no one party ever succeeds in gaining all of them. In October 1974, Labour won office with the positive endorsement of only 28.6 per cent of the electorate, and in 1979, the Conservatives did so with 33.3 per cent.[22]

3. *Individualist* theories of representation emphasize the importance of each citizen's role in the political process. MPs are meant to represent constituencies in which each individual has a vote of equal value. Because ministers are considered accountable to a House of Commons in which each MP is accountable to constituents, individual voters, or at least a plurality of voters at one remove, can control—if not positively direct—government.

Individualist values are more appropriate for a small society or one in which few people have the right to vote, such as early Victorian England. In an electorate of more than 40,000,000, no one English person can today expect his or her vote to exert a large amount of influence. Individuals must accept having their views aggregated by political parties in order to organize government.

The liberal doctrine is often conveniently invoked by the winning party after a general election. Its leaders claim that the government's policies must be 'what the people want', because they were contained in the party's manifesto. Popular support, whether given because of *or* in spite of specific party commitments, is said to constitute a mandate for the governing party to act upon the intentions declared in its election manifesto. (Cf. Table IX.2.)

The idea of individual decision-making is also a stimulus to citizen activity, and is particularly suited to 'participatory' institutions. In England, in contrast with America, it is less often invoked to justify policies intended to leave or return choice to individuals in the market place. While England is the birthplace of *laissez faire* economics, such doctrines now flourish better on other continents.

[21] 'Models of English Politics', p. 59.
[22] That is, the Conservatives' 13,697,000 votes were little more than one-quarter of the total number of registered electors, 41,093,000.

In the 1970s the British government introduced referenda giving individual voters the opportunity to express their views on the Common Market (1975), and on Scottish and Welsh devolution (1979). The use of referenda does not signify a conversion of politicians to faith in popular decision-making. Instead, it reflects a desire of the Labour government of the day to minimize the costs of intra-party divisions by asking the electorate to endorse what the Cabinet proposed, but some Labour back-benchers opposed. Many MPs oppose the principle of the referendum, believing that it undermines their position as trustees of authority. The late Labour politician R. H. S. Crossman argued against the referendum on the grounds that majority opinion is often opposed to many reforms that can secure party and parliamentary approval, but not endorsement by a referendum majority:

> Better the liberal elitism of the statute book than the reactionary populism of the market-place. Referenda or plebiscites notoriously confirm right-wing acts: they do not voice left-wing opinions.[23]

When asked directly, the great majority of MPs say that individual citizens ought to influence government. For example, 91 per cent say that people ought to be allowed to vote even if they cannot do so intelligently. The great majority of MPs, however, tend to see their primary role as that of a group representative, or as a trustee for the nation. Only one in five MPs thinks that a political leader should primarily respond to the views of followers. In the words of a Labour MP:

> The essential thing in a democracy is a general election in which a government is elected with power to do any damn thing it likes and if the people don't like it, they have the right to chuck it out.

A Conservative Member with an aristocratic background endorses the same view in a characteristic mock-diffident manner:

> I personally consider myself capable of coming to decisions without having to fight an election once every four or five years, but on the other hand, the people must be allowed to feel that they

[23] *New Statesman*, 7 August 1970. On referenda more generally, see David Butler and Austin Ranney, eds., *Referendums* (Washington, D.C.: American Enterprise Institute, 1978), shows that Crossman was characteristically arguing against the evidence.

can exercise some control, even if it's only the control of chucking somebody out that they don't like.[24]

Popular beliefs about who *does* govern similarly emphasize the importance of collective power, and of political trustees. In a Gallup Poll undertaken in 1976, the most influential groups in Britain were reckoned to be trade unions and big business. (See Table IV.3.) Leaders of the majority party—the Prime Minister and Cabinet ministers—were ranked next, followed closely by civil servants and newspaper proprietors. The average MP, the only directly elected spokesman of the individual voter at Westminster, was ranked ninth in influence, trailing behind the House of Lords and the Royal Family. This sample of voters considered people like themselves the least influential group in British government; only 5 per cent thought they had a 'lot of influence'. This perception of government is not regarded as ideal, for 72 per cent think people like themselves ought to have more say in the way the government runs the country.[25]

Different views about who should govern can coexist, because the institutions of British government are composite, rather than mono-

TABLE IV.3   **The influence of groups upon Britain's future**

	Percentage saying group influence is:			
	A lot	A little	None	Don't know
Trade unions	85	10	1	4
Big business, the City	65	20	4	11
Prime Minister	64	30	3	3
Cabinet ministers	43	45	4	8
Newspaper proprietors	41	38	9	12
Civil service	37	33	17	13
House of Lords	21	50	17	12
The Royal Family	17	43	34	6
The average MP	14	64	16	6
The Church	13	47	33	7
Generals and Admirals	9	39	37	15
People like myself	5	34	57	4

Source: Gallup Political Index, No. 187 (London: February 1976), p. 11.

[24] Quoted from Putnam, *The Beliefs of Politicians*, pp. 172–3.
[25] See *Gallup Political Index* No. 215 (June 1978), p. 11. Similar responses were given in the somewhat different political climate of February 1973, thus showing that the views are not a simple function of the party in office.

lithic. Some political institutions give pre-eminence to politicians acting as trustees on behalf of those they represent. Collectivist parties and pressure groups are important constraints upon politicians acting as trustees. Individual judgments are intermittently and crucially important at a general election.

Culture and sub-cultures

Writing a year after the General Strike of 1926, a former Conservative Prime Minister asserted, 'Our whole political machinery presupposes a people so fundamentally at one that they can safely afford to bicker; and so sure of their own moderation that they are not dangerously disturbed by the never-ending din of political conflict.'[26] Yet neither Balfour nor latter-day social scientists writing about consensus (i.e. a unanimity of views) make clear what it is that the English people are fundamentally at one about.

The foregoing survey of cultural attitudes shows that there is a consensus supporting the institutions of authority and basic political laws. Moreover, while Englishmen do *not* agree about *who* should govern, they do agree about *how* their governors should be chosen. The ability of Englishmen in times past to resolve disagreements without disrupting the regime leads Englishmen to expect to do so today as well.

Consensus about a very few political attitudes coexists with disagreement about major issues of contemporary politics. The several norms described above are consensual because they do *not* determine specific positions on policies. To the ordinary party politician, it is the differences about issues that are important, rather than agreement about a few basic cultural norms. Disagreement about policies can be conducted peaceably because politicians agree about the rules of the game for resolving political disagreements.

Every political culture combines a mixture of political outlooks or sub-cultures. By definition, any political issue will reveal conflicting opinions about the tempo, the form and the direction of choice. Political parties institutionalize the articulation of differing political views; differences in outlook can be found within as well as between political parties.

Within the Conservative sub-culture, the most clear-cut outlook belongs to those who are natural conservatives. Their view of social change is simple: they are against it. The known is always preferred

[26] Earl of Balfour, 'Introduction' to Walter Bagehot, *The English Constitution*, p. xxiv.

to the unknown; the present, however good or bad it is, is preferred to the risks of an unknown future, or a vain reactionary attempt to turn back the clock of history. *Laissez-faire* Conservatives are similarly sceptical about any purposeful attempts by government to change society, for fear that intended improvements will only turn out for the worse. They accept that the world is changing, but believe that the process of social change, like that of economic change, is best left to decisions taken by individuals and groups independently of government. Both groups of Conservatives agree that the less government does, the better; its actions should maintain rather than change society. This is pre-eminently a philosophy of political opposition, expressing distaste for policies propounded by a Labour government.

Adaptability is the characteristic outlook of Conservatives in office, for contemporary governors cannot pursue a pure do-nothing policy. One group of Conservative politicians takes the ambiguous position of favouring the existing order—in so far as possible. When circumstances appear to require government action, they will react with positive, and sometimes innovative, policies. For example, in the closing phase of the Second World War, the Conservative-dominated coalition government under Winston Churchill endorsed major changes in education, welfare and full employment policies. Another group of Conservative politicians is actively reformist, believing that a Conservative government can best promote economic and social programmes that will improve the conditions of society. Particularly in the field of economic policy, Conservatives believe that they can be more effective promoters of growth. To the Conservative reformer, the best argument for an institution is not the traditional view—Because it is there—but the instrumentalist view—Because it works.[27]

The adaptability of Conservative values has made the party ready to change to maintain political consensus, and, incidentally, to assure its survival through the centuries. The Conservative Party has survived by accepting many policies and values advocated by its opponents, whether nineteenth-century Whigs or Liberals or twentieth-century Socialists. Lord Hailsham describes this as

[27] Cf. Robert Eccleshall, 'English Conservatism as Ideology', *Political Studies*, XXV:1 (1977); Lord Blake and John Patten, eds., *The Conservative Opportunity* (London: Macmillan, 1976); William Waldegrave, *The Binding of Leviathan* (London: Hamish Hamilton, 1978) and Maurice Cowling, ed., *Conservative Essays* (London: Cassell, 1978).

accepting 'the true lessons taught by their opponents'. Conservatives, he argues,

> . . . see nothing immoral or even eccentric in catching the Whigs bathing and walking away with their clothes. There is no copyright in truth, and what is controversial politics at one moment may, after experience and reflection, easily become common ground.[28]

Because the Labour Party was formed by two generations of opposition, its early leaders developed ideas about the society that they wished to see without worrying much about the difficulties of translating ideas into practice. This habit of mind remains strong within the party, even leading the party's National Executive Committee to attack a Labour government for failing to do what it ought to do according to the party's traditional principles. Socialists wish to create new relationships in the economy; government ownership and planning is expected to provide a more efficient and equitable mechanism for economic growth. Socialists are also concerned with promoting greater social equality by reducing differences between educational institutions, as well as by reducing income differences. The most aggressive Socialists have viewed the economic difficulties of the 1970s as a practical argument for adopting the radical changes they support.[29]

The Labour Party is an inclusive party, seeking to appeal to all members of society. However controversial the policies of the Labour Party may be, they are not based upon the doctrine of class conflict. The party's Constitution states (Clause IV.5) that it wishes to promote the 'political, social and economic emancipation' of workers 'by hand or by brain', a broad appeal to 99 per cent of the electorate. The Labour Party does not draw its vote equally from all classes, but it has always sought to win middle-class as well as working-class support, and this moderates the potential for class conflict inherent in some theories of Socialism.

Labour governments have often rejected the prescriptions of Socialist theory because they are reckoned to be administratively or

---

[28] Quintin Hogg (intermittently, Lord Hailsham), *The Conservative Case* (Harmondsworth: Penguin, 1959), p. 16.

[29] Cf. C. A. R. Crosland, *The Future of Socialism* (London: Jonathan Cape, 1956); John Gyford and Stephen Haseler, *Social Democracy: Beyond Revisionism* (London: Fabian Research Series No. 292, 1971) and the files of various left-wing publications, especially the *New Left Review*.

politically impracticable. In foreign policy, Labour governments have repudiated any claim to a distinctively 'Socialist' foreign policy, basing policies on calculations of national interest. The so-called revisionist school of thought that characterizes Labour's outlook in government supports policies that, at the margin, favour redistributing income and wealth to the less well off. But its economic policies, as the 1974–9 Labour government has demonstrated, can accept higher levels of unemployment and stringent anti-inflation measures.[30] Left-wing critics of Labour's record in government argue that it lacks ideological coherence. Defenders like Herbert Morrison argue: 'Socialism is what the Labour Government does.'[31]

A liberal outlook is not confined to supporters of the Liberal Party; a stress on individual rights and individual involvement in politics can be found among supporters of all British parties. Contemporary liberals no longer adhere to strict nineteenth-century doctrines of economic and political *laissez-faire*. Today, the Liberal party offers a home to individuals wishing to promote all kinds of reforms, such as co-determination in industry, that cut across the conventional Conservative–Labour pattern. Liberals have also been first to advocate some policies, such as British membership of the European Community, later taken up by their two larger opponents.

Liberals complain that their electoral weakness is a product of an electoral system biased against third parties, arguing that if everyone who thinks like a liberal voted Liberal, the party would be the largest in Parliament. Liberal critics assert that the party encompasses so many different viewpoints that it deserves no following of its own, and that the two largest parties can respectively cater for the views of right-wing and left-wing Liberals.[32]

The differences between political sub-cultures rarely set Englishman against Englishman, because individuals, like parties,

[30] See e.g. R. Rose, *The Relation of Socialist Principles to Labour Foreign Policy, 1945–51* (Oxford, D.Phil in Social Studies, 1960); Wilfred Beckerman, ed., *The Labour Government's Economic Policy, 1964–1970* (London: Duckworth, 1972) and Peter Townsend and Nicholas Bosanquet, eds., *Labour and Inequality* (London: Fabian Society, 1972).

[31] Quoted in Peter Jenkins, *The Battle of Downing Street* (London: Charles Knight, 1970), p. 101.

[32] On the difficulties that Liberal MPs had in developing policies that were distinctive and practicable, see Alistair Michie and Simon Hoggart, *The Pact* (London: Quartet Books, 1978).

are often divided in their own minds about what politics ought to be about. Surveys of public opinion repeatedly show that individuals can endorse policies of all three parties, differing with each of them in turn, according to the issue. The Civic Culture survey of basic political outlooks attempted to classify English respondents according to three ideal-type categories: the participant citizen, the loyal undemanding subject and the parochial person remote from government. But more than two-thirds of the respondents could not be fitted into any of these three categories, because in their own minds they mixed values, beliefs and emotions from each of these outlooks.[33]

Cultural limits upon policy

The diffuse legitimacy that English people confer upon government does not endorse doing anything or everything that leaders might wish. The norms of the political culture include a set of limitations upon the scope of political authority. From the time of Magna Carta in 1215, English people have expected the Crown to recognize limits to what it may do. In theory, Parliament can enact any policy that the government of the day recommends; in practice, the government is limited by what people will stand for.

Chief among the things that government is expected *not* to limit is the liberty of the subject. Cultural norms about freedom of speech are an effective inhibition against political censorship. Allegations of police interference with the liberties of individual English people are rarely heard, by comparison with the situation in the United States, where statute laws are less effective constraints upon police actions than are the cultural inhibitions of England.

Increasingly permissive cultural values have widened the individual's freedom from government regulation of social behaviour. Even before a series of permissive legislative acts in the 1960s, the enforcement of moral norms by statute law was severely limited. For example, while the United States and Scandinavian countries were experimenting with the legal prohibition of alcohol to curb drunkenness, England adopted the simpler tactic of requiring public houses to close at specified hours each day. In the 1960s laws against homosexual relations between consenting male adults were

---

[33] The proportions with a mixed outlook varied from 63 to 87 per cent, depending upon classification criteria, see Rose and Mossawir, 'Voting and Elections', pp. 191ff.

repealed, and censorship of books, films and plays was virtually abandoned. Abortion was legalized in 1968. What individuals do in private is not considered a matter suitable for public regulation today.

Concurrently with reducing moral legislation, British governments have greatly expanded social welfare programmes. English people expect to enjoy the benefits of health, education and pensions, whether they are poor, wealthy or of average income. Government collects taxes and spends money on welfare benefits in an effort to give every citizen the freedom to enjoy a better life, without regard to income or circumstances. Increasingly, government seeks to regulate economic affairs to ensure that the freedom of corporations to do what they wish in the market-place does not create 'external' costs for others. In particular, strict control of land use offers collective protection against the sacrifice of general amenities for the short-term cash gain of a few.

The Labour and Conservative parties differ in the relative value they place upon promoting individual freedom to act, as against promoting freedom from regulation by government. The contemporary Labour Party tends to favour government provision of more welfare benefits, and to oppose government regulation of private morality. By contrast, Conservatives are readier to maintain government regulation of private morality, and believe that individual initiative, rather than government measures, is the best way to disperse the benefits of welfare widely.[34]

Today, the most significant constraints upon the scope of government are practical, not cultural. While government is responsible for the economy, it is not all-powerful over it. By expanding its commitments, the British government has exchanged the authority of command for the uncertainties of influence. Government can influence individual behaviour by taxes, and by the way it spends tax revenue in the provision of benefits. It can also influence corporations and trade unions by stating policies on wages and prices. Through international negotiations, it can influence measures of the European Community, and claim short-term benefits from the International Monetary Fund.

The economy that the British government seeks to direct is

[34] For an analysis of the contradictions between permissiveness in morality and regulation of the economy, see Samuel Brittan, *Capitalism and the Permissive Society* (London: Macmillan, 1973).

determined in many crucial respects by forces outside the control of government. Citizens may vote with their feet against government economic policies, engaging in unofficial strikes in violation of government pay policy or simply refusing to work harder to produce more goods. Companies may invest less rather than more, notwithstanding government exhortations, and trade unions may officially challenge government norms for pay. In the international economy, government policies to improve Britain's balance of trade between exports and imports may be frustrated by changes in world prices or by the falling value of the pound.

The practical limit upon government's power over the economy is best illustrated by the fact that for decades successive Labour and Conservative governments have exhorted citizens to produce more, and failed to achieve this goal. The growth rate of the British economy has been slower than government has planned, and is among the lowest in Europe. The most significant debate about the economy today is not so much about Conservative and Socialist economic goals, for both parties are pledged to promote greater economic growth, rising take-home pay and higher levels of publicly provided welfare benefits. The crucial question is: how can this be achieved in the face of the country's economic limitations?

While Englishmen agree about many things that government ought to do (e.g. provide schools and police services) and many things it ought not to do (e.g. regulate tastes in food and reading matter), at any point in time there is always political controversy about the boundaries of state intervention. For example, Englishmen disagreed for centuries, strongly and sometimes violently, about the extent to which government should regulate religion. Today, both bishops and politicians accept that a policy of non-interference in each other's affairs is the best way to manage the relationship of church and state.

Today, the economy is the subject of greatest debate about the limits of government. Neither party politicians nor pressure group leaders follow a consistent line about government involvement in the economy. At times, the interests of party politicians lead them to intervene, if only to avoid being blamed for pursuing a do-nothing policy in the face of economic difficulties. At other times, government tries to avoid taking responsibility for economic problems beyond its power to resolve.

Pressure groups want the 'mix' of interventionist and non-interventionist government policies to be their net advantage.

Whereas government proclaims a concern about the national interest, businessmen are concerned about the interests of their own firms. For example, during a sterling crisis, a part-time director of the Bank of England told a private client to sell sterling short, noting, 'This is anti-British and derogatory to sterling but on balance, if one is free to do so, it makes sense to me.'[35] Sometimes free trade has been in the interest of most British manufacturers, and they have supported it. At other times, high tariffs have been thought advantageous, and businessmen have favoured government erecting trade barriers. In the 1970s, most businesses have favoured relatively free trade through membership in the European Community. Problems of profitability have made many companies ready to accept specific government benefits provided as regional, industrial or investment subsidies.

Trade unions have sought to use their political influence to promote government ownership of major industries. When the 1945–51 Labour government nationalized the coal mines and the railways, it became the employer of the members of two of the country's largest trade unions. Unions have also lobbied for high levels of welfare benefits, as part of the 'social wage' of citizenship. Unlike Continental and American unions, British unions have reacted to their nineteenth-century experience of judicial constraints upon the right to organize and strike by refusing to recognize any claim of government to legislate about their affairs. The unions have resolutely opposed both the 1969 proposals of the Labour Government and the 1971 Conservative Industrial Relations Act. One Labour MP, Norman Atkinson, asserted that while ordinary laws must be obeyed, 'political or ideological law . . . should never be enforced by threat of surcharge, fines or imprisonment.'[36] In 1975, a Labour government repealed this act, at the behest of the trade union movement.

A recurring problem of postwar British governments has been how to reconcile the employers' and workers' expectations of the right to determine wages and prices in the market-place with the government's own responsibilities for preventing inflation. Succes-

---

[35] Quoted in Mackenzie, 'Models of English Politics', p. 60.
[36] Quoted in Gavin Drewry, *Law, Justice and Politics* (London: Longman, 1975), p. 21.

sive Conservative and Labour governments have vacillated between allowing market forces to determine wages and prices, and trying to limit their increase by more or less binding policies. Both unions and employers have tended to oppose the government becoming involved in the setting of wages and prices. They argue that government intervention only complicates already difficult labour–management negotiations, and that government ought not to interfere in this aspect of the mixed economy. The unions' determination to pursue their own interests in the market-place has been bluntly expressed by the General Secretary of the Trades Union Congress, Len Murray:

> As Frank Cousins once said in Congress, 'If it's a free-for-all then we are part of the all'. We will do our thing like other people will do their thing. If we take the view that the way in which the government is operating through its impact on employment, or prices, or the social wage or whatever is against the interests of our members, then we shall get up and say so, and if necessary we'll go and walk up and down the streets to say so.[37]

Governments have difficulties in regulating wages and prices because they are asking workers and investors to pay a direct and visible price to support this policy. In wartime, when national survival is at stake, firms and unions have been willing to make economic sacrifices for the common good. Today, there is no overriding national value to sustain sacrifices comparable to those made in more than five years of world war from 1939 to 1945. Government is also handicapped in trying to fix wages and prices because it is expected to be fair, but there is no agreement in Britain about what, specifically, constitutes a 'fair' wage or a 'fair' profit. Philosophers have been arguing inconclusively about this subject since the Middle Ages. John Goldthorpe notes that for a government to seek to enforce standards of 'fair wages' when consensus is lacking 'would carry the very real threat of extending economic into political instability'.[38]

Among British politicians, there is recognition of real political differences about particular issues of policy, as well as a belief that

[37] Brian Connell, 'Len Murray: A Life in the Movement', *The Times*, 22 August 1977.

[38] 'Social Inequality and Social Integration in Modern Britain', in R. Rose ed., *Studies in British Politics*, 3rd ed.

these differences can be readily accommodated within the existing political system. MPs do not concentrate attention upon the particular symbols and long-term goals that differentiate Conservatives and Labour. Instead, five-sixths concentrate upon the political acceptability and administrative practicality of programmes directed at immediate problems. MPs do not see their differences as zero-sum conflicts in which the gains of one side equal the losses of the other. Their outlook is aptly illustrated by an MP's calm characterization of partisan opponents thus:

> Well, they're different men with different policies, and some of them I quite like. They seem decent chaps, but I don't know. . . . I don't agree with their policies.[39]

The everyday discourse of politics tends to concentrate attention upon political differences, because politics by definition concerns conflicting opinions. But British political parties are also noteworthy for their readiness to assimilate ideas from their opponents once routine parliamentary battles are over. When an election transfers complete control of government from one party to another, the winning party maintains intact nearly all the legislation of its predecessor. The boundaries of what one party wants overlap substantially with the positive wants of its opponents and what they are prepared to accept and tolerate.

The question for politics in England in the 1980s is whether the mixture of partisan differences and consensus about the basics of government will remain as before. The legitimacy of political authority has survived the challenges of student unrest in the late 1960s and of economic difficulties in the 1970s. (One reason for this is that it was *not* put to the test in the confrontation between the Conservative government and the National Union of Mineworkers in 1974, as it would have if the Conservative government had won an election called to determine: 'who governs?'.) In a non-totalitarian society there must always be limits to government, and in England the courts cannot determine what these are. The customary way to resolve disputes in England is by an appeal to tacit assumptions and implicit understandings. At the beginning of the 1980s, these assumptions and understandings are more and more being scrutinized in the spotlight of political controversy.

[39] Putnam, *The Beliefs of Politicians*, Part II.

V
Political Socialization

People who learn slowly learn only what they must. The best security for a people doing their duty is that they should not know anything else to do.

The values, beliefs, and emotions of the political culture are transmitted from generation to generation through a series of socialization experiences in the family, at school and at work. The political outlooks of Englishmen today reflect attitudes learned early in life as well as responses to contemporary events. Socialization influences the anti-system outlook of the youthful radical as well as the positive allegiance of ordinary Englishmen. Because of the continuity of English social institutions, many values thus transmitted antedate the birth of the individual.

Most agencies of political socialization are not political in intent. Parents teach their children about many things besides politics, and there are very few couples in England who would have children for the good of the party. Schools are established to teach children reading, writing, arithmetic and other skills valued in non-political contexts. Neighbours may influence political outlooks, but a house is rarely chosen on political grounds. Political parties are the only social institution primarily concerned with political socialization, for parties have an interest in encouraging as many lifelong supporters as possible in the electorate.

Political socialization is a continuing process. When an English person begins to learn about politics in childhood, he or she may first respond emotionally to the monarch, or to symbols of Parliament. By the time a person becomes 18, the minimum age for voting, many political predispositions have been developed. But adult political behaviour is not determined by these predispositions. Adult life provides many opportunities to make new discoveries about politics and to learn from experience as a citizen. In addition, political events may force an individual to alter views and actions. For example, a person predisposed to vote for the Liberal Party will have to adopt another party if the Liberals fail to contest the constituency, and a person with a Scottish identity can only translate this into a vote for the Scottish National Party if voting in a Scottish constituency. Individuals are always potentially open to learning new ideas or altering old ones. While political socialization is a continuing process, what is newly learned often reinforces what was learned previously.

Content is more important than process. What an Englishman learns about politics has greater significance than how an outlook is acquired. In England a history of legitimate government emphasizes support for authority and compliance with basic political laws; in Bagehot's phrase, Englishmen hardly 'know anything else to do'. Allegiance to authority is a cause not a consequence of the pattern of political socialization. In Northern Ireland similar institutions socialize youths into conflict.[1]

Socialization influences the political division of labour. Children learn early that people differ from each other; these differences gradually become salient in political contexts. A young person not only learns about differences between political parties and political roles, but also the part that he or she may be expected to take in politics. Socialization differentiates persons into Conservative and Labour supporters, and into a small minority actively involved in politics or a large group of marginally or intermittently active citizens. This chapter begins with sections about socialization in the family and how sex roles influence political participation. Schooling provides a bridge between the family and the adult world and is considered next. Examining the complexities of class shows that its influence cannot be understood in isolation from other socialization influences. The final section summarizes the cumulative effect of all these socialization influences.

The influence of family

The influence of the family comes first; political attitudes learned within the family circle become intertwined with primary family loyalties. A child may learn little of what the Labour or Conservative party stands for except that it is the party of Mum and Dad. Like religion, party loyalties can be passed from parents to children; even if a young person breaks with parental loyalties, this usually

---

[1] See Richard Rose, *Governing without Consensus* (London: Faber & Faber, 1971), ch. 11, and James L. Russell, *Socialization into Conflict* (Glasgow: University of Strathclyde Ph.D thesis in Politics, 1974).

involves an emotional strain. Family circumstances dictate the class milieu in which a child grows up, and the class assigned to a youth years before going out to work.

The influence of parents upon children is most readily registered in the persistence of party loyalty from generation to generation. Politics does not need to be charged with deep emotional overtones for children to follow the partisan cues offered by their parents. But for this to happen, parents must show enough political interest to make clear to their children what the family's party is. However, this does not usually happen (Table V.1). The party preference of both parents is remembered by less than half the voters. Adults whose parents were both Conservatives tend to be Conservative, and those with both parents Labour tend to be Labour. But the relationship is not invariant; among the 42 per cent voters whose parents agree in their party, 39 per cent none the less rejected parental choice.[2]

TABLE V.1   **The persistence of party identification within the family**

	Respondent				
	Con. %	Lab. %	Lib. %	None %	Total %
Both parents:					42
Conservative	67	15	6	12	
Labour	10	71	6	14	
Liberal	39	33	18	10	
One parent unknown, other:					29
Conservative	55	30	7	8	
Labour	19	61	9	12	
Liberal	43	28	18	11	
Parents disagree	40	37	13	9	6
Neither parent's choice known	33	42	11	14	24

Source David Butler and Donald Stokes, 1964 British Election Survey.

A simple theory of intergenerational determinism fails because 61 per cent of the electorate does not acquire a lasting party identification from its parents. Most voters acquire a party identification

[2] These figures probably understate the amount of intergenerational change because of misreporting of recollections. Cf. Ivor Crewe, 'Do Butler and Stokes Really Explain Political Change in Britain?', *European Journal of Political Research*, II:1 (1974), pp. 83–7, and David Butler and Donald Stokes *Political Change in Britain* (London: Macmillan 2nd ed., 1974).

without parental direction or in opposition to it. Because less than half the support for the Conservative and Labour parties is, as it were, delivered by the obstetrician, each party has an incentive to seek recruits; once gained, they cannot be regarded as inevitable lifelong supporters.

A religious identification is likely to be acquired in childhood from parents, and in so far as religious differences affect party loyalties, this can influence political behaviour. In the nineteenth century, laws and customs reserved many civic and social benefits to members of the established Church of England, excluding non-conformist Protestants as well as Roman Catholics, Jews and atheists. Conservatives and Liberals in late nineteenth-century England tended to divide into Anglicans and non-conformist Protestants respectively. In the twentieth century, salient political differences between religions have been gradually eroded. Politicians have negotiated settlements of issues such as state aid to religious education, thus defusing a potentially disruptive force within Parliament. Clergy of many denominations have tended to stress common beliefs more than doctrinal differences. And church attendance has visibly waned. In the 1970s, only 13 per cent of a national sample said that they were very religious and another 18 per cent that they were to some extent religious. By contrast, 49 per cent said they were very religious as children, and 33 per cent somewhat religious.[3]

Notwithstanding the decline in the visibility of religion in England, it retains some influence upon party loyalties. Systematic studies of electoral behaviour from 1918 through 1979 have found that at each election Conservatives have tended to poll disproportionately well in areas with a relatively strong Anglican tradition and Labour has done disproportionately badly, even after allowance is made for the independent effect of class. The Liberals are no longer so dependent upon non-conformist votes as heretofore. While religion is a less important influence than class upon contemporary English politics, it remains significant.[4]

[3] Calculated from data contained in the October 1974 British Election Survey, variables 4:49, 4:50.
[4] For data on religion and voting, see Richard Rose, 'Britain: Simple Abstractions and Complex Realities', in R. Rose, ed., *Electoral Behavior: A Comparative Handbook* (New York: Free Press, 1974), p. 518; William L. Miller, 'The Religious Alignment in England at the General Elections of 1974', *Parliamentary Affairs*, XXX:3 (1977) and William L. Miller and Gillian Raab, 'The Religious Alignment at English Elections between 1918 and 1970', *Political Studies*, XXV:2 (1977).

Religious differences continue to show up among MPs.[5] The Conservative Party, the party historically closest to the established Church of England, is even more Anglican than the population at large. No Conservative MP admits to being an agnostic or an atheist. The Labour Party has inherited Liberal ties to non-established religions. Among non-conformist Protestants in the Commons, the great bulk are Labour. Among Catholic MPs, Labour supporters outnumber Conservatives by a ratio of about two to one. Catholics are in the Commons in approximate proportion to their numbers in the population. Jews are greatly over-represented, constituting less than 2 per cent of the electorate, but in 1974 contributing 45 Jewish MPs, 7 per cent of the Commons. Although Jews tend to be disproportionately middle class, 33 of the 45 Jewish MPs were Labour.[6]

Parental influence is also evident when a person born into a politically active family enters politics. Entering politics is then the equivalent of going into a family business. The eldest son of a hereditary peer knows that he is guaranteed a seat in the House of Lords if his father predeceases him. Sir Anthony Wagner, Garter King of Arms, argues that hereditary membership in the House of Lords is desirable because a peer may be groomed from childhood for adult political leadership. This view is rejected by the 55 per cent who favour the abolition of hereditary titles. Attitudes differ on party lines; 67 per cent of Labour supporters are against hereditary titles compared with 43 per cent of Conservatives.[7]

The number of members from political families is disproportionately high in every Cabinet. In Harold Wilson's first list of appointments in 1964, 10 of the 43 persons named to ministerial posts had parents sufficiently involved in public life to merit noticing this in their own biographies. Among Conservatives in 1979, 8 of the 22 Cabinet ministers had family ties with politics. Prime Ministers, too, are disproportionately drawn from political families. Winston Churchill's ancestors had been in the Commons or the Lords since the early eighteenth century. His son and grandson (as

[5] Some religious data is given in the candidates section of each Nuffield election study. The most recent full data is in David Butler and Michael Pinto-Duschinsky, *The British General Election of 1970* (London: Macmillan, 1971), p. 298.

[6] Cf. Herschel Katz and Ofira Seliktar, *Jewish Political Behaviour: Two Studies* (Glasgow: University of Strathclyde Survey Research Centre No. 12, 1974).

[7] Cf. Sir Anthony Wagner, 'Hereditary Peers Defended', *The Times*, 30 January 1969 and National Opinion Polls, *Monthly Bulletin* (June 1972), p. 27.

well as two sons-in-law) have also sat in the Commons. Harold Wilson's parents and grandparents, though never in Parliament, were also keenly interested in politics; he claims, 'I was born with politics in me.'[8] Margaret Thatcher's father was active in local politics as a Liberal.

Each generation does not follow blindly the path of its elders. One reason for this is that each generation differs significantly in the primary political events that influence it. The oldest generation in the electorate today was first exposed to politics before Labour was established as a major party, and early memories are likely to be of the inter-war depression. The earliest political memories of some middle-aged voters concern wartime, or postwar austerity; others have grown up in a period when prosperity has been the norm.

Differences in historical experience influence party support. The Conservatives have registered disproportionate strength among the elderly because elderly voters first became politically aware at a time when Labour was weak electorally and organizationally. Both parties enjoy stronger support among middle-aged voters than among young voters, because the former have had political loyalties fired in the crucible of major political changes during and around the Second World War.[9]

A second source of generational differences is the greater openness of young people to change. As young people become older, their party loyalties become more fixed, for the experience of one election tends to reinforce previous experiences. In the 1970s, however, young Conservative and Labour voters not only identified less strongly than their elders with the party they voted for, but also identified less strongly than their older brothers and sisters did a decade before. Younger people were also readier to engage in unconventional or unorthodox forms of political protest, and in Scotland, to vote for the Scottish National Party.[10]

Extrapolating the political future from generational differences is

[8] Quoted from 'The Family Background of Harold Wilson', in Richard Rose, ed., *Studies in British Politics* (London: Macmillan, 3rd ed., 1976), p. 192.
[9] See e.g. Richard Rose, 'Britain: Simple Abstractions and Complex Realities', p. 521, Paul R. Abramson, 'Generational Change and Continuity in British Partisan Choice', *British Journal of Political Science*, VI:3 (1976) and Ivor Crewe, Bo Sarlvik and James Alt, 'Partisan Dealignment in Britain, 1964–1974', *British Journal of Political Science*, VII:2 (1977), pp. 161ff.
[10] See Alan C. Marsh, *Protest and Political Consciousness* (London: Sage Publications, 1977), especially chs. 3 and 8, and Jack Brand, *The National Movement in Scotland* (London: Routledge & Kegan Paul, 1978), p. 150.

dangerous. Age-related differences are matters of degree, not kind, and differences in degree are often small. Parties and pressure groups normally draw some support from people of all ages. Groups that are specifically for one age-bracket, like the National Union of Students or organizations of pensioners, represent minorities. Moreover, students are a rapidly changing category within society. As students enter adult jobs, they may change their outlooks. Moreover, since the student 'generation' of 18- to 21-year olds changes every three years, its political character can also change rapidly. Consistently, party loyalties, not age, is the more important influence upon political outlooks.[11] (See Table XII.1.)

Sex similarities and differences

From childhood, boys and girls learn about different sex roles, and often go to separate secondary schools. But a major study of youthful political attitudes found virtually no difference in political interest or attitudes among boys and girls in secondary school. Class differences are more significant than sex differences.[12]

Adult differences in the political activities of men and women cannot simply be explained by attitudes formed in childhood. Nor can differences in the adult political outlook of women be explained by the fact that women secured the right to vote later than men. The vote was given women in 1918. Women voters today have had the right to vote for half a century, and most grew up at a time when their mothers as well as fathers had the right to vote.

The chief influence upon the voting behaviour of women in England is class, not sex. While studies have consistently shown that in each of the ten elections since 1950 women are slightly more likely to vote Conservative than men, the average difference has only been 6 per cent. This is much less than class differences in party support. Part of the small apparent sex difference can be explained by the fact that women tend to live longer than men, and in England the elderly are disproportionately Conservative. Cross-national comparisons emphasize that cultural and institutional differences are also more important than sex differences. For example, national considerations make voting turnout among men and women lower in England than in Continental European countries, but higher

[11] Note particularly Philip Abrams and Alan Little, 'The Young Voter in British Politics', *British Journal of Sociology*, XVI:2 (1965).

[12] R. E. Dowse and J. A. Hughes, 'Girls, Boys and Politics', *British Journal of Sociology*, XXII:1 (1971).

than in America. The absence of religious parties found in Germany and Italy also limits the choices that women (or men) can make.[13]

All political parties are interested in the votes of women, but they do not seek them by emphasizing feminist policies. Women's votes are sought on much the same ground as those of men. Economic issues, discussed in a multitude of ways, are given far more prominence than feminist issues. Because women constitute slightly more than half the electorate, all parties wish to avoid offending women, and are thus open to lobbying by women's rights pressure groups. For example, the 1975 Sex Discrimination Act, making discrimination in employment unlawful, was enacted by a Labour government following a 1973 consultative document of a Conservative government.

Women are about as likely to be interested (or to lack interest) in politics as men; 15 per cent of women describe themselves as having a great deal of interest in politics, and 24 per cent of men.[14] Given the influence of political interest upon political participation, one might therefore expect to find large numbers of women in public office.

In fact, women are under-represented in public office, by comparison with their number in the electorate. Moreover, women have a competitive advantage in seeking the unpaid office of local government councillor, for freedom from full-time employment (the position of half of England's women) is a positive asset, given the large number of day-time committee meetings. The flexible hours of local government work are less likely to conflict with family obligations than the duties, say, of serving in Parliament. Although women win votes about as well as male candidates of the same party, they are less likely to be nominated. Women constitute about one-sixth of the total membership of local councils, and are most likely to be elected to rural county councils, where the Conservative Party is particularly strong. Women are less likely to be appointed to important committee chairmanships than men, and differ in their

[13] See the Gallup Poll, 'Voting Behaviour in Britain, 1945–1974', in Rose, ed., *Studies in British Politics*, 3rd ed., and national studies in Rose, ed., *Electoral Behavior*.
[14] See October, 1974 British Election Study, variable 1:54. Note also, John G. Francis and Gillian Peele, 'Reflections on Generational Analysis: Is there a Shared Political Perspective between Men and Women?', *Political Studies*, XXVI:3 (1978), pp. 363–74.

attitude toward local council work, tending to prefer dealing with problems of individuals.[15]

In national politics, women are about 6 per cent of all parliamentary candidates. When a women seeks nomination for Parliament, she is likely to face prejudice in the selection of candidates. Women who are adopted as parliamentary candidates are less likely to be elected than men, because they more often fight for a party whose chances are hopeless in their constituency. The proportion of women in the House of Commons is low, since 1945 averaging 2.7 per cent.[16] There are usually more Labour than Conservative women in the House of Commons, but the differences between parties are slight. In the 1979 House, there were 8 Conservative women and 11 Labour.

At Cabinet level, there is an expectation that the Prime Minister will appoint at least one woman, a figure in proportion to the number of women in the Commons. From 1964 to 1979, four women served in Cabinet—Margaret Thatcher, Barbara Castle, Judith Hart and Shirley Williams. Each of these persons is a politician whose stature is not derived from her sex, or the expression of feminist views. The offices each held were determined by competitive abilities; none was confined to a department considered somehow 'appropriate' for women. Margaret Thatcher's election as leader of the Conservative Party in 1975 underscored the readiness of MPs to judge women in the Commons on political grounds. Both her friends and critics react most strongly to her pronounced political views.

The relatively low proportions of women in national politics (including the senior civil service)[17] is the result of a combination of influences. Marriage and child-rearing occupy many women in the years when young men can build the foundations for a political career. Within the Labour Party, men are at an advantage, because they are more likely to enter occupations that are unionized, and to be elected to office within a union, a stepping-stone to a Labour parliamentary career. A woman who wants a career in national

[15] See articles by Stephen L. Bristow in the *County Councils Gazette*, November and December 1978.

[16] See F. W. S. Craig, *British Electoral Facts, 1885–1975* (London: Macmillan, 1976), ch. 10; Melville E. Currell, *Political Woman* (London: Croom Helm, 1974) and Pamela Brookes, *Women at Westminster* (London: Peter Davies, 1967).

[17] On women in the civil service, see the Fulton Committee, *The Civil Service*, Vol. III:7 (London: HMSO, 1968).

politics can succeed, but the effort required is disproportionately great.

Schooling

While there is no formal educational requirement for voting or holding public office, education is potentially a major influence upon political outlooks, for school is important to young people from early childhood until they go out to work, and hundreds of thousands of voters are also students. Because schools are the product of society, education is best considered an intervening rather than an independent influence upon political outlooks.

English schools teach 'life adjustment' as well as academic subjects. Implicitly as well as explicitly, schools prepare young persons for adulthood by emphasizing behaviour and attitudes appropriate to adult roles, as well as by teaching basic skills, such as reading, writing and arithmetic. Because English people take their national identity for granted, there has been no need to teach British government, as American schools have taught civics in order to make Americans of children from a multiplicity of backgrounds. Studies of the influence of civics courses have found that they do not give their students any better understanding of political issues than that gained by youths who had only learned about politics informally.[18]

In England[19] education has always assumed inequality. Historically, the great majority of the population has been considered fit for only a minimum of education, until the end of the Second World War leaving school at 14, and today compelled to stay at school until 16. The highly educated minority, a small fraction of the population, are expected to play a leading part in politics. Speaking as Conservative minister of education, Lord Hailsham argued:

> Equality of opportunity in education or life does not mean either equality of performance or ability or uniformity of character. The object of education is to bring out differences just as much as to

[18] See Geoffrey Mercer, *Political Education and Socialization to Democratic Norms* (Glasgow: Strathclyde Survey Research Centre Occasional Paper No. 11, 1971). On civic education, see *Teaching Politics*, the journal of the Politics Association, a body of secondary school teachers, and their report, *Political Education and Political Literacy* (London: Longman, 1978).

[19] The discussion that follows explicitly excludes Wales, where education has historically been valued differently and language presents separate issues, and Scotland, where education is organized differently, both on academic grounds, and also by state-supported segregation by religion.

impose standards, and the democracy of the future will not be a drab mass of second-rate people in which distinction of intellect or character is decried as egg-headedness. It will be a society governed by its graduates—science and arts and social sciences—and largely run by people who put public service in front of enjoyment, profit or leisure.[20]

When secondary education was made compulsory by the 1944 Education Act, pupils were streamed into separate schools by an examination at age 11-plus according to academic ability, with about one-quarter attending academic grammar schools, where they would be expected to pass external examinations to qualify for university. The remainder were said to have 'failed', attending secondary modern schools, emphasizing an education for manual workers, or a very routine white-collar job.

For more than a generation Conservative and Socialist politicians have disagreed about the fundamental nature of education. Conservatives, as Lord Hailsham's remarks emphasize, see education reinforcing existing social differences within society. Conservatives defended academic selection at 11-plus because, they argued, it offered a means for the bright working-class child as well as the bright middle-class child to get ahead in the world. By contrast, Socialists have viewed schooling as a means of changing society. Socialists wish to create a society in which social differences are less marked, and believe that this required the abolition of segregation at age 11 into separate academic and non-academic secondary schools.[21]

In 1965 a Labour government circular requested all local authorities to reorganize secondary education in order to abolish the selective 11-plus examination. While the circular met with opposition from Conservative-controlled local educational authorities, it has gradually become effective throughout the country. From 1971 to 1976, including a period of Conservative gov-

---

[20] 'A Society Governed by Graduates', *The Times*, 24 January 1962.

[21] For the viewpoint of ministers, see Maurice Kogan, *The Politics of Education* (Harmondsworth: Penguin, 1971). Cf. Paul E. Peterson, 'British Interest Group Theory Re-examined', *Comparative Politics*, III:3 (1971) and Raphaella Bilski, 'Ideology and the Comprehensive Schools', *Political Quarterly*, XLIV:2 (1973). No serious test of whether comprehensive schools are achieving their social or political aims has yet been designed, let alone published. See Guy Neave, 'Sense and Sensitivity: The Case of the Comprehensive Education System', (Sheffield: Paper to the Annual Conference of the British Sociological Association, 1977).

ernment, the proportion of young people in selective schools fell from 55 per cent to 22 per cent. In 1976, 70 per cent of pupils in state secondary education were attending comprehensive schools, in which pupils of all abilities were enrolled. Pupils may, however, be streamed into different classes within comprehensive schools by self-selection of subjects or by their teachers.

Any effects of this change, such as they are, can only work slowly through the society, for the majority of voters will be products of the old selective system until about the year 2000.

Secondary schools discriminate on grounds of social status as well as intelligence. Today, about one-twelfth of young persons are in public schools, that is, private, fee-paying schools independent of the state. The majority of these schools are chosen by parents because they believe the schools offer a better formal academic education than neighbouring state schools.[22]

Whereas Americans would typically seek a better education for their children by moving house to a suburban school district providing a better state education, the limited variation within the state system leads English parents to seek a better education by paying for private tuition. If only because they do not have to take students of all abilities, private schools usually have a disproportionate number of students do well in examinations.

Within the category of private schools are a small number of extremely prestigious public schools, such as Eton, Harrow and Winchester. These public schools developed in Victorian times to provide young persons from higher social strata of society with the education appropriate to a gentleman, emphasizing character, good manners and sports as much as intellectual achievements. Today, a minority of public schools continue to attract pupils whose parents value their social character as much (or more) than their educational achievements. One of the hundreds of formally denominated public schools, Eton, has become well known for producing a disproportionate number of Conservative MPs, Cabinet Ministers and Prime Ministers. But the great majority of former public schoolboys today seek careers in industry or commerce, which offer the most numerous job opportunities.[23]

[22] See Tessa Bridgeman and Irene Fox, 'Why People Choose Private Schools', *New Society*, 29 June 1978.
[23] See S. G. Danks, 'Destination of Last Year's School-leavers', *Careers Bulletin* (Camberley: a publication of ISCO, the Independent Schools Careers Organisation No. 161, 1976), pp. 10–17, and, historically, T. J. H. Bishop with Rupert Wilkinson,

Higher education further differentiates young people, for only one in eight young persons leaving secondary school goes on to further study, and only 6.5 per cent follow a degree course at a university or polytechnic.[24] England has historically had few universities. As recently as 1956, half of English university students were attending one of three institutions: Oxford, Cambridge or the University of London. A university degree was not required for entry to business or to such professions as the law, or for a commission in the Army. In the 1960s, rising birth-rates and a rising demand for higher education caused the swamping of the ancient universities by the foundation of new institutions: 16 of the 33 English universities existing today were founded between 1961 and 1967.[25] New institutions could not claim to have the social prestige of ancient institutions, but they can compete in academic terms.

The explosion in the number of university graduates (and the provision of state scholarships for all students, scaled according to financial need) has meant that graduates are no longer so socially distinctive. To be a graduate is no longer synonymous with being a gentleman.[26] Professions formerly open to non-graduates now tend to recruit only graduates, thus raising barriers against the career advancement of young people who have not attended university. One writer has described the new class of graduates as a meritocracy.[27]

The stratified nature of English education has encouraged many social scientists to study the political attitudes of pupils, expecting research to demonstrate a strong influence of different schools upon youthful political attitudes. However, the research has demonstrated the opposite: schools appear to have limited influence upon youthful political outlooks independent of the family and class backgrounds of the pupils at school.[28]

Winchester and the Public School: A Statistical Analysis, (London: Faber & Faber, 1967).

[24] For statistics on educational achievement, see the annual HMSO publication, *Social Trends*, from which data cited here are taken.

[25] See Richard Layard, John King and Claus Moser, *The Impact of Robbins* (Harmondsworth: Penguin, 1969).

[26] See Margaret Stacey, *Tradition and Change* (London: Oxford University Press, 1960), p. 14.

[27] See Michael Young, *The Rise of the Meritocracy* (Harmondsworth: Penguin, 1961).

[28] For a socialization study of young people that also interviews parents, see Robert E. Dowse and John Hughes, 'The Family, the School and the Political Socialization Process', in Richard Rose, ed., *Studies in British Politics*, 3rd ed. The book includes at pp. 514–21 a bibliography of socialization studies.

The most striking evidence of the relative importance of home as against school is found in a survey conducted by Ted Tapper of pupils in a variety of English secondary schools, from the most to the least prestigious. Young persons did differ in their partisanship, but parental influence explained 41.0 per cent of the variance, as against school influences, which accounted for only 2.0 per cent of the variance. Young people also differed in their degree of political interest, with 37 per cent describing themselves as interested in politics. Here again, parental interest in politics was a more important influence upon attitudes, explaining 13.2 per cent of the variance.[29] When young persons were asked whether they might some day become active in politics, 42 per cent said they could conceive of someday becoming an MP. A belief in a political career was found in all types of schools; parental and school differences together could only explain 7.6 per cent of the variance. This emphasizes how widely diffused is the ideal of equality of political opportunity within schools very unequal in their educational character.[30]

Students at university have shown considerable volatility in their political outlooks. In the 1960s, surveys at a variety of institutions found more students ready to support Labour than would be expected of a disproportionately middle-class group. There were also significant differences in party preference between students in different faculties, with social scientists tending to be disproportionately Labour, and engineers the most Conservative. In 1976 however, a nation-wide student survey by Market and Opinion Research International found that undergraduates, while still leaning to Labour, were less pro-Labour than the general public, and very much less pro-Labour than young people not at university.[31] University teachers themselves are disproportionately pro-Labour; at the other end of the scale, primary school teachers are strongly Conservative.[32]

[29] In addition, youthful commitment to further education reflecting intelligence more than the school environment explained a further 12.5 per cent of the variance in political interest.

[30] All findings from Tapper's work are based upon this author's AID analysis of the original data, weighted to adjust numbers of respondents to proportions in different types of secondary schools at the time of fieldwork. For Tapper's account, see Ted Tapper, *Young People and Society* (London: Faber & Faber, 1971).

[31] See 'Unmilitant', *The Economist*, 23 October 1976.

[32] See *Teachers in the British General Election of October, 1974* (London: Times Newspapers Ltd., 1975); National Opinion Poll, *Political Social Economic Review* No. 13 (February 1978), p. 24, and 'Majority of Teachers to Vote Tory', *Daily Telegraph*, 30 April 1979.

The extent of change in student political attitudes, once they leave university, is aptly illustrated by members of the Labour Cabinet from 1964 to 1970. Many members had been contemporaries of the Prime Minister, Harold Wilson, at Oxford in the 1930s. But in their student days, these various Labour ministers had belonged to the Labour, Liberal, Conservative and Communist parties. Harold Wilson himself was a Liberal.

Differences in schooling imply differences in adult life. These most obviously affect occupational choice. A doctor or a teacher requires a formal education in order to follow his career, whereas a businessman, a bookmaker, or a lorry driver does not. The literature of political socialization states clear hypotheses about the expected political influence of education. The more educational advantages a person has, the more a person is expected to: (1) favour the party most closely identified with the educationally advantaged, the Conservatives; (2) show interest in politics; and (3) be active in politics. Because education affects occupation and this in turn affects position in the class structure, education can be important indirectly as well as directly.

Education is positively related to party preference: the more education a person has, the more likely a person is to vote Conservative. This is true when class is held constant. Among the upper middle class, those with further education to age seventeen or beyond are 5 per cent more likely to favour the Conservatives than those with the state minimum of education. Within the lower middle class the difference is 10 per cent, and among the working class, those with higher education are 18 per cent more likely to favour the Conservatives. But class differences are much more important than educational differences. Among upper-middle-class persons with a minimum of education, 66 per cent are Conservatives whereas among working-class people with low education, 35 per cent are Conservatives.[33] Length or type of education has little influence upon interest in politics; it can explain less than one per cent of the variation between those most and least interested.

Education is more strongly related to active participation in politics. The more education a person has, the greater the possibility of rising up the political career ladder. Englishmen with a minimum of education constitute nearly three-quarters of the electorate but less than half the number of local government councillors, and less

[33] See Rose, 'Britain: Simple Abstractions and Complex Realities', Table 10.

than one-tenth the number of MPs, ministers and administrative civil servants.

Those with a maximum of education, the 3 per cent with a university degree, constitute more than half the MPs, ministers and high-ranking civil servants (Table V.2). The pre-eminence of university graduates among the ranks of senior civil servants is hardly surprising, given the recruitment of these officials by competitive academic examination. But education also greatly facilitates entry to the House of Commons, even though there is no formal educational qualification for electoral victory. The Labour Party, claiming to represent working-class interests, draws more than half its MPs and ministers from the very small fraction of its supporters who are university graduates.

Education is neither a necessary nor a sufficient cause of a political career. It is not necessary, because at every rank some persons enter without any formal academic qualifications. This is most notable in local politics; it even applies to a few administrative civil servants who have worked their way up from the lower ranks. Higher or prestigious education is also not a sufficient determinant of a political career.

Education often reflects family background and, in the case of public schools, social status independent of formal learning. One must therefore separate the influence of family and schooling. One way to do this is to examine the proportion of persons in politics whose education is prestigious and meritocratic (i.e. attended both public school and university), purely prestigious (public school only), purely meritocratic (grammar school and university), or lacking both prestige and high merit.

Table V.3 emphasizes the differences between the Conservative and Labour politicians, as well as between politicians and those who elect them. Leading civil servants are university graduates and a majority also have a prestigious secondary education. The median Conservative MP and minister has 'jam on one side and butter on the other', that is, a public school education and a university degree. The modal Labour MP has no education to brag about, whether viewed in terms of prestige or merit. But the modal Labour minister had an education that is meritorious.

Educational differences between Labour MPs and ministers increased in the life of Harold Wilson's administration. By 1970 graduates outnumbered non-graduates in the Labour Cabinet by a

TABLE V.2 **Educational differences by political role**

Highest level of education	Voters	Local Councillors	MPs		Ministers		Administrative civil servants
			Con.	Lab.	Con.	Lab.	
	%	%	%	%	%	%	%
University	2	9	69	54	82	87	71
Other further education	4	6	3	16	0	0	17
Military, commercial, etc.	3	4	–[a]	–[a]	7	0	–
Public or direct-grant school	5	18	20	1	9	4	–
Grammar school	9	12	8	15	9	4	–
Technical, intermediate	5	5	–	9	0	0	10
Elementary	72	45	–	5	0	4	2

Note [a] Data not available.
Sources Voters and Councillors, Louis Moss and Stanley Parker, *The Local Government Councillor*, Vol. 2 (London: HMSO, 1967), p. 27; MPs derived from D. E. Butler and Dennis Kavanagh, *The British General Election of October 1974* (London: Macmillan, 1975), p. 214; ministers calculated by the author from *Who's Who* data on the Conservative Cabinet of 1979 and Labour Cabinet ministers appointed in October 1974. Civil servants include persons promoted from lower ranks; based on A. H. Halsey and Ivor Crewe, *The Fulton Committee*, Vol. III (1), pp. 64ff.

TABLE V.3 **Prestige and merit in the education of politicians**

Type of education	MPs		Ministers		Administrative civil servants
	Con.	Lab.	Con.	Lab.	
	%	%	%	%	%
Pure merit	16	37	14	65	44
Pure prestige	20	1	5	4	—[a]
Prestige and merit	53	17	77	22	56
Neither	11	45	5	8	—[a]
Numbers	339	269	22	23	—[a]

Note [a]In default of full details, all civil servants are classified as if graduates.

Sources MPs derived from D. E. Butler and Dennis Kavanagh, *The British General Election of 1979* (London: Macmillan, 1980); ministers calculated by the author from *Who's Who* data on Conservatives in Cabinet appointed in 1979 and Labour Cabinet ministers appointed in October 1974. Civil servants include persons promoted from lower ranks; based on *The Fulton Committee*, Vol. III (1), pp. 64ff.

margin of 17 to 4. When Home Secretary, James Callaghan, could complain that his life was 'less complete than it might be' it was because he had not gone to university.[34]

Schooling has a limited effect upon political attitudes; at most it is an intervening influence. English schools reflect social differences among parents. Parental outlooks influence party preferences and interest in politics, and secondary education does little to alter or reinforce parental influence. Schooling exerts influence at a point relatively remote in time from the political world in which adult English people find themselves today. For example, the average voter at a general election has left school a quarter-century before polling day. Whatever the ethic a school emphasizes, it makes little difference to young persons. The concept of citizenship, implying equality independent of educational achievement, appears to dominate political learning. A young person learns about common rights and duties rather than differences in political roles and duties. The differences become prominent when young people move from school to adult life.

[34] 'Farmer Jim from the JC Ranch', *The Guardian*, 6 June 1970.

Class

To speak of class is to invoke a concept as diffuse as it is meant to be pervasive, for it is sometimes a label for the cumulative effect of all socialization experiences. Occupation is the most common indicator of class in England and will be employed henceforth in this study.[35] But to group people together in terms of a single economic attribute does not mean that they are identical in every other respect. While a coal miner usually lives in a mining village where his occupation is integrally related to a whole network of social relations, with family, friends, and neighbours, a bus driver working in central London but living in a suburb outside will find work relationships divorced from other ties.

Nearly every definition of occupational class places about two-thirds of English people in the working class and one-third in the middle class. In politics it is particularly important to distinguish differences among non-manual workers. The handful of upper-class people living solely on inherited capital are politically less significant than the five per cent of upper-middle-class people who dominate the professions and large organizations, including government. The 'middle' middle class, holding less important positions in business and industry, is numerically larger although politically less important. The lower middle class, holding routine white-collar jobs, is larger than the other two sections of the middle class combined. Within the working class, sociologists often discriminate between skilled, semi-skilled, and unskilled groups. Studies of voting and political recruitment show differences between the upper middle class and lower middle class. Substantial political differences are not found among strata within the working class.

Using occupational criteria to assign people to classes ignores the influence of personal evaluations. But in T. H. Marshall's definition, 'The essence of social class is the way a man is treated by his fellows (and, reciprocally, the way he treats them), not the qualities or the possessions which cause that treatment.'[36] Subjective class assessments can differ from objective assessments based on occupa-

[35] For a historical review of changing sociological indicators of class, see Mark Abrams, 'Some Measurements of Social Stratification in Britain', in J. A. Jackson, editor, *Social Stratification* (Cambridge: University Press 1968). More generally, see W. G. Runciman, *Relative Deprivation and Social Justice* (London: Routledge, 1966).

[36] T. H. Marshall, *Citizenship and Social Class*, p. 92.

tion. Surveys consistently find that nine-tenths or more of the population are prepared to place themselves in one or other class category. But about one-third subjectively place themselves on the wrong side of class lines defined by sociologists; more people upgrade than downgrade themselves. The criteria people use to place themselves are much more heterogeneous than the sole criterion of occupation. For example, some working-class people use Socialist standards to assign people to classes by their contribution to social well-being, rating farmers, doctors and coal miners higher than company directors, accountants or civil servants.[37]

Whatever measure is used, class differences result in significant differences in party preference, political interest and participation. Those differences not only reflect the importance of what Weber called 'life chances in the market';[38] they also reflect the interaction of occupation and other socialization experiences.

The influence of occupational class upon party preference has been documented by every voting study ever undertaken in England (Table V.4). Three qualifications must be made. First a proportion of the electorate has no party preference or prefers the Liberal or Nationalist parties, which cannot readily be fitted into the conventional dichotomy of middle class and working class. Within the working class, this non-aligned group can prevent Labour from being the party of a majority. Second, the relationship between class and party is asymmetrical. The middle class is more Conservative than the working class is Labour; the most electorally homogeneous group is the upper middle class. Thirdly, whereas the Labour Party draws three-quarters of its support from the working class, the Conservatives draw upwards of half their vote from the working class. The relationship between party and class is partial, not complete.[39]

The relationship between class and party increases when account is taken of parents' class. People in the same class as their parents are likely to be Conservative if middle class and Labour if working

[37] See Michael Young and Peter Willmott, 'Social Grading by Manual Workers', British Journal of Sociology, VII:4 (1956).

[38] H. H. Gerth and C. Wright Mills, From Max Weber (London: Routledge & Kegan Paul, 1948), pp. 180ff.

[39] For a systematic analysis of measures of class and varying influence upon voting, see the survey study in Rose, 'Britain: Simple Abstractions and Complex Realities', and the aggregate data analysis of William L. Miller, 'Social Class and Party Choice in England: A New Analysis', British Journal of Political Science, VIII:2 (1978).

TABLE V.4   **The influence of class on party preference**

Class	Conservative	Labour	Liberal	Nationalist or none	Total in population
	%	%	%	%	%
Middle	59	14	16	8	13
Lower-middle	50	26	15	10	23
Working	35	42	12	11	64

Source   Calculated by the author from unpublished Gallup Poll, May, 1979.

class. Upwardly mobile people will favour the Conservatives, but by a lesser margin than those born into the middle class. A plurality of downwardly mobile Englishmen are Labour, but they are less strongly Labour than are those born in the working class. They also tend to favour their new class less strongly than upwardly mobile people favour their new class. The effect of social mobility remains when one controls for differences in parents' party preference within each class. Working-class children from Conservative homes are more likely to be upwardly mobile than those from Labour families.[40]

One reason for the limited relationship between class and party preference is that Englishmen differ in the degree to which they regard class as salient to their everyday concerns. When people are asked whether or not they think of themselves as belonging to a particular class, the proportion answering yes is 53 per cent. On this basis, the electorate must be divided into three groups: those who think of themselves as working class, those who think of themselves as middle class, and those who do not articulate a sense of class consciousness. The largest single category consists of persons who do not think of themselves in class terms. Among the consciously middle class, Conservatives outnumber Labour voters by 4 to 1. Among the consciously working class, Labour voters outnumber Conservatives by more than 2½ to 1. Among those for whom class is not particularly salient, the Conservatives have a small advantage. Table V.5 shows that 43.5 per cent conform to class-typical roles, as middle-class Conservatives, working-class Labour voters or persons refusing these party alternatives and not regarding class as salient.

[40] Recalculated from data in Paul Abramson, 'Intergenerational Social Mobility and Partisan Choice', *American Political Science Review*, LXVI:4 (1972), Tables 1–2.

TABLE V.5 **Subjective class identification and party preference**

	Con.	Other, none	Lab.	Totals
	%	%	%	%
Middle-class identifier	8.5	4.0	2.0	14.5
Low class-salience	19.0	12.0	16.0	47.0
Working-class identifier	8.5	7.0	23.0	38.5
Totals	36.0	23.0	41.0	100.0

Source David Butler and Donald Stokes, 1964 British Election Survey, combined answers to Q.69a and Q.69a*.

More complex theories of the influence of class emphasize the role played by class-specific institutions, for instance trade unions, in socializing people into political attitudes. Persons who belong to a trade union are expected to be more likely to vote Labour than persons whose nominal class position is not reinforced by involvement in a class-specific organization. Approximately half the working-class families in England include members of a union. In the families of manual workers in trade unions, 60 per cent favour Labour. In those working-class families without a union member, voters divide evenly between the Conservative and Labour parties.[41]

The tendency of people to cluster together in class-specific neighbourhoods also influences political outlooks, for individuals who live among people of a similar social class are subject to more consistent pressures to vote for the party of that class. People who live in disproportionately middle-class constituencies are more likely to vote Conservative than are those living in socially mixed areas, and voters in heavily working-class constituencies are disproportionately Labour.

Government housing policy encourages the creation of socially homogeneous neighbourhoods. One-third of families live in municipally owned council houses. Council houses are usually grouped together in substantial numbers. This clustering not only creates individual identification with the council estate but also makes persons identifiable as council tenants by those who live elsewhere. About four-fifths of council-house tenants are working class. A Gallup election survey found that 63 per cent of working-class

[41] See Rose, 'Britain: Simple Abstractions and Complex Realities', Table 11.

council tenants supported Labour, but only 40 per cent of working-class voters who owned their own homes. Among the lower middle class, a majority of council tenants favoured Labour and a majority of home owners favoured the Conservatives.[42]

Analysing the relationship of class and political participation is difficult, because full-time politicians by definition have middle-class jobs; trade union officials too are engaged in non-manual work. The influence of class is most apparent when one examines the family background of politicians. Educational data show that the great majority of Conservative MPs come from comfortably middle-class homes. Politics neither raises nor lowers their occupational status. The Labour Party, by contrast, has always drawn a significant proportion of its MPs from working-class families. Educational changes since the Second World War have created a third type of Labour MP, a person born into a working-class home but with an assured middle-class career because of a university education. The administrative civil service draws disproportionately from the offspring of middle-class families, because it recruits primarily from the universities, whose students are disproportionately middle class. The higher the political office, the greater the likelihood that it will be filled by someone who began working life in a middle-class job. One-fifth of the nation is employed in professional or managerial tasks, but 45 per cent of local councillors and more than half the MPs and ministers in both parties began their working careers at this level.[43]

Leading Labour politicians, even more than Conservatives, are drawn from the professions, especially teaching, the law and journalism. Stated negatively, Labour politicians have virtually no experience as managers of large organizations. Because trade unions can sponsor candidates by giving cash support to members nominated as candidates, a substantial number of Labour MPs and Cabinet ministers have been of working-class origin. But the proportion drawn from working-class occupations has declined steadily since the party's foundation. In 1906, 86 per cent of Labour MPs were from working-class backgrounds. Since 1945, the proportion has been less than half, reaching 26 per cent in 1970. Moreover, at the 1970 general election, more than two-fifths of the MPs returned with trade-union sponsorship were not themselves working-class

[42] *Ibid.*, Tables 14–16 and Miller, 'Social Class and Party Choice in England'.
[43] See sources cited in Tables V.2, 3.

people; they were adopted by unions seeking to strengthen their political voice in Parliament.[44]

While class differences do affect party loyalties and, even more, recruitment into active political roles, they do not lead to the view that politics is about class conflict. When people are interviewed about their attitudes toward class-related issues, differences are found within the middle class and within the working class; the two groups are not cohesively opposed to each other. While a majority in each class thinks it difficult to rise in the English class system, this is not perceived as a major source of frustration. When asked to say whether one class is happier than another, 69 per cent think that people are equally likely to be happy in either class. Among those who think one class happier, those in each class see their own class as happier than the other class.[45]

A majority of voters say that they do not think there is bound to be political conflict between the classes. After an intensive analysis of party images, Butler and Stokes conclude that approximately one-fifth of the electorate base their party choice on class concerns; fewer still see politics in terms of mutually exclusive class interests. Moreover, a majority rejects the idea that class interests are defined by the social characteristics of their MPs. Voters think it much more important that an MP should live in the constituency that elects him than that their MP should be of the same social class as most of his supporters.[46]

The cumulative effect

In the course of a lifetime, every Englishman is subject to a great variety of social experiences; some emphasize differences between citizens, whereas others emphasize an identity of concerns. For example, until the past decade, racial differences were not a basis for differential socialization, because virtually the whole English population was white. Today, differences in religious socialization are not translated into significant political differences, and in any event almost 90 per cent of the English population is nominally Protestant. Differing national identities within the United Kingdom

[44] For interpretations of these data, see e.g. William D. Muller, *The Kept Men* (Brighton: Harvester Press, 1977) and Colin Mellor, *The British MP* (Farnborough: Saxon House, 1978).
[45] See National Opinion Polls, *Bulletin No. 109*, June 1972, pp. 17–18.
[46] Data from a 1972 National Opinion Polls survey commissioned by Granada Television for the programme 'State of the Nation: Parliament'.

are of limited aggregate significance today, for England constitutes 83 per cent of the United Kingdom. Within England, four-fifths of Englishmen live in urban areas.

Cumulatively this results in a society that is very homogeneous in terms of race, religion, national identity and urban life-style. By contrast, European societies such as Germany, Belgium, and the Netherlands—not to mention America and Canada—are pluralist. More dimensions of social structure are politically salient, such as race in America and language in Belgium and Canada, and there is a more even dispersal of the electorate among these groups.[47]

Englishmen are said to differ along class lines, because class-related differences are the only politically salient differences substantial in size. Because the differences are strongest among the smallest groups, the aggregate effect is limited. The greatest degree of partisanship is shown by the smallest social groups within English society: middle-class rural Protestants (Conservative advantage, 45 per cent) and middle-class rural Catholics (Conservative advantage, 43 per cent). The largest group—urban Protestant manual workers—shows an almost even division of partisanship; the Labour advantage is 9 per cent.

The relative importance of different socialization experiences upon political outlooks is best summarized by a statistical analysis that gives precedence to experiences that come first in time. With a computer, one can use a statistical technique known as AID (Automatic Interaction Detector) to measure the influence a variety of social factors have upon party loyalties. In Table V.6, a national adult sample of British voters is divided successively by generation, sex, and other socialization categories, in order to identify the influences most likely to affect voter preferences. The influence of four adult factors—union membership, housing, region and religion—is considered at the end of the analysis. At each stage, the amount of additional variation explained by a given influence is computed.

Cumulatively, more than two-thirds of the explained variation in party preference can be accounted for by early childhood influences. Neither generation nor sex explains as much as one per cent of variation. Father's class and, independent of class, parents' party preference are of substantial importance, together accounting for

[47] For an illustration of these points, see national studies in Rose, ed., *Electoral Behavior*.

TABLE V.6 **The cumulative effect of socialization experiences**

Stage	Division	Conservative proportion Con.–Lab. %	Variation explained at each stage %
1. Generation	Born pre-1935	48	0.4
	Born, 1935 and after	41	
2. Sex	Male	43	0.2
	Female	48	
3. Father's class	Middle	69	9.2
	Working	36	
4. Father's party	Conservative	73	9.9
	Labour	25	
	Other, none	55	
5. Religion	Church of England	55	2.1
	Other	41	
6. Education	Academic	66	1.2
	Minimum	37	
7. Current class	Middle	62	2.4
	Working	29	
Other influences			
8a. Housing	Owners	61	5.5
	Tenants	29	
8b. Union membership	Yes	28	0.8
	No	60	
8c. Nation	England	48	
	Non-England	31	0.0
Total			31.7

Source October 1974 British Election Survey, analysed by the author with AID (Automatic Interaction Detector) III. The first seven items were entered in sequence, to simulate their order in the socialization process.

more than half the total variance explained. Staying at school past the minimum has little additional effect upon party preference. In adult life, where one lives is more important than how one works; owner-occupiers are disproportionately Conservative, and council tenants very heavily Labour. Collectively, all of these influences explain 31.7 per cent of the major party preferences of voters; 68.3 per cent of voters' preferences must be explained by other factors independent of the socialization influences discussed here.

One reason for the absence of voting strictly along class lines is that a majority of Englishmen do not have a set of socialization experiences consistent with ideal-type definitions of class.[48] Models of class determinism presuppose that working-class people have a minimum education, a trade-union member in the family, rent their home and think of themselves as belonging to the working class. Middle-class people are expected to have the opposite set of experiences. In fact, only 21 per cent of the British electorate meets all of these ideal-type criteria. Middle-class Englishmen are more likely to conform to their class stereotype than are manual workers. The average middle-class Englishman has three of the four attributes expected to reinforce the influence of a non-manual job; the average working-class Englishman has two. The experience that most unites the working class is a minimum of education; membership in a trade union is the characteristic most often lacking among manual workers. As the number of reinforcing attributes increases, the likelihood increases of an individual voting for the party typical of his class. The greater homogeneity of social experiences within the middle class explains the greater political cohesion of middle-class voters.

Deviations from mechanical consistency in political socialization are also caused by changes in political institutions. In party politics, the collapse of the old Liberal Party and the organizational growth of the Labour Party altered the alternatives among which voters could choose. A new party preference was forced upon persons brought up as Liberals who found no Liberal candidate in their constituency. In international affairs, politicians brought up to think of Germany as an enemy and Russia as an ally changed their minds in response to post-1945 events.

Youthful socialization is relatively important in the recruitment of a small proportion of persons to political offices and as party activists. As one goes up the ladder of office-holders from voter to councillor, MP, senior civil servant and Cabinet minister, the social distinctiveness of politicians increases. National politicians are better born, better educated and have had higher status jobs than the average voter. Yet the same evidence also shows that whatever their social origins, no one is barred from seeking office. Contrasting socialization experiences produce differences in degree, not

[48] See Rose, 'Britain: Simple Abstractions and Complex Realities', Table 13, and Elizabeth Bott, *Family and Social Network* (London: Tavistock, 1957).

differences in kind. Moreover, the great majority of middle-class male university graduates, the group most disproportionately found in politics, does not enter politics.

Socialization influences the probabilities of political action; it does not produce certainties. Because socialization is a continuous process, individuals remain open to change in their political outlook at any time in adult life. The likelihood of change depends upon the degree of an individual's involvement in politics. The mass of people are carried forward by inertia in whatever political role they find themselves. They have enough interest and knowledge to vote, but not enough involvement to learn new political roles and ideas readily. Pre-adult and para-political influences are likely to be most important.

Among active political participants, intense socialization into the role of politician is likely to override other influences. This is illustrated by what happens when an opposition party enters office. The new governors can alter the policies of government. But accession to office may also alter the men. Lord Balniel, the heir to one of the oldest titles in Britain, has noted that existing patterns of politics are preserved 'not so much by the conscious efforts of the well established, but by the zeal of those who have just won entry, and by the hopes of those who still aspire'.[49]

The speed and the direction of many political changes in England since the end of the Second World War raises questions about the extent to which past experiences are a suitable basis for coping with future political problems. In so far as continuity is desirable, then the absence of abrupt changes in social life in England results in the gradual adaptation of the political system. But novel problems require novel responses, as is shown by the wartime recruitment to office of politicians who had not been previously socialized to Westminster and Whitehall norms. In so far as England in the 1980s faces fundamentally different problems than in the preceding era of burgeoning affluence, problems may arise from politicians socialized into outlooks inconsistent with new difficulties.

[49] 'The Upper Classes', *The Twentieth Century No. 999* (1960), p. 432.

VI
Recruiting Participants

The principle of popular government is that the supreme power, the determining efficacy in matters political, resides in the people—not necessarily or commonly in the whole people, in the numerical majority, but in a chosen people, a picked and selected people. It is so in England.

Socialization can only predispose individuals to take part in politics; whether or not a person does participate depends upon recruitment procedures as well as individual aspirations. For example, in the early nineteenth century civil servants were recruited on the basis of kinship and friendship with political patrons. Today they are recruited by examination. Each procedure gives special advantage to a minority—but minorities with different social characteristics.

Before analysing how politicians are recruited, one must first ask: who are the politicians? If a politician is defined as an individual whose actions influence policy outcomes, then a housewife influences economic policy by her market-place reaction to prices, differently but perhaps as effectively as a back-bench MP. In this study, politicians are defined by their role and not by their office; they are individuals who expect and are expected to participate in policy making. Ministers and MPs are politicians by virtue of their office, as are senior civil servants. Individuals holding important offices outside government, for instance, trade union officials, heads of important industrial firms or national newspaper editors, act as politicians by participating in deliberations about central government policy. They differ from ministers because they are only intermittently active in politics.[1] In addition, individuals whose full-time job has no political standing may follow politics as an avocation, becoming active in their local communities. At election time the great bulk of the population temporarily become politicians, voting to decide who will represent them between elections.

Once active in politics, whether on a full-time, intermittent or

[1] For a full discussion of the roles of politicians, illustrated with British and American examples, see Richard Rose, *People in Politics* (London: Faber & Faber, 1970), ch. 3–4.

voluntary basis, a person undergoes intensive socialization into a political role. This experience differentiates all politicians, whatever their social origins, from non-politicians. Political socialization in the family, in school, or at work, can at most influence predispositions. Role socialization within political institutions, whether local government, parties or Parliament, is on-the-job learning. An individual's political career depends upon the ability to do what is expected. These expectations are less the product of individual ideas and more a reflection of the chief institutions of government.

In this chapter the recruitment of politicians is analysed in terms of the institutional opportunities provided to individuals and the differential response of persons to these opportunities. The first section considers the extent to which members of the peripheral public—that is, persons without a full-time political office—take a political role in their local community. The second considers socialization into central political roles. The extent to which high social or economic status is converted into political office is reviewed in the third section. The final section considers the significance of a process that selects in some people and selects out others.

The peripheral public

Everyone in England has a multiplicity of roles in society today, as spouse and parent, worker and consumer, and tax-payer and beneficiary of public services. Most people do not view their lives in terms of what can be achieved in political roles. Any analysis of political recruitment tends to distort the significance individuals give to political activities. Instead of speaking of individuals as voters, it would make more sense to speak of the behaviour of ordinary individuals in electoral situations. The role of voter or citizen is not the chief defining characteristic of English people.[2]

The majority of the population have strictly peripheral political roles. Members of the peripheral public are linked to central politics by local activists who represent them, and by the field staff of central government, whose offices (e.g. the post office, employment exchange, the army recruiting station, or the constituency party) are local outlets for central political institutions. In every Western

---

[2] For symposia about political participation, including empirical studies, see e.g. Geraint Parry, ed., *Participation in Politics* (Manchester: University Press, 1972) and Colin Crouch; ed., *British Political Sociology Yearbook Vol. III* (London: Croom Helm, 1977).

nation the peripheral public and local activists constitute the majority of the citizenry. Problems of scale and specialization make it impossible for the majority of people to participate full-time in central political roles.

Nearly every Englishman sees himself as a consumer of local government services, but knowledge and interest conducive to effective participation in local politics are limited. (Table VI.1.) In a survey commissioned to provide information for the reform of local government structure, one-quarter of the respondents could name their local council leader, and one-fifth said they were 'very interested' in what goes on in their local area. Only one-tenth said that they had ever attended a local council meeting, and fewer knew the usual date and place of their local council meetings.

An Englishman has few opportunities to vote at the local level: by comparison with Americans, a citizen is not concurrently a voter in local, county, and state elections, as well as a voter in school board and sewer district elections. An Englishman is offered no opportunity to vote for legislative or institutional reforms in local referenda, nor is there a public ballot on tax increases or bonds to finance capital expenditure for local services, as happens in many American local jurisdictions. When local government elections are held, a voter elects only councillors; the senior administrative officials of local government are appointed rather than elected, as often happens in America. The concentration of authority in the hands of a small council of elected persons and a large body of professional local government civil servants makes the town hall a mirror of arrangements found in Whitehall.[3]

The majority of Englishmen are passive subjects, not active participants in local politics. Less than half vote at local elections; in many wards, seats are uncontested, so that an election is unnecessary. A total of 25 per cent said they had been in touch with local authority officials within the year. The problems that lead people to their council office are housing, welfare services, education and such environmental services as refuse collection. Local councillors are sought out less often. When people were asked whether they might succeed if they tried to influence a local council decision, 36

[3] Local government officials are involved full-time in public affairs, and often have salaries and qualifications equal to, but different from, senior civil servants in Whitehall. See e.g. Jeffrey Stanyer, *Understanding Local Government* (London: Fontana, 1976), ch. 6.

TABLE VI.1 **Involvement in local politics**

Level	Estimated number of people	Estimated % of electorate	Source
Consumer of local government services	40,200,000	98	LGE, p. 44
Votes at local election	17,000,000	42	LGE, p. 78
Knows name of council chairman/mayor	11,500,000	28	LGE, p. 24
Very interested in local affairs	8,000,000	20	CAS, p. 29
Ever contacted local councillor	6,800,000	17	LGE, p. 51
Confident of influencing local council	5,000,000	12	LGE, p. 75
Knows date and place of council meeting	3,200,000	8	LGE, p. 54
Member, reorganized local council	21,695	0.05	

Sources LGE = Mary Horton, *The Local Government Elector*, Vol. 3 (London: HMSO). CAS = Royal Commission on Local Government, *Community Attitudes Survey: England* (London: HMSO, 1969).

per cent said they would not bother trying and another 18 per cent said they would be unsuccessful; 46 per cent thought they might be able to exercise influence.[4]

When a local authority takes an action that affects and offends strongly a group within the community, this can stimulate political activity among individuals who might otherwise take no interest in local affairs. The issues likely to stir people up—such as unsafe roads, housing problems or refuse collection—may affect any class of citizens. 'Sporadic interventionists' are unwilling participants in politics. They do not become involved in local affairs because of a general interest in politics, but because they feel government is threatening to do something that they wish to stop or change.[5]

About one in twenty persons has at some time thought of taking an active part in local politics by standing for local office; less than

[4] See Mary Horton, *The Local Government Elector* (London: HMSO, 1967), ch. 2 and Louis Moss and Stanley Parker, *The Local Government Councillor* (London: HMSO, 1967), Vol. 2, p. 45.
[5] See e.g. Robert E. Dowse and J. Hughes, 'Sporadic Interventionists', *Political Studies*, XXV:1 (1977) and Paul E. Peterson and Paul Kantor, 'Political Parties and Citizen Participation in English City Politics', *Comparative Politics*, IX:2 (1977).

half of these have ever in fact held local office. The constraint upon participation is not electoral defeat, but the unwillingness of potential community leaders, when it comes to the point, to stand for election. People exclude themselves from local politics for three major reasons: 36 per cent lack the time or the health to do the work, 32 per cent lack the self-confidence and temperament, and 24 per cent lack knowledge and interest in local politics.[6]

A seat on the local council represents the height of participation for an amateur politician. The job has no salary. Councillors receive an attendance allowance but are expected to remain in the workaday world outside politics. The average councillor spends about twelve hours a week on political work, but leading councillors spend far more. Studies of local councillors find that most achieve a high degree of satisfaction from their work. Some see council work as a complement to other community activities; some see it as compensation for a dull job; others, such as retired persons and housewives, see council politics as a substitute for full-time employment. Because of the limited willingness of people to enter council politics, a determined Conservative or Labour activist has a reasonable chance in most parts of the country to become a councillor.

The government commission that sponsored these surveys of citizenship rejected the argument that the best way to reform local government was decentralization, increasing the number of elective offices, and bringing local government closer to the consumers of its services. Instead, it recommended amalgamating local authorities into larger units, resulting in fewer elective posts and a higher ratio of electors to representatives. The new councils took power in 1974. The amalgamation of smaller authorities was intended to improve the efficiency and effectiveness of local government services, and not to encourage participation in local affairs.[7]

The extent to which individuals are deemed to participate in central government depends upon the definition of participation. If government is to live up to its name, everyone must participate if only as a compliant subject. Virtually everyone does participate if participation is defined as paying taxes and drawing benefits. The mixed-economy welfare state provides benefits at every stage of life, from maternity and children's allowances through schooling,

[6] See Horton, *The Local Government Elector*, chs. 5–6; cf. Moss and Parker, *The Local Government Councillor*, chs. 4, 9.
[7] See below pp. 295ff.

housing, and health to a pension in old age and a death benefit for the next of kin. More than three-quarters of the population live in a household drawing a weekly cash benefit from government and even more are part of a family that annually enjoys such major welfare benefits as health care, education or a pension.[8]

Parliamentary elections provide the one opportunity a person has to participate directly in central government. Virtually every British citizen eighteen years old or over is eligible to vote. Citizens of Commonwealth countries from Australia to Zambia and of the Irish Republic are also entitled to vote while residing in Britain.[9] The burden of registration is undertaken by local government officials, and registers are revised annually to maintain accuracy. Election day is not a legal holiday, but the wide dispersal of polling stations, the compactness of the territory, and the individual sense of citizen duty result in a high turnout of voters by comparison with American standards, though not by European standards.

In ten general elections since 1950, turnout has averaged 77.4 per cent; when figures are adjusted to allow for the effect of mortality and other technical considerations, the average turnout is 81.3 per cent.[10] Turnout has been falling since 1959. Many who do not vote at an election are prevented from doing so by temporary illness or holidays. There is no substantial group of people who persistently refuse to vote because of apathy or disaffection. Englishmen are well advised to vote when a parliamentary election is held. Casting a ballot for a single candidate for one seat in the House of Commons is a person's only chance to participate in a nation-wide election.

Between elections people can be vicariously involved in national government by taking an interest in politics. Nineteen per cent of the electorate say they have a great deal of interest in politics outside an election campaign; at the other end of the scale, 34 per cent describe themselves as not much or not at all interested in politics. When voters are asked to identify major party politicians,

[8] See Richard Rose and Guy Peters, *Can Government Go Bankrupt?* (London: Macmillan, 1979), Table A3.2, and Central Statistical Office, *Social Trends* (London: HMSO, 1977), Vol. 8, pp. 110–12.

[9] See H. W. Wollaston, *Parker's Conduct of Parliamentary Elections* (London: Charles Knight & Son, 1970 edition) pp. 40ff.

[10] See Richard Rose, 'Britain: Simple Abstractions and Complex Realities', in R. Rose, *Electoral Behavior* (New York: Free Press, 1974), Table 5. For an exhaustive study of the subject, see Ivor Crewe, Tony Fox and Jim Alt, 'Non-Voting in British General Elections 1966–October 1974', in Colin Crouch, ed., *British Political Sociology Yearbook Vol. III*, pp. 38–109.

the median respondent names three persons; only 5 per cent can name three Conservative, three Labour and one Liberal front-bencher.[11] Because of its size, the working class constitutes a majority of those very interested in politics, as well as of those not at all interested.

Another way in which people can be vicariously involved in politics is by belonging to an organization that sometimes acts as a political pressure group. These organizations range in character from an anglers club concerned with the pollution of a local stream to the Automobile Association, representing motorists. An estimated 61 per cent of the population belong to at least one organization; 9 per cent belong to four or more groups. The most popular organizations are leisure, social, and sports clubs, but 19 per cent report that they belong to an 'issue' organization, that is, a trade union, a professional association, or a group concerned with a policy question. A total of 14 per cent are officers or committee members of a voluntary association. Although educated people are most likely to belong to an association, a majority of people in all age and educational strata belong to a voluntary association.[12]

Political parties provide one means by which individuals can participate in national politics. Both the Conservative and Labour parties maintain constituency associations throughout England, and the Liberals wish to do so. There are no restrictive entrance rules; the parties seek as many members as are willing to join. With a little effort, a person can become a ward secretary of a local party or a member of its general management committee. The great majority of Englishmen identify with a political party, but not so strongly that they become members. Both political parties define membership in terms of dues paid to constituency organizations. In the Labour Party, nearly nine-tenths of the party's 6.6 million nominal members are affiliated by trade-union headquarters. Party dues are paid as part of union dues; trade unionists automatically become party members unless they take the trouble to contract out of their union's wholesale application to the Labour Party. Many do not know that they belong to the Labour Party and some even vote Conservative or Liberal. In 1978 the Labour Party reported 659,000 nominal members joining independently of paying union

---

[11] Cf. Mark Abrams, 'Social Trends and Electoral Behaviour', *British Journal of Sociology*, XIII:3 (1962), p. 234, and the October 1974 British Election Survey, Deck 1: Col 54.

[12] See *The Local Government Elector*, pp. 113ff.

dues. The Conservatives do not claim to know how many members they have. A study of consituency associations conducted in 1975 estimated the actual number of individual members of the Labour Party at 300,000 and of the Conservative Party, 1,500,000. The Liberals have no more than 200,000 members.[13] For most party members, paying annual dues is the maximum extent of their participation in politics.

A variety of party and pressure group organizations are kept alive by the efforts of a small number of political activists, for whom politics is their principal avocation. A survey by Market and Opinion Research International concluded that 7 per cent of the electorate can be classified as political activists, taking part in at least five of ten common political activities. A majority of these activists vote, help in fund-raising efforts, urge people to vote, hold office in an organization, advise people to get in touch with an MP, make public talks and present their views to an MP. The activists are almost evenly divided between Conservative and Labour supporters. The activists are not an exact social cross-section of the population but include substantial numbers from all ages, classes, educational backgrounds, and both men and women. The activist is distinctive in what he or she *does* rather than for what he or she is.[14]

In the 1970s *ad hoc* protest groups appeared in local and national politics. Many of these groups reflect localized concern with a single issue, whether in a univeristy, or about a local council's failure to assure pedestrian safety at a busy crossroads. The concentration of politics in London has also made it possible for London-based protest organizations to appear as nation-wide organizations. In a city of seven million inhabitants, it is not especially difficult to attract several hundred people to a protest meeting on almost any kind of issue. One requires a cause, a speaker with a name or a recognizable status, and money to hire a hall and advertise the meeting. Overall, only 6 per cent of the electorate say they have taken part in a lawful street demonstration and even fewer in illegal protests.[15]

[13] See the report of the Houghton Committee, *Financial Aid to Political Parties* (London: HMSO, Cmnd. 6601, 1976), pp. 31ff. Note also *Gallup Political Index* No. 200 (March 1977) pp. 12–15.

[14] See Robert M. Worcester, 'The Hidden Activists', in Richard Rose, ed., *Studies in British Politics* (London: Macmillan, 1969), 3rd ed., and Robert M. Worcester and E. J. Dionne 'Political and Social Activism in Britain' (London: MORI unpublished manuscript, *c*. 1975).

[15] See Alan C. Marsh, *Protest and Political Consciousness* (London: Sage Publications, 1977), p. 45.

The majority of Englishmen participate in national politics by voting and belonging to a voluntary organization. (Table VI.2.) A number of indicators converge to show 5 to 14 per cent of the electorate regularly involved in politics. If holding elected office is the measure of being a politician, the proportion drops below one per cent. By this standard one could argue that the proportion of the adult population actively participating in politics in England today is scarcely higher than it was before the passage of democratic franchise reforms in the late nineteenth century.

TABLE VI.2 **Involvement in national politics**

	Estimated number of people	Estimated % of adult population
Eligible electorate, 1979	41,000,000	98
Voters, 1979	31,221,000	76
Organization members	24,000,000	61
Receiving weekly cash benefit	12,800,000	47
Great deal of interest in politics	8,000,000	19
Official post in organization	5,500,000	14
Political activists	2,800,000	7
Protest demonstrations	2,500,000	6
Individual party members	2,000,000	5
MP, senior civil servant	4,000	0.1

Source As cited in footnotes of text. Some figures are derived from surveys and others are precise counts; all have been rounded off.

There is more than one place in Table VI.2 where one can draw the line between politicians and those outside politics. For example, if officers of organizations are considered to be at least intermittently politicians, because their representative status enables them to voice pressure-group demands, more than five million citizens are politicians. Even if one reduces the total to activists or to those who have stood for election to local or national office, there remains the 'as many as/but only' problem. Does one say, 'as many as 2,800,000 people are political activists', or does one say, 'but only 2,800,000 people are political activists'? By any criterion other than a totalitarian one, active participants in politics constitute a limited but significant fraction of the Crown's subjects.

Central political roles

There are two contrasting approaches to the study of central political roles. Prescriptively, one might first define a political job in terms of specific tasks and skills, then consider how individuals might be recruited. This is the approach of management theory. Alternatively, one might proceed inductively, analysing the attributes that influence the recruitment of English politicians, and then ask: given their skills, what kind of job can they do? Because of the constraints of history and convention upon political recruitment, the inductive approach is more suitable.

The holders of central political roles can be grouped under three broad headings: Cabinet ministers, senior civil servants, and intermittent public persons. Members of Parliament are not central to government; they become so by attaining ministerial position. But ministers must be elected to Parliament before being selected for promotion. Civil servants first compete by examinations and then gain promotion by seniority plus selection. Some intermittent public persons depend upon patronage for appointment to public bodies, while others owe their prominence to holding office in major pressure groups independent of government.

Three generalizations can be made about recruitment to central political roles. Experience is positively valued. Starting early in a political career is almost a pre-condition of success. Civil servants normally enter Whitehall immediately after taking a university degree in their early twenties. Aspiring Cabinet ministers had better gain entry to the House of Commons at an early age, because an MP must usually accumulate seniority in the House of Commons before gaining a ministerial post. For example, members of Margaret Thatcher's first Cabinet in 1979 were on average thirty-three years old upon entering the Commons, and fifty-three upon appointment in 1979. In the first Cabinet of Harold Wilson in 1964, the average Labour appointee had entered the House at thirty-eight and was fifty-six when appointed minister. Intermittent public persons also serve long apprenticeships before gaining political eminence. For example, a trade union leader will usually enter his trade in adolescence and needs thirty to forty years to reach the general secretaryship of a union. In making appointments to the chairmanship of *ad hoc* government committees, Whitehall officials consider sound judgment to increase with age.

Secondly, persons who seek leading political roles are not expected to start at the bottom in local politics and work their way gradually to the top in London. Instead, early in a career an individual must gain 'cadet' status in a central political role, then gradually accumulate seniority and skill. The process might be described as 'working one's way sideways', inasmuch as seniority will carry a cadet politician a substantial distance forward. The process is most evident in the senior civil service, for no one is recruited from the ranks of local government. Similarly, Cabinet posts are not given to individuals because of their stature in local or regional politics, as might happen in a federal system such as America or Germany. Among MPs, 71 per cent have not had local government experience prior to election to Parliament. Among Cabinet ministers the proportion is higher.[16] The local councillor's office is the high point of a peripheral citizen's career; membership in Parliament is the beginning point for a central political role.

A third influence upon recruitment is geographical. MPs, senior civil servants, and most intermittent public persons spend all their working life in London. In industry and finance as in trade unions, London is the centre. Jobs elsewhere are regarded as in a backwater. MPs are not required to have lived in the constituency that nominates them or to take up residence there upon election. Among Conservative candidates selected for winnable constituencies, 22 per cent had a direct constituency connection; in the Labour Party the proportion is little more than one-quarter.[17] A defeated MP or candidate can move to another constituency to re-enter the House and regain national political status.

Election to the House of Commons is virtually a precondition for becoming a Cabinet minister. MPs are self-recruited, in the sense that aspirants for a parliamentary nomination are expected to put themselves forward. They are selected, in that nomination for winnable or safe seats involves competition among aspirants for the favour of the selection committee in the dominant party of a constituency. A young man anxious to take a central political role does not need to become an MP. He can make a more certain career in

---

[16] See Michael Rush, *The Selection of Parliamentary Candidates*, pp. 60, 181 and Peter G. Richards, *The Backbenchers* (London: Faber, 1972), p. 22. On the overlapping of local councillors' and MPs' roles in the scrutiny of constituents' problems, see Ronald Munroe, 'Where Representatives Meet: Conflict or Co-operation?', *Public Administration Bulletin*, No. 27 (August 1978).

[17] See Rush, *The Selection of Parliamentary Candidates*, pp. 74, 181.

Westminster by winning entry to the administrative civil service in his early twenties. Both Harold Wilson and Edward Heath were administrative civil servants before seeking entry to the House of Commons. About half the post-1945 Prime Ministers have shown sufficient academic ability to have won entry to the senior civil service instead of the Commons if they had wished.

The motives leading persons to seek election to Parliament are multiple, combining public and private concerns.[18] Case studies, statistical analyses, and novels have been written about the trials of entering the House of Commons. An MP, his parliamentary agent, his wife and his biographer might each emphasize a different motive. One thing is certain: ambition for power is not the sole motive. The majority of candidates at each general election are defeated, not elected. In the Liberal Party, defeat is so likely that the party's headquarters 'discourages any potential candidate who indicates he is interested in standing because he hopes to get into Parliament'. A study of Conservative and Labour candidates found that more than three-quarters of those defeated none the less considered their campaign enjoyable and satisfying.[19]

Once elected, upwards of three-quarters of MPs can count on a career of fifteen years or longer in the Commons, because most parliamentary seats are safe against electoral tides.[20] National influences determine the movement of much of the floating vote; an MP can do little to increase (or decrease) his majority. It is, moreover, unusual for a sitting MP to be denied the party's renomination. Career MPs constitute the pool of individuals eligible for a ministerial post when their party has a parliamentary majority.

In promoting individuals to a ministerial post, a Prime Minister may use any of three criteria: representatives, loyalty or competence.[21] An MP may be offered an appointment as a representative of women, Scots or of a political tendency within the parliamentary party. Even factional opponents may be offered posts to gain their

[18] Note the catalogue of motives in Sir Lewis Namier, *The Structure of Politics at the Accession of George III*, (London: Macmillan, 2nd edition, 1957), ch. I.

[19] See Dennis Kavanagh, *Constituency Electioneering in Britain* (London: Longmans, 1970), pp. 81ff, and Jorgen Rasmussen, *The Liberal Party: A Study of Retrenchment and Revival* (London: Constable, 1965), p. 212.

[20] See Jorgen Rasmussen, 'The Implications of Safe Seats for British Democracy', *Western Political Quarterly*, XIX:3 (1966).

[21] See Richard Rose, *The Problem of Party Government* (London: Macmillan, 1974), ch. 14, for a detailed development of points summarized here about the making of Cabinet ministers.

silence through collective responsibility. Loyalty to the Prime Minister is important to counterbalance potential opposition in the Cabinet and to encourage back-bench MPs in the belief that loyalty brings rewards. Competence is an abstract term. It begs the question: competence in what—parliamentary debate? administration? the subject matter of the department?

The discretion that a Prime Minister can exercise in recruiting ministers is limited by the fact that there are upwards of one hundred jobs to distribute among approximately two hundred MPs. The remainder of the party's back-benchers are ruled out of consideration by parliamentary inexperience, old age, ideological extremism, personal unreliability or even lack of interest in office. One analysis of Conservative and Labour MPs found that a chief requirement for securing office was survival in the Commons. A majority of all MPs elected three times or more achieved a ministerial post.[22] A Prime Minister is likely to spend as much time deciding what posts are to be offered individual MPs as in deciding which MPs are suited to office.

Experience of the Commons does not lead naturally to the work of a minister, as preparatory school leads to public school. The chief concerns of an MP are dealing with people and talking about ideas. These attributes are also useful in Whitehall, but a minister must have other skills as well: knowing how to handle the paper work required by a major administrative post; the ability to appraise policy alternatives, the consequences of which will not be clear until long after he has left office; and a capacity to relate political generalities to the specifics of a technical problem. A minister may find the transition from the back benches to government greater than the shift from being a party activist to a back-bench MP.[23]

An MP joining the government is usually first appointed to a junior ministerial post. Because the convention of ministerial responsibility places authority in one man, a junior minister will usually be given little responsibility by comparison with political overlords or senior civil servants. The job of a junior minister is not intended as a training ground for Cabinet ministers,[24] as a junior

[22] See P. W. Buck, *Amateurs and Professionals in British Politics, 1918–59* (Chicago: University Press, 1963), pp. 114ff.

[23] For an example of one minister's feelings of inadequacy in office after 19 years as a back-bench MP, see R. H. S. Crossman, *Diaries*.

[24] See D. J. Heasman, 'Ministers' Apprentices', *New Society*, 16 July 1964.

executive post in a non-governmental organization can be a conscious apprenticeship for higher responsibilities. A newly appointed minister must learn 'on the job' what to do.

When ministers are asked what they think their task is, nearly every minister makes some reference to policy making and to maintaining parliamentary support. Half think it important to protect or advance their department against other departments in Cabinet deliberations. Half emphasize the importance of maintaining morale and efficiency within their department. One-third stress the need for public relations work among pressure groups and the general public. Different definitions of the job lead to differences about the skills considered most important in recruiting ministers. Half think that a good minister is a man with a specialist's ability to handle Parliament and a gifted amateur's approach to the problems of his department. But the other half think that a specialist's knowledge of a department's tasks, plus general managerial ability, is most important.[25]

The recruitment of Cabinet ministers from the ranks of MPs ensures that they have had ample experience to meet one important task: handling parliamentary business. But the restriction of appointments to established MPs prevents a nation-wide canvass for persons with specialists' skills for particular posts. Little more than one-tenth of ministers are appointed to departments where they can claim some specialized knowledge.[26]

The one way in which a minister can be sure of learning about a department's work is to learn on the job. The amount of time required to learn the ropes of a department varies with its complexity. Anthony Crosland, a Labour minister with an unusually analytical mind, reckoned: 'It takes you six months to get your head properly above water, a year to get the general drift of most of the field, and two years really to master the whole of a department.' A Fulton Committee study reckoned that the time from appraising a policy to implementing a solution could be as much as five years. But the conventions of Prime Ministerial patronage result in the frequent reshuffling of ministers from department to department. From 1955 to 1970 the average minister in major departments stayed 2.2 years in one office. The rate of ministerial turnover has

[25] See Headey, *British Cabinet Ministers* (London: George Allen & Unwin, 1974), pp. 59ff.
[26] *Ibid.*, pp. 90ff.

been increasing since 1900; it is one of the highest in Western nations. In nearly every instance in which a minister is moved, he goes to a job in a department where he lacks previous experience. The process of 'on-the-job-learning' must start again.[27]

The recruitment of ministers has come under criticism as part of a general cry for reform. Industrialists argue the need for more businesslike ministers; economists, the need for more economic expertise; and some academics praise the American system of 'in-and-outers', with persons moving between the federal executive and large organizations outside Washington—whether state government, universities or profit-making companies. In 1964 Harold Wilson named five individuals without previous parliamentary experience to ministerial posts, a practice that had previously been followed only in wartime emergencies, when men with management experience were required to run the administrative apparatus of modern war. The most prominent appointee, Frank Cousins, resigned less than two years after his appointment. Edward Heath did not emulate the tactic in 1970, nor did Wilson or Thatcher repeat the practice. Reviewing the recruitment of ministers, F. M. G. Willson concludes, 'The pattern not only remains overwhelmingly similar to that established over the last hundred years, but if anything has moved slightly towards more orthodoxy in terms of parliamentary and administrative experience.'[28]

A very small proportion of those in central political roles are temporary recruits to a full-time post in government. The closed-shop conventions of Parliament virtually debar anyone from moving to a prominent ministerial post without an apprenticeship in the House of Commons. In addition, the civil service has been opposed on principle to recruiting staff from outside its ranks, especially at higher levels. It is argued that such recruitment could make high-paying Whitehall jobs patronage plums to be awarded to party sympathizers. Civil servants expect that they will receive the top jobs in Whitehall as the reward for years of accumulated seniority.

Temporary administrative appointments of a mixture of econom-

---

[27] See Rose, *The Problem of Party Government*; Crosland's discussion in Maurice Kogan, *The Politics of Education* (Harmondsworth: Penguin, 1971), pp. 155ff; *The Fulton Committee*, Vol. II, p. 20ff; and, more generally, Valentine Herman and James E. Alt, eds., *Cabinet Studies: A Reader* (London: Macmillan, 1975).

[28] 'Entry to the Cabinet, 1959–1968', *Political Studies*, XVIII:2 (1970), p. 238. See also, by the same author, 'The Routes of Entry of New Members of the British Cabinet, 1868–1958', *ibid.*, VII:3 (1959).

ists and journalists were attempted by the 1964–70 Labour government. Samuel Brittan, an economic journalist turned Whitehall irregular, concluded from his experience that the contribution of any irregular is limited by the vice of his virtue. The more novel the perspective he brings to Whitehall, the greater the things he must learn in order to operate effectively within the confines of Whitehall. Yet the more an individual learns, the less he has a distinctive contribution to make. New men by themselves cannot make a 'new' style of government. To change government they must learn the strengths as well as observe the weaknesses of the old ways.[29]

In the 1970 Conservative government, and subsequently in the 1974–9 Labour government, special advisers were recruited from outside Parliament and the civil service. The advisers have been intended to compensate for the tendency of ministers to become so involved in administrative complexities that they ignore the broader concerns of the party they claim to represent. Their appearance as political experts is thus a reversal of the trend of the 1960s, when it was assumed that technical expertise was lacking in Whitehall. Civil servants have grudgingly accepted political advisers in small numbers.[30]

The recruitment of senior civil servants has been a controversial subject for generations. Most of the controversy has concerned the class origins of recruits to the Home Civil Service and, even more, to the Foreign Office. Less attention has been given to the skills required of recruits. Lord Macaulay stated the traditional view in commenting on civil service reform in the middle of the nineteenth century:

> We believe that men who have been engaged up to twenty-one or twenty-two in studies which have no immediate connection with the business of any profession, and of which the effect is merely to open, to invigorate and to enrich the mind, will generally be found in the business of every profession superior to men who have, at eighteen or nineteen, devoted themselves to the special studies of their calling.[31]

[29] See Samuel Brittan, 'The Irregulars' in Richard Rose, ed., *Policy-Making in Britain* (London: Macmillan, 1969), and varied comments in Hugh Thomas, ed., *Crisis in the Civil Service* (London: Anthony Blond, 1968).
[30] See Rudolf Klein and Janet Lewis, 'Advice and Dissent in British Government'.
[31] Quoted in Anthony Sampson, *Anatomy of Britain* (London: Hodder & Stoughton, 1962), pp. 222–3.

For a quarter-century after the Second World War, the majority of young recruits to the administrative class of the civil service could rightfully claim that their educational specialization in Greek, Latin and medieval and modern history had been intended as a general enrichment of the mind, and not as a specific preparation for the work of the civil service.

In 1968 the Fulton Committee recommended that administrative class civil servants should have 'relevant' knowledge of the work of government, 'minds disciplined by the social studies, the mathematical and physical sciences, the biological sciences or in the applied and engineering sciences'. It did not, however, indicate why scientific or engineering subjects should, of themselves, be more relevant to the work of Whitehall administrators. The Committee's uncertainties about what a civil servant should know were revealed when the Committee failed to agree about a straightforward way to test for 'relevant' knowledge.[32] The Civil Service Commission has since remedied this deficiency. Candidates for the highest administrative posts are now examined for their ability to summarize lengthy prose papers; to resolve a problem by fitting specific facts to general regulations; to draw inferences from a simple table of social statistics; to follow logical diagrams; and to display verbal facility.

Because bright young men enter the civil service with no specialized skill and spend decades before reaching senior posts, role socialization is specially important. Civil service recruits, whether their fathers were coal miners or members of the aristocracy, are expected to learn what to do by following the procedures used by those senior to them. Senior civil servants determine the promotion of their juniors. Co-option ensures the transmission of established assumptions about *how* government work should be transacted; it need not imply agreement about what should be done in particular policy areas. An individual gains promotion because of knowing how things should be done and not because of views about policies. A young civil servant is inoculated against deep involvement in subject matter by frequent transfers from post to post; on average an administrator is 2.8 years in a particular job.[33]

In the course of a working life, civil servants become as much

---

[32] See *The Fulton Committee*, Vol. I, pp. 27ff; and Appendix E, especially p. 162.
[33] See *The Fulton Committee*, Vol. II, pp. 20ff. On the formal training of civil servants, see E. Grebenik, 'The Civil Service College: The First Year', *Public Administration*, L (Summer 1972).

specialists as economists, lawyers or scientists. They become specialists in a difficult and abstruse field: the management of Whitehall. Their knowledge of public administration extends far beyond what can be learned in textbooks.

They know how to deal with the Treasury in annual negotiations about departmental estimates, how to remind a minister tactfully that his preferred policy may be a political disaster, how to produce a cover-up answer for an awkward parliamentary question, and how to arrive at a departmental policy when the mind of the minister is blank.

The more sophisticated critics of the civil service do not deprecate the value of knowing how to work the Whitehall machine. But they question whether this knowledge is sufficient. Much of the work of Whitehall concerns large-scale management. While civil servants are often advising others who manage nationalized industries or local authorities, their careers do not include experience in working for government outside the departmental framework of Whitehall.

More than a decade of criticism of senior civil servants as individuals, combined with visible and increasing difficulties in the policy outputs of government, has been reflected by dissatisfaction and demoralization within Whitehall. Many younger civil servants have begun to question whether the work they have to do is what they want to do. In 1966 a study undertaken for the Fulton Committee found that one-fifth of those recruited to the administrative class a decade earlier had resigned, and another fifth were applying for jobs outside the civil service. Subsequently, a study of recruits two years after they had joined the administrative class found that about half were ready to consider leaving the civil service if a good job came up elsewhere.[34] It would be an unintended and unpleasant irony if the shortcomings of the British economy in the 1970s encouraged dissatisfied younger civil servants to remain in Whitehall by default, because there were few satisfactory employment opportunities elsewhere.

Many individuals are only intermittently involved in politics and may not even think of themselves in a political role. If all persons holding government appointments were defined as political, then such diverse persons as the Archbishop of Canterbury, the Director General of the British Broadcasting Corporation, the Regius Pro-

[34] See R. G. S. Brown, 'Fulton and Morale', *Public Administration*, XLIV (Summer 1971), p. 193; R. A. Chapman, 'Profile of a Profession' in *The Fulton Committee*, Vol. III:2, pp. 1, 13; Peta E. Sheriff, 'Outsiders in a Closed Career', *Public Administration*, L (Winter 1972).

fessor of Greek at Oxford and the Astronomer Royal would be considered politicians. If challenged, each would probably deny that he was a politician, yet also claim that he carried out his duties with regard for the public interest.

Tens of thousands of people are recruited into part-time government service by appointments to bodies concerned with public policy. Most part-time appointments are without salary. Civic-minded people are expected to give advice gladly on a council, committee, or commission, or assist law enforcement as lay magistrates. Many members of government committees sit by virtue of full-time employment in an organization affected by the committee's deliberations. Pressure-group officials are involved in politics informally as well as formally. Pressure-group appointees are often balanced by having as committee chairmen a 'lay gent', a person whose amateurism implies neutrality in his conduct of government work. The Treasury is said to keep a list of 'the great and the good' to act as lay representatives of the public on specialist committees.[35]

An official tabulation of public boards staffed by intermittent public persons found 310 variously denominated bodies with a total of more than 10,000 full and part-time members appointed by the Whitehall departments 'sponsoring' the bodies. Most individuals held only one appointment and this in an area of their interest or expertise.[36] Less than half the appointments carry a part-time salary or honorarium; the holders of other posts may be rewarded by an honour, ranging from the lowly rank of OBE (Order of the British Empire) up to a 'K' (that is, knighthood) or, occasionally, a seat in the House of Lords.

Intermittent public persons come from a wide variety of backgrounds. Analysis of a sample of members of *ad hoc* Royal Commissions shows that nearly half (46 per cent) had social origins so ordinary that they did not note their father's status or occupation in standard biographical sources. While 42 per cent had an Oxford or Cambridge education, 30 per cent had no education beyond secondary school. Among those on Royal Commissions, less than half were drawn from the old professions, such as the law, the civil

[35] See K. C. Wheare, *Government by Committee*, (Oxford: Clarendon Press, 1955) pp. 15ff; Peter G. Richards, *Patronage in British Government* (London: George Allen & Unwin, 1963).
[36] Public Appointments Unit, Civil Service Department, *A Directory of Paid Public Appointments Made by Ministers* (London: HMSO, 1976); Alan Doig, 'Public Bodies and Ministerial Patronage', *Parliamentary Affairs*, XXXI:1 (1978).

service, Parliament, landowners or the military, even though many Royal Commissions are concerned with the reform of old established institutions. The varied careers of these recruits to intermittent public posts suggest that they bring to Westminster a wider variety of viewpoints than are found within the ranks of full-time politicians.[37]

The varied forms of intermittent political participation can best be shown by giving short biographies of a few such prominent public figures.

Lord Goodman. Born 1913. Educated at secondary school in London, University of London and Cambridge. Solicitor. Entered Royal Artillery as enlisted man, 1939; left as Major, 1945. Solicitor to Harold Wilson for various personal matters. Chairman, Arts Council of Great Britain, 1965–72. Member, Royal Commission on Working of Tribunals of Enquiry (Evidence) Act, 1966; Chairman, Committee of Inquiry on Charity Law, 1974. Member, British Council, 1967—; President, National Book League, 1972—; Chairman, Observer Newspaper Trust, 1967–76; Newspaper Publisher's Association, 1970–75; Member, Industrial Reorganization Corporation, 1969–71; Chairman, Housing Corporation, 1973–7; Chairman, English National Opera, 1977—; Master, University College, Oxford since 1976. Created Life Peer, 1965.

Len Murray. Born 1922. Educated Wellington Grammar School, University of London, National Council of Labour Colleges, Oxford. Joined Economic Department of Trades Union Congress, 1947, rising to become General Secretary, 1973. Member: Social Science Research Council, 1965–70; National Economic Development Council, 1973—; National Savings Committee, 1974—; Committee to Review the functioning of Financial Institutions, 1977—; Governor: National Institute of Economic and Social Research, 1968; London School of Economics, 1970; Visiting Fellow, Nuffield College, Oxford, 1974—; Vice-President, European Trade Union Confederation, 1974—; Created Privy Councillor, 1976.

Lady Plowden. Born *c.* 1910. Educated Downe House. Director, Trust House Forte Ltd., 1961–72. Chairman, Central Advisory Council for Education (England) 1963–6. Justice of Peace,

---

[37] Calculated from data in Charles J. Hanser, *Guide to Decision: The Royal Commission* (Totowa, N.J.: Bedminster Press, 1965), Appendix 3, an analysis of members of every sixth Royal Commission, 1900–64.

1962–71. Chairman of Governors: Phillippa Fawcett College of Education, 1967–76; Governor, BBC, 1970–75; Member, Houghton Inquiry into Pay of Teachers, 1974. Advisory Committee for Education of Romany and other Travellers; Working Ladies Guild; National Theatre Board, 1970—; Chairman, Independent Broadcasting Authority, 1975—; Created Life Peeress, 1978.

Different as the careers of these three public persons are, all have two things in common. None has ever been a candidate for elective office, nor held a post as an established civil servant. Their absence from conventional categories of politicians does not involve them any less in central political roles.

Politicians and society

Traditionally, the leaders of English society were simultaneously leading social, political, and economic personages. Aristocrats born into high social status could claim seats in Parliament by virtue of noble birth and financial eminence by virtue of inherited wealth, plus such riches and honours as might be added by their own efforts. When the chief tasks of government were traditional tasks, social leaders could easily double in political roles. The Industrial Revolution not only created specialized economic institutions but also increased the specialized work of government. The twentieth century has accelerated the rise of the full-time professional politician, just as it has brought professionalization to many other social roles, from sport to scholarship.[38]

Politicians and students of politics may feel that political leaders are superior to economic leaders—but businessmen, economists, and trade unionists may believe the opposite. Those with inherited social status may feel superior to both and disdain a career in politics or industry. The attractions of public office may be weighed against the attractions of other work and found wanting. Even more important, the attractions may not even be considered, because of the repute of politics or because of an Englishman's positive interest in things non-political. Political, economic and status leaders may each be amazed that the others regard their rewards as worth seeking.

In contemporary England it is necessary to ask: to what extent are those who have achieved high social status or leading economic positions recruited into politics? This is not a question about the

[38] See J. M. Lee, *Social Leaders and Public Persons* (Oxford: Clarendon Press, 1963).

social origins of politicians but rather about the political inclinations of those with high non-political status.

The qualities and achievements that confer social status are today multiple and diverse. There does not appear to be any agreement about what it is that puts 'top' people on top.[39] Prestige can be accorded persons on grounds as different as traditional honour (the Queen), statesmanship (a former Prime Minister in old age), television personalities (David Frost), and achievement in sports, whether one is a jockey in the sport of kings or a football hero in the sport of the working class. People with very different criteria of prestige live without conflict because they do not meet. For example, the wife of an Army colonel welcomed a newcomer to a village of five hundred in rural Oxfordshire with the statement that, except for three families, 'nobody' lived in the village, that is, no one else significant in terms of her criteria of status. In working-class communities, people with middle-class attributes may find themselves similarly isolated.[40]

Individuals with high social status cannot claim to govern by virtue of their celebrity. They may tell the government what to do in a public speech or a private conversation, but this right is also claimed by political activists, whatever their social status. To be effective politically, social leaders must translate their diffuse status into specific public office.

Interest in politics is a minority taste among persons of high social status. Among members of the House of Lords, about one-third do not bother to attend a single sitting in a year, and only one-fifth attend as many as half the sittings in a session of the House of Lords. Moreover, hereditary peers are less likely to attend and speak in the Lords than newly appointed life peers.[41] The proportion of arts graduates seeking to enter the senior civil service is but a small fraction of each year's crop of graduates. Similarly, the proportion of Etonians in Cabinet is an infinitesimal fraction of Old Etonians in London society at any one time.

In the days before franchise reform, office holding could be considered a form of *noblesse oblige.* Now it means seeking favour

[39] See National Opinion Polls, *Monthly Bulletin,* No. 109 (June 1972).
[40] Margaret Stacey, *Tradition and Change* (London: Oxford Univ. Press, 1960), p. 145. See also Brian Jackson and Dennis Marsden, *Education and the Working Class,* pp. 53ff.
[41] See Bernard Crick, *The Reform of Parliament* (London: Weidenfeld and Nicolson, 2nd ed.), p. 137, and *Social Trends,* Vol. 8, 1977, Table 14.6.

among the democratic mass. Individuals may prefer to pursue less controversial and plebeian activities. This is especially true to urban government. A study of local notables in Bristol found that 73 per cent had never thought of seeking election to the local council, and only 11 per cent had become councillors. They avoided politics because of a dislike of party politics; many also held councillors in low esteem as a group.[42] The Conservative Party in Parliament has changed too: 'The pre-war influence of aristocrats and of very rich capitalists has given way to the dominance of the ordinary upper middle classes.'[43]

The incentives for translating diffuse status into political position must be weighed against drawbacks. For a person of high social status, the title of MP confirms but may not enhance his prestige. A politically important position in the civil service may be looked upon as less prestigious than a politically unimportant post in the Royal Household. In status terms, political life is most rewarding to those who *lack* high inherited status. For them, to become an MP is to rise in status. For some people, even being a defeated parliamentary candidate can confer prestige. Because of its traditional status, an administrative job in the Treasury would have more social status than managing a factory, because the former work is for public good, not private profit.

Once an individual has been recruited into politics, prestige is not so much measured by social origins as by political accomplishments. A local councillor will have more prestige than a ward secretary. MPs have more political prestige than a local government councillor, and ministers sworn into the Privy Council take precedence over back-bench MPs. The civil service has a much larger number of status gradations and status symbols. The most successful of politicians and civil servants raise their social status by earning honours or titles for their political and public service. The honours list, issued twice a year by the monarch on the advice of the Prime Minister of the day, can be used to provide incentives to undertake arduous intermittent public duties. When asked what he would do with his newly conferred middle-rank honour, one public person smiled and

[42] See Roger V. Clements, *Local Notables and the City Council* (London: Macmillan, 1969), pp. 51, 156ff and D. C. Miller, 'Decision-Making Cliques in Community Power Structures', *American Journal of Sociology*, LXIV:6 (1958).

[43] David Butler and Michel Pinto-Duschinsky, 'The Conservative Elite, 1918–1978: Does Unrepresentativeness Matter?' (Unpublished duplicated manuscript, Oxford, 1978), p. 16.

said, 'work to improve it'. Honours can also soften the blow of forced retirement. A Cabinet minister fired for inefficiency or old age can be consoled with a peerage.

The financial rewards that politics can offer are limited, and usually less than what could be earned by the same effort in other occupations. An MP's salary of £9,450 a year is much less than that of an administrative class civil servant or a political journalist. A Cabinet minister's salary (£19,650) is low by comparison with salaries paid persons with similar responsibilities outside government. The heads of nationalized industries are paid more than the Prime Minister—and even then can complain that their pay is less than they could earn in private industry. In private industry success usually brings valuable capital gains. A politician cannot realize money profits when the 'stock' of his party rises. When it falls, he loses both office and official salary.

While the financial rewards of politics are not comparable with the financial rewards of business, politicians do have one thing in common with contemporary economic leaders: they must specialize in their work to succeed. It is no longer easy, as was the case two or three generations ago, for an individual to move back and forth between careers in several different worlds.

The proportion of businessmen with any political experience is limited, and has been falling greatly. A study of company chairmen, the most 'political' office in a large company, found that before the First World War a sizable minority of about three in ten had been an MP at some stage in their career. But in contemporary England, only one company chairman in 25 had been a Member of Parliament, usually well prior to becoming a company chairman. Another study of industrial managers concludes, 'All in all top managers have not had marked experience outside industry, outside their own firm, or outside their own line of work.'[44]

Most steel men, for example, have worked all their lives in the steel industry. They are not intermittently steel men and politicians: their very lack of political skills has been demonstrated by the 'unprofessional' (in the political sense) nature of their campaign against nationalization. Of the 164 directors of the dozen steel

[44] R. V. Clements, *Managers* (London: George Allen & Unwin, 1958), p. 151; Philip Stanworth and Anthony Giddens, 'An Economic Elite: A Demographic Profile of Company Chairmen', in Stanworth and Giddens, eds., *Elites and Power in British Society* (London: Cambridge University Press, 1974), pp. 87, 90.

194   RECRUITING PARTICIPANTS

companies that were privately owned prior to nationalization in the late 1960s, only 5 had ever been MPs. The only company with a board of directors having substantial political experience had acquired this asset by recruiting very senior former civil servants.[45]

Trade union leaders, like businessmen, have dedicated a working lifetime to their job. Unlike businessmen, their institutions are integrally involved in party politics, because unions are almost invariably affiliated to the Labour Party. It is unheard of for a union leader to be a Conservative, whereas a minority of businessmen are Labour supporters. Some union leaders who are not Labour Party supporters prefer the Communist Party or other Marxist groups. While trade union leaders and Labour MPs are meant to support each other—or at least recognize a common Conservative opponent—there are strict lines of demarcation between the industrial and political wings of the Labour movement. Union leaders are very rarely MPs; of the 38 members of the Trades Union Congress General Council in 1978, not one was an MP. Similarly, union leaders cannot sit on the National Executive Committee of the Labour Party, because its monthly meetings occur at the same time as that of the General Council of the TUC. The leaders send their deputies to NEC meetings. Unions sponsor more than 100 Labour MPs, but few of these are national officers of their union, and a union member, once elected to Parliament, exchanges hopes of rising in the union hierarchy for ambitions of parliamentary success.

Industrial firms and City banks, like trade unions and Co-operative societies, are not anxious to see able young men in their employment seek parliamentary careers. When this happens, it is usually assumed that the aspiring politician will lose his chance of promotion to high office in the employing organization. Just as the House of Commons is jealous about the need for a minister to have served an apprenticeship on the back benches, so those in industry, commerce, and the trade unions expect a person to have acquired experience in economic affairs before being rewarded with a top position.

An examination of the careers of Cabinet ministers since 1945 emphasizes the distance between political and economic leadership. No leader from the business world has been a senior minister since the end of the Second World War, and only two leading trade union

[45] See Richard Rose, *Influencing Voters* (London: Faber & Faber, 1967), pp. 147ff.

officials have sat in Labour Cabinets (Ernest Bevin, 1945–51, and Frank Cousins, 1964–6). In Harold Wilson's 1964 Cabinet, no one could be described as a businessman by occupation; seven were trade unionists. By the time Wilson left office in 1976, his Cabinet had become more professionalized; there was but one trade unionist. In Margaret Thatcher's 1979 Cabinet, few ministers were businessmen by occupation; no leader from the business world sat there.

Similarly, the number of ministers with high social status has declined substantially since 1945. In the 1945 Labour government, there were four products of major public schools, and in Sir Winston Churchill's 1951 Cabinet, 6 of 16 Cabinet posts were held by members of the House of Lords and many were at major public schools. In the 1974 Labour Cabinet, the only members from the House of Lords were those practically required to sit there, the Lord Chancellor and the Leader of the House of Lords. In 1979, Mrs. Thatcher appointed three peers to her first Cabinet.

Intensive apprenticeship is a prerequisite for success in many aspects of English life today. Just as a Cabinet minister must usually spend years as an MP, so a bishop must serve as a clergyman, a general as a lieutenant, a professor as a university lecturer and a managing director must work under the authority of others. The result of specialization is that leadership positions are today far more differentiated in England than they were at the beginning of political reform, when the local lord might also appoint the local clergy, lead the militia, sit as a magistrate and send his son to the House of Commons, while himself attending debates in the House of Lords. After years of interviewing men in leading positions in many different areas of English life, Anthony Sampson concluded:

> My own fear is not that the Establishment in Britain is too close, but that it is not close enough, that the circles are overlapping less and less and that one half of the ring has very little contact with the other half.[46]

Selective recruitment

The extent to which political recruitment is selective depends upon the size of the political class within society. Nothing could be more

[46] Sampson, *Anatomy of Britain*, p. 632 and end papers. If Sampson had included leaders in local government or leaders in Scotland, Wales and Northern Ireland in his 'British' study, the lack of contact would have been even greater.

selective than a parliamentary election that results in one person becoming Prime Minister of a country of 55 million people. Yet nothing is considered more representative, because an election is the one occasion in which every adult Englishman can participate in politics with equal effect. The greater the scope of activities defined as political, the greater is the number of people who must participate in politics. Growing government intervention in the economy has made company directors and shop stewards at least intermittently politicians. Yet their economic position gives them freedom to act independently of government. Workers can vote with their feet by an unofficial strike. Businessmen can vote with their wallets by investing money outside the United Kingdom.

The most analysed features of political recruitment in England are the social origins of politicians. Whatever the criterion chosen —age, sex, education or occupation—politicians differ in profile from those whom they represent. If the good fortune of Old Etonians in gaining a disproportionate number of nominations in safe Conservative seats is one form of 'class nepotism',[47] then trade-union sponsorship of workers in safe Labour seats can also be seen as class nepotism, albeit favouring a different class. Today, the most significant social change in the recruitment of Cabinet ministers is the increasing emphasis upon university education, resulting in a decline of working-class ministers in Labour Cabinets, and opening up Conservative cabinets to politicians without a prestigious public school education.[48]

Knowledge of the social origins of politicians cannot, however, be used to predict confidently the outlooks of individual politicians. If social origins were all powerful, then Conservative MPs would hardly ever disagree, because they are socially similar. Determinism would deny the existence of politics—that is, disagreement about issues—within the Conservative Party. Yet the Conservatives are never all of one mind. For example, in the late 1950s Harold Macmillan suffered the resignation of three Old Etonians from his government on political grounds. Their replacements were also Old Etonians. In the Labour Party, disagreements are frequent, but they are not easily related to social characteristics. The radical left-wing

[47] H. R. G. Greaves, *The British Constitution* (London: Allen & Unwin, 2nd ed., 1948), p. 164.
[48] See e.g. R. W. Johnson, 'The British Political Elite 1955–1972', *European Journal of Sociology*, XIV:1 (1973), and Dennis Kavanagh, in William B. Gwyn and Richard Rose, eds., *Britain—Progress and Decline*.

MP with a public school and Oxford education, like Anthony Benn, is as familiar as the working-class MP with a conservative view on many major issues. Labour politicians with non-prestigious social backgrounds are sometimes more conservative politically because less secure socially, seeking to prove that Socialists can govern just as well as (and even, just like) the well born.

Like success in polo, success in national politics is ultimately due to skill and experience. But the readiness and opportunity to play the game and develop the skills are not determined simply by natural aptitudes. They depend also upon particular personal and family circumstances, as well as upon general social characteristics.

The resulting contrast between the egalitarian basis of the electoral franchise and the selective nature of political recruitment is undoubted. Its political significance is, however, controversial. Economic efficiency dictates that some persons be selected to specialize in major political offices. The need for competent government justifies selection for some posts, as in the civil service, by criteria that favour university graduates. Yet the need for communication between representatives and the represented—by imaginative sympathy as well as by face-to-face dialogue—implies the need to select some politicians because they are socially representative of the electorate.[49]

Debates about the recruitment of politicians cannot be resolved by stating that competence should be the criterion for selection. This begs the question: What is competence? In recruiting for the civil service, academic achievement is the customary sign of competence. Experience is highly valued for promotion. Seniority not only provides an impersonal basis for selection but is also proof that an individual has undergone lengthy socialization into the norms of Whitehall. MPs too gain preferment by demonstrating to the Prime Minister and the Chief Whip that they can conform to the expectations specific to parliamentary and party politics. They gain promotion by demonstrating skills specific to Whitehall and Westminster, and not by conforming to the expectations of their former public school headmaster or their parents.

The openness of the political class to new recruits, however unlikely their backgrounds, has caused changes in the social character of politicians to be gradual. This gradualness has made it easy to

[49] For an expansion of these criteria for recruiting governors, see Robert A. Dahl, *After the Revolution?* (New Haven: Yale University Press, 1970).

transmit informal norms of political behaviour from generation to generation. The importance of past outlooks is intensified by the lengthy period of role socialization that career politicians must undergo. Civil servants spend most of their adult lifetime being socialized into Whitehall norms *before* receiving senior posts. MPs undergo role socialization for a decade or more before becoming important ministers. This continuity helps make the routine work of government, including party politics, move forward easily. Each politician knows what he can and cannot do within the confines of his current role, and what should be done to secure promotion. The resulting continuity is impressive, whether it is viewed as a means of preserving national traditions or as an obstacle to change when unfamiliar political problems arise.

In the 1980s, optimists hope that the recruitment of innovators from outside the familiar pathways to office might resolve some of the chronic difficulties that have plagued British government for a generation. Pessimists fear that only a time of national crisis would permit this, and that in any event the greater need is to ensure the continuity of institutions and traditions, lest worse befall through change.

VII

Communication and Non-communication

A parliamentary minister is a man trained by elaborate practice not to blurt out crude things.

Communication is the hyphen that joins parts of the political system. Government wishes its subjects to know what is expected of them and needs information about what citizens are doing and thinking. Citizens wish government to know what they want or, at least, what they will not stand for. Because politics is about differences in opinion, communication does not resolve conflicts. With perfect knowledge of everyone's views, it would still be necessary to decide which should prevail. Non-communication can also be decisive. A minister cannot act without knowledge that a problem exists, and a voter may ignore the views of politicians.

Political communication is simple in outline form: Who says what to whom how?[1] A sender transmits messages to an audience through one or more channels or media. The channels of communication include public media, such as the press, television and Parliament, and private media, such as letters and conversations in the corridors of Whitehall. The influence of an audience tends to vary inversely with its size: small private audiences usually include more influentials than mass audiences reached through television. Only at election time does a mass audience determine political outcomes.

The roles of communicator and audience are often exchanged. Those who speak often, such as MPs, are also expected to listen to those who seek to influence them. Those who usually listen, such as voters, can speak at elections. The dynamics of the policy process often require politicians to propose a course of action, then listen for reaction from those affected. Once reactions are registered, they can speak again, revising ideas in the light of what they have learned in a continuing feed-back process.

Every political figure, whether a politician or an ordinary citizen, is part of both horizontal and vertical communications networks.

[1] See Colin Seymour-Ure, *The Political Impact of Mass Media* (London: Constable, 1974), ch. 1–2.

Horizontal communication involves persons of a similar political status, such as Cabinet ministers, meeting together. Vertical communication involves communication between individuals differing in their political status. For example, a minister for employment must ensure that his views reach down to the local office where the unemployed live. Reciprocally, a citizen's views must travel up to where decisions are taken.

The greater the number of horizontal levels and vertical channels in the communications process, the greater the opportunity for distortion. In so far as messages move simultaneously through many channels, redundancy makes it less likely that a message will be lost; it also increases the burden of monitoring information. The greater a person's political involvement, the more complex his communications network will be. In theory, this offers more information. But it also creates a difficulty in attending to all the information that flows to, around, or by a person.

Trying to keep political discussions quiet also creates difficulties. Not only is there the risk that private negotiations will leak to the press, but also of a loss of ideas available in an open discussion. For example, in the period 1964–7 the Labour government did not wish to discuss the possibility of devaluing the pound, fearing that news of this possibility would itself lead to a speculative run on the pound. Devaluation was none the less under consideration in the Treasury, but, as one minister concerned noted, it was 'a very difficult subject to discuss because it was absolutely essential that nobody should know that it was being discussed'.[2]

In the liberal model of English politics, government is expected to communicate freely because the public has the right to know. The greater the flow of information, the better informed the public is expected to be. As the public is meant to be the ultimate arbiter of policy, better information is also expected to make the actions of government better. The Whitehall model, by contrast, takes a very different view of supply–demand relationships. Information is assumed to be a scarce commodity, and 'like all scarce commodities, it is not freely exchanged'.[3] Publicity is thought to be costly, not only because of the time required to carry out extensive public-relations

[2] George Brown, *In My Way*, (Harmondsworth: Penguin, 1972) p. 105. See also Peter Jay, 'Devaluation—Who was to Blame?', *The Times*, 23 November 1967; Henry Brandon, *In the Red* (London: Deutsch, 1966), p. 43.

[3] Samuel Brittan, *Steering the Economy* (London: Secker & Warburg, 1969), p. 29.

campaigns but also because public discussion of difficult policy questions might interfere with private Whitehall negotiations. Many laws and conventions assume publicity is 'not in the public interest'.[4] In the words of David Butler, an academic and media commentator on politics, 'Conducting the whole business of advising and policy-forming in public just wouldn't work'. In the blunter words of a Foreign Office official: 'It is no business of any official to allow the government to be embarrassed. That is who we are working for.'[5]

In this chapter, attention focuses first upon the mass public: to what extent do individuals have political views that they wish to communicate to government? The second section examines the structure of the public media—broadcasting and the press—and how they communicate information about public affairs. Horizontal communication within government, the topic of the third part of this chapter, depends to a large extent upon what is *not* communicated. The costs and benefits of the distinctive Whitehall approach to political communication are reviewed in conclusion.

Public opinion

Discussion of the role that public opinion ought to play in government usually starts from the assumption that members of the public have opinions to communicate, and that there are no obstacles in translating public opinion into public policy. Both these assumptions are belied by the evidence.

Every survey of public opinion first divides citizens into two groups: those who have an opinion about a given issue, and those who do not. The proportion of opinionated citizens is likely to be highest for issues immediately concerning the great mass of the population. For example, when people are asked whether or not they are satisfied with their standard of living, 99 per cent usually state a view. When they are asked to evaluate how well government handles different issues, the proportion of don't knows rises. When voters are asked to choose between alternative policies for handling a problem, the proportion of don't knows tends to be even higher.[6] Moreover, if the same question is put to the same person at two

[4] The title of a book by David Williams (London: Hutchinson, 1965).
[5] Quoted by Anthony Sampson, from a 1970 Official Secrets Act Trial, in *The New Anatomy of Britain* (London: Hodder & Stoughton, 1971), p. 369. See also David Butler, 'Cabinet Secrets', *The Listener*, 29 February 1968.
[6] See the monthly *Gallup Political Index*.

different points in time, a different answer may be given, even though no major political events have occurred to cause a change in outlook. Some political opinions expressed are almost random responses to passing events (including an opinion survey), and not opinions held strongly enough to justify action.

In so far as opinions are meant to be based on knowledge, there is good reason for many to withhold judgment on issues of the day. In nineteenth-century England, it was probably easier for the electorate to understand issues than it is today. There were fewer big political problems facing government, and often those required a straight decision in principle, for instance, whether or not to expand the franchise. Today, there are many more problems defined as political. The alternatives among which the government must choose are complex, and many choices involve highly technical considerations. For example, most voters do not inform themselves about the fine points of Keynesian, monetarist or other models of the economy. They are concerned with political goals, for instance, the achievement of steady prices and a rising standard of living, and not with technical means to these ends.

Knowledge of politics reflects interest in politics; the higher the interest, the more likely a person is to hold opinions about issues. There are many reasons for citizens not to take an interest in politics or even to avoid discussing the subject. People may feel that talking about politics leads to arguments, threatens friendships, or reveals civic ignorance. Low interest may also reflect reasoned calculation. Because the ordinary individual can exercise so little political influence, it is not economical to spend substantial sums and many hours each week reading books, papers, and periodicals specializing in political information. Instead, the best value-for-money strategy is to delegate responsibility for gathering information to full-time politicians.[7] A citizen need only acquire sufficient information about competing parties to choose between them. This knowledge may be gained free by living where one political party is constantly referred to as the party for 'people like us'. During election campaigns, television, the press and conversations will remind voters which party best suits their predispositions.

When individuals hold views on public issues, their opinions can affect their voting behaviour only if one party is perceived as differ-

[7] See Anthony Downs, *An Economic Theory of Democracy* (New York: Harper & Row, 1957).

ent from and superior to the other in its policies. In order to avoid giving offence to sections of the electorate, British party leaders may avoid taking a clear-cut position on a current controversy, such as the choice between trying to reduce unemployment and risking higher inflation, or reducing inflation and risking more unemployment. Upon occasion voters may impute their own political views to their favoured party, in order to avoid inconsistency between party choice and issue preference.

The public debate about British entry to the European Common Market—a seemingly straightforward question—illustrates the several difficulties that arise in efforts to relate public opinion to government. When the issue was first mooted in the early 1960s, the don't knows were sometimes the single largest group and, when augmented by those with views but no knowledge, often formed an absolute majority of the electorate. In the subsequent decade, the proportion of don't knows decreased as the Common Market became the object of much discussion in the media. Public opinion fluctuated greatly. The proportion endorsing entry to the Common Market ranged from a Gallup Poll high of 71 per cent in July 1966 to a low of 16 per cent in November 1970.

At the time of the 1970 general election, voters had no choice of pro- and anti-market parties, for all three parties were then in favour of entry. The Labour and Conservative parties subsequently adopted contrasting positions, but MPs within each party disagreed among themselves about whether the terms negotiated were satisfactory or not. As the parties shifted, the views of voters altered. Voters with shifting, uncertain, or confused opinions could claim with justice that their views reflected the views of their party's leaders.

When the country entered the Common Market, the median Englishman was literally a don't know; those with opinions were nearly evenly divided, 39 per cent for entry, and 45 per cent against. Confusion was not confined to the ranks of the less informed. A survey of university economists found 40 per cent favouring entry on economic grounds, 42 per cent against, and the median economist undecided.[8] There was however, one person who was without doubt of his view: the Prime Minister, Edward Heath. He knew

[8] See 'The Dons who want to go to Market', *The Observer* (London), 24 October 1971, *Gallup Political Index*, No. 149 (December 1972), p. 205, and *British Attitudes towards the Common Market, 1957–1971* (London: Gallup Poll).

what he wanted: British entry to the Common Market. Britain joined.

The British public was able to pronounce its views—unstable and partially informed as they were—in a 1975 national referendum on continued membership in the Common Market. This popular consultation was not undertaken because of politicians' deference to values of 'direct democracy' or a belief that the ordinary person in the street knew better than politicians in the House of Commons. The referendum was called because the Labour government of the day was deeply split on the question, and the Prime Minister Harold Wilson reckoned that a referendum might resolve disputes between his Cabinet ministers at a minimum cost to the party and to his own personal position.[9] Similarly, the 1979 referenda on devolution for Scotland and Wales were meant to overcome immediate difficulties in the House of Commons.

A general election is the principal occasion at which the majority of the public speaks its mind. Elections, however, are blunt instruments infrequently used. Counting votes can decide who governs, but it does not tell governors what to do. Election results are only a rough judgment for or against a party. For propaganda purposes the winning party speaks of receiving a mandate—as if every voter necessarily read and agreed with its pre-election proposals before casting his ballot. On a few issues, a majority of a party's voters can have more confidence in the party they vote against than in the party they vote for.[10] The doctrine of an electoral mandate is a dignified symbol rather than an effective means of expressing popular opinion.

Between elections voters can communicate their views directly to their MPs, by letter or in person. But only one-tenth of the electorate says that in fact it has ever done so. More than nine-tenths of these communications are to ask the MP's assistance in dealing with administrative actions that directly affect the writer, such as a disability pension or the allocation of a council house. In a majority of cases, these problems concern local government institutions, and not Westminster. In short, when an individual voter turns to his or

---

[9] On the referendum and the background to it, see David Butler and Uwe Kitzinger, *The 1975 Referendum* (London: Macmillan, 1976), and Anthony King, *Britain Says Yes: The 1975 Referendum on the Common Market* (Washington, D.C.: American Enterprise Institute, 1977).

[10] See Richard Rose, *The Problem of Party Government* (London: Macmillan, 1974), ch. 11.

her MP, it is for help with personal problems involving government, and not to discuss political issues.[11]

Party headquarters commission public opinion surveys in efforts to learn what the silent majority of voters think, feel and want. The Conservative Party was the first to show an interest in market research techniques in 1959. The Labour Party attacked the Conservatives for allegedly trying to sell policies like soap, and then showed itself better able to use market research in the 1964 election campaign. Since then, both parties have made regular use of their own private opinion surveys to complement traditional party mechanisms for sounding opinion. Opinion researchers prepare profiles of the social characteristics of floating voters, analyse the relative importance or unimportance of issues, the appeal of party leaders, and the appeal of particular slogans and campaign themes.

Ironically, the use of public opinion surveys of voters has demonstrated the extent to which British politicians are ready to ignore the views of those whose votes they seek.[12] In the words of Labour Party market researcher Robert Worcester, a party leader is 'a relatively unlistening client, who is much more at home talking than listening'. Many politicians believe that, by virtue of popular election, they know what ordinary voters think, and rate opinion polls well down the list of useful sources of information.[13] Politicians also tend to ignore evidence that does not point in the political direction that they wish to head. For example, public opinion polls have for years shown that the nationalization of more industries is unpopular with voters, and revisionist Labour politicians have sought to have the party abandon this policy. Proponents of nationalization have denounced both the propriety and validity of opinion poll evidence, and successfully lobbied for the extension of nationalization.

Government departments differ enormously in the directness of their communication with the peripheral public. The two chief departments, the Treasury and the Foreign Office, have no domestic channels of communication. Their listening posts are in Washington, Paris, Brussels and elsewhere abroad. Only through

[11] See e.g. Robert Worcester, 'The Hidden Activists', *New Society*, 8 June 1972, p. 200; Robert E. Dowse, 'The MP and his Surgery', *Political Studies*, XI:3 (1963).

[12] See Robert Rose, *Influencing Voters: A Study of Campaign Rationality* (London: Faber & Faber, 1967).

[13] See Dennis Kavanagh, *Constituency Electioneering* (London: Longmans, 1970), pp. 56ff; Robert Worcester, 'Interview', *British Politics Group Newsletter*, No. 8 (Spring 1977), p. 10.

market-place reactions to economic policies can the public and Treasury officials speak to each other. By contrast, a department such as Social Security has an elaborate domestic network of communication, because its local offices apply government policy to thousands of individuals. The problem of such a ministry is a surplus of information. It must have fixed bureaucratic procedures in order to handle multitudes of individual communications. But emphasis on routine, essential in a bureaucracy, can lead officials to ignore unanticipated factors of substantial consequence in individual cases.

When the majority of Englishmen speak out politically, they use actions not words. Popular sayings about voting with your feet or voting with your purse have real meaning in economic policy. A trade union can take strike action even after the government of the day—Conservative or Labour—declares that a strike is not in the national interest. Company directors can similarly act against government economic policy. They can withhold investment at times when the government wishes to stimulate investment, and push investment when the government wishes to curb such spending.

Citizens voice demands for welfare services by actions undertaken without political intent. For example, when people who formerly relied upon public transport buy cars the extra traffic they add to the road constitutes a demand that something be done about the road network that they help overload. When people have larger families, the resulting rise in the number of children demands an increased provision of education and other child-related services.

To provide information about the changing market demand for government services, the Central Statistical Office collects large quantities of information about social conditions in regular censuses and, increasingly, by sponsoring sample surveys.[14] The information-gathering work of the Central Statistical Office is policy relevant, but does not determine policy. It provides basic facts about conditions in society, but the facts *never* speak of themselves. Politicians evaluate and interpret their significance for government policy.

The right to be heard is not equivalent to the right to determine

[14] See Andrew Shonfield and Stella Shaw, eds., *Social Indicators and Social Policy* (London: Heinemann, 1972).

public policy. When individuals find that the government of the day does not share their opinion, it is the government's view that becomes law. A citizen may conceivably communicate dissatisfaction by leaving the country; in fact few English emigrate, though emigration is well publicized. More often, an individual seeks to exit from the effects of a single policy. For example, parents dissatisfied with the government's education policy may send their children to an independent fee-paying school. In many circumstances, a citizen cannot avoid the effects of public policy; for example, if a new road is built, it will affect all home-owners close to the right-of-way. In such circumstances, individuals can voice their protest against a measure. If the government of the day remains firm in its commitment, protesters are expected to accept the decision loyally. The government's view of the public interest takes precedence in a conflict with individual views.

Public media

The media, as their name implies, are means of communication. Among the media, television is the most popular means of following political news. It is preferred by 48 per cent of Englishmen: 20 per cent prefer newspapers, 19 per cent private conversations, and 5 per cent radio broadcasts.[15] People do not rely upon only one medium of political communication exclusively; they are exposed to politics through television, the press *and* private conversations.

The major media are large and complex industries, and politics is not the sole concern of publishers and broadcasters. Communicators are concerned with audience ratings, profitable balance sheets and proficiency in technical skills. Very few media organizations specialize in political reporting and many news and feature stories are remote from the world of Westminster. Technical considerations—for instance, the need for visual materials to illustrate TV news—also affect how the media operate.

Television and radio (collectively described as broadcasting) are highly centralized but competitive channels of political communication. The British Broadcasting Corporation provides two network television services and four radio services throughout the United Kingdom. Its regional branches provide local programmes, especially in non-English parts of the kingdom. Local radio stations,

[15] David Butler and Donald Stokes, *Political Change in Britain* (London: Macmillan, 1969 edition), p. 220.

inaugurated in England in 1967, are a specialized news medium. The Independent Broadcasting Authority licenses fifteen television companies, each producing programmes for one regional audience; they exchange programmes to provide network services. Independent Television News provides central government and international news for the IBA stations. Commercial local radio stations also exist on a limited scale.

Because of technical limitations on channel availability and the economics of programming, the broadcasting industry is subject to government licensing. The BBC's Board of Governors is appointed by the government, as are the members of the Independent Broadcasting Authority. Each body operates under a government charter, subject to periodic review and renewal. Because the BBC depends for much revenue upon the licence fee required of each household receiving programmes (in 1978, £21 for colour TV), the government can affect operations by determining when this fee may rise. The annual profits of independent television companies, derived primarily from advertising, are affected by financial provisions in their licenses. Moreover, the renewal of a licence is not automatic. The government of the day may influence broadcasting by licensing additional competition (e.g. a fourth television channel), or by legislation that changes programming or finance.

Because broadcasting authorities can never be sure which party will be in office when their licence is up for review, they have a substantial incentive to report politics impartially, and statutes require companies to maintain a fair balance between differing points of view. The bias toward caution in choosing party politicians is balanced against the view that novelty makes news. A study of the October 1974 general election campaign found that BBC–1 divided its news coverage equally among the two major parties, with 35 per cent for the Conservatives and 35 per cent for Labour; the Liberals received 26 per cent of attention and other candidates 5 per cent. Independent Television News acted similarly, with Labour 4 per cent ahead of the Conservatives. Parties and candidates are not permitted to purchase time to advertise themselves. The parties are allocated time for party political programmes on radio and television roughly in accord with their electoral strength. This allocation continues between elections too. In non-election periods, BBC television devotes 6 per cent of its viewing time to straight news and 16 per cent to documentaries and information programmes.

This equals the time devoted to films and light entertainment.[16]

The general public trusts the impartiality of the broadcasting media. In one national survey, only 9 per cent attributed any political bias to BBC news, and 7 per cent attributed bias to ITN.[17] Weekly current affairs programmes are similarly considered impartial. This confidence is not shared by all politicians. One set of complaints is non-partisan. It alleges that the broadcasting authorities do not give enough time to programmes that the viewers ought to watch, that is, programmes concerning Parliament. Yet MPs themselves have been singularly unhelpful in providing live programmes. Repeatedly, they have rejected proposals to permit the televising of Commons debates, and radio broadcasting of excerpts of debates was allowed only in 1978. Politicians' complaints against television may also be motivated by the hope that unpopularity rests not with themselves but with those who communicate news about them.

There is no agreement among broadcasting staff about the best way to treat political news. The BBC still reflects in part the ethos of Lord Reith, the director-general during its formative years between the wars. Lord Reigh once commented, 'It is occasionally indicated to us that we are apparently setting out to give the public what we think they need—and not what they want—but few know what they want and very few what they need.' Lord Reith's high-minded ethic has resulted in few people 'at the top of the Corporation knowing, or indeed caring what the audience makes of the service it receives'.[18]

Competition from commercial television for audiences has made some BBC staff more audience conscious. But this has only intensified differences within the BBC. In a study of BBC current affairs election staff, Jay Blumler found a 'sacerdotal' approach among a group who saw elections as intrinsically important events and the BBC as the priestly intermediary between politicians and people. 'Pragmatic' producers, by contrast, wished to report the election

[16] See chapters on broadcasting in successive volumes of the Nuffield election studies written by David Butler and others, and the annual *BBC Handbook* (London: BBC).

[17] Marplan, *Political Index* (London, January 1970) Table 5, and BBC Audience Research Department Report, 'The February 1974 General Election on Television' in R. Rose, ed., *Studies in British Politics* (London: Macmillan, 3rd ed., 1976), p. 304.

[18] Tom Burns, 'Public Service and Private World', *The Sociology of Mass Media Communicators* (Keele, Staffordshire: Sociological Review Monograph No. 13), p. 71.

only in so far as events were newsworthy; an aeroplane crash could be given more prominence than a Cabinet minister's repetition of a familiar campaign theme. As the campaign progressed, the communicators agreed on one thing: politicians rather than broadcasters were the would-be manipulators of public opinion, because of their efforts to influence campaign coverage. The communicators saw themselves as public watchdogs guarding against manipulation of the media.[19]

Studies of audience reaction to political television emphasize how little effect programmes have upon political outlooks. People judge programmes in the light of their prior party loyalty; they do not choose a party in response to their current programme preferences. Long-time Conservatives like Conservative programmes best, and established Labour supporters like Labour programmes best —regardless of programme content. Notwithstanding the effort the parties have made to produce 'popular' party-political broadcasts at election time, there is a tendency for viewers' reactions to become less favourable.[20]

The expectations that viewers bring to televised politics are several. Some hope the programmes will provide guidance for voting; others wish to be informed about what politicians are thinking, gain reinforcement for their partisan loyalty or seek excitement in an election race. Programmes can alter voters' impressions of individual political personalities—though not necessarily for the better. For example, in 1964 Harold Wilson altered public perception of his personality, but the change emphasized 'malevolent dynamism'.[21] The less well known the personality or, in the case of the Liberals, the less well known the party, the more important television becomes as a means of increasing popular awareness, if not popular appeal, of a political cause.

By contrast with America, Canada and many continental European countries, the English press is centralized. Morning newspapers printed in London circulate throughout England[22] thanks to

[19] Jay G. Blumler, 'Producers' Attitudes towards Television Coverage of an Election Campaign', in Rose, *Studies in British Politics* (3rd ed.)

[20] See successive studies of audience reactions to election TV by the BBC Audience Research Department; cf. note 17 above.

[21] Jay G. Blumler and Denis McQuail, *Television in Politics* (London: Faber & Faber, 1968), p. 243.

[22] What follows explicitly excludes the media in Scotland and Northern Ireland; see Richard Rose and Ian McAllister, *United Kingdom Facts*, ch. 7.

special night transport facilities. London-based papers account for two-thirds of daily newspaper circulation and nearly all Sunday newspaper circulation. The concentration of production is made necessary by the high costs of newspaper production and competition for advertising. A popular newspaper cannot break even financially with a circulation of one million. National papers with circulations smaller than one million require a specialized readership justifying premium advertising rates.[23]

Today, no national daily paper except the Communist Party's *Morning Star* is tied to a political party financially, though none is without political bias in its editorial columns. The view of the old-fashioned political proprietor such as Lord Beaverbrook, publisher of the *Daily Express*, was, 'I ran the paper purely for the purpose of making propaganda,' but he also believed, 'I do not think a paper is any good for propaganda unless you run it as a commercial sucess.'[24] Today, some proprietors state that they run newspapers to make (or lose) money, and boast of the independence given editorial staff. Overall, newspapers tend to be less partisan than a quarter-century ago, reflecting a reduction in strong party feelings in the electorate, and the competition with television reports providing an impartial, or at least a bi-partisan view of politics.

The criteria for defining political news are broad. While ministers complain that bad news is always news, claims of success will also be printed, if the speaker has high political status. In the words of a lobby journalist, 'You may not believe what a man is saying, but if he is Prime Minister, he has a right to have his views known.' While the criteria of political news are broad, they exclude certain types of events, as well as publicizing others. Activities are newsworthy if they are:

—Immediate (the latest economic figures, not trends of the decade)
—Novel within a familiar context (a Liberal party victory in a by-election)
—Of concern to lots of people (an increase in pensions) or to a high-status individual (an increase in the Queen's grant from Parliament)

[23] On the economics of the press, see Fred Hirsch and David Gordon, *Newspaper Money* (London: Hutchinson, 1975) and the Final Report of Lord McGregor's *Royal Commission on the Press* (London: HMSO, Cmnd. 6810, 1977).
[24] Quoted in Colin Seymour-Ure, *The Press, Politics and the Public* (London: Methuen, 1968), p. 95.

212   COMMUNICATION AND NON-COMMUNICATION

—Factually ascertainable (a change in Cabinet ministers, rather than a changing mood of ministers)

—Close at hand (poor rubbish collection in London rather than in Newcastle-upon-Tyne)

—Related to recognized areas of reporting (the wedding of a celebrity, but not the restaurant meals of a celebrity)

—Occur when little else is happening (a politician's speech when Parliament is not sitting).

News criteria also define the way in which events are reported. A demonstration may be reported because of its potential for disorder, rather than in terms of the issue that the demonstrators are marching about.[25] Sometimes the opportunity to write a major story occurs fortuitously, for example, a slum property millionaire became newsworthy by being on the fringes of the Profumo scandal. Because the slum landlord was dead, an unfavourable account of his property dealings could be given without risk of libel actions. The resulting exposé won a prize, and the publicity led to government legislation.

The Westminster lobby correspondent is the central figure in a paper's political reporting. He usually writes the paper's main political news story each day, because it is assumed that Parliament is the focal point of government. Because a lobby journalist mixes daily with ministers and MPs on a privileged basis at Westminster, he can write with authority and inside knowledge. His professional role breeds detachment and scepticism. One survey of lobby staff found that they divided almost equally into three groups: Labour, Conservative and those who voted Liberal or abstained.[26]

A lobby journalist learns to report political news by learning how politicians think, spending fifty to sixty hours a week in and around the Palace of Westminster. Like back-bench MPs, a lobby man has limited time for Whitehall departments. He depends for the most part upon ministers to provide background to government policy, whether the issue is technical or not. Specialist correspondents in such fields as economics, defence and education provide supplementary coverage of public affairs, basing their stories on techni-

[25] See James Halloran, Philip Elliott and Graham Murdock, *Demonstrations and Communication* (Harmondsworth: Penguin, 1970).

[26] For details, see Jeremy Tunstall, *The Westminster Lobby Correspondents* (London: Routledge, 1970), pp. 20, 35 and 59ff.

cal experts in and out of government, rather than MPs. The lobby man, a paper's chief political correspondent, cannot act as a watchdog in Whitehall because he 'stands guard in the wrong place'.[27]

Although their professional interests are different, communicators and politicians need each other. Journalists need politicians as news sources. Politicians need journalists to give publicity to their views and themselves. In this process, the communications loop can be complete if it only includes politicians and journalists; members of the general public may neither note nor care about the publicity that results.

If a lobby man runs the risk of having his perspective affected by too close contact with politicians and events, the occupational hazard of a leader writer is detachment. Involvement in the daily routines of a newspaper office plus heavy reading in fields of special interest allow limited time to confront at first-hand the problems about which editorial writers pronounce. The content of the day's leader page is likely to be decided by intra-office discussion in the light of the paper's past position and readership. In face-to-face discussion, idiosyncratic influences enter. By-line columnists may gain an audience by virtue of expert knowledge of one subject or, more often, by cultivating a striking prose style. A by-line columnist is likely to command interest the more original his or her point of view; to follow a party line is to be predictable, and thus to run the risk of dullness.

In the case of most of the daily press, the label newspaper gives a misleading description of its contents. The four popular tabloid papers—the *Mirror, Sun, Express* and *Mail*—carry little political news. Political stories consist primarily of headlines, photographs and catch phrases, rather than detailed analysis. These papers are sold for entertainment rather than information. Only the readers of the four serious papers—the *Telegraph, Times, Guardian* and *Financial Times*—receive sufficient domestic and international news each day so that they might be reasonably informed about events. (See Table VII.1.)

The readership of the national press is determined partly by education, and partly by style. The popular press appeals to readers with a minimum of education; inevitably, this makes a majority of

[27] Seymour-Ure, *The Press, Politics and the Public*, pp. 176ff, 311. Cf. Jeremy Tunstall, *Journalists at Work* (London: Constable, 1971).

their readers working class. By contrast, up to five-sixths of the readership of the serious papers is middle-class. Within each category, papers compete on stylistic grounds; political orientation is part of their image. Surveys show that however much an editor protests a paper's independence, readers tend to associate papers with parties. Moreover, readers of different popular papers differ in their party support: a majority of *Mirror* and *Sun* readers vote Labour, and a majority of *Express* and *Mail* readers favour the Conservatives. A paper's editorial line tends to match the distribution of views among its readers. The press today contains pro-Conservative (e.g. the *Express*) and pro-Labour (e.g. the *Mirror*) papers, and it is not lopsided in favour of one party.

TABLE VII.1   **National daily newspaper readership**

	Paid circulation[a]	Share of adult readership[a]	Readers, working-class[a]	Readers' partisanship[b]	
				Con	Lab
		%	%	%	%
Popular papers					
Mirror	3,851,000	29	76	27	57
Sun	3,723,000	29	77	23	59
Express	2,385,000	16	54	58	26
Mail	1,865,000	13	49	55	26
Serious papers					
Telegraph	1,318,000	8	21	70	10
Times	298,000	2	19	47	22
Guardian	273,000	2	21	33	33
Financial Times	178,000	2	9	79	–

Sources   [a] = *National Readership Survey, January–December 1977* (London: Joint Industry Committee for National Readership Surveys, 1978).
[b] = Derived from MORI September 1975 Survey, as reported by J. Tunstall, 'The Constrained Freedoms of the Britishers', *The Times Higher Education Supplement*, 24 June 1977.

Media consumption is affected by an individual's political role. Politicians concerned with courting popular favour give most attention to television, because it reaches the largest audience. Those anxious to court favour within the ranks of the party faithful give particular attention to papers read by their followers, whether local weeklies published in their constituency, or national dailies. Civil servants read serious and specialist papers. Among administrative class officials, a survey found 88 per cent read *The Times*, 72 per cent the *Telegraph*, 36 per cent the *Guardian* and only one-quarter a popular paper. By contrast, among the clerical grade, the majority read a popular paper; only one-quarter read the *Telegraph*, and only four per cent *The Times*. Whereas only a few per cent of the adult population read a serious weekly offering news and comments, 88 per cent of administrative civil servants do. *The Economist* is read by 68 per cent, and *New Society*, specializing in welfare services and social problems, by 33 per cent.[28]

Studies of the short-term influence of the press upon political outlooks have emphasized the importance of the class and party loyalties that lead individuals to become readers of a newspaper. Class influences the choice of both party and paper. Within a given class, individuals socialized into Conservative families are more likely to read pro-Conservative papers as adults, and those from Labour families pro-Labour papers.[29] Class differences also influence the choice of broadcasting media, and of particular programmes. The public media do not create public opinion; if anything, they reinforce predispositions that their audience already has.

Communication in Westminster

Politicians in central roles are involved in horizontal communication with their political peers in Westminster and Whitehall as well as vertical communication with those who elect them as their representatives. Whereas vertical communication is usually public, in English politics horizontal communication is usually private.

Any minister who wishes to seek advice from informed opinion outside Whitehall can easily establish contact with experts who provide a market-place of ideas relevant to the department's work. For example, defence policy involves a feedback of information and values between government ministers, senior military officers, defence correspondents of serious papers, members of the International Institute for Strategic Studies, a few MPs of each party

[28] A. H. Halsey and I. M. Crewe, 'Social Survey of Civil Servants', The Fulton Committee *Report*, Vol. III.1, pp. 32f.

[29] See David Butler and Donald Stokes, *Political Change in Britain* (London: Macmillan, 1969), pp. 232ff.

specially interested in defence, and spokesmen (sometimes former military officers) for firms producing armaments.[30] This elite network has few vertical contacts with the mass of the population. But within its terms, it is open to a wide variety of ideas and influences. Communication can be formalized by a department establishing an advisory committee in which pressure-group spokesmen and experts meet periodically to discuss both present and future problems facing the minister.

If a government wishes advice about a major issue of policy, it can establish an *ad hoc* Royal Commission or departmental committee; they have deliberated upon topics such as the press, metrication, the export of animals for slaughter and the distribution of income. A Royal Commission is often constituted when government is unable or unwilling to assume immediate responsibility for a policy decision. It can acquire information; recommend a course of action likely to be agreed by the majority of affected interests appearing before it; gain public support for a policy that the government wishes to adopt eventually; or stall decisions about a controversial matter. The government of the day will construct terms of reference so that the Commission does not publicize issues that the government wishes to leave unexamined.

An experienced committee man, Sir Andrew Shonfield, has described how these bodies proceed:

> Just plunge into your subject: collect as many facts as you can; think about them hard as you go along; and at the end, use your commonsense, and above all your feel for the practicable, to select a few good proposals out of the large number of suggestions which will surely come your way.[31]

Like a judge, a committee usually confines itself to listening to the views of those who wish to testify before it. It may lack time, money, staff or inclination to undertake any other form of inquiry or research. For example, the Pilkington Committee on Broadcasting held 120 meetings in a two-year period. It listened to dozens of pressure group spokesmen, but it did not commission any sample survey of the attitudes of listeners and viewers. After it reported, a survey showed public opinion divided about a major Pilkington

[30] See L. W. Martin, 'The Market for Strategic Ideas', *American Political Science Review*, LVI:1 (1962).

[31] 'In the Course of Investigation', *New Society*, 24 July 1969.

proposal. The pro-Pilkington group—those with education beyond the age of eighteen—constituted about 4 per cent of the population, and the anti-Pilkington group about 96 per cent of the population.[32]

Government departments may commission research but impose censorship upon it, specifying questions that *cannot* be asked. For example, two academic researchers, undertaking a study of the civil service on behalf of the Fulton Commission, said in the second paragraph of their report, 'Enquiry into such matters as political allegiance, religious affiliation, attitudes to career and promotion opportunities was ruled out as too delicate and difficult.'[33]

When a Whitehall committee publishes a document, it may effectively restrict communication by publishing it in 'code', that is, everything important may be stated indirectly or by implication, so that only those who already have private knowledge of public affairs can interpret the full significance of the document. The great majority of the public cannot.

A report on *Control of Public Expenditure* by a committee under Lord Plowden, himself a former civil servant, illustrates how communication in code operates. The committee prepared private memoranda as well as the formal report, so that the Treasury, the chief object of criticism, could decide which parts and how much of the comment should be published.

Following publication of the coded report, Professor W. J. M. Mackenzie, a former classicist and wartime civil servant, published a 'translation'. The first paragraph of the official report reads:

For these studies we co-opted the Permanent Secretaries of the Departments with whose expenditure we were concerned or who had special experience of the general problems under review. In some cases we sought specialist advice from outside the civil service. We decided, however, not to take evidence from outside bodies: our review was primarily concerned with the inner working of the Treasury and the departments, and was necessarily confidential in character, and we decided that the group itself (except on certain specialist matters) provided a sufficient body of outside opinion to bring to bear on this task.

[32] Cf. Pilkington Report of the Committee on Broadcasting (London: HMSO, Cmnd. 1753, 1962) and Harry Henry, *Public Opinion and the Pilkington Committee* (London: Sunday Times, 1962).
[33] A. H. Halsey and I. M. Crewe, 'Social Survey of Civil Servants', p. 1.

Mackenzie translates it thus:

> We proceeded on two principles: no dirty linen in public: outside critics are bores.[34]

Many conventions and laws of British government emphasize non-communication. The philosophy is summarized in a White Paper entitled *Information and the Public Interest*.

> It does not follow, of course, that public consultation on tentative proposals is invariably the right course. It may result in slower decisions and slower action when prompt action is essential. Sometimes, too, conflicting views and conflicting interests are already well known. In such cases a prolonged period of consultation will merely impose delay without any compensating advantages. Each individual case has to be considered on its merits.[35]

The government declares that it favours the publication of information about policy matters 'whenever reasonably possible'.[36] Whitehall remains the sole judge of what is reasonable and possible.

It is standard operating procedure for government departments to refuse the press information that it requests. For example, when a *Times* reporter sought to find out details of cases investigated by the Parliamentary Commissioner's (Ombudsman's) office, it was prevented by statute from even giving the name of the MP who had endorsed a complaint, thus effectively preventing the press from investigating the extent of 'consumer satisfaction' with the Ombudsman's work. Similarly, when the National Council of Civil Liberties wrote to heads of each of 46 police authorities in England and Wales requesting copies of their annual reports, only 18 replied.[37]

Members of Parliament too are frequently frustrated in their enquiries into government policy. Question time in the House of Commons is of limited value in probing Whitehall's actions, because questions are not permitted on many topics ranging from

[34] Cf. W. J. M. Mackenzie, 'The Plowden Report: A Translation' in Rose, *Studies in British Politics*, and the original *Control of Public Expenditure* (London: HMSO, Cmnd. 1432, 1961).
[35] *Information and the Public Interest* (London: HMSO, Cmnd. 4089, 1969), pp. 6–7.
[36] *Ibid.* p. 7.
[37] See Tony Smythe, 'Police Report', *New Society*, 9 November 1972; George Clark, 'Official Secrets of Britain's Ombudsman', *The Times*, 7 May 1970.

details of arms sales and purchases made by the National Health Service to regional figures for money invested in National Savings certificates. Even when the Speaker allows a question on a delicate subject, the minister involved may refuse to answer. For example, during the Suez crisis, Sir Anthony Eden refused Parliament an answer to a question asking whether or not the country was at war with Egypt![38] Because only a few minutes are allowed each question, a minister can reply with a form of words that does not illuminate the topic. In the opinion of a former civil servant:

> The perfect reply to an embarrassing question in the House of Commons is one that is brief, appears to answer the question completely, if challenged can be proved to be accurate in every word, gives no opening for awkward supplementaries and discloses really nothing.[39]

Faced with such constraints, 91 per cent of MPs believe that they are not adequately informed about the actions of government. Moreover, five-sixths of MPs think their lack of knowledge is in part caused by ministers wishing to limit what the Commons is told. In the words of one back-bencher:

> The tendency of paternalism towards Government backbenchers is strong: 'If you knew what I know you'd see I'm right.' Meanwhile, father knows best.[40]

In economic policy, the government frequently publishes forecasts of the state of the economy for the next year or two. Whatever the immediate difficulties, official forecasts almost invariably stress favourable signs for the future. No government wishes to publicize the danger that it is steering the economy in the wrong direction. Upon occasion, the Treasury can avoid risks by presenting forecasts so vague as to be meaningless for practical purposes. For example, in 1970 a Labour Government divided about British entry into the Common Market issued a White Paper estimating the cost of entry at anything between £100 and £1,100 million. A Labour minister

---

[38] See House of Commons *Debates*, Vol. 558, cols. 1452–4 (31 October 1956) and cols. 1620ff (1 November 1956). Note also, 'Speaker Helps MP to Update List of Questions Government Departments Refuse to Answer', *The Times*, 24 April 1978.

[39] H. E. Dale, *The Higher Civil Service of Great Britain* (London: Oxford University Press, 1941), p. 105.

[40] See Anthony Barker and Michael Rush, *The Member of Parliament and his Information*, pp. 150, 363ff.

commented that this was like saying the score of a football match would be anything from 10 to 0 for one side to 10 to 0 for the other.[41]

The constitutional justification for the secretive character of Whitehall is the doctrine of ministerial responsibility. Everything that a department does is said to be done in the name of its minister. The convention that the department reflects the mind of a single individual has as a corollary that no one else can speak for the department. Both junior ministers and senior civil servants in the department are expected to make no public statement committing the department to a particular policy unless authorized by the minister. This convention is strengthened by Section 2 of the Official Secrets Act of 1911, which makes it a crime for any person to communicate any information that he has received by virtue of being a minister or civil servant. This Act even covers such matters as a restricted (sic) circular from the minister to hospital authorities, asking them to convey Christmas greetings to all the staff on Christmas Eve. Libel laws are also interpreted in ways that inhibit press comment on personalities, for fear of having to pay substantial damages. Occasionally journalists get around these restrictions, but official resistance to 'unreasonable' publicity remains strong.[42]

The doctrine of ministerial responsibility is not valid empirically. Time is one obstacle to communication to and from the minister. There are not enough hours in the day for any minister to read everything about the work of a department or to draft or sign every statement issued in his name. A minister must communicate views in general terms, so that staff can apply them in particular instances without direct communication. When departmental scandals occur, the minister is formally responsible, but can plead with truth that he did not know about what was being done in his name. This plea can even be made on behalf of the Prime Minister. For example, Lord Denning's inquiry into the 1963 Profumo scandal exculpated Prime Minister Harold Macmillan from blame on the ground that he was not told by the security services what was going on.[43]

[41] George Thomson, 'The Game's the Same', Guardian, 9 July 1971.

[42] For a review of small-scale changes in official practice, see Maurice Wright, 'Ministers and Civil Servants: Relations and Responsibilities', Parliamentary Affairs, XXX:3 (1977). Cf. the views of 'Group of Crusading Reformers Intent on a British Freedom of Information Act', The Times, 6 June 1978.

[43] Lord Denning's Report (London: HMSO, Cmnd. 2152, 1963).

The flow of information between central and local government is also inhibited by geographical distance. In the extreme case of Northern Ireland, the Prime Minister may not take official cognizance of events reported for weeks in Belfast newspapers until someone such as Bernadette Devlin camped overnight on the doorstep of 10 Downing Street.[44]

The doctrine of ministerial responsibility remains powerful politically because it appeals to the most important people in government: ministers and civil servants. Ministers do not wish to have news of differences within their department discussed in public prior to decision. They are also glad to take credit and blame for all that happens, trusting that a well-run department will more often than not make them look good by actions taken in their name. Civil servants regard confidentiality as the basis of trust in their exchange of opinions with ministers. Any alteration of arrangements would raise 'major constitutional issues'.[45]

When the Franks Committee was deliberating upon liberalizing or amending the Official Secrets Act, very senior civil servants testified about the necessity to continue restricting public knowledge of departmental deliberations. Sir William Armstrong, then head of the Civil Service, favoured disseminating more information, but only if dissemination was controlled at a single point. Only this, he said, could prevent the free flow of information from being 'good, bad or indifferent, inaccurate or accurate, embarrassing or unembarrassing'. Sir Burke Trend, the secretary of the Cabinet, opposed publication of news of the existence of Cabinet committees because this might breach collective responsibility by leading to questions to ministers who are members of the committees.[46] Subsequently, a leading English academic lawyer, Professor Harry Street, commented that Whitehall's regulations prohibiting the publication of information meant:

Watergate could never have been exposed here. Our laws—the Official Secrets Act, contempt, libel and breach of confidence

---

[44] See Richard Rose, *Governing without Consensus* (London: Faber & Faber, 1971), pp. 123f, and Frank Burton, *The Politics of Legitimacy* (London: Routledge & Kegan Paul, 1978), ch. 4.

[45] *Information and the Public Interest*, p. 10.

[46] See the report of Lord Franks's Departmental Committee on Section 2 of the Official Secrets Act 1911 (London: HMSO, Cmnd. 5104). Cf. Hugo Young, 'But Who is Responsible for Burials?', *Sunday Times*, 12 April 1978.

—would have prevented any journalist from investigating too closely.[47]

The complexities of contemporary government and changing standards of behaviour among politicians have led to a reduction in the height of the wall of secrecy, as well as occasional cracks lower down. Upon occasion, a government that has narrowed down its policy options but not yet made a selection between them may publish a Green Paper to canvass political reaction to the choices before it. Doing this gives a minister the benefit of criticisms of various alternatives before officially committing a department. Individual civil servants sometimes take part in public discussions of pending legislation, in an attempt to increase public understanding of government measures. In doing this, however, officials have been cautioned that they 'should not be drawn into expressing personal views on policy matters which could be represented as in conflict with those of their ministers, or as reflecting any political (that is, party political) bias'.[48]

Contemporary politicians are more interested in publicizing themselves than in protecting Whitehall. A determined politician can publish what he wishes without judicial punishment, for 'the rules to be observed are voluntary obligations, known in advance and dependent for their observance upon no more than the decency and honour of those concerned'. A former Labour Cabinet minister, Richard Crossman, established this point when three volumes of his political diary of six years as a Cabinet minister were published shortly after his death, notwithstanding objections from Whitehall about the frequent references therein to civil servants who had worked with the minister, and the ex-minister's accounts of what was purportedly said in Cabinet.[49]

The 'leak' is the characteristic way in which a politician pays lip service to the doctrine of non-communication, while ensuring that friendly journalists print his version of current political controversies. The distinction between a leak, which is a breach of convention, and briefing, which is accepted as a necessary means of giving

[47] Quoted in 'Fear that judges may become "political"', The Times, 29 September 1975.
[48] Information and the Public Interest, p. 10.
[49] See the symposium, 'After Crossman', The Sunday Times, 30 March 1975, and Anthony Lewis, 'The Crossman Diaries and the Legal Lessons of the Pentagon Papers', The Sunday Times, 3 August 1975.

background information to journalists, has been defined by James Callaghan thus: 'Briefing is what I do; leaking is what you do'. Technically, such disclosures are violations of the Official Secrets Act. But, as the Director General of the Security Service has complained: 'The chances of their being prosecuted . . . are minimal, if they exist at all, because the ministers can always say that they authorized themselves to disclose the information.'[50]

What price communication?

The costs and benefits of secrecy and publicity differ from issue to issue. The greater the numbers who will be required to cooperate in a policy if it is to work (e.g. voluntary wage and price restraint) the greater the need to seek information in advance, and to publicize the reasons behind the policy in hopes of thus mobilizing consent. The fewer the numbers involved in carrying out a policy, whether in domestic or foreign policy, the less the need to communicate widely in advance of a decision. In every decision there is a trade-off between the speed gained by non-communication and the risk of acting without widespread understanding and support.

Communication and non-communication are complementary and concurrent. There is never enough time or enough incentive to talk to every group about every policy that government is considering. In theory, representatives of all who need to know will be consulted, and those unaffected need not be consulted. Decisions about who should and should not be informed are usually taken within Whitehall. Those in the know have a chance to act or react to a pending policy in their own interest. Those not consulted may sometimes consider that what they don't know will hurt them.

The most economical form of communication requires understanding not talk. When individuals know each other's minds, a wink and a nod may be sufficient, or one person may put himself in another's place and take the decision that the other would have taken had he been personally informed. British government requires much virtual communication. MPs speak for their constituents by virtue of election, ministers speak for their departments, and departmental civil servants write letters speaking for ministers.

[50] Quoted in Rudolf Klein's note in *New Society*, 5 October 1972. See also Hugo Young, 'A Practised Leaker meets his match', *The Sunday Times*, 30 April 1978.

It is deceptively easy for people in Westminster to mistake the echo of their own voices for the views of a much larger public. In an essay on government in wartime, Sir Norman Chester noted how the intense concentration of horizontal communication in Whitehall tended to isolate it from the general public.

> What can come to be important, if one is not careful, is not how decisions affect people, but how they are thought to operate by people in the Whitehall circle. The leader or letter in *The Times* or *Economist* can become the reality by which one's actions are judged.[51]

The habits of wartime persist in peacetime. A study of the control of public expenditure by the Treasury is aptly titled *The Private Government of Public Money*.[52]

Increasing the extent of political communication is often urged as a good in itself, but even perfect communication cannot of itself resolve all political problems. By definition politics is about conflict. Canvassing views on any issue of political significance will inevitably produce arguments and evidence supporting conflicting policy choices. The more thorough and representative the process, the greater the likelihood that the result will be stalemate, or a three-, four- or five-way division of opinion. In many political contexts, agreement is more important than anything else. For example, an economist has described how wartime estimates of aircraft production were not reconciled by more information, but rather by statistical bargaining leading to agreement upon a figure that all the Whitehall groups involved would accept.[53]

What busy policy-makers want is help, not information for its own sake. Upon occasion, Whitehall departments are prepared to spend months or years seeking information; at other times, they react to straws in the wind, or ignore facts that appear as palpable as handwriting on the wall. Politicians attend to information if the benefits of doing so are likely to be greater than the costs of ignoring it. A policy maker's attention to communication is not so much a function of the quality of information, but of immediate political requirements. In a political crisis, when the costs of inaction are

[51] 'The Central Machinery for Economic Policy', in D. N. Chester, ed., *Lessons of the British War Economy* (Cambridge: University Press, 1951), p. 30.
[52] By Hugh Heclo and Aaron Wildavsky.
[53] Ely Devons, *Planning in Practice* (Cambridge: University Press, 1950), pp. 155ff.

great, then any kind of information—statistical, literary or half-baked—will be seized upon for clues of what to do.[54]

The relative secrecy of Whitehall has been sustained by the view that Whitehall knows what is best for the country. This confidence has been increasingly undermined by the difficulties of British government in the 1960s and 1970s. The habits of the past do not disappear quickly, however, especially when they are integral to the status of both ministers and civil servants. The immediate issue is not whether it is in the interest of the mass public to receive more information about what government is thinking and doing. The arguments for and against doing so have hardly changed in a generation. The question for the 1980s is whether it is in the interest of the country's governors to provide more information about the problems of governing England today. The less their confidence that things are going well, the more important it is for politicians to warn the electorate in advance, rather than let it learn of troubles only when the loud noise of failure shatters Whitehall's customary pose of knowing silence.

[54] See Richard Rose, 'The Market for Policy Indicators' in Shonfield and Shaw, eds., *Social Indicators and Social Policy*.

VIII
Group Pressures

The unsectional Parliament should know what each section in the nation thought before it gave the national decision.

Millions of people may be of the same mind politically, but without organization they will have no means of expressing their views and no one to represent their opinions in Westminster. With organization, the same people will have spokesmen pressing government to act, and government will consult those who speak on their behalf. For example, the organization of trade unions from the late nineteenth century greatly increased the political influence of millions of formerly unorganized workers, and employers too have had to organize in order to present a case on their own behalf to government.

Both parties and pressure groups present demands to government: the chief distinction between the two is that pressure groups do not seek to control government by contesting elections. Because a pressure group does not seek the responsibilities of public office, its officials are free to press their sectional interest without regard to any notion of the public interest. By contrast, when a party moves from opposition to office, it can no longer act simply as an agent of a pressure group; it faces conflicting demands from different groups, and must try to reconcile these in ways acceptable to the electorate.[1]

A clear-cut distinction between parties and pressure groups cannot be maintained in England, because of the interpenetration of these two kinds of institution. This is particularly notable in the Labour Party, which regards itself as one wing of the labour movement, complementing the activities of the trade unions and Co-operative societies. The labour movement is two parts pressure group and one part political party. In the picturesque words of Ernest Bevin, the Labour Party grew out of the bowels of the

[1] On the origins and evolution of group demands, see e.g. Samuel H. Beer, *Modern British Politics* (London: Faber & Faber, 1965) and Graham Wootton, *Pressure Groups in Britain, 1720–1970* (London: Allen Lane, 1975).

trade-union movement.[2] The party was founded in 1900 when trade-union leaders decided that they needed political power to achieve economic goals that could not be obtained by collective bargaining alone. Gradually Socialists in the new Labour Party won over the great majority of union leaders to endorsing Socialism as a political means to gain their major economic objectives.

Today, trade unions affiliate seven-eighths of the membership of the Labour Party, elect 18 of the 29 members of the Party's National Executive Committee and provide more than three-quarters of its income. In some parliamentary constituencies, the local lodges of the National Union of Mineworkers *are* the Labour Party. At Westminster, the unions sponsor financially more than one-third of Labour's MPs. These MPs are expected to follow the policy of the Parliamentary Labour Party as laid down by party whips, but they also constitute a block of spokesmen for trade-union interests on industrial matters. Trade-union and party interests can be at loggerheads, if a Labour government seeks to legislate upon matters of immediate industrial concern. When the Labour government in 1969 proposed a major industrial relations bill, acting with the support of union-sponsored MPs, trade-union leaders successfully forced the government to withdraw the proposals.[3]

The Conservative Party existed long before industry rose to political influence, and its structure is independent of business groups. Businessmen disliking a Labour government have no choice but to support the Conservative cause: the Liberals' weak position gives them little appeal to business interests. There is no formal institutional connection between business groups and the Conservative Party; support is chiefly in the form of financial contributions. Businessmen who believe in a 'free enterprise' alternative to Socialism can be sharply distinguished from Conservative politicians; the former sponsor free enterprise publicity campaigns; the latter seek to be the governors of a mixed-economy welfare state.[4]

[2] *Labour Party Conference Report, 1935* (London) p. 180. For implications of this, see D. W. Rawson, 'The Life-span of Labour Parties', *Political Studies*, XVII:3 (1969).

[3] See Martin Harrison, *Trade Unions and the Labour Party* (London: George Allen & Unwin, 1960) and William D. Muller, *The 'Kept Men'* (Brighton: Harvester Press, 1977).

[4] See Richard Rose, *Influencing Voters* (London: Faber & Faber, 1967), chs. 2, 5–7; Wyn Grant and David Marsh, *The Confederation of British Industry* (London: Hodder & Stoughton, 1977), and Stephen Blank, *Industry and Government in Britain* (Farnborough: Saxon House, 1973).

The blurring of institutional distinctions is intensified by the blurred distinction between principle and interest, the motivations that theoretically distinguish parties and pressure groups. One person may regard as an interest what another regards as a principle. For example, class-conscious demands are viewed by some as statements of sectional interest, but by others as the articulation of party principles. Some groups promote causes in which they have no financial interest, like the Howard League for Penal Reform; members may none the less draw 'psychic income' from the advocacy of a cause.

The interpenetration of party principles and pressure-group interests can clearly be seen in the resolutions sent by activists to the annual Conservative and Labour Party conferences. Pressure-group demands unrelated to party principles appear prominently among the resolutions submitted in both parties; constituency parties ask for better treatment for farmers, pensioners, or motorists without reference to larger ideological concerns.[5] Reciprocally, the influence of party politics in interest groups can be seen in elections to national trade union offices which can turn on left-wing *vs.* moderate orientation within the Labour Party, or on questions of overt or covert Communist influence.

Parties and pressure groups are not independent, as conventional terminology implies; they are interdependent. Both are parts of a single political system, and both are concerned with advancing political demands within the same policy process. Controversies about particular political issues often find pressure-group officials and party politicians working together. A pressure group that has a variety of organizations as its constituent members, such as the Confederation of British Industry or the Trades Union Congress, aggregates interests in a fashion resembling a political party. Reciprocally, a party may present as a point of principle demands arising from the interests of steel workers threatened by unemployment or manufacturers faced with declining markets.

Although pressure groups and parties are interdependent, pressure groups seek to shape policy rather than become office holders. By not contesting elections, pressure groups reduce the scope of their potential influence in government. But for the same reason, they also reduce the extent of their accountability. Pressure groups

[5] See Richard Rose, 'The Political Ideas of English Party Activists', *American Political Science Review*, LVI:2 (1962).

are not accountable for every aspect of public policy: instead they are only accountable to their members for what affects their immediate interests.

In order to understand the work of pressure groups, we must first of all understand the nature of their organization. But organization alone will not achieve political goals. The second section of this chapter considers the political context within which groups advance their interests, and the economic constraints that influence both the voicing of demands and government's response. The concluding part of this chapter examines how pressure groups and government exchange influence in the continuing process of making policy.

The organization of group pressures

Organization is necessary to capitalize potential resources. Without organization, interests exist, but there is no means by which they can be pressed upon government, nor are there any means by which public officials can negotiate with interests to reach a satisfactory agreement. For example, in Northern Ireland, while there are Protestant and Catholic interests, there is no organization to speak on behalf of either interest *and* bind those whom they claim to represent to an agreement.

Categories of people with common interests vary greatly in the ease with which they can organize to advance their interests. For example, producer interests are more readily organized than consumer interests because they are specific and immediate. Individuals and companies derive immediate and material personal benefits from joining producer groups, whether trade unions or trade associations. By contrast, consumer groups are difficult to organize because their interests are general, and the benefits of organization long-term. An individual does not need to belong to a consumer pressure group to enjoy any benefits it negotiates; these will be available to everyone in the market-place. Alternatively, instead of joining a pressure group, a person can vote for lower prices by refusing to buy goods if there is an abrupt price rise. The Consumers Association organizes only 3 per cent of the nation's consumers, whereas trade unions organize more than 40 per cent of the same people in their role as producers.

The *commitment* of members is one of a pressure group's most important resources. The greater this is, the more confident a group's leaders can be that they speak with a united membership behind them, and that any bargain reached with government will be accepted by the group itself. While all pressure groups maintain a nominal facade of unity, their members, whether individuals or organizations, have a multiplicity of interests, dividing their loyalties among many different competing groups.

The country's major pressure groups—trade unions and business firms—have difficulties in maintaining group loyalty. Trade unions are perennially subject to conflicts of interest between members of different unions. From time to time unions dispute which one should have jurisdiction over workers in a given field. They perennially disagree about wage differentials between members of different unions, a problem exacerbated by the large number of craft unions dividing workers in a factory into many competing groups. For example, the railways have separate unions for locomotive drivers, clerks and unskilled workers, each with its own idea of the proper wage differentials between them.

The Trades Union Congress, the co-ordinating organization of unions, is internally weak, because of differences between its major members. It cannot make a contract with government about wages, because its members are not committed to accept any agreement it might make. The comparative weakness of the TUC is illustrated by the fact that it has the lowest ratio of headquarters staff to union membership of any peak labour organization in the Western world.[6]

Nominally capitalist institutions differ in many ways, and nationalized industries are not even in private ownership. There are major functional and social differences between the banks and financial institutions in the City of London; there are manufacturers wishing to borrow money cheaply for investment in the production of goods and the development of new technologies; and there are retailers wishing to supply consumers with goods bought from the most economical sources of supply. The name of the Confederation of British Industry implies a unity of industry that is lacking in fact. Corporate members of the CBI prefer to rely upon trade associations or, in the case of larger firms, upon direct contacts with government, to advance their particular and pressing interests.[7]

The *organizational cohesion* of a pressure group is a second major

---

[6] See Bruce W. Headey, 'Trade Unions and National Wages Policies', *Journal of Politics*, XXXII: (1970) pp. 428–9, and Gerald A. Dorfman, *Government Versus Trade Unionism in British Politics since 1968* (London: Macmillan, 1979).

[7] See Grant and Marsh, *The Confederation of British Industry*.

resource. The more durable, the more frequent, the more numerous, and the more intense the contacts among individuals, the easier
they are to organize for cohesive political action. Miners have all the
characteristics that lead to cohesive organization. They usually
work at mining all their lives; they always work in contact with
fellow miners, and they frequently meet miners outside the pits,
because of living clustered together in mining villages. The future of
a mine becomes, in effect, the future of their community. By contrast, members of an air charter group are virtually incapable of
organization, for they meet only once when waiting at an airport to
board an aircraft.

Whitehall prefers to deal with cohesive pressure groups, because
it is administratively convenient for it to do so. An agreement made
between a government department and a cohesively organized
pressure group is more likely to be carried out—or so it is believed
in Whitehall. But decades of attempting to organize agreement
about plans for the British economy demonstrate that pressure
group leaders cannot guarantee that a bargain they make will be
carried out. Pressure group leaders can articulate members'
demands but they cannot force their members to accept them if they
deem it against their interest. As one experienced British economist
has noted:

> Neither the trade unions nor management have systems of pri-
> vate government that can send plenipotentiaries to negotiate on
> their behalf and commit them to settlement, save on limited
> issues and particular occasions, when the negotiators can keep in
> touch with their constituents as the negotiations proceed.[8]

The third major resource of pressure groups is *strategic location* in
society.[9] This does not depend upon a group's efforts, but upon the
nature of its activities. An organization occupies a strong strategic
position if it commands resources—energy, money or food—that
are indispensable to the conduct of society. How much a group
extracts from a strong strategic location depends upon several considerations. The first is whether it has a monopoly in the provision of
a service. For example, communication is a necessity of modern

[8] E. H. Phelps-Brown, 'The National Economic Development Organisation',
Public Administration, XLI (Autumn 1963), p. 245.
[9] For a detailed elaboration of this point, see S. E. Finer, 'The Political Power of
Organised Labour', *Government and Opposition*, VII:4 (1973).

society, but there is no monopoly. In England a postal strike has been circumvented by greater reliance upon telephones and private messenger services, and a newspaper strike by use of radio and television. Unionized buses and trains compete with private automobiles and bicycles for the movement of people and goods. By contrast, electricity generating stations have a monopoly in producing a form of energy upon which England, like every modern society, is uniquely dependent. Coal miners have a national monopoly for extracting one of the country's basic energy needs and, given co-operation of other unions in refusing to handle imported coal, constitute the sole source for the country of this vital fuel. When the miners struck in 1974, the nation's industry was put on a three-day working week.

A pressure group can extract the private benefit of its public monopoly in so far as it is prepared to use its strategic location for its own members. Groups representing occupations with a service ethic, such as doctors, nurses or teachers, have professional norms that inhibit them from refusing their services to clients in need. However, in the 1970s these groups have increasingly sought ways to influence government—by working to rule, refusing all but emergency cases, threatening or actually striking—in pursuit of interests regarded as important as their service ethic. At all times, professional service groups enjoy the strategic advantage of monopolizing expertise in an important field of public policy. Generalist politicians and civil servants cannot claim that they know more about education than teachers or about medical care than doctors, and are thus inclined to let them have their way on matters of professional concern.[10]

Three resources of pressure groups—money, votes and publicity —are of relatively limited importance in England. Money can ensure that an organization exists and, in the case of a highly technical subject, that experts are available to analyse and present the group's case in the best light. Money can also be given to political parties. But money does not buy favours from parties; it is given openly in recognition of mutual interests. An MP may speak for a pressure group employer, but party discipline ensures that the

[10] See e.g. T. R. Marmor and D. Thomas, 'Doctors, Politics and Pay Disputes: Pressure Group Politics Revisited', *British Journal of Political Science*, II:4 (1972) and Maurice Kogan, *Educational Policy-Making: A Study of Interest Groups and Parliament* (London: George Allen & Unwin, 1975).

MP votes with his party in the Commons. Parties also know that many economic interest groups are tied to them, because the alternative in a two-party system is to let the other side in.

No pressure group in British politics can confidently claim that its members are so committed to it that they would switch votes from one party to another at the direction of group leaders. Even trade-union leaders, who are Labour (or occasionally Communist) party members, must face the fact that less than three in five of their members vote Labour, and about one trade-union member in four votes Conservative.[11] A pressure group leader risks revealing organizational weakness by threatening that members will swing their votes from one party to another, if the threat does not work because members put their party loyalties first.

Pressure groups with a weak strategic position and few other organizational resources may turn to the media. Media publicity gives the appearance of mass support by the multiplying effect of mass circulation. The simplest and cheapest publicity device is to issue a press release or write a letter to *The Times* signed by prominent persons, for names make news. But any publicity, even free publicity, is of little avail, in so far as it is a sign that the group in question is unable to advance its claims through quiet negotiations in Whitehall.

Political organization carries with it the risk of stimulating counter-mobilization. The more strongly one group presses its claims, the greater the pressure it puts upon opponents to organize pressure from an opposing interest. In so far as pressure groups are concerned with political issues, there will always be potential interests that may mobilize against them. For example, the political successes of trade unions place pressures upon business groups to improve their lobbying activities. Upon occasion, lobbying can have an effect opposite to what was intended. In 1968 a large Vietnam War demonstration at the U.S. Embassy in London turned into a publicity victory for the London police, because it gave the police an opportunity to show it could handle a large demonstration in an orderly fashion.[12]

[11] See Richard Rose, 'Britain: Simple Abstractions and Complex Realities', in R. Rose, ed., *Electoral Behavior: A Comparative Handbook* (New York: Free Press, 1974), Table 11. Subsequently, the proportion of trade unionists voting Labour has dropped to about half.

[12] See James D. Halloran *et al.*, *Demonstrations and Communication* (Harmondsworth: Penguin, 1970).

The political context

Pressure groups do not work in a vacuum; they can only influence public policy within a given context of political values and institutions. Cultural values determine the extent of broad political support for a group's claims. Political institutions determine how groups exercise influence.

The fundamental value of pressure groups is that all affected interests have a right to be consulted before the government of the day announces a decision. For example, when a government decision about the future of the British Museum was announced without consulting its trustees, the chairman, Lord Radcliffe, denounced this action as 'almost unbelievable administrative incompetence', being 'not only a grave constitutional impropriety that all these agencies should be ignored and despised, but also a gross discourtesy'.[13] Pressure group officials concede that their demands will not always be met by government, but they do expect that the government of the day, whatever the party, will listen to what they have to say before making firm policy commitments.

The likelihood of a pressure group gaining political support for its claims depends upon the congruence between its demands and values in the political culture. The more consistent pressure-group goals are with general cultural norms, the easier it is for a group to equate its interest with the national interest. The greater the clash with cultural norms, the more difficulties a group will face in pursuing its aims. At least six different relationships can occur:

1. *Harmony between pressure-group demands and general cultural norms.* Since animal pets command respect, affection and support, the Royal Society for the Prevention of Cruelty to Animals is in a favoured position. It does not need to devote much of its resources to gaining popular endorsement of its aims; they are already popular. Its resources are instead devoted to the very different (and far from easy) tasks of negotiating details of legislation and administration, and seeking priority for its demands in competition with other groups making claims on government.

2. *A gradual increase in the acceptability of political values supporting pressure-group demands.* For example, groups lobbying for colonial independence saw their position change in the 1950s and 1960s, as the claims of native nationalists for self-government

[13] House of Lords *Debates*, Vol. 287, cols. 1130ff. (13 December 1967).

became accepted, first within the Labour Party, and then widely throughout the political system. Similarly, proponents of permissiveness in the 1960s and 1970s have increasingly found government prepared to endorse their demands for changes in the law governing divorce, homosexuality, theatrical censorship, drinking and abortion.

3. *Bargaining with fluctuating support from cultural norms.* While there is always some pro-union and some pro-employer sentiment in society, the balance of support fluctuates in response to events, sometimes favouring one group or another in industrial relations disputes, or not sympathizing with either. Leaders of pressure groups with fluctuating popular support must be adaptable, pressing claims when support is high and acting defensively when their opponents are popular.

4. *Advocacy in the face of cultural indifference.* Indifference is a greater handicap than opposition. A pressure group fighting opposition at least has its views discussed. A group facing mass indifference will have no audience in government or outside it. For example, the National Society of Non-Smokers suffered for years from such public apathy that, although it claimed to represent 15 to 20 million non-smokers in the country, 'the majority of them have no knowledge of this society'.[14] It took the publication of evidence by medical experts that cigarettes can cause cancer to give political salience to the anti-smoking policies.

5. *Advocacy in opposition to long-term cultural trends.* A pressure group that finds cultural norms changing to its disadvantage is forced to fight a holding operation. For example, groups such as the Lord's Day Observance Society were once strong enough to secure legislation regulating Sunday activities, and some of these laws remain on the statute books. In view of diminishing cultural support for the political enforcement of religious values, the Society now must concentrate on forestalling or delaying the repeal of Sunday observance laws.

6. *Conflict between cultural values and pressure-group goals.* Any group may advocate demands in conflict with prevailing norms in the hope that cultural values will change and its goals will be realized. But groups advocating absolute values are handicapped because they cannot bargain with opponents in hopes of partial

[14] See Allen Potter, *Organized Groups in British National Politics* (London: Faber & Faber, 1961), p. 87.

accommodation; their goal of all or nothing makes even partial success appear a defeat. For example, leaders of the Irish Republican Army and British politicians from time to time have met to discuss their mutual interest in Northern Ireland, but these talks have always broken down, because the objectives of the two groups are in fundamental conflict.

Because they wish to secure benefits from government, the first rule of pressure groups is to exert pressure where decisions are made in the policy process. They concentrate attention upon civil servants and ministers in Whitehall, because, as the Devlin Report on Industrial Representation explained, 'All executive policy and most legislation is conceived, drafted and all but enacted in Whitehall.'[15]

Pressure groups give most attention to senior civil servants and departmental ministers, because the largest number of decisions of concern to pressure groups are made within a departmental context. For instance, regulations concerning industrial injury claims in the glass industry are unlikely to be discussed at Cabinet. They can most easily be settled by negotiations between the department concerned and representatives of affected groups. To achieve success in such circumstances, employers' or workers' representatives need only (sic) convince departmental officials that their position is reasonable, not contrary to Cabinet policy, and unlikely to cause conflict with other pressure groups.

A direct approach to ministers and civil servants is the normal channel of communication between established pressure groups and government departments. The channel may be institutionalized by the appointment of group spokesmen to departmental advisory committees. Group spokesmen accept this way of working because, if they are successful, those having power to act will immediately be in accord with them. Public officials prefer private approaches because this exposes them to a minimum of public criticism or unwelcome publicity about complex negotiations. Discussions carried on through channels allow each side to negotiate without a public and sometimes acrimonious exchange of demands.

Competition tends to constrain the influence of any pressure group. Whitehall officials receive different and often conflicting demands. They are aware that a concession, say, to commercial broadcasting interests will be opposed by newspaper proprietors

[15] Quoted in Grant and Marsh, *The Confederation of British Industry*, p. 2.

fearful of losing advertising revenue to broadcasting. Moreover, they are adept at playing off competing pressure groups against one another in search of an agreement that will be acceptable to the department's own interests, as well as those of groups lobbying it.

The influence of a particular pressure group upon government policy depends chiefly upon the scope and scale of the decision. The wider the scope of an issue, the greater the likelihood it will be controversial among conflicting pressure groups. All departmental decisions requiring public expenditure must be examined and approved by the Treasury before being presented to Parliament. The more complex the problem, the greater the likelihood that a number of Whitehall departments will be affected, thus requiring inter-departmental negotiations as well as negotiations between pressure groups and departments. Once a matter requires inter-departmental negotiations, the department initiating proceedings becomes an interest, seeking to advance claims on behalf of its preferred policy. The greater the importance of a question, the greater the likelihood that the Cabinet will be consulted, because its members will be collectively responsible for whatever is agreed. Once the Cabinet has taken a decision, then the sponsor department, like the pressure groups associated with it, must accept the policy made in the collective name of the government.

Within the political context of British politics, pressure groups find that the centralized institutions of Whitehall are relatively difficult to influence, by comparison with the highly permeable institutions of Congress and the executive branch in Washington. Moreover, the existence of very distinctive economic approaches in the alternative parties of government is a substantial countervailing force against many group demands. Pressure groups rarely expect to supplant government's authority. What they want to do is to influence specific details and particular procedures of policies to which the government is committed. In the words of a director-general of the Confederation of British Industry:

> Industry may or may not like the policy; and the CBI will say so on its behalf. But when the issue is decided, it may make a world of difference to industry how the policy is implemented and translated through administration into action.[16]

[16] Quoted in Samuel H. Beer, 'Pressure Groups and Parties in Britain', *American Political Science Review*, L:1 (1956), p. 8.

Government officials do not mechanically weigh the pressure that groups exert. The assessment of pressures and political consequences is inevitably uncertain. At a minimum, Whitehall influences policy by deciding how much weight competing groups can claim, and what should be the most appropriate bargain or deal for a settlement. At a maximum, government's power to enact laws and allocate public funds can change the weight of pressure groups by putting public power in the scales on behalf of otherwise weak groups. In the extreme case of the nationalization of an industry, the party in office can use the lawful powers of government to take over assets of a non-governmental organization, thereby fundamentally changing the forces with which it negotiates.

No pressure group, however favourable its position at the moment, can regard itself as static. The strength of a pressure group is ultimately determined by the complex influences that constitute the policy process. Even when these are favourable, a group must work hard to maintain its position against competition from other groups and prospective changes in the wider political environment.

The overall *pattern of policy* of the government of the day is the most important and variable influence upon pressure groups. The variability of policy is limited by long-term commitments made by previous governments, and by established practices of civil servants. But it is also subject to sudden shocks when party control of government changes at a general election. For example, in 1945 a Labour government entered office committed to nationalizing a number of major industries. It was not concerned with negotiating the question of principle—whether the mines or the railways should be nationalized—but with deciding how nationalization should take place.

The fortunes of every pressure group are much affected by whether or not its claims are considered partisan. A pressure group regarded as partisan will find its fortunes fluctuating depending upon which party is in power. In exceptional cases, a pressure group may enjoy bi-partisan support, as the National Farmers Union did for decades. But the NFU learned that this support was not permanent, for the Conservative government of Edward Heath was not prepared to put protectionist British agricultural interests ahead of its overriding commitment to negotiate entry to the Common Market.[17]

[17] Cf. J. Roland Pennock, 'Agricultural Subsidies in Britain and America', *American Political Science Review*, LVI:3 (1962) and Robert J. Lieber, 'Interest Groups and Political Integration: British entry into Europe', *ibid.*, LXVI:1 (1972).

In contemporary England, most pressure groups claim to be 'non-political', that is to say non-party-political, because they wish to be on good terms with the government of the day whatever its party. One study of urban pressure groups found that more than four-fifths of their demands had little relevance to party controversy.[18] But the growth of government's influence upon the mixed economy has tended to politicize many issues that pressure group leaders would prefer to regard as non-political.

Parties rather than pressure groups decide whether or not a group can secure non-partisan status for its claims. By making a political issue of a group's activities, a party draws a group into the arena of party conflict against its wishes. The Labour Party tendency to consider the totality of society's conditions as the concern of government often leads it to take the initiative in politicizing everything from secondary education to foxhunting.

Pressure groups face a perpetual dilemma: should they seek non-partisan or bi-partisan status by following a strategy of responsibility, co-operating with the government of the day in the implementation of its policies, in the hope of securing amendments in the group's interest? Or should they be outspoken in articulating their demands, even when this leads to controversy with the government of the day, and threatens the loss of concessions in private by Whitehall? The controversy about the reorganization of secondary education by the 1964–70 Labour government showed educational groups that there was no escape from this dilemma. Because the policy was a major commitment of the governing party, education groups that chose a non-partisan status found themselves on the sidelines when major decisions about the future of education were made.[19]

The exchange of influence

In contacts between pressure groups and government, influence moves in two directions: government seeks to influence pressure groups, and groups press claims upon government. An exchange of influence occurs because each has things that the other wants, and each can offer things that the other needs.

[18] See Kenneth Newton and David Morris, 'The Politics of Four Thousand Voluntary Organizations in a British City', Comparative Politics, VII:4 (1975) p. 587.
[19] See e.g. Paul E. Peterson, 'The Politics of Comprehensive Education in Three British Cities', Comparative Politics, III:3 (1971).

Pressure groups seek four things from government. First they seek information about government attitudes so that members can be informed of likely shifts in policies affecting them. Second, groups seek the goodwill of Whitehall officials who have discretionary power to decide whether or not a host of actions are allowable under established laws and regulations. The greater the amount of government supervision of a particular field, the greater the importance a pressure group places upon frequent and friendly contacts in Whitehall. Third, pressure groups seek to influence government policy. The most dramatic examples of influence are the introduction of legislation. More usually, a pressure group seeks to influence one element in a government decision. For example, when a new tax is imposed, pressure groups will clamour to have their own products exempt from its provisions. Fourth, pressure groups seek status. This may be given symbolically, by allowing an organization to add the prefix Royal to its title or by the award of a knighthood to its general secretary. A group's status also rises by virtue of membership in official committees, even if its actual influence does not change.[20]

Government seeks four things from pressure groups. Information is the simplest of its needs. By virtue of contacts with members, pressure groups accumulate much information that does not otherwise come to the attention of Whitehall, and which it will want to consider when reviewing a policy. Secondly, Whitehall wants advice, so that it can know what pressure groups think ought to be done and how they would react to various policies being canvassed within a department. Thirdly, once a decision is taken, a department expects pressure groups likely to benefit from the measure to give it support. Finally, when a policy has been made formally binding, government looks to pressure groups to co-operate in administering the law. In extreme instances, a government may want a group to carry out policies on its behalf. For example, the Marriage Guidance Council receives an annual government grant to do things that government considers in the national interest but unsuited to civil service procedures.

Because of the complementary nature of most of these needs, pressure groups and government find it easy to negotiate. The

[20] On the importance of status, especially to business groups, see J. P. Nettl, 'Consensus or Elite Domination: The Case of Business', *Political Studies*, XIII:1 (1965).

negotiations proceed without threats of coercion or bribery because each needs the other. The interdependence of pressure groups and government results in an exchange of influence in which policies can be the product of the dialectic, and not the specific product of one or the other group.

The object of negotiations is agreement. Public officials and pressure group spokesmen know it is a matter of great convenience for a general consensus to be achieved among all affected interests. Agreement is convenient for participants because it avoids decisions being taken by remote outsiders who know and care less about details than do those most involved. Agreement may not be in everyone's interest. It might be agreement about practices mutually convenient to producers and government, but not to consumers. Agreement can concentrate on conserving the community of interests of the bargainers without regard to the policy interests of those outside this close circle.

Tripartite (or so called corporatist) institutions of government, business and trade unions give concrete expression to the presumed mutuality of interest among the major participants in pressure group politics in England. In place of competition between conflicting interests or coercion by government or party, corporate institutions are expected to resolve major public policy questions by bringing together the major institutions outside government and government itself, to arrive collectively at decisions.[21]

Since the necessities of the Second World War forced the British government to take responsibility for mobilizing both labour and industry, Whitehall has been negotiating continuously with the Trades Union Congress and with a variety of business interest groups. Tripartite discussions have been primarily concerned with two sets of issues: How to increase economic growth by changes within British industry? How to prevent the inflation of prices and wages from destabilizing the economy, both domestically and internationally? The fact that tripartite institutions are recurringly established *and* abandoned demonstrates the seemingly ineluctable difficulties of framing institutions that can resolve these major problems of political economy.

[21] For a review of trends and literature, see Wyn Grant, 'Corporatism and Pressure Groups', in Dennis Kavanagh and Richard Rose, eds., *New Trends in British Politics* (London and Beverly Hills: Sage Publications, 1977). For a comparative discussion of corporatism, see the special issue of *Comparative Political Studies* X:1 (1977), edited by Philippe C. Schmitter.

The great bulk of tripartite deliberations are not corporatist, because they are meetings to discuss and advise, rather than to take legally binding decisions. Government is hesitant to delegate effective decision-making powers to councils in which Cabinet ministers are outnumbered by trade union and business spokesmen. Moreover, leaders of these pressure groups do not wish to be committed there to decisions that their own members may strongly oppose. Furthermore, questions of wages, economic growth and inflation cannot be decided by laws or corporate decrees alone; they are determined effectively by a complex process of influence outside as well as within government. When tripartite bodies do have effective executive authority, they tend to deal with the less controversial elements of manpower, industrial health and safety.[22]

Tripartite institutions appear most effective when their conclusions are consistent with the mutual interests of all three groups. For example, in 1975 high rates of inflation, combined with an actual contraction in the economy, brought about widespread acceptance of short-term measures to limit wage and price increases. Events allowed government to force groups to do what they accepted as desirable, but would not demand.

Just as government is hesitant about binding itself to accept decisions taken by economic pressure groups, so too pressure group leaders are hesitant about promising to deliver what is beyond them. Elite discussions between the heads of institutions become meaningless if the goodwill generated there cannot be translated into specific practical agreements implicating group members. This cannot be assumed, for as Lord Watkinson, former chairman of the CBI, has admitted, neither the Confederation of British Industry nor the TUC 'has effective control over its membership, to the extent that it can undertake to deliver a policy by ensuring that all its members will implement it'.[23]

All partners to tripartite bargaining tend to be constrained by the limited economic resources of society; this is especially true of England. When the economy is booming, every pressure group can hope to gain at least a little more in publicly financed benefits, paid for by the fiscal dividend of economic growth. When the economy is in trouble, as has been the case for most of the 1970s, pressure

[22] See Grant, 'Corporatism and Pressure Groups', pp. 173ff.
[23] Lord Watkinson, *Blueprint for Survival* (London: George Allen & Unwin, 1976), p. 88.

groups may concentrate upon defending their current standard of living, rather than demanding a relative or absolute increase in benefits.

Cumulatively, the granting of demands to many disparate groups adds up to big bills in aggregate. A pressure group sees only the particular benefits of any measure it advocates; the costs tend to be widely dispersed in society. By contrast, the government must be conscious of the total costs of all the demands made upon it. In 1977, a harried Labour minister for Health and Social Security was faced with demands to adopt dozens of well-intentioned pro- grammes for diverse disadvantaged groups, many of which were in principle attractive to Labour supporters. The minister responded by calling representatives of all these pressure groups together for a meeting. The agenda listed in detail the requests and the costs of each group's proposals. At the end of the paper, it added up the total bill; approximately £13 billion, more than twice as much as it was currently spending on social services. To have said yes to each group individually would have required an increase of almost 30 per cent in income tax to pay the aggregate bill.[24]

In the 1980s, both government and pressure groups face the challenge of reconciling the merits and costs of particular group demands with the total resources available to society. Pressure group leaders have no difficulty in urging their specific claims, arguing that their relatively small costs are not the major cause of the government's public expenditure difficulties. But what is true in isolation is not true in aggregate. The government of the day is the institution in society responsible for finding the resources to meet the sum total of group demands. It seeks to make claimant groups accept that the general interest of citizens in maintaining the mixed-economy welfare state must sometimes be set against the particular interests of pressure groups. The government must do more than respond to particular group demands; it must also articu- late policies that it regards as in the interest of the country as a whole.[25]

[24] Calculated by the author from an unpublished DHSS briefing paper for a Seminar on Social Security Priorities, London, 5 July 1977.
[25] For a detailed discussion of this point, see Richard Rose and Guy Peters, *Can Government Go Bankrupt?* (London: Macmillan, 1979), especially chs. 5, 9, 10.

IX
The Choice of Parties

Party organization is the vital principle of representative government, but that organisation is permanently efficient because it is not composed of warm partisans. The body is eager, but the atoms are cool.

British government is party government. Parties organize the selection of candidates, the preparation of programmes and the conduct of elections. At a general election, a voter does not vote for the policies that he or she wishes government to carry out; instead, votes must be cast for the party deemed best at aggregating the interests and values of millions of citizens. Individuals cannot expect any party's programme to match their own views perfectly. The aggregation of views in party manifestos forces voters to search for the party that best represents (or least misrepresents) their political outlook.[1]

Voters do not determine who governs, but rather which party names the governors. The leader of the party with the most seats in the House of Commons is invited to choose a Cabinet. Once in office, governors rely upon their party position to secure parliamentary support for their policies. If no party can secure an overall majority, as was the case in February 1974, another general election is likely to occur shortly, for the conventions of British government assume that party loyalty gives the executive the continued confidence of Parliament.

Political parties are complex organizations. Their members can be concerned with everything from majorities in the House of Commons to cake sales to raise funds for their local branch. Because parties are complex organizations, the motives that lead people into party politics are several. Making policy is but one of many things that can bring satisfaction to a party member. Making a career is another. The intensity of personal contacts among full-

[1] For a full elaboration of the intricacies of party politics, see Richard Rose, *The Problem of Party Government* (London: Macmillan, 1974) and *Do Parties Make a Difference?* (London: Macmillan, 1980).

time politicians can make the party dominate a person's social life too.

Collectively, parties constitute a system, for their actions are interdependent. What happens to one affects the others. For example, if the governing party loses popularity, then the opposition is likely to gain support as the means of 'turning the rascals out'. If one party announces that it favours a policy, such as increasing pensions, the pressure is on its opponents to adopt the same objective, or risk losing votes of the elderly. When one party in a system favours trade unions, there is scope for a competitor to seek votes by favouring interests not represented by trade unions.

For generations, writers about British politics have praised the virtues of the party system as a means of fixing responsibility for government, and assuring effective legislative support for whichever party proved most popular with voters. In the 1970s, the British party system has come under criticism. Writers with strong left-wing or right-wing views criticize the established Conservative and Labour parties for not offering voters a wide enough political choice; both are said to seek the 'middle ground' in the competition for votes. Others complain that established parties offer the wrong choice, neglecting the views of individuals who do not accept orthodox trade union or business policies. The two 1974 British general elections showed there were many who shared this dissatisfaction, for the votes of 'third force' parties, the Liberals plus Scottish, Welsh and Ulster nationalists, rose to 25 per cent of the total. While the Labour Party won office, it did not win a secure parliamentary majority.[2] In 1979, the combined vote of the two major parties rose, but 'third force' parties secured nearly one vote in five.

In order to understand the choices that the party system offers, we must first consider the way in which elections translate individual votes into parliamentary strength or weakness. Secondly, we must consider how the parties organize themselves to formulate policies and choose leaders to carry out policies. The third section of this chapter systematically compares the views of voters and the views of the parties for which they vote to see how good is the fit between representatives and represented. Finally, examining coalition and competition between parties emphasizes the extent of differences within, as well as between parties.

[2] For a collection of critical academic views, see S. E. Finer, ed., *Adversary Politics and Electoral Reform* (London: Clive Wigram, 1975).

Electoral choice

The decision of one person—the Prime Minister—determines the date at which an election is held. While an Act of Parliament states that an election must occur at least once in every five years, the Prime Minister is free to request the Queen to dissolve Parliament and call a general election at a time of the governing party's choice. Thus, the person with the most to win or lose by a general election seeks to select the most favourable date for the party in power. In search of re-election, a Prime Minister can try to manage the economy to increase prosperity and use opinion polls to gauge popularity. Both Labour and Conservative Prime Ministers have won re-election even though their party trailed the opposition during most of the Parliament.[3] But in six of the eleven elections since 1945, the party in power has lost the election it called.

The ballot offers a very simple choice. A voter is presented with a small sheet of paper giving the name, address, occupation and party description of several persons, each of whom seeks to become the single MP from the constituency. The ideas and arguments of thousands of political activists and the decisions of a multiplicity of party committees are aggregated by the ballot paper into a choice between a few partisan standard-bearers. Until 1970, no reference to party affiliation appeared on the ballot paper. Nomination requires only the written endorsement of ten of the constituency's electors. To discourage frivolous contestants, each candidate is required to post a deposit of £150 with nomination papers. This deposit is forfeited if the candidate does not secure at least one-eighth of the vote in the constituency. In the 1979 general election, the Liberal Party lost 304 deposits in the 577 seats it contested, the Conservatives 3 deposits, Labour 22, the Welsh Nationalists 29 in the 36 seats they contested, and the Scottish Nationalists 29 in the 71 seats they contested.

There is always a third choice, even when only two parties are on the ballot: not voting. The level of voluntary or involuntary abstention from voting is low in England by comparison with the United States but high by European standards. While non-political reasons

[3] See the compilation of opinion poll data in D. E. Butler and A. Sloman, *British Political Facts, 1900–1975* (London: Macmillan, 4th ed., 1975), pp. 204–18, and for interpretation, see William L. Miller and Myles Mackie, 'The Electoral Cycle and the Asymmetry of Government and Opposition Popularity', *Political Studies*, XXXI:3 (1973).

appear to explain most abstentions, it is noteworthy that the proportion of eligible voters not voting at a general election rose from 16 per cent in 1951 to 24 per cent in 1979.

How a person votes reflects the cumulation of a lifetime of influences, and not just the events of a single election campaign, or a single Parliament. Ninety per cent of British voters identify with a political party, and when a general election is announced, those who have identified with a party are already predisposed to vote for it. In an election campaign parties canvass their established supporters to turn out to vote. An increasing proportion of voters, however, have not been loyal to one party through a series of elections. The great majority do not change sides completely. Most floating voters move between voting and non-voting, or between voting for the Liberals and one of the two largest parties. Few cross from Conservative to Labour ranks or vice versa.[4]

Voters identify parties by their generalized image, and not by carefully weighing all the actions for which a party is responsible in government, or all the pledges that an opposition party makes. Party images are relatively stable, for they are derived from the past achievements of the parties and the past experience of voters. The characteristics that voters cite when asked what they think about a party usually imply a judgment that past performance will persist in the future: 'Knows how to get along with business', 'Knows how to get along with the trade unions', 'United party', 'Experienced leaders', and so forth.

Individual party leaders contribute relatively little to party images, for they are ephemeral figures. Not only are party leaders changed from time to time, but also esteem for an individual fluctuates during a period of party leadership. While the person remains the same personality, voters' opinions change more or less in tandem with the evaluation that they put on the government's record. As Prime Minister, Harold Macmillan saw his approval by Gallup Poll respondents fluctuate from 30 to 79 per cent; Harold Wilson saw his swing between 27 and 66 per cent, and Edward Heath from 31 to 45 per cent. Margaret Thatcher led the winning party at the 1979 election, even though opinion polls consistently gave James

[4] See David Butler and Donald Stokes, *Political Change in Britain* (London: Macmillan, 2nd ed., 1974), and Ivor Crewe, Bo Sarlvik and James Alt, 'Partisan Dealignment in Britain, 1964–1974', *British Journal of Political Science*, VII:2 (1977).

Callaghan a higher popular rating. The influence of a leader's personality upon the electorate is much less than it is in America, where the less well-defined image of American parties and the freedom from party discipline of elected officials make personal considerations more important.

Voters tend to relate their party identification and party images to relatively unchanging perceptions of social class. The Labour Party is most often perceived as a party standing for class interests. The Conservatives see themselves as a 'national' party; their opponents attack them as the party of the wealthy or middle class. The Liberals like to appear as a party rejecting a class-based appeal or as standing for a class in between the wealthy and the lowest class. More than one half of the electorate votes for the party with a class image that is not strictly consistent with the voters' own class. (Cf Table V.4.) The difference between sociological expectations and individual behaviour indicates the scope for choice free from crude social determinism.

In aggregate, the differences in class size and electoral cohesiveness result in an asymmetrical profile of party supporters. In terms of its vote, the Labour Party is a class party, for more than 75 per cent of its vote comes from working-class electors. By contrast, the Conservative Party draws 46 per cent of its vote from the middle class, and 54 per cent the working class. The greater social cohesion of the Labour vote gives that party's leaders a relatively clear indication of issues and interests that concern its supporters. There is also the risk that Labour concentrates exclusively upon the working class, ignoring the middle-class third of the electorate. The Conservatives must appeal to a more heterogeneous group of voters, and party leaders must consider the implications of their policies for working-class voters, as well as for their well-defined middle-class supporters.[5]

Because many movements of voters tend to offset each other, the net fluctuation in the vote for the two major parties is small by absolute or comparative standards. Since 1945, the Conservative share of the national vote has varied by 13.9 per cent, and the Labour share by 11.9 per cent. (See Figure IX.1.) By comparison, since 1948 in America the Republicans' share of the Presidential vote has varied by 22.2 per cent between its peak and trough, and

[5] See Richard Rose, 'Britain: Simple Abstractions and Complex Realities', in R. Rose, ed., *Electoral Behavior* (New York: Free Press, 1974).

the Democratic Party's share by 23.6 per cent. Both the Conservative and Labour parties fell below 40 per cent of the total vote in both 1974 elections, and in 1979 Labour recorded 36.9 per cent of the popular vote, its lowest since 1931.[6]

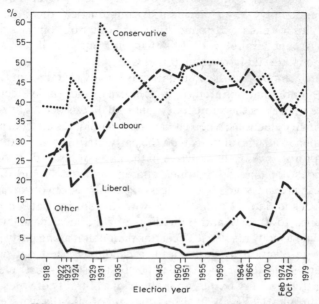

FIGURE IX.1   **Votes cast at British General Elections 1918–1979**

The two major parties are very evenly matched in their national electoral appeal. In the eleven elections since 1945, Labour has won an average of 44.2 per cent of the vote, and the Conservatives 43.5 per cent. The margin of votes between the two parties is usually small, averaging 3.8 per cent. In the 34 years from 1945 to 1979, Labour was in office for 17 years, and the Conservatives for 17.

The logic of the electoral system favours the single strongest party, however small or large its share of the vote. The net swing in votes between the two major parties has averaged only 2.6 per cent in post-war elections (that is, 26 votes in 1,000). Election results make it appear that big political changes are taking place because a swing of one per cent of the vote can deliver about 15 seats from the Conservatives to Labour or vice versa, thus altering

[6] For the definitive text of election results, used in all calculations in this book, see F. W. S. Craig, *British Electoral Facts, 1885–1975* (London: Macmillan, 1976).

the government's majority in the Commons by 30. A swing of two or three per cent is usually enough to change control of government from one Parliament to the next.

The evenness of the national strength of the parties is not, however, matched by competition at the constituency level. The evenness nationally is an accidental consequence of large local majorities for each party cancelling each other out on the national scale. At a general election less than one-tenth of all seats in the Commons are likely to change hands.

In such circumstances, nomination is usually tantamount to election. But nominations are not the concern of the whole electorate, nor are they even the subject of a public ballot as occurs in American primary elections, when each party's candidates are chosen by a vote open to all who identify with the party. In England, nomination is the prerogative of those active in the party organization. A voter who does not like the nominee chosen by his local constituency party can abstain, vote none the less on party lines, or vote against his party's candidate. Voters faced with a conflict between their allegiance to a party and their dislike of the local parliamentary candidate usually resolve it by casting their ballot along party lines.[7]

To win election to Parliament, a candidate need not gain an absolute majority of the votes; the 'first-past-the-post' electoral system gives victory to the candidate with a plurality of votes. From 1945 through 1970, about three-quarters of all MPs were elected with more than half the votes in their constituency. But the proportion of MPs elected with an absolute majority fell to 36 per cent elected in February 1974, rising again to 40 per cent in October 1974.

The electoral system usually manufactures a majority party in Parliament from a minority of votes. No party has won more than half the popular vote since the 1935 general election; the post-war high is the 49.7 per cent share of the vote gained by the Conservatives in 1955. Yet at ten out of eleven elections since the war, one party has won an absolute majority of seats in the House of Commons. In the extreme case of October 1974, the Labour Party won a bare majority of 318 seats with only 39.2 per cent of the total popular vote. By contrast, the Liberals won only 13 seats with 18.3 per cent of the vote. The 1979 election was more typical. The

[7] See Philip M. Williams, 'Two Notes on the British Electoral System', *Parliamentary Affairs*, XX:1 (1964).

Conservatives won 53.3 per cent of the seats in the Commons with 43.9 per cent of the vote, and the Liberals 1.7 per cent of the seats with 13.8 per cent of the vote.

The electoral system is not intended to provide proportional representation for the parties, allotting seats in the Commons in accord with each party's share of the national vote. It is a system of *dis*proportional representation, intended to vest control of government in the hands of one party by giving it an absolute majority in the House of Commons. To criticize the system because it does not produce an exact ratio of seats to votes is to miss the political point. It is not meant to treat all parties equally; it is intended to give all the power of the Crown to the largest party however large or small its support may be. In the 1970s, some students of British politics have come to regard the abrupt reversal of control of government as more destructive of stable policies than the changes likely to arise in a system of coalition politics, as is found in many Continental European countries, and also in the United States Congress.

Britain can be said to have a two-party system by one measure only: the number of parties that have formed a government since 1945. Since then, government has been in the hands of either the Labour Party or the Conservative Party; no other party has shared in office. In 1977–8, when the Labour government depended upon the votes of 13 Liberals for a working majority in the Commons, Liberals could discuss pending legislation with the government, but not sit in government nor, as it turned out, exert significant positive influence upon that legislation. Except in war or national crisis, Labour and Conservative politicians would rather accept the perils of governing without a parliamentary majority than share power in a coalition government.

In electoral terms, Britain has a multi-party (that is, more than two-party) system. This is clearly and consistently shown in four different ways:

1. In most constituencies there are normally three or more candidates contesting the seat: Labour, Conservative, and Liberal or Nationalist. In 1979, there were 2,576 candidates contesting 635 seats, an average of 4.1 candidates per seat.

2. The two major parties do not monopolize the popular vote. They came closest to doing so in 1951, when the Conservative and Labour candidates collectively secured 96.8 per cent of the popular vote. The two major parties have not secured more than 90 per cent

of the vote since 1959, and since 1970, have taken no more than 81 per cent of the total vote.

3. The two major parties do not monopolize seats in the House of Commons. The electoral system has on average awarded Conservative and Labour parties 97 per cent of the seats in the House of Commons. But in 1950, 1964 and February 1974, the existence of a small third force group prevented the government from holding a Commons majority large enough to make a government secure for five years.

4. Outside England, a multiplicity of parties win significant numbers of seats and votes. In the extreme case of Northern Ireland, parties tend to organize around two religions—Protestant and Catholic—and since 1974, the British Labour and Conservative parties have failed to nominate any candidates there. In Scotland, the Scottish National Party and the Liberal Party between them won 26.3 per cent of the popular vote in 1979, and in Wales, the combined strength of Welsh Liberals and the Welsh Nationalists took 18.7 per cent of the Welsh vote in 1979. (See Table II.2.)

The party system is better described as multi-party than three-party, because the name and number of relevant parties differs from election to election, as well as from area to area of the United Kingdom. The Liberals have consistently run third in total votes in the United Kingdom, but they have not won more than 14 MPs at any election since 1945. Nationalist parties, confining their appeal to one part of the United Kingdom, can win more seats than the Liberal Party, because the nationalists bunch their constituency vote, thus increasing their chances of coming first in a few seats. In October 1974, the Welsh Nationalists won an average of one seat in the House of Commons for every 55,000 votes, the Scottish Nationalists won one seat for every 76,000 votes, and the British Liberals, one seat for every 411,000 votes. In 1979, the ratios changed again. The Welsh Nationalists won one seat for every 66,000 votes, the SNP one seat for every 252,000 votes, and the Liberals, one for every 392,000 votes.

The Liberal Party, which rotated in office with the Conservatives for most of the century up to the First World War, has the most substantial claim to be the country's third party. It consistently contests constituencies throughout Great Britain and has fought at least 300 seats at every election since 1964. Since 1945 its share of the total national vote has ranged from 2.6 per cent in 1951 to 19.3

per cent in February 1974. In eleven post-war general elections it has averaged 9.8 per cent, and in six since 1964, 11.5 per cent. The Liberal vote total is depressed by the fact that potential supporters cannot vote Liberal where the party does not nominate candidates. Liberal membership in the House of Commons has ranged from 6 to 14.

If the Liberal Party were contesting elections in a proportional representation system, such as applies in most Continental European countries, it would be one of the country's three major parties, winning one hundred seats or more at a typical general election. Voters consistently indicate that they would be readier to vote Liberal if they thought the party had a reasonable chance of victory.[8] The Liberals would expect to participate in coalition governments frequently, if Britain were to conduct elections by proportional representation. The very reason that encourages the Liberals to support proportional representation—the fact that it would increase their influence in British government—is the reason for Labour and Conservative MPs to vote overwhelmingly to retain the existing first-past-the-post electoral system.

The persistence of two parties alternating in government is not a reflection of class structure or of a psychological predisposition to favour choices of an either/or type. Nor is it even a necessary consequence of the first-past-the-post electoral system, for the non-English parts of the United Kingdom consistently have more than two parties represented in Parliament. The pre-eminence of two parties reflects first of all the small size of the non-English parts of the United Kingdom. Secondly, it reflects the inability of the Liberals to break through the threshold dividing gainers and losers in a plurality-vote electoral system. To achieve a breakthrough, the Liberals would need to win one-third of the national vote or more, rather than one-sixth or one-eighth of the vote as tends to be the case. As it stands, the electoral system faces voters with much the same choice as a vote of confidence in the House of Commons: a choice between two parties, the Ins and the Outs. A voter can vote for or against the governing party and the opposition. The great majority of voters are prepared to accept this choice, some with a

[8] For studies of the Liberal voter, see Peter H. Lemieux, 'Political Issues and Liberal Support in the February, 1974 British General Election', and James Alt, Ivor Crewe and Bo Sarlvik, 'Angels in Plastic: The Liberal Surge in 1974', *Political Studies*, XXV:3 (1977).

marked preference for one party, and others reduced to choosing between the lesser of two perceived evils.[9]

Control of the organization

Because British government is party government, control of the party promises control of government. But neither the Conservative nor the Labour Party can be controlled from any single central position, for each is a complex set of plural institutions. Each party can be divided into three major parts: the party in Parliament, the party at headquarters and a network of constituency parties. Each part is differently composed and differently controlled. Much of the effort within parties is not directed against the electoral enemy, or at the government of the country. It is intended to keep together the disparate parts of a complex party structure. Fragmentation, not mechanical integration, is the chief feature of party organizations.

The party in Parliament enunciates and applies party policy routinely and in crises at Westminster. Events and issues arise so fast that speed greatly limits consultation between the party inside and outside Parliament. Sometimes, there is also little prior consultation among front-benchers in Parliament or Cabinet, and between these leaders and their own back-bench MPs. Once party leaders in Parliament have made a commitment, it is an important political fact. Other sections of the party are expected to go along with the decision of party leaders, particularly if they form the government of the day.

The organization of a party in Parliament varies with its electoral fortunes. The leader of the majority party automatically becomes Prime Minister and forms a Cabinet that constitutes the front bench or leadership stratum in Parliament. When out of office, the Parliamentary Labour Party elects a Parliamentary Committee of twelve to act as its executive committee. The party leader allots shadow ministerial posts to the Committee members, as well as to those not elected to it. In the Conservative Party, the party leader distributes shadow posts as the leader thinks best; the back-benchers elect a chairman of their own group, the 1922 Committee.

The party headquarters of both major parties are symbolically opposite each other in Smith Square, slightly removed from the

[9] On popular attitudes toward parties, see the national survey data reported in the Appendix of the report of Lord Houghton's *Committee on Financial Aid to Political Parties* (London: HMSO, Cmnd. 6601, 1976).

central axis of Whitehall and the Palace of Westminster.[10] The size of the staff working for each party differs substantially. (Table IX.1.) The Conservatives have more than twice the staff of Labour, and Labour five times that of the Liberal Party. Only the Conservative Party has a full-time official in a majority of constituencies. The Labour Party maintains a full-time worker in less than one-quarter of the constituencies in which it returns MPs. In all three parties, the bulk of officials are agents, specialists in organization. The influence of agents is limited by their dispersion throughout the country; they represent a relatively small proportion of staff at party headquarters. At headquarters, the research staff is the largest single group: it consists of university graduates. The research department is not so much concerned with long-term policy analysis as with briefing MPs and front-bench spokesmen and serving on party policy committees. The briefing work overlaps the efforts of the publicity department, concerned with press releases, advertising and television.

TABLE IX.1   **Full-time party staff by activity, 1979**[a]

	Con.	Lab.	Lib.
Organization			
National headquarters	18	11	3
Regional offices	42	39	6
Constituencies	335	80	15
Research	32	20	3
Publicity	14	16	6
Finance	14	4	1
General administration	14	12	2
Total	469	182	36

Note [a] Labour figures for Great Britain; Conservative and Liberal for England and Wales only. Clerical and ancillary staff excluded.

The Conservative Party has a dual structure; two organizations share common facilities in Smith Square.[11] One organization is the Conservative Central Office, which services the Conservative Party in Parliament. The chairman of Central Office is appointed by the

[10] For a full discussion of party organization, see Rose, *The Problem of Party Government*, chs. 6–10.

[11] See particularly Michael Pinto-Duschinsky, 'Central Office and "Power" in the Conservative Party', *Political Studies*, XX:1 (1972).

leader of the party in Parliament. He is usually a front-bench MP, and when the party is in government, also in the Cabinet.

The second organization is the National Union of Conservative and Unionist Associations, which brings together constituency parties. At the Annual Conference of the National Union, individual constituency associations express their views about party policy. Votes at the Annual Conference are allotted in equal numbers to each constituency association. The leaders in Parliament have no voting rights; the gathering is technically not their conference. The parliamentary leadership exercises influence informally, by the exclusion of resolutions that could embarrass the leadership and by speaking frequently in Conference debates. Because resolutions are usually phrased to avoid splits within the party, and few delegates wish to vote against their parliamentary leadership, it is rare for a Conference debate to conclude with a formal ballot. Between 1950 and 1964, no such ballot was held; from 1967 to 1976 there were eight occasions in which intra-party differences were pushed to a conference ballot.

The Labour Party* is an amalgam of diverse organizations. It incorporates independent centres of power in one body, thus institutionalizing a potential for disagreement that is averted by the dualistic Conservative structure. The constitution of the Labour Party states, 'The work of the party shall be under the direction and control of the Party Conference.' The five-day meeting of the party's Annual Conference concentrates upon debating policy resolutions. Resolutions and amendments are not fixed by the platform, and controversial resolutions are usually pressed to a vote. Votes are distributed according to notional figures of membership. Approximately five-sixths of the Conference vote is in the hands of trade unions, distributed in proportion to the money that each union pays annually as a per capita affiliation fee for membership. The vote of each union is cast as a single unit, even though the union's membership and delegation may be divided almost evenly about how to cast its bloc vote. The five largest affiliated unions—the Transport and General Workers, the Amalgamated Union of Engineering Workers, the General and Municipal Workers, the Electrical and Plumbing Trades Union, and the Shop, Distributive & Allied Workers—together have an absolute major-

* Described as of the 1979 general election, prior to the party's 1979 Annual Conference approving resolutions involving major changes.

ity of the Conference vote. The bloc vote thus concentrates far more power in the hands of a few political caucuses than is done in an American presidential nomination convention.[12]

Between Annual Conferences, the National Executive Committee directs the Labour Party's headquarters. Its membership is also dominated by trade-union votes. The unions elect twelve of the committee's twenty-nine members in their own name, and their votes dominate the selection of the five women's representatives and the party's treasurer. The constituency parties elect seven representatives, often back-bench MPs, and the Co-operative Societies and Young Socialists, one each. Seats are also reserved for the leader and deputy leader of the Parliamentary Labour Party.

The full-time headquarters staff at Transport House works under the direction of the National Executive Committee and its sub-committees. The party chairmanship rotates annually by seniority; this limits its political importance and adds to the stature of the party's general secretary, the senior full-time staff official. The leader of the Parliamentary Labour Party remains the chief spokesman for the party as a whole, but lacks the formal authority to issue directives to Transport House staff or to countermand decisions of the National Executive Committee.

The headquarters staff in each party must try to satisfy two distinct groups: the party in Parliament and the party in the constituencies. (In addition, Transport House staff must consider the views of trade unions affiliated to the party.) To keep headquarters and constituency groups in contact, the parties maintain regional offices. Regional offices are directed by headquarters and do not control constituency parties. They act as observers and advisers to constituency associations but cannot issue orders, nor are their staffs sufficiently large to provide organizational assistance to constituencies where the party is weak.[13] It is illustrative of limited contact that no party headquarters can estimate accurately how many individuals are members of their party at the constituency level.

The local organizations of the parties are defined by parliamentary constituencies but usually these boundaries do not encompass a natural geographical unit or community. The constituencies are larger than wards comprising urban neighbourhoods, yet are rarely

[12] Cf. Richard Rose, 'Between Miami Beach and Blackpool', *Political Quarterly*, XLIII:4 (1972).

[13] See David J. Wilson, *Power and Party Bureaucracy in Britain* (Farnborough, Sussex: Saxon House, 1975).

the same size as a city or county. Where a party controls local government, there are immediate incentives for members to give priority to affairs within their own community. A high level of membership does not necessarily indicate great interest in parliamentary politics. It may indicate that the local party provides a good social club, can organize garden fêtes and bazaars, or runs a well-organized football pool. The interest of headquarters in developing a mass-membership organization in every constituency need not be matched by constituency officials.

Constituency parties are important nationally inasmuch as each separately selects a parliamentary candidate; collectively, the choices of constituency parties constitute the House of Commons, and provide the pool of mixed ability from which a Prime Minister selects a Cabinet. National party headquarters compile lists of would-be parliamentary candidates, vetting applicants more on personal grounds than on strict policy grounds (whether the individual has a criminal record, evidence of recent or current membership in another political party, and so forth). A constituency party then compiles a list of persons to interview, some of whom are locally known and some from outside the constituency; there is no requirement that a parliamentary candidate lives in the constituency. In a hopeless seat, a constituency may have to hunt hard to find anyone to be the party's standard-bearer. The selection of the constituency candidate is made after interviewing up to a dozen prospects, sometimes in as brief a space as a single afternoon or evening. The final choice is made by a constituency party committee, which may have a dozen members or up to several hundred.

The decentralization of candidate choice to more than 600 associations in each party results in the selection of a wide variety of candidates and prevents party headquarters from favouring any one faction or tendency within the party. Some constituencies favour local worthies, others the individual who promises to attend to constituency interests in a professional way or celebrities from the media, and others consciously seek a potential Cabinet minister to represent them. Intra-party differences on policy appear more important in Labour constituency parties than in Conservative ranks.

Once selected and elected to the House of Commons, an MP from a safe seat—about three-quarters of the total—need not fear rejection by the voters. A small number may find their security upset by population movements leading to boundary changes of their constituency. The great majority need only fear rejection by their local constituency party. The Conservative Party does not require that MPs submit to re-selection before each general election; Labour procedures are under review.

There are three major grounds for the constituency rejecting a sitting member, and thus ejecting him or her from the House of Commons. Personal delinquencies—heavy drinking, financial irregularities, etc.—are the most frequently cited reason. Old age or laxness in attending to constituency requests is a second reason. Political differences between the MP and the constituency have been a third basis of controversy. Historically, constituency parties have been expected not to 'interfere' with the political judgments of their MP at Westminster.[14] Today, there are more articulate constituency activists with views at variance with their Member, and an increasing number of Labour MPs are under pressure to adapt views to suit constituency association inclinations.

To ask who controls the party organization is to assume that someone must be in effective charge. Yet it is logically possible that no one official or committee controls all of the disparate institutions described above. The most obvious claimant to control is the party leader in Parliament. In both parties, the position of the leader is strongest when the leader is also Prime Minister, with authority enhanced by constitutional conventions and Cabinet patronage. Moreover, an open attack upon a Prime Minister threatens the party with loss of office through internecine conflict. But only one party leader can enjoy the status of Prime Minister at any one time. The opposition leader has no powers of patronage, and influence will depend upon whether the leader is expected to become Prime Minister after the next election.

The dynamics of electoral competition alter the status of the leader during the lifetime of a Parliament. The leader of a newly elected government can claim popular justification for authority. Conversely, the leader of the opposition has just had his efforts repudiated, with disastrous effects on the ministerial ambitions of colleagues and a wait of four or five years before it is possible to try to reverse the defeat. Midway in the life of a Parliament, the positions are usually turned around, as the governing party becomes

[14] Cf. A. D. R. Dickson, 'MPs' Readoption Conflicts: Their Causes and Consequences', *Political Studies*, XXIII:1 (1975).

unpopular. The Prime Minister is no longer the person who led the party to victory, and may appear as the person who will lead it to defeat if not replaced before the next election. The Prime Minister's influence is discounted appropriately. At the same time, the leader of the opposition becomes the Prime Minister apparent and the value of shadow patronage appreciates. As another general election approaches, the need to unite a party—whether in government or opposition—increases the leader's influence, as the person around whom others must rally.

The influence of the party leader is a variable, not a constant. It fluctuates according to the personality of the individual. For example, at the height of his wartime success, Winston Churchill had far greater influence upon Conservatives than did one of his Conservative successors, Sir Alec Douglas-Home. But influence varies even more during one man's tenure of office. For example, after his stroke in 1953, Churchill passed the last eighteen months of his Prime Ministership without the physical ability to exert such influence as he retained. In theory, a party leader could retire at the height of his influence. Stanley Baldwin, who left office voluntarily in 1937, was the last party leader to do so until Harold Wilson retired voluntarily in 1976. Every leader in between has retired after ill health had visibly reduced his influence, after political failures had reduced his followers' confidence, or after his standing had diminished on both counts.

The influence of the Labour Party leader is complicated by the status accorded the party's Annual Conference. R. T. McKenzie has argued that the party's constitution is at variance with the British constitution. He claims that a non-elected party conference has no right to dictate to an elected Parliamentary Labour Party, whether it is in office or in opposition. The party's constitution also recognizes that in practice the Annual Conference cannot bind MPs dealing with complex and changing events; they are expected 'to give effect as far as may be practicable to the principles from time to time approved by the Party Conference' (Clause IV.3).

Because Labour's National Executive Committee is dominated by the same extra-parliamentary constituency that dominates Annual Conference, there are continuing opportunities for the extra-parliamentary organization to take positions opposed to the Parliamentary Labour Party, and controversy can ramify throughout all the institutions of the Labour movement. For example, in

1960 the Annual Conference endorsed unilateral nuclear disarmament, overriding the wishes of Hugh Gaitskell, then opposition
leader. Gaitskell denied the right of the Annual Conference to
dictate to popularly elected MPs. But he and his friends also paid
silent respect to the Annual Conference, by organizing support
within the extra-parliamentary party so that the decision was
reversed by the Annual Conference the following year. At the
height of the dispute, the party's general secretary summarized the
practical political moral:

> Within the party there are three centres of decision making: the
> Annual Conference, the National Executive Committee and the
> Parliamentary Labour Party. . . . None of these elements can
> dominate the others. Policy cannot be laid down: it must be
> agreed.[15]

The problem does not arise in the Conservative Party because of the
absence of formal accountability of the party leader to the Conference of the National Union. Moreover, Conservative Central Office
does not issue policy statements in the manner of Labour's National
Executive Committee.

The autonomy of different parts of the two major parties is most
clearly demonstrated by an analysis of party finance. Of all commodities, money is in principle among the easiest to transfer. Yet
neither the Conservative nor the Labour party has any institutional
mechanism by which money can be centrally allocated. The problem of finance affects both the relatively affluent Conservatives and
the Labour Party, which operates in a chronic state of financial
difficulty even though individual trade unions simultaneously
accumulate large reserves in their own political funds. For example,
in 1972 the unions held in aggregate £2.9 million in their separate
political funds, equal to more than two years' revenue for an under-
financed Transport House. Of the total revenue the unions raise
by their political levy on members' dues, little more than half is
contributed to Labour headquarters or constituency parties. The
remainder is spent directly by the unions or hoarded in cash
reserves.[16] In the Conservative Party, constituency associations

[15] Cf. Morgan Phillips, *Constitution of the Labour Party* (London: Labour Party,
1960), p. 4, R. T. McKenzie, *British Political Parties* (London: Heinemann, 2nd ed.,
1963) and Lewis Minkin, *The Labour Party Conference* (London: Allen Lane,
1978).
[16] See Rose, *The Problem of Party Government*, ch. 9.

raise more than twice as much money as Central Office, and retain five-sixths of these funds to spend on local activities, no matter how safe the seat. Similarly, Central Office spends most of its money centrally.

Stratarchy is the best term to describe the distribution of power within British political parties. Parties are not hierarchical organizational 'weapons', led from the top like an army. They are stratarchies,[17] characterized by different groups ruling at different levels or strata of the organization. Local councillors tend to run their local party as an adjunct of local concerns; the party's chief full-time officer in Smith Square can be primarily concerned with bureaucratic problems of co-ordination; and the parliamentary leader can run the party in the Commons in the way deemed best suited to the environment of Westminster.

Party organizations are often referred to as machines, but the term is a misnomer. The parties do not have a machine to manufacture votes at election time, nor can a party headquarters necessarily manufacture support for a party leader under criticism. Nor does party organization convert the preferences of voters into government policy by any process recognizable as mechanical, even in a metaphorical sense. By the standards of American political parties, British parties are organizations, that is, they have formal institutions and offices, established by a written constitution and staffed by long-service bureaucrats whose careers depend upon organizational loyalty rather than loyalty to an individual politician. But by comparison with party organizations in such countries as Germany and Sweden, British parties are outdated and under-capitalized organizations. The Houghton Committee on Financial Aid to Political Parties, judging parties by the requirements of a healthy democracy, concluded: 'British political parties frequently operate below the minimum level of efficiency and activity required.'[18]

Policy preferences

Whether and to what extent parties stand for different policies is a matter of theoretical and practical controversy.[19] To deny differ-

---

[17] See Samuel J. Eldersveld, *Political Parties: A Behavioral Analysis* (Chicago: Rand, McNally, 1964).

[18] See p. 54.

[19] See Richard Rose, *Do Parties Make a Difference?*

ences of opinion among parties and partisans is to deny that parties are concerned with politics, that is, making decisions about matters of public choice. But it is often argued that some issues, such as foreign policy, should be above party dispute; all Englishmen are said to have a common interest *vis-à-vis* other nations. In domestic affairs, differences may be matters of degree: even a seemingly clear-cut ideological issue such as nationalization can become a matter of degree: how many industries should be nationalized? Parties can also differ on matters of timing. Typically, Conservatives are inclined to argue that the time is not yet right for change, whereas Labour MPs may argue change is overdue. Even if parties agree about both means and ends, they will disagree about which is best qualified to carry through policies in the national interest.

At a very high level of abstraction, parties differ about their vision of an ideal society. But none of the parties is so explicitly ideological that it presents an election manifesto as a logical conclusion deduced from a theory of society. The Conservative Party does not even offer a statement of goals in the constitution of its National Union, as the Labour and Liberal parties do. Many of the goals enunciated in party constitutions are not specific to a single party. For instance, the Liberals' endorsement of peace, prosperity and liberty, and denunciation of poverty and ignorance could be echoed by almost any party anywhere.[20]

Statements of principle must be general if they are to be of enduring significance. But generality reduces their applicability to day-to-day politics. The gap between abstract ideals and everyday reality is such that goals may best be considered symbols to inspire partisans to battle. Harold Wilson aptly caught the symbolic flavour of much debate about party principles when he said, concerning efforts to abandon Labour's symbolic commitment to total nationalization:

> We were being asked to take Genesis out of the Bible. You don't have to be a fundamentalist in your religious approach to say that Genesis is part of the Bible.[21]

If contrasting political philosophies are to affect everyday politics, then the policy preferences of partisans should differ, as do the

[20] See John D. Lees and Richard Kimber, eds., *Political Parties in Modern Britain* (London: Routledge & Kegan Paul, 1972), pp. 14ff.
[21] In a radio interview reprinted in *The Listener*, 29 October 1964.

outlooks of conservative, liberal and socialist philosophers. A review of popular attitudes to a variety of political issues —economic, social and moral—shows that a plurality of both Conservative and Labour voters hold the same views on a majority of eighteen issues.[22] Many issues on which supporters of the two parties are in agreement have moral overtones: treatment of immigrants, capital punishment, control of political demonstrations and abortion. Agreement usually involves endorsing the more conservative of the two policy alternatives. Disagreement between Labour and Conservative supporters is greatest about issues with economic overtones, a pattern that has persisted for decades. It is especially noteworthy that the two issues showing the highest measure of inter-party difference—steel nationalization and the power of trade unions—do *not* reflect clear-cut conflicts between partisans. Inter-party difference appears high because of a major division of opinion among Labour voters, and the unanimity of Conservative opposition.

Overall, Conservatives are more likely to agree with each other than are Labour voters, who tend to divide into two almost equal-sized and opposed groups. One reason why the Conservative Party draws support across class lines is that its supporters tend to agree on political issues. By contrast, Labour draws support because of social solidarity within the working class, and less because of agreement with Labour policy. Moreover, since 1964, there has been a tendency for Labour voters to be less inclined to agree with Labour policy on major issues.[23]

While party leaders depend upon the mass electorate for votes, they depend upon party activists to keep the party alive at the grass roots. Some political scientists have argued that active party workers tend to hold extremist views; only people with both strong and extreme ideological commitments are expected to be prepared to do the humdrum voluntary work of local party organization. The absence of 'jobs for the boys', as in a patronage party system, is assumed to increase the importance of extremist ideology in recruiting party activists. In fact, this is not the case. For example, one survey study of ward activists found that less than one-third gave

[22] See Rose, *The Problem of Party Government*, ch. 11 for a full presentation of the survey data of voters and MPs discussed herein.

[23] See Crewe, Sarlvik and Alt, 'Partisan Dealignment in Britain 1964–1974', Tables 6, 7.

'working for a cause' as a principal satisfaction derived from their political activity. Helping people, helping the community, and the social pleasure of organization were more important satisfactions.[24]

The chief constitutional way in which activists make their policy views known nationally is by submitting resolutions to their annual Party Conference. An analysis of resolutions submitted to Conservative and Labour party conferences through a six-year period found that 46 per cent of all resolutions were non-partisan. They concerned matters agreed across party lines, such as the need to reduce road accidents, or pressure-group views that can be advocated within both parties, such as demands for more teachers in schools. Among the resolutions advancing strictly partisan views, 24 per cent favoured policies agreed within the party. Overall, more than two-thirds of resolutions from activists are non-partisan or moderate.[25]

During election campaigns, politicians do not compete with each other by comparing the relative merits and demerits of their own policy, and the policy of the opposition party. A study of the election addresses circulated by Conservative and Labour parliamentary candidates found that of the top ten issues mentioned by the candidates, only one issue— housing—appeared on the lists of both parties. Candidates tend to stress the issues on which they feel their party is popular, for instance anti-inflation policies on the Conservative side, and education and health on the Labour side. The candidates are not so much advocating different policies for the same problems as describing the country's problems in ways that make their respective party policies seem most attractive.[26]

The emphasis upon tactical differentiation rather than alternative strategies for governing is also clear in the speeches of the two party leaders. In 1970, the defending Prime Minister, Harold Wilson, devoted 75 per cent of his major speeches and broadcasts to attacks on the Conservative opposition, and Edward Heath, leader of the Conservative opposition, devoted 70 per cent of his major speeches to attacks upon the Labour government.[27] The choice that party leaders stress is negative: reject my opponent.

[24] Rose, *The Problem of Party Government*, Table VIII.4.
[25] Richard Rose, 'The Political Ideas of English Party Activists', *American Political Science Review*, LVI:2 (1962), Tables 1a–c.
[26] See David Robertson, Appendix IV, in David Butler and Michael Pinto-Duschinsky, *The British General Election of 1970* (London: Macmillan, 1971).
[27] See Rose, *The Problem of Party Government*, Table XI.2.

MPs are much more likely than voters to differ on party lines. The greater involvement of MPs in politics gives them a higher degree of commitment to party policies than is found among the electorate as a whole. MPs' views have been analysed by examining private responses to survey questions and parliamentary votes on conscience questions when party whips are not invoked. A majority of Labour and Conservative MPs disagree with each other on ten of fifteen domestic and foreign policy issues.[28] Ironically, MPs in different parties disagree more consistently on conscience issues, such as divorce law reform, abortion or hanging, where the party whips are not on, than about issues for which there is a party line.

The extent to which the policy preferences of MPs differ from the electorate can be demonstrated by comparing the attitudes of voters and MPs in each party for seven issues for which a complete range of attitude data is available. Table IX.2 shows that the bulk of Conservative voters and Conservative MPs tend to agree on three issues, and disagree about four issues. The same is true in Labour ranks.

Voters supporting different parties are more likely to agree with each other than with their own MPs. Whereas the average difference[29] between Conservative and Labour voters on issues is 18 per cent, the average difference between Conservative voters and Conservative MPs is 27 per cent, and between Labour voters and Labour MPs, 38 per cent (Table IX.2). It is also noteworthy that the average difference in opinions of Labour voters and Conservative MPs is 4 per cent less than the difference between Labour voters and Labour MPs.

Another way to compare the views of voters and MPs is to ask: what proportion in each group are reform-oriented, that is, in favour of changes in the abortion law, comprehensive schools, joining the Common Market, etc. The replies reported in Table IX.2 indicate that on average Labour MPs endorse reformist views 83 per cent of the time. In doing so, Labour MPs are far ahead of popular opinion in their own party, as well as distant from the opposition. Among Labour voters, reform views are endorsed 46

[28] See Allan Kornberg and Robert C. Frasure, 'Policy Differences in British Parliamentary Parties', *American Political Science Review*, LXV:3 (1971) and, on free votes, P. G. Richards, *Parliament and Conscience* (London: George Allen & Unwin, 1970), p. 180, as summarized in Rose, *The Problem of Party Government*, Table XI.3.
[29] That is, the difference between the positive answers to a question given by Conservative and Labour voters.

TABLE IX.2 **Differences in policy preferences, MPs and voters**

Policy favoured	Conservative			Labour		
	MPs %	Voters %	Difference, Con. MPs/Voters % Plurality	MPs %	Voters %	Difference, Lab. MPs/Voters % Plurality
Hanging to punish murder	68	89	21 Agree	—	80	79 Disagree
Coloured immigrants to go	38	67	29 Disagree	6	56	50 Disagree
1967 Abortion Act	34	48	14 Disagree	85	47	38 Agree
Comprehensive schools	8	32	24 Agree	92	61	31 Agree
Trade union reform	97	87	10 Agree	81	48	33 Disagree
Join Common Market	66	28	38 Disagree	60	42	18 Disagree
No Rhodesian independence before majority rule	4	57	53 Disagree	74	69	5 Agree
Average difference			27			38

Source See R. Rose, *The Problem of Party Government*, Tables XI.1, 3.

per cent of the time, a figure little different from the 43 per cent endorsement given by Conservative MPs and the 41 per cent endorsement by Conservative voters.

At a general election, voters are not offered a chance to say yes or no to questions about different policies, as might be done with a massive referendum ballot. Instead, voters concerned about policy issues can only choose between parties on the basis of their record, and what they promise in their election manifestos. Election manifestos are taken seriously by both party leaders and parliamentary candidates.[36]

The two parties do differ on a range of specific issues and these differences are often reflected by differences in action while in government. An analysis of party manifestos for the 1970 general election found that the Conservative platform was in agreement with the views of the majority of Conservative voters in 12 of 15 instances. By contrast, the Labour platform agreed with the majority view of its partisans on only four issues: foreign affairs, comprehensive schools, farm incomes and pensions.[31]

Comparing statements in party manifestos with public opinion surveys confirms the proposition that Bagehot advanced a century ago: leaders at the top of parties are readier to emphasize different policies than are the mass of the electorate. While party manifestos often disagree sharply about priorities, it is rare for a majority of Labour and Conservative voters to disagree about policies.[31]

Coalition and competition

Coalition and competition are opposites, but the two co-exist within the British party system. Competition and coalition occur first within each party. Before a parliamentary party asserts apparent agreement in a whipped vote on a major issue, groups within the party compete to determine the line around which they are to coalesce.

Parliamentary parties divide into factions, tendencies, and non-aligned partisans. *Factions* are self-consciously organized persisting groups that collectively advance a programme for government and a leader to govern. Factionalism gives stability to intra-party disputes and may even stimulate controversy, in so far as old factional

[30] See the discussion in Richard Rose, *Do Parties Make a Difference?*, chs. 3–4.
[31] See Rose, *The Problem of Party Government*, Table XI.4.

enemies continue conflict by transferring their enmities to new issues. The left-wing Bevanite faction in the Labour Party in the 1950s, often called a party within a party, is the outstanding post-war example of a faction. A *tendency* is a stable set of attitudes rather than a stable collection of politicians. The names and numbers of MPs adhering to right-wing or left-wing tendencies within a party can vary greatly from issue to issue, for some politicians identify with contrasting tendencies on different issues. *Non-aligned* MPs ignore intra-party differences on policy to emphasize differences between parties. A Conservative who concentrates on attacking Socialism aligns himself against the opposition, and not with a divisive position within his party. When factions or followers of tendencies dispute, they seek to convince non-aligned partisans that their own position is most nearly in accord with the principles and interests of the party.

The Conservatives are pre-eminently a party of tendencies. An analysis of resolutions signed by back-bench Conservatives found that 'such disagreements as arise are struggles between *ad hoc* groups of members who may be left or right on specific questions: but as new controversies break out, the coherence of the former groups dissolves, and new alignments appear, uniting former enemies and separating old allies'.[32] The chief tendencies within the party favour reaction, defence of the *status quo*, and gradual reform.

Factionalism rarely occurs within the party. The leaders of the Bow Group, youthful Conservatives of potential front-bench stature, have carefully refrained from becoming a faction promoting specific causes and personalities. The members of the Monday Club have sought to change the party's policy in right-wing directions —but they have not become a fully-fledged faction, for lack of a leading figure in Parliament. Enoch Powell, the Conservative politician potentially most suited to lead a faction within the party, has never been able to gain broad parliamentary support. The absence of factionalism within the Conservative Party reduces institutionalized rivalries, but it also makes it more difficult for party leaders to anticipate how much disagreement will arise within the party on a controversial issue.

The Labour Party always has competing views put forward within

[32] S. E. Finer, Hugh Berrington, and D. J. Bartholomew, *Backbench Opinion in the House of Commons, 1955–59*, (Oxford: Pergamon Press, 1961), p. 106. See also Robert C. Frasure, 'Backbench Opinion Revisited', *Political Studies*, XX:3 (1972).

its ranks by politicians grouping themselves into identifiable factions, such as the left-wing *Tribune* Group or the moderate Campaign for Democratic Socialism, subsequently the Manifesto group. Labour politicians differ about immediate priorities as well as about the nature of the party's ultimate goal, a socialist society. The persistence of controversy illustrates the truth of the late Lord Samuel's remark, 'There is only one way to sit still, but there are many ways to go forward.' From 1951 until the return of a Labour government in 1964, factions remained stable, whether the issue was the H-bomb or nationalization. Clement Attlee led the party for the first part of this period by reserving his personal position until it was clear which faction would dominate. Hugh Gaitskell was the leader of the right-wing faction as well as of the party. Harold Wilson sought to be non-aligned within the party, straddling differences or shifting from side to side according to the issue. As Prime Minister, however, he could not avoid taking responsibility for major decisions.

Reform, a doctrine of change for the sake of improving society, has a great historical tradition in England. This tendency antedates change in accord with Socialist ideas and at times may be in conflict with received ideas of Socialism. Today, parties disagree about which is best qualified to introduce reform. On specific issues, reform can create *ad hoc* alliances across party lines. This is illustrated by the coalition of a minority of Conservative MPs with a majority of Labour MPs on a variety of conscience issues.[33] Coalition is made easier by the fact that reform often concerns issues excluded from party manifestos. Occasionally on a major issue, notwithstanding contrasting party policies, cross-party alignments can occur. Entry to the European Community (progress to some, disaster to others) was carried in Parliament in 1971 by a cross-party coalition consisting of 282 Conservative MPs and 69 Labour MPs; 39 Conservatives and 189 Labour MPs voted against entry.

Individuals as well as parties find competing claims for allegiance pressing upon them, because the coalition of policies that each party represents does not match exactly their personal combination of preferences. For example, one person might favour reformist moral policies usually advocated within the Labour Party but liberal economic doctrines usually advocated within the Conservative Party. Conversely, another voter might favour government inter-

[33] Cf. Richards, *Parliament and Conscience.*

vention in the economy, a Labour tendency, yet also favour Conservative views on moral issues. In such circumstances, an individual must abstain from voting or choose a party notwithstanding agreement with its opponents on some issues. The largest single group of voters is in the middle on a scale measuring attitudes toward the two parties; people tend to find some things that they like and dislike about each of the parties.[34]

The competing attractions of major parties are felt by political leaders as well as political followers. A list of party leaders who have switched from one party to another includes such Prime Ministers as Sir Robert Peel, William Gladstone, David Lloyd George, Ramsay MacDonald, Winston Churchill, and the youthful Harold Wilson, a Liberal as an undergraduate but Labour when he stood for Parliament less than a decade later.

Competition between the Conservative and Labour parties has led to a long-term reduction in the distance between the parties on policy issues.[35] For decades, the Gallup Poll has asked voters whether they think there are important differences between the parties; the proportion believing that there are important differences has declined from 74 per cent in 1955 to 54 per cent in May, 1979.

Policy statements of the two major parties have also tended to show a narrowing of differences. A content analysis of party manifestos since 1923 found that the difference between the two parties on the management of the economy reduced by half from its prewar level in the period from 1955 to 1966; the distance also dropped by more than two-thirds on issues concerning welfare policies. The changes primarily reflected Conservative shifts in policies.[36] Many Conservatives are proud of the adaptiveness of their party, arguing that it is a good party tactic to campaign for 'Tory men and Whig measures'. The economic policies of successive Labour governments have also shown that it is possible to have a government with 'Labour men and Tory measures'.[37]

[34] Cf. Samuel Brittan, *Left or Right: The Bogus Dilemma* (London: Secker & Warburg, 1968).

[35] *Gallup Political Index*, No. 203 (June 1977), p. 10, and No. 225 (May 1979) p. 16.

[36] David Robertson, *A Theory of Party Competition* (New York: John Wiley & Sons, 1976), ch. 4.

[37] See e.g. Wilfred Beckerman, ed., *The Labour Government's Economic Record 1964–1970* (London: Duckworth, 1972).

The extent of coalition and competition between the parties can be measured by voting in the House of Commons. While the convention of party discipline requires MPs to vote together, it does not require that opposition MPs vote against all measures of the governing party. A vote takes place in the Commons only if there is an explicit request to divide the House. When the object of legislation is likely to be popular, for instance, the provision of greater welfare benefits, the opposition party will hesitate before going on record against a benefit. It will confine criticism to amendments challenging the operation of a bill, but not its principles. Refusing to request a division, in effect, gives tacit consent to the government's legislation.

Many measures coming before the Commons are of a procedural or administrative kind. In a detailed analysis of parliamentary legislation, Ivor Burton and Gavin Drewry have identified approximately two dozen bills in each annual session that are policy bills, that is, they introduce a new line of action. In the 1969–70 session, the last of that Wilson government, Labour introduced twenty-three such bills which received a second reading in the Commons. The Conservatives gave tacit support to eighteen measures; only five were the subject of a second-reading division. In the next session of the House, 1970–71, the Conservatives introduced twenty-six policy bills, including fourteen similar or virtually identical with measures that the previous Labour government had been promoting.[38]

Notwithstanding the rhetoric of confrontation between the parties that rose in the 1970s, the practice of legislation shows very limited competition between parties. In the 1970–74 Parliament, the Labour opposition voted against the principle of only 17 per cent of the bills introduced by the Conservative government of Edward Heath. Of the total bills introduced, nearly half were primarily concerned with administration rather than policy. When the Labour government returned to office in March 1974, it faced a Conservative opposition that only divided the House against the government on three of the first 26 government bills it introduced. Although in the 1974–79 Parliament Labour was often without an

[38] See Ivor F. Burton and Gavin Drewry, 'Public Legislation: A Survey of the Session 1969–70', *Parliamentary Affairs*, XXIII:4 (1970) and '1970–71', *op. cit.*, XXV:2 (1972). The 1974 Labour government also re-introduced a majority of Conservative bills stranded by an election.

overall majority, the Conservatives only divided the Commons against the government on 23 per cent of bills. One reason for this is that two-fifths of the Labour bills dealt with administrative rather than policy concerns.[39]

The extent of agreement between parties on particular policy issues is contingent upon events; it is not a necessary feature of the British party system. The party system that has dominated Britain since 1945 appears strong, but tensions within and between parties could lead to abrupt changes, perhaps to a system as in earlier times. From 1914 to 1945 three parties were important in the House of Commons—Conservatives, Labour and Liberals—with minority governments or coalitions more frequent than single party majority governments. Before 1914, the Irish Nationalist Party consistently won more than 80 seats at each election, and used their numbers to advance a policy that did not permit compromise, namely, the break-up of the United Kingdom.

By comparison with party systems in the European Community, Britain is distinctive because of the pre-eminence of two large parties. One reason for this is the use of an electoral system that over-represents the strongest parties; nearly all European countries have proportional representation. In the June 1979 direct election of members of the European Parliament, the Conservatives won almost three-quarters of the British seats with half the vote. Another reason is that religious and linguistic differences important to large blocs of voters on the Continent concern small numbers within the United Kingdom. The British Labour Party has not had to divide working-class votes with a Communist competitor, as is the case in France and Italy. The Conservatives differ from their European counterparts in not being an explicitly religious party, as are the Christian Democrats in Germany or Italy.

By comparison with America, British parties cover a different ideological spectrum. American parties include a larger right-wing element, whether this is defined in political, economic or cultural terms. There is no British electoral equivalent for the relative success of George Wallace in presidential and primary contests in 1968 and 1972. The Labour Party has a larger left-wing element on economic issues than would be found in the Democratic Party in America. The most persistent distinction between the parties of the

[39] See Burton and Drewry's continuing analyses in *Parliamentary Affairs*, XXVIII:2 (1975); XXIX:2 (1976) and XXXI:2 (1978).

two nations is the greater organization and policy cohesion of the two largest British parties. In England, the voter chooses *between* the parties. In America, in primaries and general elections, a voter chooses *within* as much as between parties.

The crucial issue for the 1980s is not whether the British party system will change to resemble that of other nations, but whether it will continue to resemble the two-party system that prevailed unchallenged from 1945 until the shock loss of support by both major parties in 1974. The five per cent rise in support for the two major parties in the 1979 election may be interpreted as a sign of increasing confidence in the two-party system, or as a blunt recognition by voters of the facts of life under an electoral system that is intended to manufacture majority rule in the House of Commons.

X
Making Policy

If we think what a vast information, what a nice discretion, what a consistent will ought to mark the rulers of that empire, we shall be surprised when we see them. We see a changing body of miscellaneous persons, sometimes few, sometimes many, never the same for an hour.

Government policies are statements of intent, not accomplishment. A policy indicates what politicians would like to do about a particular condition in society. A policy usually aggregates a multiplicity of demands by parties and pressure groups (including those of Whitehall departments) into a more or less agreed statement of intent. Stating a policy intention is meaningless, if it is not followed by actions intended to direct government institutions toward the realization of policy objectives. Passing an Act of Parliament is not proof that intentions will be realized; the record of any Parliament includes monuments to good (and sometimes bad) intentions that never came to pass.

Making policy is but one stage in a lengthy political process. Analytically, we can start by conceiving a 'steady state' routine, when no decisions are required of politicians; Whitehall's only task would be to supervise and administer policies determined by past choices. Routine administration is challenged by political statements defining a given social condition as in need of change. For example, from the passage of the 1944 Education Act guaranteeing free secondary education for all until the mid-1950s, the system of selective but universal secondary education was routinely praised by all parties. But beginning in its 1955 election manifesto, the Labour Party began to urge a policy of comprehensive schools instead. In 1965, a Labour government made this government policy as well. Comprehensive education had become routine by the mid-1970s, when the Labour Prime Minister of the day, in a speech on 18 October 1976, announced the de-routinization of this policy by inviting a 'great debate' about the methods and results of secondary education.

Making policy is far more difficult than stating policy intentions.

To translate a statement of good intentions into a specific programme requires running what has been described as 'the Whitehall
obstacle race'.[1] Within Whitehall a determined minister must secure agreement within a department that a proposal is administratively practicable. He must then gain consent from other departments affected by the proposal. The Treasury must grant its
approval if money is to be spent. Once over these hurdles, the
minister will ask Cabinet for formal approval and to find room in a
crowded parliamentary timetable to introduce and pass a bill, if
legislation is required. The effort necessary to secure an Act of
Parliament can be so great that politicians come to regard it as an
end in itself, without regard to the results of implementation.

To understand how policies are made we must look within the
black box of government. Instead of treating government as a
unitary decision-maker we must face up to the realities. The formal
unity of the Crown is not matched by a unity of decision-making in
the policy process. Government is best conceived as a plural noun; it
is not a singular organization. It embraces a myriad range of organizations in central London, as well as local authorities, separate
institutions for Scotland, Wales and Northern Ireland, and nationalized industries.

To understand how policies are made, we should first consider
the different criteria of choice that politicians can have in mind
when formulating policy intentions. Given the formal unity of British government, it is then necessary to look at the limits of central
control of the policy process, starting with constraints upon the
Prime Minister. In a complementary manner, we then turn to consider the limits of decentralization within England, and then elsewhere in the United Kingdom. The final section asks: who or what
groups wield the power of the Crown-in-Parliament?

Criteria for choice

Making public policy is a question of both means and ends. It raises
normative questions about the purposes of public policy, for the
ceaseless activity of governing is not an end in itself. It is also the
means to achieve larger public purposes.[2]

[1] Hugh Dalton, *Call Back Yesterday* (London: Muller, 1953), p. 237.
[2] For an outline of the policy process and discussion of relevant concepts, see
Richard Rose, *What is Governing? Policy and Purpose in Washington* (Englewood
Cliffs, N.J.: Prentice-Hall, 1978).

In England, as in any modern society, there are always differences of opinion about the extent to which the government of the day should adopt policies to conserve or change societies. The very name of the Conservative Party identifies it with a belief that many things are better left as they are. But such a belief cannot justify a 'do nothing' policy in government, for British society is continually in flux. For example, to keep unemployment or prices from rising, a Conservative Chancellor of the Exchequer must pursue an active policy of managing the economy. To prevent the English countryside from being transformed by a mass of new houses and factories, a government actively regulates land use. To conserve society as it is, a government must actively pursue many different policies.

The Labour Party's intention of changing society still leaves open many questions about the means and ends of change. In so far as the Labour Party is concerned with changing society through the conscious and collective choice of popularly elected government, Labour must make government more powerful. In so far as Labour leaders are concerned with increasing the welfare of the mass of the population by providing better education, health services and pensions, this implies a generous measure of economic growth to finance more welfare benefits. In so far as Labour leaders give first priority to reducing inequalities of income and consumption, there remain major decisions to be made about the means to such an end. Is equality to be promoted by compelling an absolute reduction in the living standards of that half of the population which is above the median, or is it to be promoted by trying to raise faster the standards of those in the bottom half of society?

Many English people believe that the primary criterion for making policy should not be what the parties want, but what the people want. Deciding what is wanted by the people (or who the people are) is no easy task. There is no way in which an organization as large as British government could hope to provide each individual with what he or she particularly wishes from government, for this would mean separate legislation for every citizen. The most and the least that British government can do is allow individuals to vote for the party that makes policy. Pressure groups claim to simplify the task of government, by telling Whitehall what is wanted by the group that they represent. But their demands inevitably reflect the views of a smaller section of society than the electorate as a whole. Politicians claim to serve each individual's wishes by promoting the collective public interest. But the definition of this interest is not left to members of the public individually. Instead, Whitehall and Westminster express what they think ought to be the will of all.

Political scientists concentrate upon asking: who (or what) makes policy? Inevitably, the decisions of government reflect what governors want. In addition to wanting to advance broad political goals, individual politicians want to advance themselves. In a Cabinet dispute between ministers advocating different views, each minister wishes his or her view to carry the day, as a demonstration of personal political power. An ambitious young MP will not only want to do what is good for the country, but also what is good in career terms. Civil servants too have a personal interest in doing things that will give them a good name in Whitehall and secure promotion. In addition, they have a collective interest in policies that protect them, such as the Official Secrets Act, which shelters civil servants from public controversy. Government departments too have readily definable interests. For example, the Treasury wishes to control the general level of public expenditure, and such spending departments as Health, Social Security and Education want to increase public expenditure in their particular policy areas.

As the scale and complexity of British government has increased, so too has concern with the means of choice. The pre-eminence of the Treasury within Whitehall and the pre-eminence of economics as *the* social science in universities makes economic analysis prominent in many debates about government policy. The creation of the Government Economic Service in 1965 and the assignment of senior economic advisers to all Whitehall departments institutionalizes this influence. Most economists believe that policies ought to be determined by a rational choice, in which monetary and non-monetary costs are balanced against benefits, whether expressed in pecuniary terms or in the 'shadow' values of cost-benefit analysis.[3]

The record of British government demonstrates that rational decision-making is far from realization in Whitehall; it is often accompanied by a miscalculation of costs and benefits, or by a mistaken faith in programme effectiveness. Experience has also demonstrated that government efforts to remove contradictions and co-ordinate decisions by planning the economy, both in total and in terms of particular industries, have often been followed by

[3] For a critique of cost-benefit analysis in the British context, see Peter Self, *Econocrats and the Policy Process* (London: Macmillan Press, 1975).

the failure of these plans. The Treasury's direction of the economy since 1945 has tended to follow a cyclical path, in which the fashion for planning has been succeeded by disillusionment, and a period of *laissez faire* has led to demand for planning as a more 'rational' basis for making economic choices.

Policy-making works most easily when an issue involves applying a known predictable technology to choices of little political importance. A known technology makes the results of a choice predictable, and an absence of political differences makes it easier to reach an accord. For example, decisions taken within the Property Services Agency about building government offices are rarely major, for the technology of the construction industry is predictable, and the state of government offices is rarely in political dispute between parties. The presence of a known technology, such as nuclear physics, does not of itself simplify choices when issues are controversial, such as the development of atomic energy. When an issue involves an uncertain technology and difficult problems of balancing conflicting political interests, then a disjointed, incremental method of policy-making may be used, with government taking a small step in one direction, and then a step in another, in the light of an after-the-fact evaluation of the wisdom of a given decision.[4]

The biggest decisions that face the most senior members of government cannot be resolved easily, because they typically have a high degree of political controversy, and there is a low level of predictability about the consequences of alternative choices. For example, in Rhodesia, the British government in 1965 decided not to try to bring down the rebel white settler regime by force. In 1979, it had to decide whether backing a black official or guerrilla army would produce fewer deaths and better government than a compromise settlement that might (or might not) end violence.

The criteria of policy making cannot be integrated in a neat manner, for the values that justify different criteria of public choice cannot readily be quantified, and may be considered 'priceless' by those who advocate them. Each of the foregoing criteria of choice is plausible; one can think of circumstances and groups arguing that they should dominate decisions taken in Westminster. At times they are incommensurable, because government is about the advance-

[4] See Richard Rose, 'Disciplined Research and Undisciplined Problems', *International Social Science Journal*, XXVIII:1 (1976), pp. 105ff.

ment of conflicting views, as well as about the reconciliation of conflict through the making of public policy.

Central choice and its limits

In theory, political parties are the institutions that unite disparate groups of people into a single governing force. But British parties have demonstrated that it is far easier to state desired goals than it is to prepare detailed programmes that show how these goals are to be achieved.

The conventions of British government inhibit the opposition party from preparing detailed plans for governing.[5] The opposition has no chance of any of its parliamentary motions becoming law; hence, it is negative rather than constructive. The more unpopular the government, the greater the opposition's incentive to make its chief policy: 'Throw the rascals out.' MPs have no staff to aid them in drawing up draft bills. The restricted flow of information from Whitehall to the Commons does not tell MPs much about the mechanics of administration. Moreover, Parliament encourages MPs to become fluent in oral discussion rather than in skills most important in drafting legislation or administrative orders. The party headquarters have research departments, but they are overworked and understaffed. The practical problems of implementing policies may not be noticed by MPs until they are installed in office. Emanuel Shinwell, a Labour MP placed in charge of nationalizing the mines in 1945, discovered:

> We are about to take over the mining industry. That is not as easy as it looks. I have been talking of nationalization for forty years, but the complications of the transfer of property had never occurred to me.[6]

Many constraints upon government policy are unlikely to be mentioned or anticipated in party manifestos. Sir William Armstrong, when permanent head of the civil service, said that ministers enter office with a vain optimism about the ease with which their intentions could be translated into achieved policies. The civil servants then call the minister's attention to 'ongoing reality', that is,

[5] See Richard Rose, *The Problem of Party Government* (London: Macmillan, 1974), esp. chs. 15–16, and, more generally, R. M. Punnett, *Front-Bench Opposition* (London: Heinemann, 1973).

[6] Quoted in Alan Watkins, 'Labour in Power', in Gerald Kaufman, ed., *The Left* (London: Anthony Blond, 1966), p. 173.

circumstances that civil servants regard as inhibiting or dooming the realization of these intentions.[7]

If a minister does have clear policy intentions *and* understands how to accommodate these with the ongoing problems of government, party policy can give central direction to government, or at least, particular party preferences can direct particular government programmes. If not, there is likely to be much continuity in policies from a Labour to a Conservative government or vice versa. As a former Conservative Chancellor of the Exchequer said of the economic policy of his Labour government successor, they inherited 'our problems and our remedies'.[8]

Elective office offers one great advantage to the winning party. If a front-bench MP can get on top of a Whitehall department, its whole weight lends authority to policies pronounced in the name of the party. What is true for individual ministers is particularly true for the party leader, who is Prime Minister as well.

The Prime Minister is the person most often named as the leading policy maker in British government. This reflects the Prime Minister's unique eminence in Parliament and in Cabinet, as well as the spotlight that the media shines upon whoever holds that office. Yet publicity should not be confused with power.

Because of the Prime Minister's prominence, some writers go so far as to argue that Britain now has Prime Ministerial government.[9] While often invoked, the phrase is rarely defined. R. H. S. Crossman, a former Labour minister, has argued that 'primary decisions' are made by the Prime Minister and 'secondary decisions' are made by departmental ministers in consultation with the Cabinet; any decision taken solely by a minister becomes by definition 'not at all important'.[10] John P. Mackintosh, a professor turned back-bench Labour MP, once asserted, 'The country is governed by the Prime

[7] 'The Role and Character of the Civil Service' (Text of a talk to the British Academy, London, 24 June 1970), p. 21.

[8] Reginald Maudling, quoted in David Butler and Michael Pinto-Duschinsky, *The British General Election of 1970* (London: Macmillan, 1971), p. 62. For a detailed account of what it feels like to be a Cabinet minister unprepared for government, see the three-volume *Diaries* of R. H. S. Crossman (London: Hamish Hamilton, 1975–7).

[9] The power of the President is often overstated. The classic American study tends to emphasize weakness; see Richard E. Neustadt, *Presidential Power* (New York: John Wiley & Sons, 1960).

[10] See R. H. S. Crossman, 'Introduction' to an edition of Bagehot's *The English Constitution* (London: Fontana, 1963), pp. 51ff.

Minister, who leads, coordinates and maintains a series of ministers.'[11] But Mackintosh immediately retracted the full force of this
statement by noting that some decisions are taken by the Prime
Minister alone, others in consultation with senior ministers, while
others still are taken by Cabinet, Cabinet committees, ministers, or
senior civil servants. Thus, even proponents of a theory of centralized power in Downing Street hedge their generalizations with
statements about the limits of the Prime Minister's authority.

The weaknesses of the theory of Prime Ministerial government
are several. The first is vagueness. The distinction between important and unimportant decisions is never clearly defined. Yet, without knowing this in advance, there is the tautological implication
that important decisions are those taken by the Prime Minister and
unimportant decisions those taken by others. While individual decisions in crises of greatest importance are usually reserved for the
Prime Minister, the decisions in which she does not involve herself
can be *collectively* more important than the dramatic but occasional
crisis.

Secondly, writers such as Mackintosh attend less to the
decision-making activities of the Prime Minister than to the incumbent's survival in office.[12] To argue that the Prime Minister's significance arises from remaining in office is to apply a criterion that
treats the incumbent as a constitutional monarch, except for the fact
that in England the monarch is more secure than a Prime Minister.
There can be times when the price of a Prime Minister's retaining
office is giving way to Cabinet colleagues, reinforced by extra-
Cabinet pressures on a major policy matter. The point is aptly
summed up in Peter Jenkins's description of Harold Wilson's position in 1969, after the Prime Minister abandoned his much resisted
proposal for a major industrial relations bill.

> The power of the Prime Minister was thus sufficient for him to
> remain in office, but insufficient for him to remain in office *and*
> have his way.[13]

Organization imposes a third constraint upon the influence of a
Prime Minister. Contemporary governors of Britain are over-

[11] John P. Mackintosh, *The British Cabinet*, 2nd ed., p. 529.
[12] The same confusion is also evident in R. T. McKenzie's discussion of the 'power'
of party leadership in *British Political Parties* (London: Heinemann, 2nd ed., 1963).
[13] Quoted in Peter Jenkins, *The Battle of Downing Street* (London: Charles Knight,
1970), p. 163.

loaded, that is, their responsibilities far exceed their ability to deal with problems of governance at first hand. Mackintosh portrays the Prime Minister as 'at the apex supported by and giving point to a widening series of rings of senior ministers, the Cabinet, its committees, non-Cabinet ministers and departments'.[14] But the view from the top of the pyramid of government can be remote as well as elevated. Only a small portion of activities occurring lower down the pyramid can filter through to the top. The Mackintosh metaphor could easily be interpreted to show that bureaux within departments are the base of government, and at the top senior civil servants and ministers are approaching in remoteness the Prime Minister's lonely eminence.

Because of the opportunity to intervene in so many affairs of government, the Prime Minister pays a very high opportunity cost for any action taken. Time is finite, and it is exhaustible. To participate in negotiations about an industrial dispute is to forego the opportunity of discussing other issues with other ministers. One person cannot keep abreast of the complexities of foreign affairs, defence, internal security, economic policy, industrial relations, the environment and housing, education, health and social security and public order— especially when there are other tasks besides. For every Cabinet minister whom the Prime Minister sees often, there will be many more who will only be seen infrequently or not at all about matters of government policy.

In their memoirs, retired Prime Ministers emphasize the time spent on foreign affairs.[15] The choice is understandable, inasmuch as a chief executive is often expected to speak for the country in international affairs. The Prime Minister receives Foreign Office papers as a matter of course; he does not similarly receive papers from domestic departments. By appointing a relatively weak Foreign Secretary, a Prime Minister can easily give directives to Foreign Office officials. Yet as long ago as 1900, Sir Henry Campbell-Bannerman commented, 'It is absolutely impossible for any man who conducts the foreign affairs of the country at the same time to supervise and take charge of the general action of the government.'[16] When Britain no longer has as much influence internation-

---

[14] *The British Cabinet*, 2nd edition, p. 531.
[15] See e.g. A. H. Brown, 'Prime Ministerial Power'.
[16] Quoted in H. J. Hanham, ed., *The Nineteenth-Century Constitution* (Cambridge: University Press, 1969), p. 69.

ally as it did in Queen Victoria's time, the Prime Minister's continuing involvement in matters which the British government can little affect is a sign of weakness not power.

The lack of a large personal staff is a fourth limitation upon the Prime Minister's ability to extend influence throughout Whitehall. Since 1964, successive Prime Ministers have had one or more personal policy advisers in Downing Street to supplement a handful of civil service advisers, but in total they number less than a dozen. Their staff provide political support for the Prime Minister, such as writing speeches, and cultivating good press relations. In terms of numbers and political status, the staff of a Prime Minister is slight by comparison with the White House staff of an American President. Downing Street staff lack both the constitutional status and political weight to give direction to well-staffed and institutionally separate Whitehall departments. The pre-eminence of the departments *vis-à-vis* Downing Street led a personal confidant of Harold Macmillan to comment that a Prime Minister 'may well ache to collar a department for himself'.[17]

In such circumstances one must conclude that the Prime Minister, while usually the most important single person in government, cannot be the dominant figure in government. Describing the Prime Minister as at the apex of government aptly symbolizes the smallness of the space that the position occupies. If success is defined in terms of achieving one's intended aims, then paradoxically, a Prime Minister may be most successful when the role is defined as doing only those things within one's immediate competence.

The Cabinet is constitutionally the chief institution for the central determination of government policy. It is large enough to include persons with day-to-day executive responsibilities for major areas of public policy, such as education, agriculture, and the social services, yet small enough so that every member can sit around a table and participate in its deliberations. In theory, the most important persons in government can deliberate in Cabinet upon the general wisdom of particular measures, and consider priorities among policies. Once a Cabinet decision is minuted, ministers are collectively responsible.

Every Cabinet minister has great incentives to de-emphasize his collective Cabinet role and bury himself in his department. Within

---

[17] See Anthony King, ed., *The British Prime Minister* (London: Macmillan, 1969), pp. xii, 96ff.

the department, he is the chief personage; the limits upon his ability to influence other departments is also a defence against interference by colleagues. A study of Cabinet ministers found that half made no mention of their Cabinet role. Only one in ten saw himself as in any way a *Cabinet* minister. Bruce Headey comments, 'In so far as the Cabinet is important to ministers, it is seen as an interdepartmental battleground rather than as a forum for collective deliberation on policy.'[18] Government policy can come to mean no more than the sum of what individual ministers will approve or defend departmentally.

Cabinet ministers head departments that compete with each other for scarce resources, such as money, skilled manpower and parliamentary time for legislation. This competition divides ministers from each other. Barbara Castle entered the 1964 Labour Cabinet believing 'in my innocence' that it would make major policy decisions in collective deliberation. But 'I was soon disabused of that. . . . I wasn't in a political caucus at all. I was faced by departmental enemies.'[19] Departments' disagreements are at bottom institutional; differences of personality or political tendency between ministers reinforce rather than cause this competition. Disagreements may arise from overlapping areas of responsibility; for instance, the Department of Education and Science, the Home Office, and the Department of Health and Social Security each have some responsibilities for children. Or they may arise from the efforts of one department to encroach upon the authority of another; for instance, the Welsh Office has interests in taking over powers currently exercised in Wales by other departments.

The chief formal mechanisms for resolving inter-departmental differences are Cabinet committees of ministers, and counterpart committees of departmental civil servants. Before 1914, there was only one Cabinet committee, Defence. Today there are more than a dozen committees on subjects ranging from nuclear defence to agricultural policy. Ministers may also privately meet each other or the Prime Minister, seeking wider support for departmental policies and to resolve disputes informally, in order to avoid the risks and potential opposition of formal committee deliberations.[20]

[18] Bruce Headey, *British Cabinet Ministers* (London: George Allen & Unwin, 1974), ch. 1.

[19] 'Mandarin Power', *Sunday Times*, 10 June 1973.

[20] See Patrick Gordon Walker, *The Cabinet* (London: Jonathan Cape, 1970), pp. 46, 176f. See also G. W. Jones, 'Prime Ministers and Cabinets', *Political Studies*, XX:2 (1972), p. 218.

If affected ministers can agree among themselves about an issue before it goes to Cabinet, the matter will be presented for information only. There is little an uninvolved minister can contribute that has not already been debated prior to reaching Cabinet. If every minister sought to speak on each item on the agenda, there would be time to discuss only two or three items per meeting. Individual Cabinet ministers engage in tacit log-rolling, remaining silent on matters outside their field of responsibility in the expectation that other ministers will be quiet when they themselves put forward proposals.

Strict control of Cabinet's agenda is necessary because of the scarcity of time for discussion. Meetings of Cabinet occupy about six hours a week. By convention, the agenda regularly includes discussion of foreign affairs and of parliamentary business, as well as issues that involve great political controversy, however transitory their significance. Before a matter can be placed upon the Cabinet agenda, the Cabinet Office must be satisfied that it is sufficiently important to merit discussion there and that the necessary preparatory work for discussion has been undertaken in committee. So heavy was the overload of business in the 1964 Labour government that at one time the Prime Minister decreed that decisions of Cabinet committees were to be final, without appeal to the full Cabinet, unless the committee chairman agreed to reconsideration.

The Cabinet can veto or delay a minister's policy if it finds it politically undesirable. When crisis requires prompt action, it cannot veto a policy unless an alternative can be found. Often there is not time for non-expert ministers to challenge a departmental minister involved in a crisis negotiation. There may not even be time for the Cabinet to be told about a decision until it is a *fait accompli*.

In Cabinet deliberations, 'The one thing that is hardly ever discussed is general policy', that is, questions of underlying priorities and objectives. 'Nothing, indeed is more calculated to make a Cabinet Minister unpopular with his colleagues, to cause him to be regarded by them as Public Enemy No. 1, than a tiresome insistence on discussing general issues.'[21] The Cabinet is not an institution for co-ordinating policies; it enforces collective responsibility but not collective decision-making. In the words of Colin Seymour-Ure:

[21] L. S. Amery, *Thoughts on the Constitution*, p. 87.

The Cabinet seems to have disintegrated in the literal sense of that word. Every member of the Cabinet is important, but his importance depends on functions that are performed almost entirely *outside* the Cabinet.[22]

In an effort to give more political direction to the co-ordination of government policy, in 1970 Edward Heath created 'super-departments' in which a single senior minister, for example Environment, was responsible for policies previously divided among three different ministries: transport, public works and also housing and local government. It was argued that the creation of super-departments could lead to the better co-ordination of major policy decisions, because a single minister could see within one large department the interdependence of policies concerning housing, roads and planning decisions. Moreover, within a super-department a minister would have to rank policies in terms of their importance; only one issue can come first at a time.[23] But changing the names of government departments and adding another ministerial layer to an already high pyramid has not centralized the making of policy. There still remains only a limited amount of time in which one minister can deal with the multitude of problems arising beneath him. The resolution of disputes within the walls of a super-department also makes it more difficult for the Cabinet to see and correct the mistakes that individual ministers inevitably make.

The Treasury has a unique co-ordinating role to play among Cabinet departments, because it has the authority to review the programmes of all other government departments annually, and to recommend how much (or how little) money they should spend on their programmes. The Treasury's formal authority is also enhanced by the fact that it tends to attract civil servants of very high calibre, and many of the leading positions in Whitehall are held by persons who have their careers in the Treasury.[24]

The Treasury's control of public spending starts before a new measure is put to the Cabinet; the Treasury must be consulted about its cost, and it must have Treasury approval before going on to be

---

[22] Colin Seymour-Ure, 'The "Disintegration" of the Cabinet', p. 196.

[23] See Richard Clarke, *New Trends in Government* (London: HMSO, 1971).

[24] See particularly, Hugh Heclo and Aaron Wildavsky, *The Private Government of Public Money* (London: Macmillan, 1974), and Samuel Brittan, *Steering the Economy* (London: Secker & Warburg, 1969), and Lord Diamond, *Public Expenditure in Practice* (London: George Allen & Unwin, 1975).

considered in Parliament. The annual budget cycle provides another opportunity for departmental policies to come under review, especially if they involve a noteworthy increase in expenditure. Long-term expenditure implications of policies are reviewed in the five-year forward look of the Public Expenditure Survey Committee. Moreover, the Treasury's responsibilities for general economic policy lead it to issue at irregular intervals directives requesting departmental spending cuts or increased public spending, depending upon whether the economy is deemed in need of deflation or inflation.

Treasury control is no longer concerned primarily with 'saving candle ends', to use Mr. Gladstone's picturesque phrase equating economics with economy. Instead, it is concerned with pervasive issues of government policy, in so far as they affect or are affected by economic considerations. This means that when there are strong national or international pressures, e.g. domestic inflation, a reaction against taxes or foreign pressure on the pound, the Treasury may be able to dictate cuts or constraints upon the programmes of spending departments. But the Treasury can be influenced by strong political pressures as well. For example, in the months leading up to a general election, the Treasury is expected to allow public spending to increase in order to provide more social benefits or, as a tax-conscious opposition might argue, to 'bribe the public with its own money'.

The Treasury finds it difficult to control exactly spending by other Whitehall departments, because it cannot control the economy. Its policy objectives are multiple, and its organizational priorities involve dilemmas of choice. All areas of economic policy are, or ought to be, interrelated. But the number of tasks involved are more than one minister can handle. Three activities of utmost importance are interrelated, yet at times can be in conflict. First, the Treasury is manager of the domestic economy. Second, it is responsible for maintaining a favourable balance of payments in trade between the sterling area and other parts of the world. A third Treasury function, budgeting annual expenditures, is no longer viewed as an end in itself; because of the influence of public sector spending upon the economy, it has now become a means to the end of managing the economy as a whole.

Because of conflicts between these activities and the often negative effects that measures taken in one field may have upon another, since the First World War British governments have intermittently sought to undertake economic planning. The history of Whitehall's efforts shows a slow but gradual increase in the Treasury's economic sophistication, with new forms of planning being introduced, then abolished, leaving behind some gain in knowledge. But administrative machinery cannot, of itself, resolve political conflicts or guarantee economic success.

The limits upon central direction to government led Edward Heath, when newly installed as Conservative Prime Minister in 1970, to establish a Central Policy Review Staff (CPRS) within the Cabinet Office. The unit was intended to provide a comprehensive review of government strategy, evaluating alternative policy options and considering how policies of different departments related to more general objectives of the governing party. With a staff of fifteen, less than one man for each government department, the CPRS cannot be compared with the Executive Office of the President in Washington. Its creation was evidence of weaknesses perceived in Downing Street. When asked to name the CPRS's major achievement, its first head, Lord Rothschild, said:

> I don't know that the government is better run as a result of our work. I think the highest compliment I ever got paid was from a Cabinet minister who said: 'You make us think from time to time.' I thought that was a great achievement, considering how much ministers have to do. They don't have much time to think.[25]

Decentralization and its limits

Decentralization exists, even within a unitary state, because central government cannot administer all its services in all parts of the kingdom without creating a great overload of responsibilities at the centre. The desire to push administration out of Whitehall—whether by functional or spatial decentralization—has become a prominent feature of administrative reorganization. Only by delegating tasks considered unimportant can the heads of Whitehall departments hope to gain time to attend to activities that cannot be delegated because of their importance for the political success or failure of the government.

Decentralization means that Whitehall departments do not have direct control of health, education and personal social services

[25] 'Thinking about the Think Tank', *The Listener* (London), 28 December 1972.

of immediate concern to citizens. Whitehall lays down the standards for the delivery of services and pays the bill, but what gets done in specific instances is usually determined elsewhere. Even in a political system in which governors believe that the Crown-in-Parliament ought to be the chief decision-making authority, there are inevitably limits to decentralization.[26]

Many different motives lead ministers to decide that they do not wish to be directly responsible for policies that have a statutory basis, affect the public, and spend public monies. Ministers may wish to insulate activities from charges of political interference (e.g. the National Theatre), to provide flexibility in commercial operations (the Gas Board), to give an aura of impartiality to quasi-judicial activities (the Monopolies Commission), to respect the extra-governmental origins of an agency (the British Standards Institution), to allow qualified professions to regulate technical matters (the Royal College of Physicians and Surgeons), to remove controversial matters from Whitehall (the Family Planning Association), or to concentrate efforts for a special purpose (a fund for disaster relief).

Decentralization can be functional or territorial. Functional decentralization gives an agency a specific power covering the whole country, for example, the National Coal Board. Territorial decentralization gives multiple powers to agencies operating within restricted areas, such as local government authorities or the Scottish Office. Some agencies may combine both attributes; for example the BBC is divided into regional units for some programme purposes, and functional for other purposes.

A great many agencies operate with government authorization, yet outside the framework of government departments. *Whitaker's Almanack*, a standard reference book, requires seventy-five double-column pages to list government and public offices. In addition, it separately catalogues commissions, banks, the armed services, churches, universities and schools, nationalized industries, museums, and art galleries, each of which also affects the public interest.

Examining the number and range of public employees calls attention to the extent of government. Overall, almost 30 per cent of the

[26] See e.g. Christopher C. Hood, *The Limits of Administration* (New York: John Wiley & Sons, 1976) and Jeffrey Stanyer and Brian Smith, *Administering Britain* (London: Fontana, 1976).

labour force works for government, an increase of one-quarter since 1965. The largest number of public employees (3.0 million) work for local government, and the largest single group of local government employees are in education. Workers in nationalized industries and other public corporations producing goods for sale are the second largest group. Some of these nationalized industries are growth oriented and make a profit, whereas others are labour intensive and often money losing, like the Post Office. The National Health Service is the largest employer in central government, with 1.2 million staff. The armed services employ no more people than public corporations supplying gas, electricity and water. The civil service in Whitehall departments, from the senior posts to typists and messengers, constitutes a relatively small block of total public employment. The very senior civil servants constitute little more than one-tenth of one per cent of all public employees.

Functional agencies of the Crown exist in a political no-man's land, because they are not immediately controlled by elected representatives, whether MPs in Cabinet or local government councillors. They are 'fringe' bodies, on the margin of central government, yet not immediately under a minister's direction. They are indubitably a part of government because their duties are sanctioned by law, and are often public monopolies; their funds are derived from taxation; and, not least, their directors are normally appointed by the Whitehall department that is ultimately responsible for them.

In functional agencies, policy-making is first of all the responsibility of its formal head. For example, the direction of the BBC (British Broadcasting Corporation) is legally vested in a Chairman and Board of Governors. The Chairman normally comes from outside the broadcasting industry; currently, it is Sir Michael Swann, a scientist and ex-University head. The Board of Governors are part-time not full-time. The Governors, appointed by the government, are meant to see that broadcasting serves the public interest, a hard-to-define term. The government of the day often claims to know best what that is. Yet the Governors are meant to protect the BBC from partisan political influence, for the government of the day may try to use broadcasting to promote its own partisan interests. The Governors also wish to exert influence upon government to increase their annual licence revenue and to constrain competition from the independent commercial broadcasting

TABLE X.1　**Public employment by category of government**

		Public Employees Numbers	%
Central government			
National Health Service		1,155,000	15.6
Armed forces		327,000	4.4
UK & Northern Ireland civil services, and other central government employees		823,000	11.1
	Total	2,305,000	31.1
Public corporations			
Nationalized industries, including Post Office		1,803,000	24.4
Other public corporations		286,000	3.9
	Total	2,089,000	28.3
Local authorities			
Education services		1,561,000	21.1
Police, including civilian employees		184,000	2.5
Other local authority services		1,254,000	17.0
	Total	2,999,000	40.6
Total public employment		7,393,000	29.7
Total private employment		17,481,000	70.3
		24,874,000	

Source 'Employment Analysed by Sector and Industry, 1972–77', *Economic Trends* (January 1979), pp. 132, 136.

companies. The BBC Governors are also expected to lay down broad policy guidelines for professional programme-makers, to respond to initiatives from the full-time professional broadcasting staff, and resolve disputes within the complex institutions that constitute the BBC. The Director-General of the BBC is the chief broadcasting official acting as the interlocutor between lay governors and experienced professionals.

The relationship of fringe bodies to Whitehall departments is influenced by their origins. Institutions that grow from the top down, created at the initiative of central government, are most likely to be subject to Whitehall influence. For example, the new universities founded in the early 1960s in consequence of a government decision to expand higher education are immediately sensitive to government policies. By contrast, an institution originating outside the public sector grows from the bottom up; its leaders are likely to be less ready to accept uncritically changes in government policy. In a self-regulating profession such as medicine, doctors think of themselves as free professionals and not as civil servants. The creation of the National Health Service has not altered doctors' insistence upon autonomy, even though their income is almost wholly derived from public funds.

In many cases, Whitehall departments and functional agencies are best described as interdependent, each wanting things from the other, and each influencing the other. For example, the fate of a minister at the Department of Industry and problems of nationalized industries are inevitably intertwined, for nationalized industries are big industries, and anything that promotes their success is good news for their Whitehall sponsors, just as any difficulties in a nationalized industry cause difficulties in Whitehall. Moreover, the Department of Employment will be concerned if a nationalized industry threatens to reduce its labour force, thus adding to the ranks of the unemployed. When major investment decisions are taken, the Secretaries of State for Scotland and Wales will be anxious that nationalized industries invest money in Scotland and Wales, whatever the economic arguments may be, for these ministers are concerned with territorial prosperity, and not with maximizing the rate of return of investments by nationalized industries.

The following catalogue of para-governmental agencies is illustrative, for the boundary between public and private is not easily drawn.

Executive agencies not directly under ministerial departments. The National Health Service and the Royal Mint are formally independent of Whitehall departments, because of the desire to retain operational flexibility and freedom from political intervention. Yet both agencies are solely concerned with applying policies decided elsewhere. The Mint cannot coin money independently of Cabinet authority, nor can the National Health Service spend money unless the Treasury is prepared to foot the bill.

Nationalized industries. The government not only owns the corporations that operate nationalized industries, but also appoints the boards that direct them, provides investment capital, and underwrites financial losses. Yet each industry is formally independent of Whitehall, and its employees are not civil servants. This is intended to increase the freedom of action of the industries; coal, electricity, gas, the railways, airlines, steel etc. The relationship between ministers and leaders of nationalized industries is confused by the coexistence of multiple and sometimes conflicting objectives: profitability, an undefined 'fair' rate of return on investment, services to consumers and the protection of the jobs of those employed in the industry.

Publicly maintained regulatory or administrative agencies. A regulatory agency such as the Independent Broadcasting Authority grants licences to commercial television companies, and monitors the programme content of the companies it licenses. An administrative agency, such as the Social Science Research Council, draws funds from the Treasury and its Council is appointed by government. But its activities are administered by staff whose work is monitored by SSRC committees composed of academic experts in the social sciences, plus a limited number of lay persons.

Publicly assisted agencies. While originating outside government, these bodies receive substantial government aid. For example, the Royal Opera House did not commence under government or royal sponsorship. Today, it can only present operas at an international musical standard thanks to a very substantial Treasury subsidy granted it by the Arts Council.

Fringe bodies are a para-governmental jungle surrounding the central departments of state in Whitehall. They are para-governmental because they discharge functions around but not in the Whitehall policy process. They are a jungle, because of their complexity and density. Any Whitehall official, whether a minister or civil servant, is well advised to secure a 'survival kit' before rushing into that jungle hunting for more influence upon the agencies to be found there.

Fringe bodies are also like a jungle because of their rapid and lush growth. One official survey of fringe agencies reckoned that they had grown from 10 in number in 1900 to 103 by 1950, and 250 in 1978. In total, these fringe bodies are spending billions of pounds each year in public funds. Fringe bodies grow around Whitehall departments because only in this way can ministers expand the activities of government without risking the collapse of policy-

making in heavily loaded (or overloaded) Whitehall departments.[27]
Local government is the chief *territorial* means of decentralization. Within a given city or county, local authorities are not the only
government agency delivering services locally. A few Whitehall
departments also have major local field offices, e.g. pensions and
social security and employment. In addition, many functionally
organized agencies are incidentally important in local areas.
Nationalized industries such as electricity, gas, transport and the
post office are prominent local employers, and in steel towns or
mining communities a nationalized industry may be the single
largest local employer.

In constitutional theory, English local government reflects a
'top-down' conception of authority. All local authorities operate on
the basis of powers and institutions prescribed by Parliament. The
boundaries and powers of all local authorities are determined by
the central government, which can transform both with a single
Act of Parliament, most recently the Local Government Act of
1972.

Efficiency has been the overriding aim in local government
reform in England. Whitehall views local government as a major
mechanism for delivering services to citizens. As such, it wishes the
services to be of a reasonable standard and the cost to be reasonable
too, for central government funds pay for a substantial portion of
local government services. Popular election of local government
leaders is recognized as politically inevitable but, in the words of
one leading expert on central–local relations, 'mayors and aldermen
and councillors are not necessary political animals. We could manage without them.'[28]

Local government reorganization in the 1970s was based upon
the assumption that there were too many small local authorities,
and that bigger local authorities would be better (that is, provide
services of a higher standard at the same or relatively less cost).
English local government reform replaced more than 1,300 county
councils, boroughs and districts with a new system of 410 local

[27] See *Survey of Fringe Bodies* (London: HMSO, 1978), *A Directory of Paid Public
Appointments Made by Ministers, 1978* (London: HMSO) and Brian W. Hogwood,
The Tartan Fringe: Quangos and other Assorted Animals in Scotland (Glasgow:
Strathclyde Studies in Public Policy No. 34, 1979).
[28] J. A. G. Griffith, *Central Departments and Local Authorities* (London: George
Allen & Unwin, 1966), p. 542. Cf. John Gyford, *Local Politics in Britain* (London:
Croom Helm, 1976).

authorities. Trebling the size of the average authority was assumed to produce economies of scale as in an assembly-line manufacturing process.[29]

The reformed local government structure divides England into three different jurisdictions: the shire counties, with 59 per cent of the population; metropolitan county councils in major cities, with 25 per cent of England's population; and the Greater London Council, with 16 per cent. Each of these top-tier local authorities has a lower tier of elected government beneath it: district councils in the counties and metropolitan areas, and borough councils in Greater London. County councils have responsibility for education, strategic land use planning, roads and transport and personal social services. In metropolitan areas, the district councils have education and personal social service responsibilities elsewhere assigned to the upper-tier county councils. Housing, a major concern when more than one-quarter of the population lives in municipally owned council houses, is primarily a district council responsibility. In the Greater London Council area, the great bulk of local authority responsibilities are in lower-tier boroughs.

Local government reform has increased the size of the average local authority and, incidentally, the distance between the citizen and responsible local officials, whether appointed or elected. The position of staff has been strengthened as local authorities secured union co-operation with reorganization plans by upgrading the salaries and responsibilities of many officials. Party politics has become more prominent, as elections are more often contested on party lines. The coincidence of galloping inflation and local government reorganization resulted in a skyrocketing of costs and of rates levied as a property tax to help meet them.

Within local authorities, elected councillors are meant to give direction to government. The effectiveness of councillors is limited by the fact that their office is unpaid, thus greatly biasing the kind of people who can afford to participate: employees in public sector agencies granted paid leave for such work; businessmen such as estate agents, solicitors and others with flexible office hours and an interest in local affairs; housewives; and retired persons. The pres-

[29] For a description and critique of local government reform, see Jeffrey Stanyer, *Understanding Local Government* (London: Fontana, 1976), and Edward C. Page and Arthur F. Midwinter, *Remote Bureaucracy or Administrative Efficiency?* (Glasgow: Strathclyde Studies in Public Policy No. 38, 1979).

ence of disciplined parties in most local authorities usually ensures a few more or less full-time politicians at the top of local authorities. Low levels of turnout at local elections—often half that at a parliamentary election—indicate a lack of popular interest in local government. Individuals are more likely to be sporadic activists, organizing friends and neighbours to lobby councillors, or taking part in unconventional protests, when their house, road or children's school is immediately affected by a policy.[30]

The politics of Westminster and Whitehall influences local politicians in two ways. In so far as local politicians take their views from national party leaders, they will seek to carry out locally policies that the party is advocating nationally. In practice, this often does not happen, for local politicians rarely meet national political leaders, and may regard themselves as more practical, experienced and better positioned to judge local needs than their Westminster counterparts. For example, in 1965 a Labour government had to issue a circular directing Labour-controlled local councils, as well as Conservative councils, to reorganize secondary education, because most Labour authorities had not already done what was within their powers.

Party politics can make co-operation between central and local governments more difficult, when the party in power is seeking to promote nation-wide a policy that the opposition rejects. For instance, Conservative councils responded slowly and sometimes negatively to the 1965 Labour circular calling for the reorganization of secondary education and some Labour local authorities carried out a guerrilla war in efforts to delay or subvert the enforcement of a Conservative Housing Finance Act in 1972. A substantial number of local authorities will normally be in the hands of the party out of office at Westminster.

The politics of professionalism is another major influence upon local government policy. The crucial political relationships within local authorities are between the councillors who chair the most important committees of the council and the professionals who constitute the chief officers directing the services that these committees provide. Within each committee, the chief local officer, a

[30] See e.g. A. P. Brier and R. E. Dowse, 'The Politics of the Apolitical', *Political Studies*, XVII:3 (1969) and C. W. Chamberlain and H. F. Moorhouse, 'Lower Class Attitudes towards the British Political System', *Sociological Review*, XXII (1974), pp. 503–25.

full-time council official appointed on grounds of expertise, merit and seniority, can exercise great influence because of technical knowledge, commitment to professional values and a strategic position in charge of operating staff. In major local authorities, chief officers can be of the same calibre as Whitehall civil servants, and be paid as much as well. But the politicians that they are meant to follow often lack the abilities of Cabinet ministers.

National professional associations of educationists, town planners, architects, social workers, traffic engineers and so forth constitute an important vertical link in the policy process. These associations can simultaneously promote policies in relevant Whitehall departments and in local authorities. Chief officers look to their professional associations for leadership in developing new programmes—and also as a defence against unwanted directives from Whitehall. In turn, Whitehall looks to professional associations to promote change on the ground in accord with what Whitehall regards as desirable standards.

Those who believe that local government should above all be efficient government look to non-elected chief officers to promote change. Yet in so far as professional officers become strong, each gives priority to the policy concern of greatest importance to his or her profession. The result is difficulty in co-ordinating decisions between architects, traffic engineers and social workers, if each is responding to different professional standards, and directives from different parts of Whitehall. In recognition of the fragmentation arising from these vertical links, Whitehall has sought to promote horizontal co-ordination on the ground through 'corporate' management in local government, that is, the adoption of institutional and policy making processes that bring together specialists within the bureaucracy and leaders of the governing party to make and co-ordinate policy on the basis of local circumstances—always within the limits of central government directives.

The framework for local government action is laid down in Whitehall and Westminster. Under the *ultra vires* rule, local authorities can only do what they are authorized to do by an Act of Parliament. This rule has tended to create a pattern of careful and cautious local government activity; many officials have feared to exceed lawful powers. Even when Whitehall is willing for local authorities to take initiatives, local authorities may be hesitant to do so, if action is not explicitly authorized in legislation. By contrast, the American Constitution leaves states the power to do anything that is not explicitly denied them.

When local authorities wish to spend money, they are normally subject to a wide range of Treasury guidelines affecting both current and capital expenditure. The Treasury gives more money to local authorities than local authorities raise in local taxes. Central government lays down standards for the cost of building local council houses, and subsidies are related to these cost standards. When inflation is the primary worry, the Treasury presses local authorities to spend less by setting cash limits, or curtailing capital spending on schools, housing or roads. When the Treasury wishes to stimulate the economy, it encourages local authorities to spend more.[31]

Central government departments exercise a variety of supervisory powers as well. Inspectors examine schools and police and fire services. Auditors examine both small and large expenditures to make sure they are sanctioned by statute. The salaries and terms of appointment of many local authority employees are also affected by central government decisions. The land-use planning decisions of local authorities may be appealed to the central government, even when the dispute lies within a single local authority area. In extreme cases, a minister can override decisions made by elected local councils, suspend councillors, or assume administrative powers directly.

Notwithstanding its right to authorize activities and set standards, the central government has consistently rejected responsibility for the administration of most major services of the welfare state. Education is administered locally, as are many services by social workers. Local authorities build and manage housing. A variety of planning, road, environmental services and police and fire protection are also locally administered. The resistance of medical doctors to local authority control led to the establishment of regional hospital boards outside the control of local authorities, but outside the immediate control of Whitehall departments as well.

The paradox of central authority and administrative devolution was aptly summed up by John P. Mackintosh:

Central government can plan, control, guide, review, audit and so on, but never actually execute. Foreign students find it scarcely credible that in Britain Ministries of Housing have never built a

[31] See the *Report* of the Layfield Committee of Inquiry into Local Government Finance (London: HMSO, Cmnd 6453, 1976).

single house and Ministries of Education have never run a single school.[32]

The centre's power to set minimum standards and maximum costs is balanced by the decentralized bodies' powers of execution. While local government officials complain about the restrictiveness of central government, ministers complain about their own lack of influence. Lord Hailsham, a minister with experience in many departments, has contrasted being a defence minister with the armed forces exclusively under central government control, and being a minister in a department whose programme is administered by local authorities.

> In the Admiralty you are a person having authority. You say to one person 'come' and he cometh, and another 'go' and he goeth. It is not so in the Ministry of Education. You suggest rather than direct. You say to one man 'come' and he cometh not, and to another 'go' and he stays where he is.[33]

Decentralization exists because the central government cannot administer all its services in all parts of the United Kingdom without overloading the centre. The desire to push administration out of Whitehall has become a prominent feature of administrative reorganization. Yet central government does not wish to reduce its power to constrain the authorities it has created. Only Whitehall supervision, it is assumed, can ensure territorial justice for its subjects, that is, an equality of services and opportunities for individuals, wherever they live within England.[34]

The positive argument for more local determination of public policy is that local citizens know best what they need. No laws drafted in Westminster can match the particular circumstances of tens of millions of people scattered throughout the United Kingdom. Local authorities can adapt laws to local circumstances and better scrutinize the delivery of local services. Policy differences that are regarded as evidence of inequalities by centralists are regarded as evidence of variety by proponents of local policy-making. In the non-English parts of the United Kingdom, national-

[32] 'The Report of the Review Body on Local Government in Northern Ireland, 1970', *Public Administration*, XLIX (Spring 1971), p. 20.
[33] Quoted in Maurice Kogan, *The Politics of Education* (Harmondsworth: Penguin, 1971), p. 31.
[34] See Bleddyn Davies, *Social Needs and Resources in Local Services* (London: Michael Joseph, 1968).

ists go so far as to argue that self-government, rather than efficient government from Whitehall, is the best form of government. But even some advocates of national independence make clear that they do not wish to do away entirely with financial aid from London.

The complexity of the contemporary policy process restricts both centralization and decentralization. Centralization in the hands of a single decision-maker is limited by the number and variety of formal organizations involved in most major decisions. For example, a proposal to establish a New Town with a population of upwards of 100,000 people will involve four or five major Whitehall departments, plus two or more major local authorities, and a host of functional agencies, both governmental and non-governmental. In such circumstances, decisions are not 'made', they emerge.[35] Many organizations influence policy at some point in the process; the more or less intended result is the outcome of inter-organizational bargaining and adjustment between groups rather than the product of a singular decision.

The dilemma of centralization and decentralization is illustrated by disputes in land-use planning between nationalized industries and local authorities. A nationalized industry may claim that the industrial use of land is in the public interest; a local authority may wish to keep land free from industry because it views green spaces as even more important for the common good. Central government cannot eliminate disagreement, but it can hear appeals and determine which of its competing substructures has the most persuasive notion of the public interest.

The United Kingdom dimension

The government of England is only one part of the government of the United Kingdom. Given the disparity in size and political influence between England and each of the non-English parts of the United Kingdom, it is practicable to think of the government of the non-English parts of the realm as an additional and sometimes complicating factor in the politics of the heartland, that is, England. The powers of British Cabinet departments and major non-departmental agencies immediately affect England. By contrast, in Northern Ireland, Scotland and Wales, Westminster has authorized distinctive forms of government that often mediate or substitute

[35] See J. K. Friend, J. M. Power and C. J. L. Yewlett, *Public Planning: the Inter-Corporate Dimension* (London: Tavistock, 1974).

institutions of governance, more or less accountable to West-minster.

Northern Ireland has consistently demonstrated the limits of central influence. Its establishment in 1921 was due to the fact that Ulster Protestants were unwilling to follow Westminster laws establishing home rule throughout Ireland, and took up arms to remain British. As a result of this, Westminster thrust autonomy upon Ulster, making the Stormont Parliament accept responsibility for all the problems of governing without consensus. The Speaker of the House of Commons ruled that matters devolved to the Stormont government could not even be debated at Westminster, and no Whitehall department had even one person full-time monitoring events in Northern Ireland. It did not wish to know what was happening there.[36]

Westminster's refusal to interest itself in the government of the Irish part of the United Kingdom was acceptable to the Protestant majority in Northern Ireland, because Unionists there were ready to undertake the most important and onerous of tasks defending the security of the state against armed attack by the IRA. In addition, Unionists were happy to govern with a majority guaranteed by the numerical preponderance of Protestants and the electoral significance of religious divisions. The Unionists were able to administer police, housing, local employment, electoral boundaries and other policies in ways that suited the majority. Members of the Catholic minority could not gain electoral influence because of their numerical weakness, nor could they use the courts to pursue their grievances, because of the absence throughout the United Kingdom of written constitutional guarantees of individual rights.[37]

The suspension of the Stormont government in 1972 meant a swing from complete decentralization to complete centralization. Westminster was now responsible for all the affairs of the Province. Formal authority was placed in the hands of a Secretary of State for Northern Ireland, but events since have demonstrated that effective authority over the troubled Province does not rest in Westminster. Killing escalated and successive efforts by Westminster to delegate specified responsibilities for government to an elected Northern

[36] See Harry Calvert, *Constitutional Law in Northern Ireland* (London & Belfast: Stevens & Northern Ireland Legal Quarterly, 1968).

[37] See Richard Rose, *Governing without Consensus* (London: Faber & Faber, 1971) and R. J. Lawrence, *The Government of Northern Ireland* (Oxford: Clarendon Press, 1965).

Ireland assembly have failed, because the Ulster majority has refused to accept Westminster's conditions. There is a political impasse, because of fundamental divisions between Protestants and Catholics in Northern Ireland about the very basis of government, and fundamental disagreement between both groups and Westminster about the 'least undesirable' if not most acceptable form of government. In default of achieving their preferred but mutually exclusive goals, both religious groups in Northern Ireland have accepted direct rule by the Northern Ireland Office whereas Westminster maintains direct rule is only temporary; its authority must be renewed annually by a vote of Parliament.[38]

In Scotland and Wales, the existence of the Scottish and Welsh Offices within the British Cabinet has institutionalized both administrative decentralization and political centralization. Administrative decentralization is justified in Scotland by differences in the legal system from England, as well as by a network of institutional, social and political differences.[39] In Wales, social and linguistic differences are both arguments for administrative decentralization. Since one in five Welsh persons is a Welsh-speaker, there is a particular need for bi-lingual education policies.

The determination of public policy for Scotland and Wales is centralized in Westminster when it is made by British Cabinet departments. A Scottish or Welsh minister is a British Cabinet minister, and as such, is bound by the convention of collective Cabinet responsibility. Any measure that either office puts forward must be acceptable to the whole of the British Cabinet. A Scottish or Welsh Secretary may try to do 'more' (for example, direct more government spending to Scotland or Wales), or try to do things differently (that is, pass laws not effective in England, or vice versa), but this can only be done with the endorsement of the whole Cabinet. Scottish and Welsh ministers seek to promote their departmental interests, as do Education or Agriculture ministers. But none has ever carried identification with territorial interests to

[38] Cf. Lord Windlesham, 'Ministers in Ulster: The Machinery of Direct Rule', *Public Administration*, LI (Autumn 1973): W. D. Birrell, 'The Northern Ireland Civil Service', *Public Administration*, LVI (Autumn 1978); and Richard Rose, *Northern Ireland: Time of Choice*.

[39] For the evolution of institutions of Scottish and Welsh government, see Richard Rose and Ian McAllister, *United Kingdom Facts* (London: Macmillan, 1980).

the point of resigning from Cabinet, let alone resigning from the Labour or Conservative party.

Devolution Acts for Scotland and Wales, adopted by Parliament in 1978, promised a major structural change in relationships. Devolution involved the establishment of popularly elected Assemblies for Wales and Scotland, though the Act of Parliament authorizing these assemblies also strictly limited their powers. The Welsh Assembly was not to have any legislative powers; it was to supervise the administration of services, like a super-local government for Wales. The Scottish Assembly was to have legislative powers within listed areas. Neither Assembly was given effective revenue-raising powers; the Treasury was to determine its funds. The Devolution Acts asserted the overriding authority of Westminster, and made provision for Westminster to override Assembly actions, if Westminster so wished.

In a March 1979 Referendum, Welsh voters unambiguously rejected the proposals for a devolved Welsh Assembly, as an unnecessary and cumbersome addition to government. In Scotland, voters split almost equally. Some Scots felt the devolution proposals did not go far enough in granting Scotland scope for autonomous policy-making; other Scots thought it went too far. In the absence of a large referendum majority, Parliament refused to put Scottish devolution into effect.

The United Kingdom dimension in Westminster politics is less a means by which Westminster can influence Scotland, Wales and Northern Ireland than it is a means of maintaining a dual polity.[40] The two parts of the dual polity are the unitary government of England, and the non-uniform and distinctive institutions for government elsewhere in the United Kingdom. When administrative or political powers are devolved within England, the authorities in receipt of them are immediately accountable to Parliament at Westminster. By contrast, devolution of powers elsewhere was meant to remove small and sometimes awkward parts of the United Kingdom from Westminster's immediate responsibility. The distinctive institutions of governance of Scotland, Wales and Northern Ireland are meant to act as a buffer between the problems of the so-called 'periphery' and the proper concerns of the government of the heartland, England.

[40] See Jim Bulpitt, 'The Making of the United Kingdom', *Parliamentary Affairs*, XXXI:2 (1978).

A ruling clique or a plurality of winning groups?

In reply to the question—Who governs?—some observers emphasize the dispersion of policy-making powers among a plurality of
groups, and others the inequalities that give a disproportionate
amount of power to a select few.

The *ruling clique* model of policy making postulates the centralization of power in the hands of one group co-ordinating major
decisions within government, and between government and other
institutions of society as well.[41] To speak of a ruling clique is much
more precise than talking about a ruling class, for the latter term can
describe a heterogeneous assortment of people who have nothing in
common except similar social origins, upbringing and status.

Pluralist models of the policy process emphasize the fragmentation of power among a number of groups, each of which wins some
struggles to influence government decisions. In the pluralist model,
winners on one issue may be losers on another or not even involved
in other decisions. To describe the policy process as pluralist is a
negative statement: it emphasizes that power is not integrated.
Pluralists leave open the questions of how many and what kinds of
groups compete for influence, and which ones are successful within
the policy process.[42]

Power cannot be examined in isolation from policy making, for
the actions and inactions of government are evidence of the wield-
ing of power. In theory, any one of six different models of policy
making could characterize England today. Because the actions of
government are continuous and multiple, a model appropriate to
one policy area will not necessarily fit another. In so far as examples
can be found for each model, neither the ruling clique nor the
pluralist model can claim universality. Within the confines of this
study, we can only briefly review the alternatives, drawing upon a
systematic analysis of major British government decisions by C. J.
Hewitt.[43]

[41] See e.g. W. L. Guttsman, *The British Political Elite* (London: McGibbon &
Kee, 1963).
[42] See e.g. Robert A. Dahl, *Who Governs?* (New Haven: Yale University Press,
1961).
[43] See C. J. Hewitt, 'Elites and the Distribution of Power in British Society', in P.
Stanworth and A. Giddens, eds., *Elites and Power in British Society* (London:
Cambridge University Press, 1974) and his 'Policy-making in Postwar Britain',
British Journal of Political Science, IV:2 (1974).

1. A *ruling clique* model is most appropriate to describe foreign policy making. Major decisions about diplomacy and defence are consistently made by a small group of people around the Prime Minister, the Foreign Office, the Ministry of Defence, and, when financial considerations are significant, the Treasury. To describe these persons as a single group is not to suggest agreement among everyone involved, but to note their relative isolation from influences outside a narrow circle in Whitehall. One constraint upon the ruling clique in foreign affairs is the dependence of British foreign policy upon limited manpower and public money. Another constraint is the military power of other nations.

2. *Balance-of-power pluralism* occurs when a few groups consistently compete in the same policy, with each winning some of the time; it characterizes the making of domestic economic policy. Typically, business and financial interests are arrayed on one side and unions on the other, with the government's senior economic officials acting as something more than disinterested brokers. The weight of each side in the balance varies with changing economic and political circumstances. For example, in the course of fifteen years, the British steel industry was nationalized, denationalized and renationalized.

3. Social policies illustrate *segmented pluralism*, in which a stable number of groups are involved with a given issue, but they tend to differ from issue to issue. The cluster of groups concerned with education are few and stable, as in the balance-of-power model. But they differ from the cluster of groups involved with health. These in turn differ from the groups involved in social services for the poor and the handicapped. The narrow scope of each group's concern —teachers and doctors, for example, have different professional associations—produces a high degree of institutional organization within each policy area, and differentiation between them. Because of this institutionalization, the policy-making process requires lengthy negotiations, and changes that cut across segmented interests are particularly difficult to negotiate.

4. *Amorphous pluralism* describes policy arenas in which those with interests to defend or articulate are constantly changing. For example, controversies arising in land-use planning always concern specific plots of land. Whereas planners are concerned with the consistency of principles from case to case, nearly all the other participants are only concerned with looking after their own gar-

dens. The personalities and groups involved in planning controversies are thus *ad hoc*, depending upon the particular site of a dispute.

5. Policy making is *populist* when the mass of the electorate is directly involved in determining the outcome. When government policy depends upon consumer response, the decisions of masses of consumers become crucial. Some mass consumer decisions affect policy unwittingly. For example, the decision of many people to buy motor cars and rely less upon railways and buses has incidentally had a great influence on government transport policy. In race relations, popular opinion, as reflected in MPs' perceptions as well as in opinion polls, has increasingly been used to justify laws intended to restrict entry to England of non-white Commonwealth citizens. Referenda are limited as a means of populist influence, because they can be used only infrequently, and only at times and for questions prescribed by the government of the day.

6. A *veto* model describes the frustration of government policy by extra-governmental groups. Occasionally, policy proposals are vetoed by the public opposition of strategic pressure groups. More often, the veto power of a group prevents an issue being put on the political agenda that would threaten one of its central interests. For example, the Trades Union Congress has successfully prevented governments from proposing legislation affecting them, as well as vetoing legislation once proposed or enacted, like the 1969 Labour government's Industrial Relations Bill, or the 1971 Industrial Relations Act of the Conservative government.

Every model of the policy process is conditional: it will fit some problems but be inappropriate to others. The political influence of a group is not only a function of its own resources but also a function of the policy area. The resources of bankers, trade unions, teachers or motorists cannot be generalized across all policy areas, though each is specially salient in some. The influence of Whitehall is a variable too; it is not constant in education, economics, and environmental planning. Hewitt's study found that of 339 extra-governmental organizations involved in his twenty case studies, more than five-sixths were involved with only one major issue, and only six per cent with three or more issues.

The groups most consistently involved in policy making enjoy both victories and defeats. Business firms, trade unions or, for that matter, government departments concerned with industrial policy do not achieve their objectives in every case—nor do they always lose. Because their interests in a given area are permanent, they are prepared to make recurring and continuing attempts to influence a wide range of policies, hoping that their positive achievements will more than offset their frustrations and defeats. Interestingly, Hewitt found that public opinion was exceptionally likely to be on the winning side; this happened in eight of the nine issues where opinion poll data did indicate a clear popular preference.[44]

The successful groups are more numerous than the unsuccessful groups in the policy process. This does not mean that majority opinion is sure to prevail in the policy process, for groups are, by their nature, led by small numbers of full-time politicians. Moreover, most mass (*sic*) membership organizations can only claim a few per cent of the population as members, or a very limited commitment from larger numbers of members. Many organizations, such as banks and manufacturing firms, have a legal personality but do not claim to 'represent' people as do political parties. Research does make clear that policies tend to favour the larger and more numerous groups, with greater claims to representativeness.[45]

The intermittent and limited involvement in policy making of many groups gives special advantage to those most consistently involved: public officials in government. Ministers and civil servants must be involved in policies that require positive state action. They are not only participants, but also persons who define the terms of any outcome. Ministers do not dominate all policy areas, for extra-governmental groups often have strong market powers. But governors can extract advantage from whatever room for manoeuvre there is, and take initiatives to which others can only react. Governors are not only experienced players but also the referees who, at the end of the day, arbitrate between group demands.

The making of policy by nominally sovereign governments is constrained at all times, however, by organizational facts of life. Government itself is a cluster of organizations, not a unitary monolith. Studies of the policy process within government emphasize that it is an *inter*-organizational process; different Whitehall departments have separate identities and distinctive interests and ideas about what the policy of that formal entity, the Crown-in-Parliament, should be. Questions of public policy are as likely to pit different Whitehall departments (or extra-Whitehall public

[44] Hewitt, 'Elites and the Distribution of Power', p. 57.
[45] *Ibid*., pp. 58ff.

agencies) in opposition to each other, as they are to concern major differences between political parties.

The division of British government into a multiplicity of organizations is territorial as well as functional. The conventional model of the Crown-in-Parliament emphasizes the locus of sovereignty at a single point in space, whether it is thought to be the Cabinet table at 10 Downing Street or the floor of the House of Commons. But the delivery of the goods and services of contemporary government is not organized there. Nor are most of these goods and services produced within Whitehall. They are provided by a host of public bodies, ranging from the National Health Service, the Post Office and nationalized industries through local government in England and devolved offices and institutions for Scotland, Wales and Northern Ireland to a host of quangos (equally well defined as quasi-governmental or quasi-non-governmental organizations). In giving direction to these organizations, Cabinet ministers have the upper hand. But they can only use this hand to point out what *should* be done; other organizations have their hands on the delivery of most of the goods and services of British government.

The organizations of government do not make policy in isolation; they are in turn part of an even more complex network of relationships with social and economic organizations elsewhere in society, concerned with all kinds of issues: business, industrial, trade-union, professional, social, cultural, humanitarian and so forth. The policy process is increasingly internationalized because of the dominance of economic problems. The international dimension in the network of organizations affecting policy-making in Britain is reinforced, but not caused, by British membership in the European Community.

Because the purpose of public policies is to influence conditions in society, government organizations must accept that they too are subject to influence from organizations outside the formal command of the Crown-in-Parliament. Inter-organizational relations between government and non-government agencies cannot be subsumed under the commanding authority of the Crown-in-Parliament. They are best understood as bargaining relationships, in which the resources of the organizations involved are unequal. There are parallels between intra-governmental bargaining and bargaining between organizations on different sides of the line (or the grey area) separating government from extra-governmental organizations. But given the value presuppositions about the scope and limits of authority in England, government finds it far more difficult to compel agreement by extra-governmental organizations than those within government.

One great problem for policy-makers in England in the 1980s is whether the network of relationships required to carry out the activities of government can effectively carry the responsibilities placed upon them. Governors may intend to make government provide more and more benefits to society, but can the organizations they direct produce the goods and services? The question goes beyond questions of the relative efficiency of public and private sector organizations. It concerns the aggregate costs of public policy. Even more, it questions whether government can actually do everything that its policy-makers declare to be their intentions. The difficulties of managing the British economy in the 1970s demonstrate that there is no guarantee that there is an effective technology at hand for every government intention. (Or if there is, government cannot discover or implement it.) Equally important, government policies—for example, maintaining rising wages, full employment, an open international economy and low inflation—may be in contradiction with each other. As the scope of government policies expands, there is the prospect of government incorporating within its own organizational goals all the contradictions that already exist within English society.

XI
Implementing Policies

What grows upon the world is a certain matter-of-factness.
The test of each century, more than of the century before,
is the test of results.

The impact of policy is not necessarily what governors intend. Measures adopted to secure peace and prosperity may be followed by war or depression. In a world of complex causation, many conditions of society change independently of or in spite of actions of governors. Any attempt to evaluate the impact of government policies upon society must start with a consideration of the resources that government can bring to bear, and the means it uses to implement its policy intentions.

If a policy is to be anything more than a minister's statement of pious intentions, Whitehall must create a programme that can plausibly be expected to advance a government's stated intention. The first test of a programme is at the choice stage: will a particular measure secure the endorsement of Cabinet and Parliament? But the greater test of a programme is at the stage of implementation: Will the programme work as intended? Can it be implemented at all?[1]

In logic, the design of programmes should follow decisions about the ends of policy, for means reflect ends. But in politics, the choice of ends often depends upon the acceptability of means. Ministers and senior civil servants spend much of their time discussing with groups inside and outside government what measures they are prepared to accept and implement. A 'good' programme can even be defined as one that is easily implemented, and acceptable to all interested parties. The process of bargaining to seal a deal can become an end in itself; programme objectives may only be settled after bargains about programme means.[2]

[1] For a general discussion, see Jeffrey Pressman and Aaron Wildavsky, *Implementation* (Berkeley: University of California Press, 1973) and Carol H. Weiss, *Evaluation Research: Methods of Assessing Program Effectiveness* (Englewood Cliffs, N.J.: Prentice-Hall, 1972).

[2] See Richard Rose, *What is Governing?* (Englewood Cliffs, N.J.: Prentice-Hall, 1978), ch. 7.

Examining the impact of public policy upon society shifts attention from government as a reactive institution responding to popular demands to government as an active force, positively trying to influence the conditions of society. The reactive model reflects liberal values. The model of the positive state is especially consonant with collectivistic values, whether of paternalistic Toryism, Socialism or aggressive technocracy. The dominant political philosophies in England today stress positive action by the state rather than a passive *laissez-faire* ideology.

While the policy intentions of governors are often unclear or confusing, the activities of government are everywhere palpably evident. Each week the multiplicity of organizations that collectively constitute the government of Britain employ millions of people to spend billions of pounds under the authority of tens of thousands of laws and regulations. To the ordinary citizen, the most important feature of these activities is the impact they have upon society. Even if governors enunciate vague or contradictory policy intentions and social scientists have difficulty in precisely measuring the consequences of government actions, it is none the less true that the actions of government do have a major impact, for better and worse, upon society.

To understand the impact of government policies upon society, we must first of all examine the resources that government has at hand to implement policies, and then how they are combined and implemented as programmes. The third section of this chapter considers the impact of government programmes upon conditions in society. The concluding section assesses how the public itself evaluates the overall impact of government in England.

The resources of policy

The resources that government has at hand to implement policies —the resources of law, personnel, money and land—are today great, whether measured in an absolute sense or in relation to the total resources of society. Before analysing how these resources are combined in specific programmes, we should examine each resource in turn.

Law is the unique resource of government. The power to make rules that ought to be binding upon all members of society distinguishes government from other institutions in society that employ large numbers of people and disburse large sums of money. Private organizations can use economic power to influence other organizations, but they cannot invoke political authority to legitimate their intentions, and to compel popular compliance. The long-standing legitimacy of government makes law a particularly valuable resource for British government. People expect to follow government directives not because they are popular, wise or successful, but 'because it is a law'.

The most familiar rules are those contained in Acts of Parliament. The continuity of government from medieval times results in a vast accumulation of legislation from many different ages, even though few laws from pre-industrial England are today significant. The official *Chronological Table of the Statutes*, giving the title of each Act of Parliament, runs to more than 1,300 pages. The earliest statute still in force dates from 1235; nearly one-quarter date from before the accession of Queen Victoria in 1837. Most important is the legislation of a century of modern government, which has never been codified. Government policies are usually based upon legislation enacted at different times without a logical and comprehensive analysis of cumulative effects.

Drafting a law is a test of how carefully policy-makers have thought about their intentions.[3] Legislation requires politicians to state precisely what it is that they intend to do about a given problem. A law is not like a speech, a form of words that can be as vague as desired. Nor do the consequences of a law disappear at the end of an evening, as often happens with the consequences of a speech. Even civil servants may find it difficult to transfer their attention from drafting speeches and White Papers for ministers to drafting legislative instruments to realize proclaimed intentions. In the words of one civil servant experienced in drafting legislation:

> Very often you don't see the pitfalls and traps until you write your instructions to parliamentary counsel. Having to be so specific, you suddenly realize you have been talking nonsense for months.[4]

The difficulties of legislation are compounded in Britain by the fact that party politicians tend to be excluded from the legislative process before entering office in Whitehall. As ordinary Members

[3] See the Report of the Committee chaired by Sir David Renton, *The Preparation of Legislation* (London: HMSO, Cmnd. 6053, 1975).

[4] Quoted in John Clare, 'Who Makes the Decisions that Change our Environment?', *The Times*, 9 May 1972.

of Parliament they can only criticize the laws that are made. Whitehall avoids detailed consultation with MPs about the drafting of legislation; legislative details are treated as official secrets. Nor do MPs individually have the influence to compel explanations or changes in clauses of statutes, as do American Congressmen.

Once a measure is introduced, it is subject to review through a series of procedural mechanisms that are not only time-consuming but also of dubious relevance to the impact of the law. For example, amendment procedures intended to clarify a bill in Parliament may be used by the opposition to reiterate differences about principles. Even though critics realize that what they dislike will become law, they often concentrate their parliamentary speeches upon criticizing the bill in principle, rather than seeking to remove particular drafting defects from the legislation.[5]

In the course of a year the majority party in Parliament has the opportunity to pass twenty to thirty bills with significance for some field of public policy. The number of bills passed each year has altered little in the last half-century.[6] Because the government can be nearly certain of success for almost any bill it cares to introduce, its relative efficiency in legislating—the ratio of bills proposed to laws enacted—is very high. But it is still greatly constrained by a short supply of parliamentary time in relation to the demand from departments for new legislation.

The government enjoys great powers to make binding rules outside the exhausting process of parliamentary legislation. In such fields as foreign affairs and defence, the government can invoke the unlimited prerogative powers of the Crown, derived ultimately from medieval concepts of royal sovereignty, to justify its actions. In domestic policy, a British government can enact legislation retrospectively to give *ex post facto* justification to what it has done.

Acts of Parliament can delegate authority to make detailed regulations necessary to implement the general principles of a given Act. Executive decrees can in some fields be issued as Orders in Council, with the full force of law. Statutory Orders and Regulations, typically rules of relatively minor importance, provide another means of executive rule-making outside the conventional

---

[5] Gavin Drewry, 'Reform of the Legislative Process', *Parliamentary Affairs*, XXV:4 (1972).

[6] See D. E. Butler and A. Sloman, *British Political Facts* (London: Macmillan, 4th ed., 1975), pp. 156–7.

parliamentary routine. Statutory Instruments must be notified to Parliament. A Statutory Instruments Committee of the Commons scrutinizes these measures and can, if it wishes, call a rule to the attention of the Commons for possible rejection if it is thought to exceed powers authorized by Act of Parliament. If this is not done, the instrument becomes binding as law. The number cited as objectionable is usually less than ten a year, hardly one per cent of the annual total.[7]

At some point in the process of implementation, policy involves the discretionary use of statutory powers. This is true for thousands of daily acts of administrative routine, concerning the grant of a disability pension or planning permission to build an extra room on a house, as well as in the management of the economy and foreign affairs. While single decisions may be limited in scope, the result can be of intense significance to the individual concerned. Many decisions involving the discretionary use of statutory powers are taken by special-purpose administrative tribunals. The volume of the work of the tribunals is great in aggregate. Even excluding Inland Revenue cases, industrial tribunals, local valuation courts, national insurance bodies, rent tribunals, supplementary benefit appeal tribunals and other bodies together hear more than 250,000 cases a year.[8]

Money is a second major resource of British government. The government's revenue depends upon the total gross national product (which in Britain is large in aggregate as well as in per capita terms), the methods it uses to secure revenue (income tax, customs and excise taxes, local rates, insurance-like contributions for welfare services, loans, etc.), and the yield from these resources, plus the amount of money it can borrow at home or abroad, augmented by the money it can create (*sic*) through its control of credit and the money supply.

The total revenue resources of the British government are vast and growing.[9] In 1951, the British government took 34 per cent of the national product to meet the costs of public policy. In 1977, it took 49 per cent, a share almost half again as high as that of the

[7] *Ibid.*, pp. 169–70.
[8] Central Statistical Office, *Social Trends*, Vol. 9 (1979), Table 15.9.
[9] For an overview and interpretation, see Richard Rose and Guy Peters, *Can Government Go Bankrupt?* (London: Macmillan, 1979). Cf. the annual Treasury announcement of public expenditure; the figures cited here come from Cmnd. 7439 (1979).

governments in the United States, and only 5 per cent less than that in Sweden, the Western society where government taxes the largest portion of national income. Because of inflation the absolute value of government revenue, when measured in current prices, has grown enormously too. From 1961 to 1977, total government revenue rose from £9.7 billion to £61.9 billion, an increase of 637 per cent. In the particularly inflationary years from 1971 to 1977, government revenue rose by 264 per cent, an increase in current money terms of £38.5 billion.

Taxes on income, including social security, are the single biggest source of government revenue, accounting for 49.5 per cent of total revenue, equal to about £480 per man, woman and child in the country; in 1966, the total take from these taxes on income was equivalent to £260 per person. (See Table XI.1.) The chief and most visible source of this revenue is income tax, most of which is deducted from weekly or monthly wages. When income tax was originally introduced, it affected only a small and wealthy stratum of the population, and took only a small fraction of their income. The concept of progressive income tax, that is, that persons earning more money should pay higher tax rates, has meant that as the income of manual workers has risen with living standards, so too the increased earnings are subject to progressively higher taxes. Today, nearly all wage earners pay income tax, and most pay income and social security tax at the rate of 36 per cent for every extra pound earned. In total, income tax yields £17.4 billion to government.

Social insurance contributions provide an additional £9.4 billion in government revenue. These taxes are levied upon the bulk of income earned, and compulsorily deducted from weekly or monthly wages. An employee is expected to contribute 6.5 per cent of his or her earnings for national insurance and the employer is expected to contribute 10 per cent. Social security taxes are distinctive because they are earmarked, that is, they are paid in return for benefits, principally an old age pension. Normally, the Treasury dislikes earmarking taxes, because this is reckoned to tie the hand of government.

A variety of indirect taxes, such as VAT (Value Added Tax), an 8 (now 15) per cent general sales tax, accounted for another £15.2 billion of government revenue. In addition to raising revenue, certain excise taxes are also meant to regulate consumption, for example, especially high taxes on petrol, drink and tobacco. Gov-

TABLE XI.1 **The revenues of British government, 1966–1977**

	1966	1977	Change 1966–77	1977 Value £ million
Central government	(As % total central govt. revenue)			
Income tax	36.7	32.1	−4.6	17,419
Social insurance levies on income	14.9	17.4	+2.5	9,453
VAT, customs, excise and other indirect taxes	33.3	28.1	−5.2	15,246
Corporation & profits tax	1.0	5.3	+4.3	2,876
Other income (taxes on capital, rent & capital income)	9.6	8.9	−0.7	4,856
Borrowing requirement	4.5	8.2	+3.7	4,465
				£54,315
Local government	(As % total local govt. revenue)			
Rates on property	29.8	26.2	−3.6	5,194
Rent	8.8	10.2	+1.4	2,022
Other income	6.6	7.3	+0.7	1,436
Borrowing requirement	20.8	8.1	−12.7	1,610
Plus Current & capital grants from central govt. revenue	34.0	48.2	+14.2	9,557
				£19,819
Total general government income (excluding transfers between sectors of government)				£61,964

Source: Social Trends, Vol. 9 (1979), Table 7.15.

ernment could not prohibit smoking or drinking without forfeiting more than £1 billion in tax revenue.

The total yield of corporation and profits taxes is variable, because profits fluctuate up and down from year to year, depending upon economic circumstances. Hence, government does not like to rely upon profits tax for substantial amounts of revenue. It prefers to tax the products that firms sell and the labour that they employ, through VAT, national insurance and other means. These taxes must be paid by a firm as a first charge upon its operating expenses, whether it is making a profit or loss. In 1977, corporation and profits tax yielded £2.8 billion, 5.3 per cent of total government revenue.

The transfer of money from central government is the largest single source of local authority revenue, accounting for 48 per cent (£9.5 billion) of its total income in 1977. By comparison, rates levied on local property yielded little more than one-quarter of local authority income, £5.1 billion in 1977. Rents from council house tenants accounted for another £2.0 billion in revenue. Overall, local authorities in Britain raise less than one pound in revenue for every five pounds raised by Westminster.

When the costs of governing exceed the revenue that government can raise from taxation, it turns to borrowing. The extent and amount of borrowing varies with government policy and with economic conditions generally. In 1966, borrowing accounted for 4.5 per cent of central government income, and in 1971, 3 per cent. In 1975 it shot up to 19 per cent of income, and in 1977 stood at 8 per cent of total income. In addition, local authorities borrowed an additional £1.6 billion in 1977. One pound in ten spent by British government in 1977 was borrowed money.

Loans to government are not gifts; they will have to be repaid from the tax receipts of future years and/or further borrowing. Foreign loans, which have been specially important in financing much British public debt in the 1970s, must be repaid in hard foreign currencies, which may appreciate in value against sterling during the life of the loan, thus further adding to the cost of repayment. For most of the postwar era, governments expected to repay current loans with the extra revenues generated by economic growth. In the 1970s, government tended to rely upon inflation depreciating the real cost of loan repayments. Because of this, interest rates too have risen; from 1946 through 1955, the bank rate set by the Bank of England for borrowing purposes ranged from 2 to 4.5 per cent. From 1956 to 1970 it ranged from 4 to 8 per cent. Since 1971 it has ranged from 5 to 17 per cent, and between July 1973 and April 1977 did not fall below 9.0 per cent.

Manpower is the third major resource of government. In wartime and national emergencies, the British government has conscripted millions of people to fight in armies, and in the Second World War it directed labour in civilian employment as well, for the whole of the economy was mobilized for the war effort. Conscription remained in effect for more than a decade after the war. The government announced its abolition and a reliance upon an all-volunteer military force as part of the reduction of the country's international commitments after the 1956 Suez War.

In aggregate, government organizations employ nearly one in three workers in Britain (see Table X.1), a proportion that has grown slowly but steadily since 1961. Folklore to the contrary, the growth of government has not been brought about by a great enlargement of political cronies and paper-shuffling clerks in Whitehall. Instead, the prime cause of growth has been an increase in the numbers of public employees outside central London, especially individuals providing services directly to the public in education and the health service, or producing goods and services in the nationalized industries.

The number of people working in a given policy area does not indicate its political importance. The Treasury, the Foreign Office and the Cabinet Office are among the smallest departments in Whitehall, employing fewer people than an average sized local authority. The number of employees is related to the type of work that a department does. For example, it requires far more people to sort the daily post than it does to manage the nation's economy.

Land is the fourth major resource of government. In addition to being a major landowner, government benefits from the traditional centralization of land ownership in the hands of the monarch and the nobility. Crown lands can be put to public use (e.g. London parks or forestry reserves) and large landed estates of nobility can be given to the National Trust for recreational purposes to avoid death duties. Even prior to the passage of government legislation regulating land use, private owners of large estates maintained planning controls by granting restrictive leaseholds to tenants in cities.

Today, government has the power to regulate the use of land through planning legislation; and, if it wishes, to acquire land by compulsory purchase. Laws on compulsory purchase and compensation tend to favour the government as purchaser. The ability of central government to allocate land has been most notably used in the creation of New Towns. Since 1945 the government has established twenty-eight New Towns on green field sites outside congested urban areas. These new towns have a population of 1.9 million people.

Analysis separates what government unites. The resources catalogued above—laws, money, personnel and land—are brought together in varying combinations in the manifold of public policies. Laws authorize government to act, and require the compliance of citizens. Laws also create government agencies to carry out programmes. In turn, these organizations bid for money, personnel and land as necessary from the pool of total resources. Policies usually combine all of these factors. For example, children are legally compelled to attend school and, whether or not they have children, citizens pay taxes to support education. Local education authorities, working under central government supervision, manage education services. Education policy combines the expenditure of billions of pounds and the employment of hundreds of thousands of teachers in tens of thousands of buildings to provide one of the many major services of government.

Implementing programmes

To implement policy intentions requires a programme. A programme assigns a policy intention to a specific government agency. A programme prescribes in bureaucratically meaningful language the means—money, laws, and personnel—allocated to achieve the ends of policy. There is often more than one programme to achieve a given policy intention: for example, several different Whitehall departments have programmes intended to promote economic growth. A programme may also have more than one purpose: for example, programmes to reduce unemployment are also concerned with protecting the governing party from losing votes. The creation of a programme is no guarantee that a policy will be a success. But without a programme, a government has not identified any means to achieve a stated intention.

Logically, the implementation of a government programme should start with a declaration of the ends of the policy. But identifying the objectives of a given government measure is not easy. There is an enormous variation in the clarity with which the intent of major laws is stated. The National Health Service Act 1946 is exceptionally clear in stating objectives—to secure improvement in physical and mental health by the prevention, diagnosis and treatment of illness—and specifying administrative means to these ends. The preamble of the landmark 1944 Education Act, making secondary schooling free to everyone, is more typical; it simply enunciates a vague intention 'to promote the education of the people of England and Wales'.[10]

There is no legal requirement that an Act of Parliament carries any statement of intent. For example, the Act to end capital punishment contains no statement of its intent; it could have been enacted to aid the rehabilitation of murderers, to reduce the danger of judicial errors or to shed governmental responsibility for taking human life. Many programmes enumerate too many objectives. There are good political reasons for this. Each Whitehall department has a distinctive set of departmental interests and pressure group clients who reinforce these interests with their demands. The Prime Minister of the day also wishes to generalize the broad appeal of the governing party, and must seek broad themes that are not only comprehensible to the ordinary voter, but also make some sense of the multiplicity of things that are done concurrently in the name of Her Majesty's Government.

Because British government has so many objectives in aggregate its actions can easily appear confusing or contradictory, when viewed as a whole. For example, the Coal Industry Nationalization Act 1946 states as objectives: to get coal from the mines, to secure efficient development of the industry, and to sell coal 'at such prices as may seem to the directors best calculated to further the public interest in all respects'. Collectively, these objectives are often contradictory. If maximizing the output of coal were the sole objective, then the Coal Board could concentrate upon increasing supplies of this major energy resource, whatever the cost. If efficiency were the sole objective, then the amount of coal extracted would depend upon the marginal cost of production, reducing the yield. If the miners' interest is reckoned part of the public interest, the Coal Board might provide good working conditions, secure jobs and high wages to the miners, whatever the cost in terms of coal production or economic efficiency. Determining *which* objective is the *dominant* objective of the moment is a political choice.

Busy public officials do not have time to be bothered by a confusing welter of programme objectives. Confusion, after all, can be a sign of intense political interest and activity. The denizens of Whitehall and Westminster are not logicians, or engineers designing instrumentally effective systems of means and ends. They are

---

[10] For preambles to major laws, including those cited here, see G. Le May *British Government, 1914–1953* (London: Methuen, 1955).

English empiricists, content to pursue a policy of 'muddling through', ready to implement programmes even if unsure about the purpose of their actions.

The first step in implementing a programme is for governors to assemble resources within the network of inter-organizational relationships that constitutes government. A Whitehall ministry may propose action, but it is likely to delegate responsibility for carrying out measures to a local authority or a non-Whitehall functional agency. English public officials are particularly skilled at inter-organizational co-operation, provided that there are no political obstacles in the way. The stability of government ensures familiarity with a wide range of standard operating procedures, informal as well as those formally laid down in the 'Estacode' of the Treasury. The relative centralization of the political system and its formal unity also encourage co-operation. The absence of a written constitution or a code of public law also allows for great organizational flexibility. At all times, organizations recognize that in the event of differences of opinion turning into a showdown, Westminster can legitimately claim the final word.

The second stage in implementing a policy requires shifting from an introverted to an extroverted view of politics. Instead of asking: What should be done within government? policy makers must ask: How can government achieve its aims in society? The world 'out there' is more complicated and far harder to control than the world within government.

From a politician or a civil servant's point of view, public policies may well be considered the final output of government, that is, the ultimate objective of months or years of political struggle and bargaining within the policy process. But from a broader sociological perspective, these programme outputs are only inputs to society. British government is, however, not the only major institution influencing English society. The multiplicity of influences affecting a given condition in society can be categorized under three broad headings: (1) government programmes, (2) other identifiable organizational activities outside the direct control of government, and (3) last but not least, all those factors that neither governors nor social scientists can identify or understand.[11]

[11] In statistical terms, the third category represents the error term. Even when social scientists can identify influences upon social conditions, many independent variables fall in the second rather than the first category.

The difficulties of implementing government economic policy illustrate how government competes with other influences in determining policy outcomes. At a given moment, the state of the economy can be influenced by government policies affecting the level of public spending, the size of public deficit, and specific policies encouraging investment and employment. But the state of the economy also reflects conditions that the British government does not control, for example, wage demands voiced by trade unions, and investment decisions of businessmen. The British economy also responds to changes in the international economic environment.

The difficulties of implementing a policy may be anticipated to some extent by planning. Every new programme of British government involves at least a measure of planning, for laws cannot be drafted and officials organized without some idea of what is meant to happen next. But planning the actions of government is only half the total story. In a non-totalitarian society, government cannot plan how citizens must respond. It can only estimate, on the basis of past experience, advice from proponents and opponents of the policy and shrewd surmise, what impact a new programme *may* have. Even the best of estimates must include a *ceteris paribus* (all other things being equal) clause. But this is often not so. Unforeseen events can work against or for the success of a programme. They are certain to complicate the efforts of those trying to implement a plan.

The simplest programmes to implement are those that call for the application of a known and efficient technology to the physical environment. For example, the British government can successfully carry out a programme of building bridges across rivers or motorways, because civil engineering technology is well understood, and the costs are calculable within limits. Moreover, these actions make an impact on the physical environment, which in England offers few difficulties to bridge-builders or highway engineers. Yet increasingly, even these seemingly simple tasks face political obstacles. Construction costs have escalated with inflation, making it more and more difficult to calculate the economics of long-term building projects. Even more important, citizens have organized environmentalist groups to protest against government civil engineering proposals, in the name of a previously mute environment.

Programmes that involve giving away money are administratively easy to implement. All that is required is a statutory definition of who is entitled to receive benefits, and Treasury appropriation of the funds to be paid out. Civil servants will also be concerned that everyone entitled to a benefit by law actually takes up the benefit. The most expensive single British government programme— pensions for the elderly—is very simple to administer. Pensioners are identified by their age, registered long before they are ready to claim a pension, and post office branches are authorized to pay cash over the counter to pensioners on the production of their claim book. Cash benefits become difficult to implement in so far as an element of discretion enters in, whether it is an estimate of how much money a family may need each week, or how much earning power has been lost by a partially disabled worker.

Many major programmes of the welfare state are easy to implement up to a point, namely, the production of programme outputs. This is true, for example, of education. From a Whitehall point of view, a new education policy is implemented when buildings are built and staff are at work at a new task, say, providing compensatory education classes for children from disadvantaged homes. But the provision of such a service is not an end in itself, as the term output implies. It is an input meant to improve the education of disadvantaged children. Because their learning is influenced by family, community and other influences beyond the control of government, it is simplest for public officials to concentrate upon producing outputs rather than to worry about the impact that their efforts have.

At any particular moment, the great bulk of government activity runs easily, because it is concerned with relatively routine activities, that is, maintaining programmes that were first implemented decades or even generations ago. The continuity and formality of government institutions constitute powerful inertia forces maintaining established programmes, once they are first implemented.

The routine programmes of government do not reflect the current choices of the party in power; instead, they reflect past decisions taken in the light of circumstances that may have since changed. Because they are established with the force of law, the government of the day is committed to spending billions of pounds to maintain them. Any newly elected government, if it is to uphold the law of the land, is immediately committed to carrying out the accumulated policies that its predecessors have left behind. No newly elected government could, in the lifetime of a Parliament, review all the programmes for which it was responsible, let alone carefully weed out the bad from the good. These programmes create the expectation among beneficiaries that they will continue. A government can make more enemies by taking away specific benefits than it can gain friends by transferring funds to new programmes, or to finance a diffuse tax cut. Programmes also continue because they are popular with the public officials charged with running them; they will oppose abolishing activities that justify their jobs.[12]

In financial terms, the inertia commitments of government are dynamic, not static. Inertia here describes the tendency of a body in motion to remain in motion. In the past quarter century, the costs of public policies in Britain have grown in seven years out of eight. The costs have been growing at an average rate of 4.3 per cent a year. Cumulatively, small percentage point increases add up to large sums of money. For example, from 1973 to 1978, total government expenditure increased from £25.2 billion to £58.5 billion in current prices. Of this increase, 93 per cent was accounted for by inflation. When allowance is made for rising prices, however, public purchasing power sometimes falls. From 1977 to 1978, total government spending fell by three per cent in terms of constant purchasing power, but because of inflation, this fall was also accompanied by a £3.5 billion increase in the actual amount of money that government actually spent.[13]

Most public expenditure in Britain pays for what people normally think of as 'good' goods. Pensions and other social security payments account for nearly one-quarter of total public spending; education and health and social services rank second and fourth in their claims upon the public purse. These three programmes, plus spending on housing, collectively accounted for 59 per cent of all government spending in 1978. These programmes continue because they are popular and provide benefits to the majority of English families. That also explains why in aggregate they cost so much money.

Second in importance, accounting for 21 per cent of public spending, are those programmes that are by definition the responsibility

[12] For a development of this analysis, see Rose and Peters, *Can Government Go Bankrupt?*, ch. 5.
[13] *Social Trends*, Vol. 9 (1979) Table 7.14, supplemented by unpublished Treasury figures.

of a modern state: maintaining a military force and representation overseas; law and order; providing common services to the bureaucracy (e.g. civil service recruitment); and paying interest on accumulated national debts. If British government today only met its minimum defining activities, it would spend £12 billion annually instead of £58 billion.

TABLE XI.2   **The growing cost of implementing public policies, 1973–1978**

Programme categories

	Current spending 1973 1978 (£ billion)		Change in constant £ %
Defining activities			
Defence	3.5	8.3	−0
Law and order	0.7	2.0	+21
Debt interest	0.4	1.9	+208
Total	£ 4.7	£12.3	+12%
Welfare			
Health and personal social services	3.0	7.9	+13
Education	3.9	8.7	+4
Social Security	5.0	13.2	+24
Housing	1.5	4.7	+43
Total	£13.4	£34.6	+18%
Mobilizing resources			
Agric. & Fish.	0.4	0.9	+0.1
Trade, Ind. & Employment	1.5	1.8	−41
Govt. lending to nationalized industries	1.0	−0.1	−632
Roads and transport	1.3	2.8	+0
Other environmental services	1.2	2.7	−2.1
Total	£5.5	£8.0	−26%
Other programmes	1.6	3.6	+12
Total	£25.2	£58.5	+7%

Sources Current spending: Central Statistical Office, *Financial Statistics* (September 1978), p. 151; Change in constant spending: Cmnd. 7049–I, T.11. As a fiscal year includes parts of two calendar years, the year given above is the second of the pair, e.g. 1978 = 1977/78.

Third in importance are programmes concerned with mobilizing the nation's economic resources. The most costly of these individual programmes involve spending on roads, transport and the environment, accounting for £5.4 billion in 1978. Second in significance are programmes providing cash subsidies for trade and industry, for farmers and fishermen, and for nationalized industries and public corporations.

In the five years from 1973 to 1978, spending on every major government activity except one increased in terms of current money values. The exception was subsidies to nationalized industries. When the effects of inflation are removed from the analysis of the growth of public spending, the pattern remains much the same —most programmes show a significant increase in costs. The most rapid increase was in debt interest, which is specially volatile, depending on the size of the government's debts and the rate of interest it must pay for the money it borrows. The most popular—and also the most costly—policies, the welfare services, tended to grow most in real terms in the 1970s.

Most of the increase in public spending does not reflect major policy initiatives by the government of the day. Instead, it reflects pressures upon established programmes. First of all, inflation drives up costs everywhere; the relative price of government programmes tends to rise faster, because they are labour intensive, or, in the case of pensions, indexed to rise with the cost of living. Secondly, demographic pressures can cause government to spend more money to honour open-ended commitments to provide compulsory education to all young people, or a pension to the elderly as long as they live. Thirdly, costs rise when relatively minor improvements or adjustments are made in established policies. Normally, these add only a small proportion to costs in any one year, but the cumulative effect of annual adjustments can be substantial.

There are three figures that government is hesitant to publish in any statement about future spending priorities. First of all, it can only guess at the cumulative rate of inflation. If inflation from 1978 to 1983 were at 18 per cent, this would increase public spending by about £27 billion in five years. Because the state of the economy cannot be known for certain far ahead, the government of the day is even more cautious about estimating its tax revenue. Whereas plans for spending more look like good news to voters, plans for raising more taxes constitute bad news. The volatility of the economy and of public spending is such that it is difficult to forecast accurately the size of the government's deficit, if any, several years ahead.

To study the implementation of public policies is to move from a world where government is formally sovereign to a realistic perspective of society, in which government organizations are only one among many institutions seeking to exert influence. The difficulties that government faces in implementing programmes are not unique to government, or to England. Only the government of a totalitarian society would want to determine everything that happens therein. And the record of history demonstrates that even totalitarian aspirations are doomed to frustration.

The impact of public policies

Even with the most careful anticipation of means and ends, events outside the foresight or control of government can produce unexpected or undesirable results. Nor does British government claim to be omnipotent. For example, sooner or later all the patients of the National Health Service will die. The work of the Health Service is best evaluated by asking questions of degree: How much longer do people live? Or about the distribution of benefits: To what extent do life chances differ between the wealthy and the poor? Or by asking questions about cost-effectiveness: How much is health improved by the money government spends? How much additional improvement would be gained by spending more?

The impact of government varies with circumstances. Its potential power is greatest when it can claim a lawful monopoly (printing money) or powers of compulsion (fixing the age for starting and leaving school). Usually, government can be confident that its programme outputs will have some impact upon social conditions, but not a monopoly of influence. For example, the government can influence transport by building roads, and by investment and pricing policies for nationalized public transport. But it does not force people to travel by rail or bus, if they wish and can afford to go by car. Nor can it force people to travel or to avoid travel. Often it relies upon market pressures—prices and rationing by queueing—to influence travel. There are also fields of life in which the impact of government is limited by its choice. For example, British government has no population policy. In the words of an ex-Cabinet minister, 'It would mean a policeman in every bed-room.'[14]

Any major policy will have an impact in a multiplicity of ways, some intended and some unintended. For example, a scheme of slum clearance will not only remove physically insanitary buildings, but also may uproot communities whose residents have lived together for years. Many consequences of a policy are not so much unintended as ignored, because they constitute the costs of implementing a programme. Politicians prefer to stress benefits, such as new houses, rather than costs, such as social dislocation. An extremely disillusioned civil servant has taken comfort from the belief, 'Thank God, the government's influence is so little', fearing that its influence would tend to be harmful rather than positive. Setting costs against benefits cannot be done with mathematical precision, as the efforts of cost-benefit economists unintentionally illustrate. Political judgments are necessary to evaluate how the impact of a programme may be beneficial, and what costs it imposes.[15]

The difficulties of anticipating, measuring and evaluating the impact of a given public policy concern the Treasury even more immediately than social scientists. In a negative sense, the Treasury is aware that spending more money on a programme does not guarantee increasing its impact proportionately. An extra £100m. or £500m. spent on health services might only reflect the success of doctors, nurses and hospital workers in pressing claims for higher wages, rather than showing that the nation's health improved by as much as the health services budget rose.

When making judgments about competing priorities of public policy, the Treasury tends to fall back upon evaluating policies by the inputs of government resources, 'numbers of staff employed, goods and services purchased, and so on . . . because of the difficulty of measuring the social output of the services'.[16] In 1970 the Heath government sought to introduce a system of Programme Analysis and Review (PAR) to ask fundamental questions about established

[14] Reginald Maudling, quoted in David Wood, 'Birth of a Population Policy', *The Times*, 8 March 1971.
[15] See 'Sir William Armstrong talking with Desmond Wilcox', *The Listener*, 29 March 1974; also Peter Self, *Econocrats and the Policy Process* (London: Macmillan, 1975).
[16] See Her Majesty's Treasury, *Public Expenditure White Papers: Handbook on Methodology* (London: HMSO, 1972), p. 23.

government policies: What is the object of this programme? Should the government be seeking to do this? What are the effects of the means used to these ends? Can the same resources be employed more effectively and efficiently?

Asking common-sense cause and effect questions is one thing. Securing answers is another, as PAR staff found out. Not only were there analytic difficulties of measuring cause and effect, but also political difficulties in securing departments prepared to put programmes at risk by evaluation. Whitehall departments do not want outsiders from the Treasury asking questions to which they have no precise answers. Nor could the Treasury ask awkward questions in all departments, for to do this would have mobilized a coalition of nearly the whole of the Cabinet (that is, all the spending departments) against it. The PAR system has lapsed into political innocuousness.[17]

The pages that follow cannot pretend to offer a definitive evaluation of the impact of major public policies upon society in England. What can be done is to review changing conditions in society since 1951, when the immediate effects of the Second World War had been largely overcome, and to ask whether these changes are in the direction favoured by major government policies. To indicate correlations is not to prove causation. Yet it is important to see whether trends in English society and government goals have been moving in the same or in opposite directions.

Welfare policies are the major programmes of government, whether judged by the money or personnel devoted to them. Questions of health, education, housing and security of income are pervasive concerns of almost all families in society.[18]

Since the Second World War made the health of the population a military resource as well as a moral value, the government has declared a positive intention to maintain and improve health conditions. The means to this end include preventative health services, such as ante-natal clinics and free milk and vitamins for infants, as well as medical and hospital services virtually free of charge to the patient. Both parties agree about the objectives of the national health service, even though they sometimes disagree about the means of policy.

[17] See Hugh Heclo and Aaron Wildavsky, *The Private Government of Public Money* (London: Macmillan, 1974), ch. 6.

[18] The bulk of the data in the following pages is from the annual Central Statistical Office volume, *Social Trends*, Vol. 9 (1979).

TABLE XI.3 **Changes in health, 1951–1976**

	1951	1961	1971	1976	Change N	%
Infant mortality (per 1000)	29.7	21.4	17.5	14.5	15.2	51
Life expectancy at birth (years)						
Males	66.2	67.9	68.9	69.4	+3.2	5
Females	71.2	73.8	75.1	75.6	+4.4	6

Sources: Annual Abstract of Statistics, 1977, Table 2.31; *Social Trends* Vol. 9 (1978), Figure 8.1, Table 8.2.

The health of the English people has improved since 1951 when judged by common measures of physical well-being. (See Table XI.3.) The number of infant deaths per thousand has fallen by one-half. The Englishman born in 1951 could only look forward to 1.2 years of life following retirement at age 65, whereas his wife, who could start a pension at 60, might live another 11.2 years.[19] A man born in 1975 can look forward to 4.4 years of life after retirement, and his wife 15.6 years from the date of first being eligible for a pension. Health is improving, as government policy intends, but it is improving more slowly than in the period 1931 to 1951.[20]

In education, government has spent massive sums to increase the amount of education received by young people. In 1944, secondary education was made freely available to every young person for the first time, and the compulsory school-leaving age raised to 15. In 1971, the compulsory school-leaving age was raised to 16. Concurrently, large sums were spent in expanding the number of places in universities, polytechnics and other colleges of further education.

Because school attendance is compulsory, raising the minimum age for leaving school has certainly increased the number of young people with eleven years of education instead of nine, the pre-war minimum. In so far as the number of pupils per class measures the quality of teaching, primary education has improved substantially in the past quarter-century, with class size falling, even when numbers of pupils are increasing (Table XI.4.) The proportion of secondary

[19] A woman qualifies to draw a pension at age 60 if she has been employed or is a widow.
[20] From 1931 to 1951, infant mortality fell from 80 to 30 per thousand and life expectancy for males rose from 58.4 years to 66.2 years.

TABLE XI.4   **Changes in education, 1951–1976**

	1951	1961	1971	1976	Change N	%
Pupil/teacher ratio	30.1	28.9	27.1	23.8	−6.3	21
School leavers with five O-level passes or better						
As % of youths	n.a.	15.8	24.7	24.8	+9.0	57
Total numbers	n.a.	97,000	151,000	186,000	+89,000	92
% Secondary school leavers going to full-time further education	6.2	11.3	18.9	23.6	+17.4	281

Sources Social Trends, Vol. 9 (1979), Tables 4.10 and 4.7: the latter table
   averages % for male and female school leavers. *Statistics of Education*, 1971, Vol. 2, Table 13; 1976, Vol. 2, Table 1.

school pupils who are academically successful, that is, pass at least
five Ordinary level examinations or better,[21] has risen from 15.8 per
cent of the age group in 1961 to nearly one-quarter fifteen years
later. Because the proportion of young people in schools has
increased, this means that nearly twice as many school leavers in
total now show good examination results. The proportion of young
people going on from secondary school to further education has
increased nearly fourfold.

Because of an inheritance of nineteenth-century houses considered sub-standard by contemporary eyes (e.g. lacking an indoor
toilet or a fixed bath) and because of war-induced shortages, British
governments from 1945 into the 1970s have sought to promote the
building of modern houses. Conservative and Labour parties have
differed about whether owner-occupied housing or council housing
should receive more encouragement; they have agreed about the
general goal of building more houses.

Government policy, implemented through market measures
affecting both local authority building and private home construction, has encouraged the construction of more housing, and
improved the physical quality of the houses. From 1951 to 1976, the
total number of houses increased from 12.5 million to 18.2 million,
while concurrently the total number of households increased from
13.3 to 17.5 million. A total of 7.3 million houses were built,

[21] Including equivalent CSE passes, introduced in 1965.

virtually all to modern standards, and 1.4 million were razed, virtually all sub-standard. In consequence, the proportion of houses lacking a fixed bath declined from 39 per cent in 1951 to 7 per cent in 1976. Concurrently, the number of people living in overcrowded housing conditions declined from five per cent of households to one per cent. (Table XI.5.)

TABLE XI.5 **Changes in housing, 1951–1976**

	1951	1961	1971	1976	Change N	%
Total number of houses (mn)	12.5	14.6	17.0	18.2	+5.7mn	46
Total number of houses built post-1945 (mn)	0.8	3.4	6.8	8.1	+7.3mn	1013
Ratio of households/ houses	1.1	1.0	1.0	1.0	−0.1	−9
Number of houses lacking a fixed bath (mn)	4.9	3.2	1.4	1.3	−3.6mn	−73

Sources Housing Policy: Technical Volume Part I (London: HMSO, 1977), Tables I.5, I.23, I.21, I.13. I.12; *General Household Survey 1976* (London: HMSO, 1978), Table 5.5.

For many people, security of income means a job, but for the elderly, it means a pension; and for those who are unemployed, disabled or otherwise unable to support themselves, it means a weekly social security benefit in lieu of wages. Since the war, maintaining full employment has been a cardinal aim of British government economic policy. Providing social security benefits to prevent want has been a major welfare policy goal, involving a variety of benefits, some given to all who meet a basic eligibility criterion (e.g. pensions), and others contingent upon need (e.g. unemployment benefit).

In the past quarter century, an expanding economy has provided more jobs; the labour force has grown primarily because of an increase in the number of married women going out to work. The growth of public sector employment has been directly responsible for a significant portion of the increased number of jobs. The proportion of unemployed who receive weekly cash benefits from government has been low by historic standards; between 1921 and

TABLE XI.6   **Changes in income security, 1951–1976**

	1951	1961	1971	1976	Change N	%
People in work (mn)	23.6	25.1	24.3	24.8	+1.2	5
The unemployed						
Numbers (000)	257	340	799	1,359	+1,102	428
Percentage	1.3	1.6	3.5	5.8	+4.5	346
Old age pensioners (mn)	4.2	5.9	7.9	8.5	+4.3	102
Supplementary benefit						
Total in families						
receiving (mn)	n.a.	2.7	4.7	4.9	+2.2	81
% of population	n.a.	5.1	8.5	8.8	+3.7	73

Sources Social Trends, Vol. 9 (1979), Tables 5.1, T 6.31; *British Labour Statistics Historical Abstract*, T. 118/118; *Yearbook of British Labour Statistics 1975*, Table 52, T. 93; *Annual Abstract of Statistics*, 1977, T. 6.1, 6.8.

1939 it ranged from 9.7 to 22.1 per cent of the work force, whereas from 1951 to 1971, it ranged from 1.2 to 3.5 per cent. Reflecting world-wide economic trends, unemployment has risen in the 1970s; even at its highest, it remains below the inter-war low. The number of old age pensioners has doubled, because of increasing longevity in the population, and an easing of the qualifications for drawing of a pension. A host of special programmes provide incomes for the sick and disabled, single-parent families and others. In addition, 4.9 million people receive supplementary benefit payments; these are given for persons who otherwise would not have a secure income and persons whose existing cash benefits are inadequate. This group has increased by 2.2 million since 1961, a fact varyingly cited as evidence of inadequacy in the basic standard of cash benefits or as evidence of the adjustment of welfare provision to individual needs. (Table XI.6.)

The longer the time span invoked, the better the welfare of the British people appears when judged by the standards used above.[22] Welfare has improved by comparison with the period of relatively full employment between 1900 and 1914, as well as the period of

[22] For a comparison of within-Britain changes in living standards, see Central Statistical Office, *Regional Statistics* (HMSO annual) and Ian McAllister, Richard Parry and Richard Rose, *United Kingdom Rankings* (Glasgow: Strathclyde Studies in Public Policy No. 44 1979).

high unemployment between the wars, and the period of full employment in the 1950s.[23] Improvements in welfare are not exclusively the cause of government policies; trends upward antedate the introduction of many major welfare policies. The positive influence of government is most clear in education, for government both compels schooling and provides most education services, and in income security, for government compels payment of social security contributions and disburses cash benefits directly to recipients. Public policy is similarly responsible for the care that people receive when ill, but this does not of itself ensure longer life. Changes in diet, smoking and other habits also influence life expectancy. The British government's influence upon unemployment is significant, but the extent cannot be measured precisely, as against other influences in the national and international economy. Full employment policies have tended to be constant, while unemployment has been rising in the 1970s. Whatever influence government may claim upon levels of employment is variable and limited, not constant.

The major welfare programmes of British government spread benefits widely: every family, and nearly every member of it, expects to benefit at some point in life from publicly provided education, health and pensions. Nearly every family also benefits from housing subsidies, whether as council tenants or by buying a home on a mortgage made cheaper by tax allowances. No political party advocates dismantling any major programme of the contemporary welfare state, for fear of the electoral consequences of threatening tens of millions of citizens with the loss of benefits.

In contemporary England, disputes about the welfare state concern how much (or how much more) government should spend, and what changes or additions should be made to its panoply of programmes. They also concern how the costs and benefits should be distributed. If welfare policies are a badge of citizenship, should all citizens be compelled to rely upon government services? If benefits are meant to help those most in need, does this mean excluding people with average as well as above-average income, and interrogating recipients about their means to make sure that they are poor enough to qualify?

Mobilizing economic resources is a second major concern of government. The large and increasingly costly programmes of the

[23] Cf. A. H. Halsey, ed., *Trends in British Society since 1900* (London: Macmillan, 1972).

contemporary welfare state were financed from the 1940s into the 1970s by the fiscal dividend of economic growth. Government can simultaneously raise more money in taxes *and* leave more money in the pockets of citizens if two conditions are met. The first is that the economy expands, rather than contracts. The second condition is that the costs of public policy do not grow more than the growth in the economy.

Ministers and MPs speak casually about the government managing the economy, but the phrase implies a power that politicians in England lack. In fact, the British economy is neither owned nor controlled by the state, as is the case in Eastern Europe. It is a mixed economy. This means that there is a substantial private sector; both trade unions and industrialists and financiers are free to make many decisions as they think best. They may (and do) take decisions that the government of the day says are against the national interest, e.g. striking for higher wages when the government is seeking to maintain a voluntary incomes policy, or by refusing to invest (or investing abroad) when the government is trying to encourage investment.

While the British government's influence over the economy has undoubtedly increased substantially, by comparison with 1939 or 1959, the influence of world economic conditions upon the British economy has increased greatly too. In the competitive world economy Britain has usually done less well than other nations. The most visible indicator of this is the falling value of the £, by comparison with other major currencies, such as the dollar and the Deutsche Mark. Germany and America, as well as Britain, have had difficulties in maintaining full employment, reducing inflation, and encouraging economic growth. But overall, both countries have succeeded better than England in balancing claims and resources. For that reason, the £ has fallen in value significantly against the dollar, and even more against the Deutsche Mark.

A Chancellor of the Exchequer, after learning that he had the responsibility for managing the economy but not the power to do so, might complain that the problem was not so much the government's lack of impact as the economists' lack of fresh ideas (or old ideas that work effectively), or the public's expectation of greater growth than was practicable. Economists disagree about the need for new ideas. Some argue that Keynesian methods for managing the economy, including a proper regard for the money supply, are still

TABLE XI.7   The changing foreign exchange value of the pound, 1948–1979

	USA ($ to £)	Germany (DMark to £)
1948	4.03	(Germany virtually bankrupt)
1958	2.81	11.7
1968	2.39	9.6
1973	2.45	6.5
1976	1.81	4.6
1979	2.16	3.8

Note 1948–1976 figures are annual averages; and 1979, as of 16 November.

adequate—if only politicians would do what economists tell them. Others reckon that perhaps the fault lies not in politicians, but in themselves, for failing to find explanations for difficulties that, according to their theories, should not or need not occur.[24] Public opinion surveys make clear that the electorate is not to blame for expecting endless or impossible growth. In fact, the problem is created by government, which itself has generated the need for growth in order to finance painlessly the rising costs of the contemporary welfare state.[25]

One explanation for the failure of British government to give more effective direction to the economy is that, unlike French planners, British politicians have been too ready to take into account the views of those meant to carry out plans, business and the unions. In England, consent has been placed ahead of effectiveness in mobilizing resources. A concern with due process has triumphed over a sense of purposeful growth. Another explanation is that British people have not wished to make the effort, as Germany and Japan had to do in the aftermath of military defeat in 1945, to increase wealth. This may reflect satisfaction with material standards of living that are higher than in the past, an unwillingness to abandon customary business or trade union practices or to forgo consumption for the sake of investment. A third explanation is that a small offshore island such as Britain lacks the natural resources to maintain its world economic hegemony of a century ago, now that

[24] See Rose and Peters, *Can Government Go Bankrupt?*, ch. 6.
[25] See Richard Rose, *Ordinary People in Extraordinary Economic Circumstances* (Glasgow: Strathclyde Studies in Public Policy No. 11, 1977).

international trade is open to competition with many other large countries, often better endowed with resources. It is possible that all three of these explanations are true.

When judged by historical standards, the British economy has succeeded in the postwar era, whether the government is given the credit for this or reckoned to be the cause of its not doing even better. From 1951 through 1978, the total national wealth available for public and private consumption has more than doubled. The economy's growth rate in the 1950s (2.3 per cent annually) rose in the 1960s to 2.9 per cent annually, then fell in line with experience elsewhere in the Western world to 1.6 per cent in the 1970s. In this period, Britain has maintained a higher annual rate of growth than at any earlier period in the twentieth century. The fact that this higher rate applies to a larger economic base increases substantially the absolute value of the fiscal dividend of each year's growth. But by comparative standards, the British economy has not grown as quickly as Britain's major European competitors. (See Table II.1.)

A third major responsibility of British government—providing security for citizens against international war or domestic disorder —antedates the welfare state. It is by definition a responsibility of every modern state, whatever its political colour.

Since 1945 English people have not been involved in a major international war. England has enjoyed a longer period of continuous peace than the period between the ending of the Crimean War in 1856 and the commencement of the Boer War in South Africa in 1899. For better or worse, its most significant military involvement has been an internal war in Northern Ireland, raging since 1971.

Britain's avoidance of war is more the result of a global balance of power than of British diplomacy. But British diplomats can claim that they played an important role in the years after 1945 in constructing this balance of power. From 1945 to 1951 the Labour government was very active in promoting the development of economic recovery in Europe through the American-financed Marshall Plan, and military security through NATO (the North Atlantic Treaty Organization). It participated in the Korean War of 1950–53 as an act of mutual security, but since then has carefully disengaged from military confrontation in Asia, and since the failure of the 1956 joint Anglo-French attack upon the Suez Canal in Egypt, it has eschewed the use of force on any significant scale. Since then the British government has successfully adapted its military commitments to the facts of its international weakness.

At home, the best measure of political security is the freedom of speech enjoyed by the citizenry. The authority of government is so secure that it does not control the press, or subvert it privately. The right to protest is respected by police, as well as avidly invoked by devotees of a cause, or those anxious to protest against social conditions generally. There are restrictions upon the reporting of activities in Whitehall. The Official Secrets Act is not so much a device protecting the state against subversive elements as it is a political convenience for the party momentarily in office and the permanent civil service.

The liberty of the individual has been further extended by government de-regulation of such activities as homosexuality, abortion, gambling and prostitution, which have long existed in England and many other societies. For generations they were regarded as breaches of *public* morality, and therefore subject to legal punishment, if persons were caught indulging in them. By repealing laws in such areas, government has facilitated a change in moral standards. It is debatable whether this change is caused by government or is merely a consequence of social pressures more powerful than government.

The rise in crime in England is almost certainly a consequence of social trends common throughout the Western world, and not distinctive to England. The fact that there are a larger number of young people in the population, and that young people are more likely to commit crime is one significant cause of the increase in crime. For a combination of reasons, the number of indictable offences known to the police has increased four times from 529,000 in 1951 to 2,136,000 in 1976. Most of the increase in crime results from an increase in theft and robbery. Crimes of violence are relatively few. The murder rate in England is only one-ninth the American murder rate.[26]

The increase in crime has occurred in spite of the growth in the size of the police force from 71,000 in 1951 to 87,000 in 1961, and 125,000 in 1977. As crime has increased, the proportion of offences cleared up by police investigation and prosecution has

[26] *Social Trends*, Vol. 9 (1979) T. 13.20. A part of the increase results from changes in the definition of indictable offences.

fallen slightly from a high point of 47 per cent in 1951 to 41 per cent in 1977.

The most intangible, yet not the least important, feature of a society is an agreed community of identification, for without a common identity, there is literally nothing to hold people together in acceptance of the authority of a given state. Within the United Kingdom, common symbols of national identity have not been as readily available as in, say, France or America, because there is no primary community of 'Ukes' (that is, people of the United Kingdom). The population divides into at least four communities: English, Scottish, Welsh and those who think themselves British, including a portion of the residents of Northern Ireland.

A distinctive feature of the 1970s has been the apparent decline in a sense of common national identity. Nationalists in Scotland and Wales claim that they belong to a different political community. They wish to remain loyal to the Crown, but as self-governing dominions in the Commonwealth, like Canada or Australia. Ulstermen do not necessarily want to do even this. The debate on Northern Ireland has also shown that few English MPs wish to accept United Kingdom responsibilities, that is, to defend Northern Ireland as if it were one community with England. The casual way in which devolution was debated for Scotland and Wales, with party advantage at least as important as what might be called 'national' considerations, is further evidence of a weakened sense of a United Kingdom identity.

The most familiar symbols of political community—the Queen, the Union Jack, the national anthem, and images of green fields and old villages— are all peculiarly irrelevant to the political problems of the moment. The problems of England today are those of an ageing industrial economy, an economy that needs to make major changes in its industrial structure and trade if it is to prosper in future as in the past. Computer scientists, export managers and coal miners are unlikely to be moved by an appeal to traditional symbols of rural England. They require different symbols or material inducements or sanctions to intensify their efforts.

As British government goes 'deeper in' to society by undertaking a wider range of policies, it increasingly reduces its claim to unilateral sovereignty. Instead of being able to achieve policies by fiat, it becomes one of many influences upon a wider range of social conditions. The nation's welfare, economic resources and security are products of complex processes influenced by government's policies—but by many other factors as well.

The inability of successive Labour and Conservative governments to achieve their policy aspirations raises questions about the limits of government.[27] Radicals and reformers respond with a plea for government to try harder, and to try different policies. Others respond by acceptance of the limits of things as they are. In the words of one student of politics, Ken Young,

> The age of reform is giving way to an age of realism. The exercise of power at both the national and local levels is becoming more self-conscious, better informed as to the indirect and unintended consequences of its exercise, and more acutely aware of the constraints of feasibility. Feasibility tempers purpose in this new governmental spirit. Its genesis is to be found in the failed or faltering policies of the 1970s, and its distinguishing characteristic is the reluctant recognition by governments of the *intractability* of the external world upon which they seek to operate.[28]

In so far as the purpose of making choices is the mobilization of national resources to achieve political goals, limitations upon government are frustrating. This encourages a search for ways to reorganize government to make it more effective. The failures of public policy in the past twenty years in Britain have precipitated a plethora of reforms concerning the Treasury, the Civil Service, Parliament, local government and Scotland, Wales and Northern Ireland. But the effectiveness of government has not increased, as judged by its ability to manage an economy upon whose growth both public and private policies depend.

If the chief purpose of government is thought to be maintaining consent, then the frustrations of government appear in a different light. Government is not an organization doing things in response to a command from the top, like a military-style hierarchy. It is meant to do what citizens want, and what they will accept. The unitary power of government is more apparent than real. Even within the network of functional and territorial institutions that constitute government, Cabinet ministers must bargain for political consent, if

[27] See Richard Rose, *Do Parties Make a Difference?* chs. 7–8.
[28] Ken Young, 'Environmental Management in Local Politics', in Dennis Kavanagh and Richard Rose, eds., *New Trends in British Politics* (London & Beverly Hills: Sage, 1977), pp. 143–4.

they wish to secure the co-operation of all involved in the policy process.

Popular feedback

The impact of government is evaluated by English citizens in the light of already established values and beliefs. People have ideas, grounded in experience, about what government ought (and ought not) to do and what it can realistically be expected to achieve. Popular evaluations of government reflect a wider and deeper range of personal concerns. Most English people are not political scientists; they are concerned first and foremost with leading a good life, and not with good government for its own sake.

Studies of public opinion consistently find that English people are generally satisfied with the life they lead. As many as five out of six English people respond positively to the question: On the whole, are you very satisfied, fairly satisfied, not very satisfied or not at all satisfied with the life you lead? (Table XI.8.) Moreover, English people are usually more likely to be satisfied with their life than citizens of other major nations in the European Community. In 1978, 85 per cent of English people were satisfied, as against 63 per cent of Italians. Furthermore, most English people are moderate in their judgments: they are more likely to say that they are 'fairly satisfied' with their life than to say 'very satisfied'. Among those at the extremes of opinion, the 'very satisfied' outnumber those 'not at all satisfied' by a margin of about eight to one.

Gallup Poll surveys asking English people whether or not they are satisfied with a wide range of specific circumstances in their lives confirm the broad finding of the European Community surveys.

TABLE XI.8   **Life satisfaction in major European nations, 1973–1978**

	1973	1975	1977	1978	Change 1973–8
	(% satisfied with life)				
Britain	85	71	87	85	0
Germany	82	79	85	82	0
France	77	75	73	71	−6
Italy	65	58	62	63	−2

Source Euro-Barometre, No. 9 (Brussels: Commission des Communautés Européennes, July 1978) p. 5.

The survey reported in Table XI.9 was particularly well timed to record dissatisfaction, for it occurred after more than a decade of media discussion about 'What's wrong with Britain?', and in the middle of a particularly sharp and disconcerting down turn in the economy.

TABLE XI.9   **Social satisfaction by class, 1976**

	Total population		Proportion satisfied	
	Satisfied	Dissatisfied	Middle class	Working class
	%	%	%	%
The leisure you have	81	17	80	81
The work you do	74	14	80	70
Your housing	74	24	79	72
Your standard of living	68	28	76	64
Your family income	57	41	63	53
Children's education	49	35	44	52
The future facing your family	45	39	47	44
Honesty and behaviour of people in this country today	21	70	25	19
Britain's world position	19	75	20	19

Source Unpublished figures from a Gallup Poll survey, January 1976.

A majority of English people with views report that they are satisfied with the leisure they have, the work they do, their housing, standard of living, family income, children's education and the future facing their family. (Table XI.9.) Only in two domains do a majority report that they are dissatisfied: three-quarters are dissatisfied with Britain's world position, and almost as large a proportion are dissatisfied with their fellow citizens' standards of honesty and behaviour.

There are class differences in popular satisfaction, but these differences are relatively small. A majority or plurality of both middle-class and working-class people are satisfied with seven out of nine domains of social life. Moreover, working-class people are more satisfied than middle-class people with the leisure they have, and their children's education. People are less satisfied with things that most directly relate to occupation: the work done, living standards and family income. On average, the proportion of satisfied middle-class people is four per cent greater than the proportion of satisfied in working-class families.

Popular satisfactions have been rising in the working-class in the 1970s, and falling in the middle class. When the questions reported in Table XI.9 were asked by the Gallup Poll in February 1973, an average of 59 per cent reported themselves satisfied with varied conditions.[29] Three years later, the proportion of satisfied middle-class respondents fell in six of the nine cases, declining on average by 2 per cent. By contrast, the average level of satisfaction among working-class respondents rose from 49 per cent to 51 per cent.

Both surveys reject the hypothesis that economic recession leads to popular dissatisfaction with society. Life satisfaction has remained high since the oil crisis of 1973, and since the economic recession of 1975. (See Table XI.8.) Satisfaction with specific domains of society, as measured by the Gallup Poll, rose on average by one per cent between 1973 and 1976. Most of the changes in life satisfaction appear to reflect normal sampling fluctuations, and certainly do not show any major change of opinion.

General life satisfaction is consistent with specific political dissatisfactions. Whereas 85 per cent of British people reported themselves satisfied with the life they led in 1973, only 44 per cent said that they were satisfied with the way democracy worked in Britain. Similar gaps were reported for other major European countries. By 1978, satisfaction with democracy had increased substantially in Britain; 62 per cent reported political satisfaction. In the case of Italy, the gap widened, for in 1978 only 25 per cent of Italians reported themselves satisfied with how Italian democracy worked whereas a majority (63 per cent) reported themselves generally satisfied with their lives. (Cf. Table XI.10, XI.8.)

The implication of these findings is important: the greatest concerns of individuals are insulated from the major political institutions of society. If we could do a content analysis of what ordinary English persons talked about we would almost certainly find that talk about the weather or sport is more frequent than talk about politics, and that phatic communion is a more common form of social intercourse than reasoned analysis of society's ills.

Time and again, when surveys ask people to evaluate their lives, the same pattern recurs: individuals report that they are most

[29] See *Gallup Political Index*, No. 151 (February 1973), p. 39.

TABLE XI.10   Satisfaction with the way democracy works in major
               European nations, 1973–1978

	1973	1976	1977	1978	Life satisfaction (Table XI.8) minus political satisfaction 1978
	(% satisfied with national democracy)				
Germany	44	79	78	76	+6
Britain	44	51	62	62	+23
France	41	42	49	49	+22
Italy	27	14	19	25	+38

Source Euro-Barometre No. 8 (Brussels: January 1978), p 17.

satisfied with their family, friends, home, and job, and least satisfied
with major institutions of society for which government is responsible. Individuals generalize their view of life primarily from face-
to-face experiences, and not from distant actions of distant institutions communicated indirectly or vicariously through the media. In
terms of knowledge, people today are aware of a far wider world
than illiterate peasants belonging to *The World We Have Lost.*[30]
But in terms of emotional values, face-to-face relationships remain
most important to most people in contemporary post-industrial
society.

If individual Englishmen put material standards of living first,
then they would emigrate to America, Canada or Australia or to
other countries of the European Community. But large-scale emigration does not take place. By contrast to the 1930s or the Second
World War, political dissatisfactions are not so intense as to lead to
massive flight. People can and do adapt in their everyday lives to
what British government does or fails to do. Yet English people
today voice concerns about their political influence, or the lack
thereof, using the term political in the broadest sense of the term.
When asked whether people like themselves have enough say in a
variety of major institutions in British society, the great majority
consistently say that they do not. More than 70 per cent say that
people like themselves do not have enough influence upon central
and local government, the nationalized industries, and the television media. People are least likely to feel powerless in the most
non-political settings, as customers in shops and, because of the high

[30] Peter Laslett, *The World We Have Lost* (London: Methuen, 1965).

degree of trade union organization, as employees. (See Table XI.11.) In all twelve fields, more English people feel lacking in influence than satisfied.

TABLE XI.11 **Social influence by class, 1978**

Do people like yourself have enough say in:	Yes %	No %	Proportion saying yes	
			Middle class %	Working class %
Services in shops	41	45	44	41
The education of their children	27	59	29	28
Working conditions	36	49	40	34
How newspapers present news	27	58	25	26
Policies of employers	28	46	32	27
Television programmes of BBC	16	76	19	14
Policies of trade unions	28	54	30	26
Television programmes of ITV	17	73	19	17
How local authorities handle things	16	75	17	16
How the government runs the country	20	72	23	20
How banks operate	23	51	24	25
Services of the nationalized industries	15	74	14	15
Average	25	61	26	24

Social Unpublished figures from a Gallup Poll survey, May 1978.

A sense of political inadequacy is not a reflection of class differences, for middle-class and working-class English people agree about their lack of influence. In none of the replies to twelve questions did a majority in either class consider that people like themselves had enough say in what was done. While working-class people are consistently less likely to see themselves able to influence major social institutions, the differences between them and middle-class people are consistently small, averaging 2 per cent.

Moreover, a sense of political inadequacy has been growing in the 1970s. The Gallup Poll has asked a cross-section of British people the same questions about political influence in 1969, 1973 and 1978. The proportion saying that they felt able to influence major social institutions has, on average, declined by 2 per cent from 1973 and by 5 per cent from 1969 to 1978. Whereas an average of 30 per cent of people thought they had enough say about things in 1969, a decade later the proportion had fallen to 25 per cent.[31]

Critics of British government in Parliament, the press and the universities usually criticize government for what it fails to do. In particular, its efforts to mobilize the nation's economic resources are judged inadequate by comparison with the economic record of other major European nations.

By contrast, popular dissatisfaction concentrates upon the inability of political institutions to give ordinary people enough say in decisions that affect them. How decisions are made can be at least as important as what decisions are made. Inevitably any large organization—whether a government, a trade union or a bank—will centralize the making of many major decisions. But the inevitability of some degree of oligarchy does not necessarily mean that the present extent is generally acceptable.

One theory of political authority emphasizes the importance of results: citizens will accept a government that produces the goods that people want. Another theory emphasizes the importance of participation: citizens will consent to do what government decides if they are involved in the means and institutions of policy making. In England in the 1970s, government has found it increasingly difficult to produce the results it wants, because of economic difficulties particular to Britain, as well as general to the world. One question for the 1980s is whether the government of England can continue to rely upon the diffuse allegiance of citizens if its economic policies do not succeed, and another is whether it can continue to exercise authority effectively if large numbers of citizens feel relatively powerless.

[31] See *Gallup Political Index*, No. 151 (February 1973), p. 37.

XII
A Changing England?

It is needful to keep the ancient show while we secretly interpolate the new reality.

Any speculation about a changing England is conditioned by what is expected to alter when politics changes.[1] Focusing upon institutions might lead one to argue that there has been no 'fundamental' change in England since the Glorious Revolution of 1688, or even since the Norman Conquest. An electoral focus might suggest that every election that results in a change in the governing party inaugurates a new (*sic*) politics. Changes in one dimension of politics do not necessarily produce changes in another. For example, England could turn from a monarchy into a republic with little alteration in public policies. The persistence of an institution in name does not mean that nothing of consequence has altered. For example, Parliament today is far different from what it was a century ago.

Political changes can be grouped into three categories: nominal, ordinal, and continuous. The biggest changes are nominal, a change in kind. For example, the reaction against immigrants represents a new way of thinking about British citizens in terms of colour not class. Some changes occur at precise points in time: the election of a new government or the enactment of an Act of Parliament. But often changes that cumulatively result in discontinuity—for example, Labour replacing the Liberals as the alternative governing party—take decades to accomplish.

Many changes of great political importance are best measured in orders of magnitude. For example, British government had been providing some health services prior to the passage of the National Health Service Act in 1946. But the comprehensive service established then was different in scale from what went before. Similarly, governments have always preferred the economy to grow rather than contract, but the increasing value that British governments have placed upon economic growth in the past generation reflects a

[1] See Richard Rose, ed., *The Dynamics of Public Policy* (London: Sage Publications, 1976), especially ch. 1.

big shift in relative priorities between economic growth, with its attendant friction and risks, and economic stability with its attendant constraints.

The everyday issues of politics often concern small increments of change along a continuum of choice. Typically, welfare policies involve changing the money value of a benefit by a few per cent. Changes in the rate of economic growth are measured in tenths of one per cent. Small changes along a continuum provide the best opportunity for compromise; for instance, in a debate about whether interest rates should be increased by one per cent or two per cent, an increase of one and a half per cent is a readily available compromise.

Some political changes have a special significance, because they are irreversible. For instance, once a government has declared war, in a literal sense it can never go back to exactly what was before. Politics in England at the end of the First World War was different from politics at the outbreak of that war; the same thing happened after the Second World War. Many policies are virtually irreversible, because of the strength of cultural values. For example, it would be legally possible to take away the vote from women or persons below a given income. But no party hoping for political success would conceivably advocate this. Similarly, it would be legally conceivable to deport non-white English residents. But practical as well as moral objections make it very unlikely that England will return to the status of an all-white society.

Other political changes are cyclical, like the movement of the Conservative and Labour parties in and out of office. There is no pendulum-like regularity to their movements, but there is a pattern of ups and downs in the fortunes of the two parties since 1945. In economics, government moves back and forth between policies giving priority to economic growth, and those giving priority to keeping down a rising cost of living. The inflation-deflation cycle is aptly known as a 'stop-go' policy.

In looking ahead, it is easier to see the pressures for and against change than it is to see the direction of change. To avoid overestimating the speed with which an established society like England can change, constraints upon change are examined first in this chapter. The next section considers pressures promoting change. Even if government cannot determine change through political planning, at a minimum it must cope with change: this is the theme of the third section. The final section of the book starts from the assumption that there will always be an England, but it makes no assumption about the character of the England to be.

Constraints upon change

Few political changes take place as quickly as a Prime Minister can change with a general election. Yet this event, occurring hours after the result is conceded, does not alter many things about the control of government. It takes several days for a Cabinet to be formed, months for ministers to become familiar with their new departments and substantially longer for them to make an imprint upon public policies. Once new men enter office, they may change more than the government, for constraints upon policy do not disappear with a new Cabinet.

Parliament, Cabinet and the civil service are shaped by laws and customs that can only be altered gradually. Even a revolution would not produce a new set of legal statutes overnight. At most, it could only repudiate laws of its predecessor. Unwritten customs and conventions embodied in the political culture are further constraining influences. Laws can be rewritten in a day; the customs and conventions of government cannot be changed in a day, because they are embedded in the minds of men. Politicians and partisans share cultural beliefs that make many political changes literally unthinkable.

When slogans of change are on many lips, sitting tight is a posture that speaks louder than words. This is aptly illustrated by proposals to reform the civil service. The appointment of the Fulton Committee in 1966 to examine the structure, recruitment and management of the civil service reflected a widely felt desire—within and outside Whitehall—for changes in an institution that had last been the subject of major structural reform in the nineteenth century.

The desire for reform could not mean a wholesale rejection of existing methods of public administration. First, there was a conscious desire to maintain positively valued features of the civil service, such as its reputation for financial probity and non-partisanship. Second, there was a desire to minimize the effects of change upon the clients of the civil service. Routine and precedent provide predictable and economical ways of dispatching its great volume of detailed work. Third, the hundreds of thousands of civil servants with permanent pensionable positions could not be fired or moved about at will without violating contractual obligations. Fourth, the civil servants placed in charge of reforms themselves reflected outlooks developed in their previous work in the civil service. The first Permanent Secretary of the 'reforming' Civil Service Department, Sir William Armstrong, had started learning on the job in the very different climate of Whitehall between the wars. Individuals first recruited to the reformed administrative ranks in 1971 are, by the normal process of seniority, not likely to reach very senior posts in government until the year 2000.

What is true of the civil service also applies to other institutions of government. In theory, English local government could be reformed in a single session of Parliament, for its structure and powers depend upon legislation. In practice, the 1974 reform of English local government was the culmination of thirty years of investigation, deliberation and discussion. The most visible changes in central government, the frequent alteration of the names of Whitehall departments, do not alter activities or personnel; they simply reshuffle units among departments and ministers, or alter the department's letterhead.[2]

Notwithstanding the readiness of some MPs to preach root-and-branch change in society, Parliament itself resists reform of its own procedures. Abolishing the hereditary House of Lords has been debated ever since its powers to obstruct legislation were greatly curbed in 1911. Liberal, Conservative and Labour governments have pondered the subject—but none has yet abolished its hereditary membership. Changes in practices of the House of Commons have been numerous, but Sir T. Erskine May's guide, *The Law, Privileges, Proceedings and Usage of Parliament*, first published in 1844, still remains, in its suitably amended nineteenth edition, the standard work on the Commons.[3]

However great the intended change, policy makers must start from what is already there. The governors of England may envy small, prosperous neutral countries the freedom from international economic and diplomatic commitments that they enjoy. Economists struggling with the problems of 'remodernizing' the world's first

---

[2] See e.g. L. J. Sharpe, 'Whitehall—Structures and People', in Dennis Kavanagh and Richard Rose, *New Trends in British Politics* (London & Beverly Hills: Sage Publications, 1977), and Christopher Hood, *The Machinery of Government Problem* (Glasgow: Strathclyde Studies in Public Policy No. 28, 1979).

[3] See the comments in S. A. Walkland and Michael Ryle, eds., *The Commons in the 70's* (London: Fontana, 1977), especially Walkland's 'Whither the Commons?'.

industrial nation may long for the advantages of developing new industries without the incubus of declining ones. For the foreseeable future, at least, these thoughts must be classifed as wishful thinking. There is no escaping the immediate fact: England is a large, old industrial society greatly affected by events outside its boundaries.

In time, almost anything can be changed. The island of Britain may even be joined to the Continent of Europe by a bridge, tunnel, or a land passage. Other things that once seemed more far-fetched may occur even sooner. But the longer the time required to alter social conditions by political action, the greater the delay in realizing benefits to set against the political costs of change. To politicians concerned with immediate events, this argues against action. To those concerned with future generations, it may be an argument for beginning work today, so that posterity may enjoy the benefits.

The time required for government policy to have an impact varies from policy area to policy area, as the following catalogue illustrates:

Immediately changeable. Many features of the economy for which government is responsible can (or must) be altered quickly. This is most notably true of bank rate and other determinants of the exchange value of the pound. If not forestalled, a run on the pound could literally bankrupt the Bank of England in a matter of days.

Changeable in a few months. The public esteem of political leaders and parties can rise or fall significantly in a few months. These fluctuations, reflecting very crude political judgments, occur at a much faster rate than substantive changes in parties or the basic personalities of politicians change. The 1970 British general election provided an especially vivid demonstration of this. In January, the Labour Party trailed the Conservatives substantially in all five opinion polls, only to be ahead in all the polls in May, and on the losing side when the election result was declared in mid-June.

Changeable in up to five years. An Act of Parliament normally takes several years to process from the point at which a minister decides that a bill should be prepared to formal enactment. Consultations must be undertaken with affected pressure groups, with the administrators responsible for the bill, and with lawyers concerned with the language of the statute. The Cabinet must give the measure priority in the queue for legislation, and Parliament will require months to discuss and propose amendments. Once the bill is

enacted, administrators require time to implement the new measure, and the public must become accustomed to it. Within the
lifetime of a Parliament there is time for a newly elected governing
party to enact a substantial legislative programme. But if it does not
commence this work within a year of election, it is unlikely to have
time to see its measures through before once again risking its future
with the electorate.

Changeable in a decade. Many major activities of government
require substantial time to plan and implement. A particularly long
lead time is required by major capital investment programmes for
school buildings, hospitals or roads. For example, to help meet the
rising demand for university education, seven new universities were
founded in England between 1961 and 1965. Because each literally
commenced on a 'green field' site, growth came slowly. By 1976,
the seven new universities had a total enrolment of only 22,000, a
figure 20,000 less than that of the University of London, and
insufficient to accommodate the growth of applicants for university
places. The bulk of additional students were accommodated by the
expansion of established universities, rather than by founding new
institutions.

Changeable in a generation or more. Any proposal to alter society
by altering education can require a generation to take effect as the
first cohort of beneficiaries progresses from nursery schools to adult
life. Life-expectancy cannot show the full effect of the National
Health Service until well after the year 2000, the time at which the
whole population will consist of persons who have had its benefits
all their lives.

Past choices limit present policies. A newly elected government
will find itself committed to many decisions that it is too late to stop
or reverse, except at a very high political or monetary cost. For
example, the roads and highways policy of any newly elected government must start from the fact that in the lifetime of a Parliament,
more than 95 per cent of all traffic will be travelling on roads
planned or built under previous governments.

Present choices constrain future actions. A newly elected government, like its predecessors, can make some major policy decisions that its successors will find difficult to reverse. For instance, it
can assume that the great bulk of the legislation that it places on the
statute books will not be repealed by its successor. In the case of
housing any change in policy will influence at least a dozen future

Parliaments, for the Treasury assumes when writing off construction loans that a newly built council house will be in use for sixty years.

The constraints of government are an inertia force. Inertia creates resistance to change; this makes it difficult to put new programmes into effect. But once in motion, the momentum of inertia also makes it difficult to stop the growth of a government.

Pressures for change

Even if the government of the day intended to pursue a policy of no change, this would not result in unchanging policies, because of alterations in the society that programmes are intended to influence. The more socially conservative a government is, the more it must *actively* pursue policies designed to negate or limit the effects of social change.

Demographic change is the most inevitable of all changes in society, the least amenable to influence by legislation, and the strongest in its pressures upon public policies. An increase of ten per cent in the population means that the economy must expand by ten per cent in order to keep constant the gross national product per capita. Problems increase disproportionately if population growth occurs among children and the elderly; these dependent portions of the population are especially heavy consumers of education, health and other welfare services. In the past forty years, both the total number and the proportion of people of pensionable age has almost doubled in Britain.

Population change creates pressures to provide more of the same public services (expanding universities in the 1960s) or different services (geriatric programmes in the 1970s). Doing nothing in response to population change also has consequences. If demand rises more quickly than supply, then the benefits of public policy will be harder to obtain whether these are conceived as a place in higher education or a bed in a nursing home for the elderly.

Today, there are very great uncertainties about the future trends of population. In 1970, the Central Statistical Office estimated that the population of the United Kingdom would grow by 2.8 million people by 1981, with all that that implied in terms of an increased demand for public services. By 1978, it was forecasting nil population growth between 1970 and 1981. Whereas in 1970 official forecasts anticipated a 6 million population increase by 1991, by

1978 official forecasts had scaled this down to a forecast increase of 1 million in the population. And in 1978, the population in the year 2001 was expected to rise by 1.8 million from the 1971 population, rather than by the 10 million forecast in 1971.[4]

The deceleration in population growth in the 1970s poses difficulties for government. The expansion of education has been based upon a continuing increase in young people demanding schooling. In the 1970s, the number of births declined by nearly one-quarter from its peak in the mid-1960s. In turn, this implies fewer children going to school in the 1980s, with the prospect of classrooms closing, and newly trained teachers without jobs because of a fall in the demand for their services. The move toward a relatively stable population also has important implications for housing policy. Instead of building new houses for additional families, housing policy may concentrate more upon the quality of housing and its size, building more homes for small or childless families.

The population of working age will continue to grow in the 1980s, for it consists of persons already born by the beginning of the 1970s or before. Moreover, because birth-rates in the 1960s were generally higher than between the wars, the numbers entering the labour market will be greater than those reaching retirement age. In consequence, the Department of Employment estimates that nearly 2 million more people will be seeking jobs in 1986 than in 1976. The number could be even greater, if the trend of women working accelerates. The increase in numbers seeking work is happening at a time when the total number of jobs in the economy has actually decreased by 0.6 million from 1966 to 1976, and the number of unemployed nearly doubled to 1.5 million from 1971 to 1978.[5]

Even if the population remains constant in number, the composition of society will inexorably change, for millions of elderly English persons die each decade, and millions of youths mature into adults. The passing of the elderly removes those who have a first-hand recollection of England's role as a world power prior to the First World War, and diminishes the proportion who recall the years of depression between the wars. The entry of youthful cohorts to the

---

[4] For basic figures, see Central Statistical Office, *Social Trends*, Vol. 9 (1979), T. 1.2. For comment, see Central Policy Review Staff, *Population and the Social Services*, (London: HMSO, 1977).

[5] See e.g. *New Society*, 16 March 1978.

ranks of adult citizens increases the proportion who have no personal experience of the Second World War, the death—let alone the political life—of Winston Churchill, or of times when affluence was not the expectation of most people in society. In the 1945 general election, the median voter was born about 1900 and had been socialized into an awareness of all these things. In the election of 1979, the median voter was born just before the Second World War broke out in 1939.

The processes of political socialization by family, old friends and established institutions of society are important in maintaining continuity in society. Population changes slowly, with less than 2 per cent of the voters entering the electorate for the first time each year, and 2 per cent of older voters dying. From one election to another upwards of 90 per cent of the electorate will be constant.

Young adults, like the elderly, are one among many minorities. Young people cannot dominate politics by their numbers. And unlike the elderly, they do not have sufficient experience to have many very firm political views. Their electoral influence is incidental or even accidental: because young voters are new voters, they are less likely to be fixed in their political behaviour, and readier to swing from party to party, or to alter political attitudes.

In so far as generational differences are a more important influence than party loyalties, young people should differ more from old people than Conservatives differ from Labour voters. However, when the attitudes of young and old people are compared on a range of twelve issues, very little difference in political outlook is found, notwithstanding an average difference of more than 30 years in age. (See Table XII.1.) The average difference between age groups in political attitudes is ten per cent, and many of the differences are within the range of sampling fluctuations. In so far as there are differences in opinions, more young people tend to favour redistributing wealth and spending on welfare. In part this reflects the greater strength of Labour support among youthful Britons.

When the views of Conservative and Labour supporters are compared on a range of twelve issues, bigger differences appear. The average difference between the two groups of partisans is 20 per cent, double the difference between the young and old. Whereas differences between young and old are often matters of degree, differences between Conservative and Labour supporters are more like differences in kind. On five of the twelve issues

Table XII.1 Age and party differences in policy preferences

Favour:	Age			Party			Greater Difference %
	Young %	Old %	Difference %	Con. %	Labour %	Difference %	
More nationalization	35	24	11	5	52	47	Party 36
Redistributing wealth	59	42	17	28	75	47	Party 30
Membership of European Community	48	50	2	69	39	30	Party 28
Comprehensive schools	42	29	13	22	54	32	Party 19
Giving workers more say at job	64	49	15	43	69	26	Party 11
Preserving countryside	82	81	1	88	81	7	Party 7
More social services needed	36	21	15	15	36	21	Party 6
Tougher measures against crime	90	94	4	96	91	5	Party 1
More foreign aid	40	34	6	34	40	6	Equal
Spending more against poverty	88	74	14	76	88	12	Age 2
Spending more on health service	86	75	11	79	85	6	Age 5
Repatriating immigrants	29	40	11	37	32	5	Age 6
Average			10			10	10

Source Derived from data collected by the British Election Survey, October 1974. Young respondents, aged 18–29; old, aged 60 and above.

reported in Table XII.1, a majority in one party favours an opinion and a majority in the other does not.

Overall, party differences are much more likely to divide the British electorate than are age differences. The distance between Conservatives and Labour is greater than the generation gap in eight of the twelve issues reviewed in Table XII.1. The effect of age differences is further diminished by the fact that the median voter is neither young nor old but of middle age, with an outlook mediating between any political differences between young and old.

By definition, the economy involves constant change. Even nil growth requires change, because the economy is continuously transforming resources into goods for sale. The importance of international trade to England makes it particularly sensitive to changes in world markets. Some major export industries have declined greatly in this century. For example, in 1913 Britain exported 73 million tons of coal and in 1977 1.8 million tons. Similarly, the export of printed cotton goods declined from 1,230 million square yards in 1913 to 57 million in 1971. Concurrently, new industries have developed as prominent export earners. For example, in 1913 Britain exported 7,500 motor cars; in 1935, 43,900; and in 1977, 562,800. In 1954 the *Annual Abstract of Statistics* did not give any entry for exports of man-made fibres; in 1960, 49 million pounds were exported, rising to 298 million by 1973.[6]

Past success is forcing change upon British government, for the economy must continue to grow in future to meet the costs of past commitments to public policy. From 1951 to 1977, the costs of public policy grew fairly steadily, averaging 4.3 per cent each year. In 1951, financing this by a fiscal dividend required a growth of 1.2 per cent in the Gross National Product, since public spending accounted for only one-third of the total national product. But by the mid-1970s, a similar percentage growth in public spending anticipated a growth of more than 2 per cent in the National Product.

The slowing down of economic growth in the mid-1970s meant that if public spending continued to grow as before and could not be financed by the fiscal dividend of growth augmented by foreign borrowing, then take-home pay would have to fall. Just this occurred from the end of 1974 to 1977. For every pound of purchas-

[6] Data from the chapter on External Trade in relevant volumes of the *Annual Abstract of Statistics*.

ing power earned by a worker in September 1973, only 90 pence was earned four years later.[7]

When future risks become immediately pressing, a government must do something to preserve individual take-home pay. To do nothing would threaten a further reduction in earnings. The 1974–9 Labour government could not try to resolve the difficulty painlessly by promoting economic growth, given the state of the world economy in the mid-1970s, and the failures of previous Labour and Conservative governments to sustain faster economic growth. Instead, it sought to protect take-home pay by putting the brakes on public spending.[8]

Proponents of Britain's entry to the European Community thought that this would provide a stimulus necessary to generate faster changes in the economy leading to higher rates of economic growth. The British economy has been changing since 1973, but not in ways expected. The great pressures for change have come from a world-wide slump in economic activity, affecting other members of the European Community as well as nations outside it, such as the United States.[9]

Membership of the European Community symbolizes the increasing influence upon British government of events outside its territorial jurisdiction.[10] In previous generations, matters of foreign policy only occasionally erupted into matters of domestic concern. By contrast, Community membership commits the British government to accept regulation of a large number of commercial practices on a day-to-day basis. As long as the law of the Community primarily concerns commercial matters and can only be made by the unanimous decision of national governments, the supremacy of Community law is of little domestic significance. Its potential import remains. With or without Community membership, Britain

[7] See *Hansard*, Written Answers, 3 March 1978.

[8] On cash limits and the difficulties of planning or controlling public expenditure, see e.g. Maurice Wright, 'Public Expenditure in Britain: The Crisis of Control', *Public Administration*, L (Summer 1977).

[9] For contrasting comparative surveys, see the relatively optimistic *Towards Full Employment and Price Stability* (Paris: OECD, 1977) and the less optimistic study by Theodore Geiger and Frances M. Geiger, *Welfare and Efficiency* (Washington: National Planning Association, 1978).

[10] See e.g. House of Lords Select Committee report, *Relations between the United Kingdom Parliament and the European Parliament after Direct Elections* (London: HMSO, HL 256–I 1978); and the Hansard Society Working Party, *The British People: Their Voice in Europe* (Farnborough, Hants: Saxon House, 1977).

must come to terms with the economic and political power of France and Germany and of non-members, such as the United States and Japan as well.

The pressures for change are neither new nor unpredictable. For decades, even generations, writers have been warning of the vulnerability of the British economy to changes in world trade, and politicians have been trying to reduce this vulnerability. But their efforts have yet to show success. In 1976, the Prime Minister James Callaghan told the Labour Party Conference:

> Britain has lived for too long on borrowed time, borrowed money, and even borrowed ideas, and we live in too troubled a world to be able to promise that in a matter of years, we shall enter the promised land.
>
> The route is long and hard, but I believe the long march has at last begun.[11]

By definition, long marches take a long time to show a change in fortunes. The more accurate forecast for the 1970s was given by Anthony Barber, Conservative Chancellor of the Exchequer, in his 1971 budget speech:

> For many years, under one government and another, the economic performance of our country has been poor. If we are realistic, we should recognise that unless there is a change in the trend—a change not only compared with the last five or six years, but with the trend over the last two decades or more—the prospect is that by 1980 our standard of living in this country will have fallen considerably behind that of most of the countries of Western Europe.[12]

When the Chancellor spoke, Britain accounted for 20 per cent of the total product of the nine nations now consituting the European Community. By the end of 1974, the year in which Barber left office, Britain's share had dropped to 17 per cent.

There is widespread popular recognition of pressures for change, but English people are more often gloomy than optimistic about the prospect for change. Since 1957, the Gallup Poll has asked a cross-section of public opinion what they expect of the year ahead; usually, the majority expect some change rather than no change. In

[11] *Labour Party Conference Report*, 1976, p. 187.
[12] *Hansard*, Vol. 814, cols. 1358–9 (30 March 1971).

every one of the 21 years since, more people have expected prices to rise than fall, and more have expected strikes and industrial disputes than industrial peace. In 6 years out of 7 in this period, a plurality of people have expected taxes to rise, and in 16 of these years more people have also expected unemployment to rise. Economic difficulties rather than prosperity have been the expectation in 17 of the past 18 years. The international situation too has appeared foreboding, for in 19 of the past 21 years more people have expected international discord than peace.[13]

The very fact that English people do *not* expect the world to be getting better every day in every way is a powerful defence against mass political disappointment or frustration. It also means that the inability of government to make conditions better is not a shock or surprise to many citizens. When things go wrong with the economy, the government is not disappointing the citizenry; it is delivering what many English people have come to expect! People have learned from the difficulties of the country in the 1960s and 1970s not to expect continuous improvements; there is what one survey describes as a 'revolution of falling (rather than rising) expectations'.[14]

Coping with change[15]

The biggest problem immediately facing politicians is not whether British government can cope with its problems, but *how* can it do so? History demonstrates that British government has succeeded, time and again, in surmounting great difficulties. After the event, coping with change looks easy and obvious. But politics is about actions taken in moments of uncertainty and conflict.

Wartime offers extreme examples of government's need to cope quickly and successfully with unexpected and great challenges. Both the First and Second World Wars imposed many burdens upon a Whitehall machine unprepared for a long war. Both wars also involved the mobilization of civilians. State intervention under-

[13] See the annual review in the January issue of the *Gallup Political Index*, e.g. No. 222 (January 1979), p. 14.

[14] See the Opinion Research Centre survey, 'Do the British Sincerely Wish to be Rich?', *New Society*, 28 April 1977. Note that every survey of expectations always has considerable ballast, provided by those who expect conditions to remain the same, and those who don't know what to expect next.

[15] For a fuller discussion, see Richard Rose, 'Coping with Urban Change', in Rose, ed., *The Management of Urban Change in Britain and Germany* (London: Sage Publications, 1974).

taken in wartime has had important carry-over effects in the years of peace that followed. Wartime brought new institutions, such as the Cabinet Secretariat and the Central Statistical Office, as well as expanding greatly the services of the welfare state.

But the success of British wartime government provides ambiguous tribute to the coping strategies of peacetime governors. Wars were not won by relying on Whitehall's standard peacetime methods of government, but by introducing institutions and personnel that were not (or could not be) adopted in peacetime. In the Second World War, for example, three of the most important members of Cabinet—Ernest Bevin, Lord Beaverbrook and Sir John Anderson—were, respectively, a trade-union leader, a press lord and a senior civil servant. None would have found himself in Cabinet but for the war. The same is true of the Prime Minister, Winston Churchill.

Some reformers or jeremiahs would argue that peacetime difficulties are just as great a challenge to government as war. This is particularly the case among those who believe that major structural reform is necessary in the British economy if England is to prosper in future as in the past. But intellectual arguments are not a sufficient condition for action. After canvassing a number of alternative arguments for action in the crisis of 1931, André Siegfried concluded pessimistically that 'what is much more likely is that England will not choose at all.'[16]

No peacetime political event can create a crisis of the intensity, scope and duration of war. Many so-called crises in domestic politics are extremely trying while they last, but very short-lived in their consequences. Few people today refer to the Profumo scandal of 1963 or the Bank Rate Tribunal of 1957, even though each at the time received great political attention. When important issues do arise unexpectedly, government must act without plans in circumstances that do not allow much time for thought about long-term consequences. For example, the British government decision to put troops in the field in Northern Ireland in August 1969 was taken under the immediate pressure of riots; there was no plan of how the troops would get out.

The standard operating procedures of Whitehall are meant to avoid the possibility of major difficulties erupting, and concentrate upon the ample supply of difficulties already at hand. The Fulton

[16] *England's Crisis* (London: Jonathan Cape, 1931), p. 311.

Report on the Civil Service describes how Whitehall copes with policies on a routine basis:

> The operation of existing policies and the detailed preparation of legislation with the associated negotiations and discussions frequently crowd out demands that appear less immediate. Civil servants, particularly members of the Administrative Class, have to spend a great deal of their time preparing explanatory briefs, answers to parliamentary questions, and minister's cases. Generally this work involves the assembly of information to explain to others (civil servants, outside bodies and so on) the policies of the department, how they are operating and how they apply in particular cases. Almost invariably, there are urgent deadlines to be met in this kind of work. In this press of daily business, long-term policy planning and research tend to take second place.[17]

Planning ahead is the remedy often proposed for dealing with major problems of government. But the environment of British government is often turbulent, and this is especially likely to be the case with important issues. In a turbulent political environment it is difficult to forecast. A former government economic adviser has argued that in such circumstances, 'the hardest thing to forecast is where you are now'.[18] In the mid-1970s, the Treasury, the central agency concerned with such planning as is done in Whitehall, was reduced to submitting three or four budgets a year to Parliament, because every few months economic developments made invalid the assumptions of its previously announced plans.

When there is world enough and time to plan what to do, there may not be any political pressure to act. The introduction of decimal coinage illustrates how slow and cautious government can be before acting upon a policy proposal. The abandonment of the old £.s.d. system of coinage was first debated in Parliament in 1817. At that time, the Napoleonic Wars had created a shortage of metal coins in England. But by the same token, the wars with France also made the introduction of an alien (i.e. decimal) form of coinage suspect. Two decades later, Charles Babbage, a Cambridge professor and pioneer of ideas basic to modern computing, offered a detailed scheme for converting the existing currency into decimal coinage.

---

[17] The Fulton Committee *Report*, Vol. I, p. 57.
[18] Lord Roberthall, quoted in Sir Alec Cairncross, *Essays in Economic Management* (London: George Allen & Unwin, 1971), p. 129.

The government did not respond positively until 106 years later, when it established a committee to review the subject once again. In 1971, 154 years after the topic was first raised in Parliament, England adopted a system of decimal currency along the lines recommended by early nineteenth-century reformers.[19]

There is always one good political argument for maintaining the *status quo*: the fact that it is there. When pressures for action mount, a government can respond by following a policy of delay. The procedures of British government provide a rich repertoire of devices for stalling action if the government of the day has a mind to do so. Unlike America, they provide virtually no methods by which the opposition party can delay government action.

The best descriptive and normative justification for standard governmental practices is given by the doctrine of 'muddling through', or as it is known in its most elaborate form, the theory of serial disjointed incrementalism.[20] Politicians are expected to take decisions one at a time, reacting empirically to problems that are immediately before them. They are not expected to worry about the further consequences of what they do, because these consequences cannot be completely known. In effect, they will constitute tomorrow's problems. If the consequences of today's decisions are bad, they should be reversed tomorrow, for this is better than consistency in pursuing unsuccessful or unpopular measures. In this model of coping with change, a policy is not so much a statement of intent, but a description of the results of a series of decisions taken over a significant period of time.

The concept of muddling through is ambiguous; everything depends upon whether one emphasizes the muddle or 'winning through'. It is more appropriate for coping with emergencies when imponderables are numerous; it is least suited for coping with long-term large-scale capital investments, like building roads or universities. The evaluation of muddling through will differ according to the perspective of persons involved. Those who are caught in the muddle are likely to be less satisfied than those who view the problem in a broader analytic framework. Cumulatively, muddling through can lead policy-makers to hit upon an acceptable and

---

[19] A. F. Timms, 'Hundred Year Delay in Completing the Change to Decimals', *The Times*, 12 February 1971.

[20] See David Braybrooke and C. E. Lindblom, *A Strategy of Decision* (New York: Free Press, 1963).

durable decision by a process of trial and error. Alternatively, a decade of trying first one policy, then another, can result in 'muddling around in circles'.

A decade of efforts to reform British government from 1964 to 1974 has created, as an unintended consequence, a loss of confidence in the capacity of British government to plan change. If government cannot develop its own institutions in ways that reformers would like, this also raises doubts about the prospect of government being able to change society.

Ordinary English people are more likely to participate in history as 'decision takers' rather than 'decision makers'. They must cope with the changes that government introduces, as well as with other changes happening concurrently in their own lives, and in society at large. Government acts in the name of the people, but it does not normally act at popular initiative. This is particularly the case in England, where the theories of representation dominant among politicians stress acting as trustees for a public interest or as spokesmen for group interests.

The victory of the Labour Party at four out of five successive general elections since 1964 placed government for eleven of fifteen years in the hands of a party nominally committed to introduce major changes in British society. Moreover, the 1970–74 Conservative government was led by an activist, reform-minded Prime Minister. During that period, the Labour government did succeed in introducing a number of laws that could change social conditions, in so far as they were 'permissive' laws making legal behaviour that was formerly illegal and covert. The attitudes of the Labour government, as well as its legislation, were also a force for change. In a few cases, such as the abolition of capital punishment for murderers, the Labour majority in the Commons voted in the knowledge that the great bulk of public opinion opposed this change. They did so because they believed this was the right thing to do.[21]

After fourteen years of government in a climate of change, the British public was in a position to judge reform measures even better than MPs could at the time they were proposed. When a bill is introduced into Parliament, it can only be evaluated hypothetically; its effects become apparent after it is adopted. In 1978, when the Gallup Poll conducted a nation-wide survey of popular attitudes

[21] See P. G. Richards, *Parliament and Conscience* (London: Allen & Unwin, 1970).

toward accomplished reforms, popular judgments could be based upon the experience of more than a decade of change.

When people are asked to say whether changes have gone too far, not far enough or about right, one would expect the median respondent to endorse the view that changes are about right. In fact, there is substantial popular resistance to government promotion of change in English society. When asked about a range of nine different reforms occurring since the mid-1960s, on six of nine issues the largest group consisted of those who thought change had gone too far. An absolute majority said that they thought there had been too much change in terms of respect for authority, going easier on people who break the law, sex in the media, and in the reduction of Britain's military strength. More people believe that government provides too much in welfare benefits and has gone too far in promoting modern methods of education than think its policies are just about right.

Only one measure—laws to promote equal treatment of women —is considered 'about right' by a majority of public opinion. In

TABLE XII.2 **Popular resistance to change**

	Attitude toward changes in British society in recent years		
	Gone too far %	About right %	Not gone far enough %
Respect of people for authority	71	13	11
Going easier on people who break the law	58	10	27
Nudity and sex in films, magazines	56	36	3
Reduction of Britain's military strength	53	25	8
Modern methods in teaching children	43	31	12
Provision of welfare benefits	43	35	18
Availability of abortion on National Health	33	43	13
Measures to ensure equality for coloured people	30	43	21
Measures to ensure equality for women	20	58	17
Average	45	33	14

Note   Percentages do not add up to 100 because of the omission of don't knows.
Source: Gallup Political Index, No. 220 (November 1978), p.11.

addition, the public is more likely to be satisfied with laws promoting equality for coloured people, and providing abortion on the national health service, than to criticize these reforms for going too far.

The proponents of further change are greatly outnumbered by the defenders of the new *status quo*, and by those who believe that change has gone too far. On average, only one in seven English persons favours further change in a major area of English life, and as few as 3 per cent wish to see an increase in the public display of sex. Those who endorse the *status quo* often hold the balance, occupying the median position. But if there is to be change, more English people would like this to be a step back, reversing measures that are deemed to have gone 'too far'.

A question of values

The most important of all political changes—alterations in the values and beliefs of the political culture—are the most difficult to measure or anticipate. They cannot be extrapolated like a line on the graph, nor can they be predicted with the actuarial certainty with which one can forecast primary school population from a knowledge of the number of infants under the age of five. Yet once the meaning of politics alters, much else changes in consequence.[22]

Many basic features of the political culture have not changed. English people still agree upon the value of liberty and the choice of government through ballots cast by universal suffrage. They continue to trust the goodwill and *bona fides* of their governors and the civil servants who do most of the day-to-day work of government. There is continuing positive belief that groups affected by government policy have a right to be consulted. All parties to government also continue to endorse evolutionary rather than revolutionary change.

Some changes in cultural values can lead to greater agreement, when change represents one group 'catching up' with the ideas of others. Measures that were once novel and controversial then become assimilated into the conventional wisdom. For example, in the 1930s the Labour Party opposed rearmament for national defence, and Conservatives opposed welfare measures endorsed by

[22] See Richard Rose, 'England: A Traditionally Modern Political Culture', in Lucian W. Pye and Sidney Verba, *Political Culture and Political Development* (Princeton: University Press, 1965).

Labour. During and after the Second World War, the majority of the Labour Party swung toward a reliance upon military force in foreign policy, and Conservatives have accepted Labour's welfare state measures.

Attempts to forecast the direction of future political change inevitably call attention to the contrasting value-assumptions of forecasters. A traditionally minded English person might emphasize the value of conserving achievements from the past, not least maintaining a form of government with fully legitimate authority. Socialists are less concerned with forms of government and more concerned with the achievements of government, especially the redistribution of wealth, status and political power. Economists assert that all talk of change is meaningless, unless society has the resources required to maintain existing material standards or attain those to which politicians aspire. Humanitarians argue that the next major development in English society should relieve the handicapped rather than the productive groups in society. Libertarians argue for the removal of government constraints upon behaviour.

Amidst the troubles between the wars, R. H. Tawney, a leading Socialist theorist, noted that the idea of reflecting upon alternative futures is 'uncongenial' to the bustling people who describe themselves as practical, because they take things as they are. He proceeded to tell his fellow Englishmen:

> The practical thing for a traveller who is uncertain of his path is not to proceed with the utmost rapidity in the wrong direction: it is to consider how to find the right one. And the practical thing for a nation which has stumbled upon one of the turning points of history is to consider whether what it is has done hitherto is wise, and if it is not wise to alter it.[23]

A prominent Conservative philosopher, Michael Oakeshott, viewed the failure of grand designs to bring about a new order in Europe from the perspective of 1951. He wrote, in an equally apposite but opposite way:

> In political activity, then, men sail a boundless and bottomless sea; there is neither harbour for shelter nor floor for anchorage, neither starting-place nor appointed destination. The enterprise is to keep afloat on an even keel; the sea is both friend and enemy;

---

[23] R. H. Tawney, *The Acquisitive Society* (London: Bell, 1921), p. 2.

and the seamanship consists in using the resources of a traditional manner of behaviour in order to make a friend of every inimical occasion.[24]

In contemporary England, political leaders are ambivalent in their attitudes toward change. A desire to conserve past achievements is often commingled with a desire to remove present grievances or promote future improvements. A study of young political leaders found that characteristically these politicians used 'the language of the future when talking of modernization, but they seek to join this with the values of the past: balance, stability, and unity'.[25] A majority of would-be innovators explicitly state that the things they like most about England moderation, tolerance, a capacity for compromise and continuity—are also the cause of what they most dislike: resistance to change.

[24] *Political Education* (Cambridge: Bowes & Bowes, 1951), p. 22.
[25] Erwin Hargrove, *Professional Roles in Society and Government: The English Case* (Beverly Hills: Sage Papers in Comparative Politics, 01–035, 1972) p. 14.

Index